Contemporary French
Cultural Studies

Contemporary French Cultural Studies

Edited by

WILLIAM KIDD
Reader in French
University of Stirling

and

SIÂN REYNOLDS
Professor of French
University of Stirling

HODDER
EDUCATION
AN HACHETTE UK COMPANY

First published in Great Britain in 2000

http://www.hoddereducation.co.uk

© 2000 Arnold

British Library Cataloguing in Publication Data
A catalogue entry for this book is available from the British Library

Library of Congress Cataloging-in-Publication Data
A catalog record for this book is available from the Library of Congress

ISBN 978 0 340 74050 7

Typeset in 10/12pt Sabon by Phoenix Photosetting, Chatham, Kent

Contents

Contributors

Helen E. Beale is Lecturer in French at the University of Stirling. She has published papers on war memorials, public sculpture and public space, and is currently working on the Scottish colourist J. D. Fergusson (1874–1961) and his links with France.

Mary Breatnach is a professional musician and independent scholar. She teaches at the Royal Scottish Academy of Music and Drama and in the French Department at the University of Edinburgh. She is the author of *Boulez and Mallarmé: A Study in Poetic Influence* (1996), and has published articles on French poetry in relation to music.

Lucille Cairns is Lecturer in French at the University of Stirling, and the author of *Marie Cardinal: Motherhood and Creativity* (1992); *Privileged Pariahdom: Homosexuality in the Novels of Dominique Fernandez* (1996), as well as articles on both French women's writing and French lesbian and gay literature and cinema.

Dougal Campbell is a Language Tutor in the French Department at Glasgow University. He also works for the Open University, Harrap's dictionaries and an A Level board. A link at http://www2.arts.gla.ac.uk/ French/french6.html will take you to his monthly cyber-column about language-related topics, from puns and headlines to the delights of translation.

Christophe Campos is Director of the British Institute in Paris, where he contributes to undergraduate and postgraduate courses on French theatre. From 1971 to 1997, he organized the annual Paris-Théâtre international seminar.

Susan Collard teaches in the School of European Studies at the University of Sussex and has published widely on French politics with special reference to French cultural policy, on which she is completing a book.

Martyn Cornick is Reader in Contemporary French Studies at the University of Birmingham. He is editor of the journal *Modern and Contemporary France*, and has published widely on French intellectual history. His book *Intellectuals in History: the Nouvelle revue française under Jean Paulhan* appeared in 1995.

Marion Demossier is Lecturer in French and European Studies at the University of Bath. She is the author of *Hommes et vins, une anthropologie du vignoble bourguignon* (Dijon 1999), has published several articles on French culture and society and is working on a project about culture and wine consumption in France.

Philip Dine, Senior Lecturer in French at Loughborough University, is the author of *Images of the Algerian War: French Fiction and Film, 1954-1992* (1994). He works on representations of decolonization, sport, leisure, and popular culture in France. Currently completing a social history of French rugby.

Alastair Duncan is Senior Lecturer in French at the University of Stirling. He has published on the French New Novel, especially Claude Simon, and on advertising in France, including articles on racism, sponsorship and television.

Elizabeth Ezra teaches in the French Department at the University of Stirling. She is the author of *The Colonial Unconscious: Race and Culture in Interwar France* (2000), and *Georges Méliès: The Birth of the Auteur* (2000) She is also co-editor of *France in Focus: Film and National Identity* (2000).

Sue Harris is Lecturer in French at Queen Mary & Westfield College, University of London. She has published articles on popular film comedy and performance, is co-editor of *France in Focus: Film and National Identity* (2000) and is the author of a forthcoming book on Bertrand Blier.

Alec G. Hargreaves is Professor of French and Francophone Studies at Loughborough University. His publications include *Immigration, 'Race' and Ethnicity in Contemporary France* (1995) and, co-edited with Mark McKinney, *Post-Colonial Cultures in France* (1997).

Brian Jenkins is Professor of French Area Studies at the University of Portsmouth. He is the author of *Nationalism in France: Class and Nation since 1789* (1990), co-editor of *Nation and Identity in Contemporary Europe* (1996), and an editor of the *Journal of European Area Studies*.

William Kidd is Reader in French at the University of Stirling. He has written extensively on twentieth-century literature and ideology, culture and iconography, war and memory, including a recently published monograph on the problematics of commemoration in Lorraine from 1871 to the present.

Jeremy F. Lane is Lecturer in French at Aberdeen University. He has published widely on many aspects of the work of Pierre Bourdieu and is the author of *Pierre Bourdieu: a critical introduction* (2000).

Susan Milner is Reader in European Studies at the University of Bath. She has published on the history of trade unions and has recently embarked on comparative studies of the impact of socio-economic change on local communities. She is currently investigating the role of cultural policies in urban regeneration in France.

Lucy Mitchell is Librarian at the British Institute in Paris where she also teaches in the English Department. Her three children have all been educated through the French state school and university system.

James S. Munro teaches in the University of Stirling, both in the department of French and the Centre for English Language Teaching. His interests and publications range from French literature of the seventeenth and eighteenth centuries to the methodology of language teaching.

Siân Reynolds is Professor of French at the University of Stirling, and works on French history and politics. Her latest book is *France between the Wars: gender and politics* (1996) and she has also published a number of translations.

Jean-Claude Sergeant is professor at the University of Paris III (Sorbonne-nouvelle), and a member of the Centre for Research on Media. He is the author of books on Britain and Europe since 1945, and Britain under Margaret Thatcher and has published widely on the British and French press and news media.

Eric Sterenfeld is a French musician and composer who works in Paris. He has played in several of the groups mentioned in chapter 19 and is an expert on electronic musical reproduction.

Bernard C. Swift (University of Stirling) has also held appointments in Canada, Geneva, and at the University of Bordeaux. He has written widely on François Mauriac, has published translations of works by Jean Starobinski and articles on French symbolism, and has worked on book censorship in France.

Acknowledgements

For permission to reproduce photographs of theatre posters from Christophe Campos's collection (Figures 15.1 and 15.2), the editors are grateful to the Comédie Française, the Théâtre du Lucernaire, the artist and Professor Campos. For the ad for Chanel's Allure (Fig. 14.1), acknowledgements are due to Chanel, Paris; Daniel Jouanneau, Mak Gilchrist and Elite Premier, London; Herb Ritts and Vernon Jolly, New York. Other photographs are by Helen Beale (Figs 11.1, 11.2, 12.1); William Kidd (Figs 3.1, 5.1, 12.2, 21.1); and Bernard Swift (Fig. 20.1). Our thanks also go to Graham Brown of Stirling University Media Services.

Sue Harris wishes to acknowledge with thanks a grant from the Carnegie Trust for the Universities of Scotland, which enabled her to research chapters 16 and 17. The editors are particularly grateful to Alison Cooper, French Departmental Assistant at Stirling, for her help in preparing the word-processed version of the final text and typing the index. They also wish to thank John Oswald for reading sections of the manuscript with the keen eye of a postgraduate. The original idea and commission came from Lesley Riddle, and the editors would like to thank her and her colleagues at Arnold, especially Elena Seymenliyska and Anke Ueberberg, for all their help and encouragement as the book went through the press. Various sharp-eyed copy-editors eliminated errors and inconsistencies, but the editors accept responsibility for any that have escaped undetected.

The Editors

Abbreviations

AIDS	Acquired Immune Deficiency Syndrome
AFAA	Association française d'action artistique
BVP	Bureau de vérification de la publicité
CAPES	Certificat d'aptitude professionnelle de l'enseignement secondaire
CNC	Centre national de la cinématographie
CREDOC	Centre de recherche pour l'étude et l'observation des conditions de vie
CROUS	Centre régional des œuvres universitaires et scolaires
CSA	Conseil supérieur de l'audiovisuel
CUARH	Comité d'urgence anti-répression homosexuelle
DB	Division blindée [(2nd) Armoured division]
DGRCST	Direction générale des relations culturelles, scientifiques et techniques
DOM-TOM	Départements d'outre-mer – Territoires d'outre-mer
DRAC	Direction régionale des affaires culturelles
DSU	Dotation de solidarité urbaine
DVD	Digital Versatile Disk
EHESS	Ecole des hautes études et sciences sociales
ENA	Ecole nationale d'administration
EU	European Union
FEMIS	Fondation européenne des métiers de l'image et du son
FHAR	Front homosexuel d'action révolutionnaire
FN	Front national
FNAC	Fédération nationale des achats des cadres
GATT	General agreement on tariffs and trade
GDP	Gross Domestic Product
HLM	Habitation à loyer modéré
IMA	Institut du monde arabe
INA	Institut national de l'audiovisuel

INED	Institut national d'études démographiques
INSEE	Institut national de la statistique et des études économiques
INSEP	Institut national du Sport et de l'Education Physique
IOC	International Olympic Committee
IRCAM	Institut de recherches et de coordination acoustique musique
IUT	Institut universitaire de technologie
NATO	North Atlantic Treaty Organization
OECD	Organization for economic cooperation and development
OJD	Office de justification de la diffusion des supports de publicité
ORTF	Office de radiodiffusion-télévision française
PACS	Pacte civil de solidarité
PAGSI	Programme d'action gouvernemental pour la société d'information
PCF	Parti communiste français
PUF	Presses Universitaires de France
RATP	Régie autonome des transports parisiens
RER	Réseau express régional
RIAS	Royal Institute of Architects in Scotland
RMC	Radio Monte-Carlo
RTL	Radio-Télévision Luxembourg
SACEM	Société des auteurs, compositeurs et éditeurs de musique
SNCF	Société nationale des chemins de fer français
SOFRES	Société française d'enquêtes par sondage
SPD	Sozialdemokratische Partei Deutschlands
SPF	Société française de production
STS	Sections de techniciens supérieurs
TDF	Télévision de France
TF1	Télévision française 1 (la première chaîne: equivalent of BBC 1)
TGV	Train à grande vitesse
TNP	Théâtre national populaire
UDF	Union pour la démocratie française
ZEP	Zone d'éducation prioritaire

PART

I

INTRODUCTION AND SOURCES

|1|

Introduction: to the reader

BY WILLIAM KIDD AND SIÂN REYNOLDS

Some people like to read introductions last. You might prefer, when you open this book, to start by looking at the chapters on, say, music, cinema or advertising, which describe what has been happening in France recently in these areas. But sooner or later the editors hope you will feel curious about the overall architecture of the collection, which is explained in this foreword. It can be summed up in the four words of the title.

The book has been written and put together in the closing months not only of the twentieth century but of the second millennium. The word 'contemporary' in the title is meant to be taken seriously. All the contributors were asked to look at what is happening in France now, as it moves into the twenty-first century. That does not mean ignoring the past – and in almost every chapter, some explanation of the past is helpful in understanding the present. But we have tried not to repeat too much of what has been very adequately written elsewhere. For instance, much past writing about sport in France has concentrated on the high-profile men's sports like football and cycling, viewed historically. The chapter on sport here starts from the 1998 Football World Cup, but draws attention to the new aspect of French football, its multiculturalism, before considering some of the newer sports like free rock-climbing and the rise of women sporting champions.

We are also conscious that the very bases of our knowledge about both past and present have changed radically in a very short time with the coming of the Internet. The students who use this book will probably be as familiar with the computer screen as with traditional paper support systems. Any cultural analysis of the future will have to take account of the globalization brought by information technology. The reader will find not only regular bibliographies but also specialized website references at the end of some chapters, while in our section on sources, we have included an introductory guide to France on the Web, with jumping off points for any subject. Despite all this, the philosophy of the book is that the 'contemporary' does not come from nowhere. In France as elsewhere, the past is all around, shaping the present, and we have tried to provide pointers to help make sense of the changes that are happening now, as in chapter 3 which suggests some ways of looking back over the twentieth century.

One of the most important questions in our time is the changing nature of national identity. The second word in the title is 'French', and this book sets out as it goes along to examine critically what 'Frenchness' means. Most of the first half of the book is devoted to this exploration. It should be stressed first that the Frenchness in question is that of the French nation-state and chiefly of 'the Hexagon'. While the implications of Francophonie, the use of the French language outside France, are briefly discussed (chapter 10), we have not attempted in a book this size to cover the cultures of other French-speaking parts of the world, such as Quebec. That probably requires a completely separate textbook.

Second, while some contributors have written from inside France on subjects where inside knowledge was particularly valuable (media and education for instance) most of us are outside observers; and readers will also be looking at a culture that is not their own. A foreign culture is always in some sense exotic, different. As Brian Jenkins remarks, outside observers of French politics have sometimes stressed the 'special' nature of French political history – taking their cue from an idea quite widespread among French commentators themselves (chapter 9). The term often used in recent times to describe this specialness is 'l'exception française' – the notion that France is somehow unique, different from its neighbours – and in particular from what is sometimes called 'Anglo-Saxon' (more correctly 'Anglo-American') civilization.

All the contributors found themselves dealing with this question, because it can crop up in almost any context. The strong sense of French culture as an inheritance to be guarded has inspired an unusual degree of state intervention in cultural matters, as described in chapter 4. The French Ministry of Culture has had a high profile over the last twenty years or so and has made a marked difference to everyday life: French films and theatre groups are subsidized, festivals have been created, rock concerts sponsored. The thrust of this activity is in part defensive. Having seen the very rapid progress of globalization, the French authorities are understandably anxious about the encroachment of the English language and in particular about the infiltration of American culture. This anxiety can be seen in strenuous attempts to promote the French language worldwide, to prevent English creeping into French advertisements, and in the imposed 40 per cent quotas of French songs on radio stations. The fact that McDonald's and Disneyland have established apparently unshakeable bridgeheads in France is seen as worrying, whereas other countries have been more eager to embrace what the French sometimes call 'Coca-colonization'.

At the same time, France has also faced what is sometimes seen as a 'crisis' of multiculturalism. France has prided itself on being a 'terre d'asile', a country which has opened its doors to refugees, especially political ones.

And along with many other European countries, especially those with a history of colonial empires, France has received many immigrants, chiefly from former colonies, whose reasons for coming are primarily economic. One form which French exceptionalism has taken, for reasons dating back to the Revolution of 1789, is that under a republic, citizens should not be singled out for special treatment. So immigrants who come into France have traditionally been expected to assimilate to the dominant patterns of living, for example abandoning their native language for French. (The same inspiration lies behind the original banning and still rather unwilling toleration of regional languages in the provinces: see chapter 8.) The term 'multiculturalism' is viewed by many French people as representing a rather dangerous kind of 'ghettoization' which they see as the pattern in countries like Britain and the US: allowing or even encouraging foreign communities to foster their own languages, customs and cultures.

It would be quite wrong however to see France as a country which suppresses other cultures. In practice, the culture of immigrant communities in France has been able to assert itself, for example in the cinema of second-generation Maghrebi immigrants. France is also more open to foreign writing, in the form of published translations, than either Britain or America. And Paris has become one of the global centres for the diffusion of African music (see chapter 19). Despite the existence of the Front National, with its extreme anti-immigrant policies, one might hazard the view that everyday life in France is much less racist in atmosphere than that of many other countries. But the subject of assimilation versus multiculturalism does provoke discussion and debate in the press, and some cultures have attracted particular attention – the famous 'affaire du foulard', concerning the right of Muslim girls to wear headscarves to school for religious reasons, is mentioned in a number of chapters.

So the idea of French exceptionalism is an important one to grapple with – these issues of identity do not crop up in quite this form in other countries. But as Jenkins goes on to say, there may be some danger of exaggerating France's uniqueness. In several chapters, our contributors have pointed out that French people's approach to culture may be not so different from that in other countries. French readers and radio listeners may be eclectic in their tastes, picking up airport novels translated from the American, watching internationally produced TV programmes or operas, listening to very multicultural world music.

All these factors, then, temper the idea of a single 'French culture'. While chapters 3–5 provide the background to French exceptionalism, in terms of history, the education system and cultural policy, we have particularly asked contributors to chapters 6–9 to explore differences within cultural activity and practices in France, sometimes using the notion of subcultures. How people 'consume' culture may depend on several variables. What sort of differences may arise because of people's age, sex, sexual orientation, income, birthplace, politics, religion and so on? We have been selective here to avoid duplication of previous textbooks. References at the end of chapters will direct the reader to further specialist reading.

In this kind of exercise, the word fragmentation comes to mind: could it be that France (like other countries) is actually seeing a previously national culture splinter into a number of fragmented subcultures? The whole debate about French exceptionalism (and *la fin de l'exception française*), which has taken an acute form at the end of the twentieth century, might be seen as a pathological response to a fear both of invasion and fragmentation. So after the section on differences we have included three chapters (10–12) which discuss some of the countervailing forces – they look at French as a national language, at 'constructing Frenchness' and at the national heritage as represented iconographically in public spaces. Is there still a strong case for arguing that a national sense of 'French culture' is consciously pursued via national symbols and traditions, spurred on perhaps by the very American challenge which is so feared?

This brings us to the third word in the title: 'cultural'. What does it mean? It is used in a bewildering number of contexts these days. In the first half of the book (chapters 3–12), we use the term in a fairly pragmatic and general way to include the world-view of various sections of French society. In the second half (chapters 13–22), it is used to designate *cultural activity*, those activities which are pursued or consumed by most people in their non-working time, yet which nowadays also *employ* many people and account for a considerable share of the national income: books and publishing, music and the music industry, cinema, theatre, TV, sport – and so on. If one takes a bird's eye macro-economic look at France, one notices at once that these 'industries' are extremely significant in the national economy and in the government budget. If one takes a worm's eye view, from the perspective of the individual's everyday life, he or she may wake up and switch on the radio or TV, listen to music or the news, see advertisements on the way to work, read a newspaper, go to a concert, a film or a play from time to time, watch (or even play in) a game of football or tennis, read thrillers or poetry before going to bed. All of these are cultural activities, engaged in sporadically and sometimes only partly consciously: French people will take for granted the singing of the Marseillaise at football matches, or seeing the image of Marianne in the local town hall (cf. chapter 12). We have therefore avoided getting drawn into the debates about so-called 'high culture' and 'popular culture' which are a feature of modern cultural theory.

This is the point to say that the term 'French cultural studies' as used in this book is not to be confused with the above-mentioned *cultural theory*, a branch of intellectual activity concerned with the general analysis of society through culture (but see chapter 22 below). Our more modest definition is to be seen in the context of the changing field of 'French' and 'French studies' syllabuses in school and university, focusing rather more on *cultural production* in the broader sense (including films, TV programmes, etc.) than on literature. Recent years have seen quite a change in the traditional field of French studies. There was a time when everyone studying French read several well-known works of French literature. Some of the writers of this book did just that. Depending on our generation, we read the plays of Racine and Molière, the novels of Balzac and Flaubert, the poetry of Baudelaire and Rimbaud, the philosophical essays of Sartre, Camus and Beauvoir, the experimental novels of Nathalie Sarraute and Marguerite Duras, the critical theory of Roland Barthes and Michel Foucault, and so on. We did not usually study French cinema, let alone popular music, sport or advertising. And in some ways it is actually harder to study other cultural forms than literature: video may have made it easier to view films (at the cost of the full-size screen experience) but there is no substitute for going to the theatre to see plays, or to the stadium truly to experience sporting culture; and how do you study festivals?

Students still study literature, we are glad to say. But their needs are very fully catered for in the number of texts, critical editions and survey works available for them to consult. On the other hand, many students of French today read comparatively little literature (and very little earlier than the twentieth century). They may be studying French as part of a joint degree with other subjects, perhaps science or business studies or vocational courses of all kinds, including other languages. They probably devote much time to language study itself, since secondary and high schools do not always take them to an advanced level. So it may be useful for them to have a contextual knowledge of the wider culture of the country they are studying, whatever form it takes, 'high' or 'popular'. This is what lies behind the choice of subjects in chapters 13–22. They arise in part from our experience of teaching cultural options, alongside literature, at the University of Stirling, where this book has been edited. 'Literature' in the broad sense is not entirely neglected, but it is tackled in three ways: in a chapter on what French people are reading today, another on the place of the French intellectual, and a third looking at the specifically French contribution to international thought (chapters 20–22). These are 'book cultures' if you like; earlier sections discuss cultural activities or productions relating more to spectacle and performance: sport, advertising, the media, theatre, cinema, festivals, music. In all of these there are some examples which appeal to minorities, others which appeal more widely, and readers will draw their own conclusions about them.

We have had to be selective here too for space reasons and there are some gaps, explained by the decision to have a contemporary emphasis. For example, if one were doing a similar book on Britain, one would have to include a large section on contemporary visual arts of all kinds, because that is a striking, if controversial part of British culture today. Unlike in France, where study at Beaux-Arts is limited and very professional, the art college culture is familiar to many in Britain, and institutions like the Turner Prize attract world-wide interest. In France, the visual arts are not quite so central today as in the past: painting and sculpture, for example, flourished particularly in the late nineteenth and early twentieth century, photography between about 1920 and 1960. The visual arts are certainly mentioned in chapters in this book, but in particular contexts (iconography, advertising, museums, festivals). Rightly or wrongly, we felt that they were not at present sufficiently prominent nationally or well enough documented to warrant special chapters (neither do they figure strongly in Hughes and Reader's 1998 *Encyclopedia*). The contributors were all asked to consider their particular field within the French cultural scene today, and to look at how these fields are changing. These chapters are not designed to provide all the answers on the subject, or to be used as plunder for essays: they are intended above all to be introductory and thought provoking.

In terms of 'studies' then, while the chapters in this book are 'studies' of particular subjects, they are located in the wider field of 'French cultural studies'. Inevitably a book of this kind is a sort of textbook, designed for students, although general readers might also find it of interest. But it is not holy writ. The point of study is to find out and acquire knowledge, but also to examine that information critically. We have tried not to take too much for granted, so that beginners will not feel out of their depth: long quotations in French have been translated for instance, though short sentences and phrases are left in the original. But the aim has also been to provoke students to want to know more, and to criticize any chapter, or the whole book, for what is *not* here – there is plenty we have had to leave out. As editors, we regret that we did not have room for chapters on either French historical culture or French scientific culture for instance, and in this introduction we have deliberately drawn attention to other gaps. By doing so, we want to suggest that no textbook is ever the last word on a subject. It will always be imperfect and incomplete. Energetic readers will complement textbooks by looking further afield. The book as a whole is simply intended to help students find their bearings before going further into whatever takes their fancy. We suggest various reference works, websites and encyclopedias to follow up particular people or topics – and in particular we hope to encourage the reader to move on to authentic French sources, written, sound or electronic. To draw attention to its aim of inspiring personal research, the next chapter you will hit, *chère lectrice, cher lecteur*, if you turn the page after this introduction is called 'France @ your fingertips' and suggests some useful ways to get started.

Further general reading: recent works on French culture in English

COOK, Malcolm (ed.) 1993: *French culture since 1945*. London: Longman.
COOK, Malcolm and DAVIE, G. (eds) 1999: *Modern France: society in transition*. London and New York: Routledge.

FORBES, Jill and KELLY, Michael (eds) 1995: *French cultural studies: an introduction*. Oxford: OUP.

FRANCE, Peter (ed.) 1995: *The new Oxford companion to literature in French*. Oxford: OUP.

HUGHES, Alex and READER, Keith (eds) 1998: *Encyclopedia of contemporary French culture*. London: Routledge.

|2|

France @ your fingertips:
print and on-line resources

BY ELIZABETH EZRA AND DOUGAL CAMPBELL

Where do you go if you want more information about France? This chapter gives an overview of resources for students of French culture, including literature and cinema; it may be especially useful for undergraduates and postgraduates planning to write essays or dissertations. First, we discuss those resources, such as reference works, magazines, newspapers, and scholarly journals, accessible in English-speaking countries; then we give examples of helpful resources, including libraries, bookstores and videothèques in France (particularly Paris); and finally, we provide a digest of 'France on the Web' – useful Internet sites that can be accessed anywhere from an on-line computer. Note, too, that suggestions for further reading and some websites are also listed at the end of several chapters in this book.

Resources at home

The daily newspaper *Le Monde*, widely available in university libraries around the world, is a respected source of news and commentary, and is sold in specialist newspaper shops in major cities in English-speaking countries. *Libération* is another widely available daily paper. Current-events magazines to watch out for include *Le Point*, *Le Nouvel Observateur* and *L'Express*. Most of these publications have websites (below). A number of scholarly journals devoted to aspects of French culture are published in English-speaking countries, though they vary in accessibility: sometimes the articles are highly specialized because they are aimed at professional researchers, but many are helpful to students as well. For in-depth research projects, the first port of call might be the *MLA Humanities Index*, which should be available on CD-ROM or in the older printed editions in most university libraries. This index allows you to locate articles in scholarly journals from past years according to subject. Journals that specialize in modern French culture include: *Modern and Contemporary France*, which publishes articles on politics, history and culture; *French Cultural Studies*, published in the UK; *Contemporary French Civilization* and *French Politics, Culture and Society*, published in the US – all of which feature essays on a variety of cultural topics, including music and film; *Sites*, which also includes some original fiction and poetry in French; *L'Esprit créateur*; *The French Review*; and the *Journal of Francophone Studies*, which focuses on literature, but also treats cultural topics of the French-speaking world outside France. Journals devoted primarily to literature and literary theory include *Yale French Studies*, *French Forum*, *Australian French Studies*, *Nottingham French Studies*, and *French Studies* (which has recently widened its scope to include more contemporary topics, both literary and cultural). Journals that cover more general ground, but also contain articles of interest to students of French culture include *MLN* (*Modern Language Notes*), which publishes a French-themed issue once a year; *PMLA* (the *Periodical of the Modern Language Association*), which publishes articles on several national literatures and cultures; *SubStance*, and *Representations*, which both include articles on French literary and cultural themes. There is fairly regular coverage of French current affairs in several English-language newspapers such as the *New York Times* and, in Britain, *The Times*, *Guardian*, *Financial Times* and *The Economist*, which often publish special features or supplements devoted to France.

Reference guides to literature include *The New Oxford Companion to Literature in French* (1995), edited by Peter France, and *A New History of French Literature* (1994), edited by Denis Hollier, which has literary and other cultural entries arranged around significant dates, rather than by author or title (both works also include many entries on arts, history, and other cultural topics). Popular French periodicals devoted to literature include *Lire*; *Le Magazine littéraire*, which often devotes special issues to individual authors; and *Littérature*. Literary supplements are published in some daily newspapers, such as *Le Monde* (on Fridays) and *Libération* (on Tuesdays). *The Times Literary Supplement* in the UK and the *New York Review of Books* often cover French themes. These supplements can provide a useful overview of the current literary and cultural scene.

For general reference works on French cultural topics, consult *Quid*, an annually updated cultural dictionary, as well as the Routledge *Encyclopedia of Contemporary French Culture* (1998), edited by Alex Hughes and Keith Reader. Collections of useful essays can be found in *Identity Papers: Contested Nationhood in Twentieth-Century France* (1996), edited by Steven Ungar and Tom Conley; *French Cultural Studies: An Introduction* (1995), edited by Jill Forbes and Michael Kelly; *Postcolonial Cultures in France* (1997), edited by Alec Hargreaves and Mark McKinney; *French Culture since 1945* (1993) edited by Malcolm Cook; and *Le Creuset français: histoire de l'immigration* (1988) by Gérard Noiriel et al., which discusses the question of cultural diversity within France, in comparison with the US and other countries.

For students of cinema (see chapter 16), useful studies of French film include *The Cinema in France: After the New Wave* (1992) by Jill Forbes; *Contemporary French Cinema: an Introduction* (1996), by Guy Austin; *Mists of Regret: Culture and Sensibility in Classic French Film* (1995), by Dudley Andrew; *The Companion to French Cinema* (1996), edited by Ginette Vincendeau; *French National Cinema* (1993), by Susan Hayward; *Republic of Images* (1994), a history of French cinema by Alan Williams; and *The Ciné Goes to Town* (1998), by Richard Abel (on film's early days). For more specialized study, Manchester University Press (St. Martin's in the US) publishes a series on the work of individual French film directors. Some of the more important French film journals are *Cahiers du cinéma*; *Positif*; and *L'Avant-scène du Cinéma,* which publishes screenplays of individual films. Journals that include coverage of early French cinema include *1895*; *Les Cahiers de la Cinémathèque*; and *Iris*, published alternately in France and the US. The UK-based *Journal of French Film Studies* is due to start publication in 2001.

For subtitled French films on video and DVD in the United States, Facets in Chicago has a large selection of French films, and will fill orders by mail. In the United Kingdom, HMV and Virgin Megastores carry a selection of subtitled French films in the 'World Cinema' section. British, American and French video systems are mutually incompatible without a multi-standard video cassette machine, so videos should normally only be purchased in the country in which they will be viewed. If you live in a country that receives satellite TV broadcasts from France, that gives a hot line to French culture.

Grant and Cutler in London is a foreign-language bookstore with a good selection of French titles; they will mail orders throughout the UK. Residents of both the US and the UK can try searching for French titles from Internet booksellers amazon.com or amazon.co.uk, as well as FNAC in France (http://www.fnac.fr) which will ship books abroad. CPEDERF is an on-line and postal service in Paris (http://www.wanadoo.fr) that, for a fee (payable in francs or pounds sterling), will help you find books, videos and other research materials in France.

Resources in France

This section concentrates primarily on resources in Paris, since most students pass through Paris during their stay in France.

Libraries: Most libraries require one or two identity photos, so it is wise to carry several around with you; many charge a small daily admission fee. Every city in France has municipal library branches open to the public, and often with open stacks. In Paris, the most user-friendly public library, the Bibliothèque publique d'information, is located at the Centre Pompidou on the rue Saint-Martin, a landmark called 'Beaubourg' by locals. The centre has a large selection of daily newspapers from all over the world, housed separately from the library. Open stacks and Sunday opening make it popular with students (it is closed on Tuesdays). You can watch videos from the centre's 2400 documentaries and educational films, or listen to some of the 10 000 music CDs. There is Internet access for those who have the time to wait for a terminal.

The largest library in France is the Bibliothèque Nationale de France, in an imposing set of buildings on the quai François-Mauriac in Paris (13th arrondissement; métro station Quai de la Gare or Bibliothèque François Mitterrand, bus line 62 or 89). For a small charge, students may use the haut-de-jardin (garden-level) area of the library, where there is access to 430 000 works in French and other languages as well as a selection of current newspapers; day passes and annual cards can be purchased at the general reception on the east or west side of the building (l'Accueil général Est or Ouest). The library is closed on Mondays and some holidays (website: http://www.bnf.fr).

Not all libraries in Paris are open to undergraduates. Among those that are, the Bibliothèque Forney, at 1 rue du Figuier in the Marais (4th arrondissement), has a good collection of material relating to decorative and graphic arts: 200 000 books, 2600 periodicals, some 23 000 posters and over a million postcards. Also in the Marais, the Bibliothèque Historique de la Ville de Paris (24, rue Pavée) houses 15 000 maps, manuscripts and printed works from the sixteenth century to the present devoted to the history of Paris and the surrounding region. The Bibliothèque Sainte Geneviève is located in a historic building at 10, Place du Panthéon; the Bibliothèque Marguerite Durand, in the 13th arrondissement, specialises in works by and about women (open afternoons only); and the Bibliothèque des littératures policières – also known as the Bilipo – at 74–76 rue Mouffetard, has a collection of crime novels. Every library has different opening hours (many, for example, are closed one weekday), and most libraries are closed for between two and four weeks in the summer, often during August, so always try to phone ahead or have a backup plan in case you arrive when the library is closed.

The Forum des Images, formerly known as the Vidéothèque de Paris, is an excellent resource for students interested in film and video. Located in Les Halles in Paris, its most useful feature is its automated video collection. The admission price (discounted for students) entitles you to two hours at one of the individual viewing stations, where over 6000 short films, newsreels, advertisements and feature films from the silent era to the present may be accessed by computer. Most of these films have some connection with Paris. Their identification numbers should be checked on the computer terminal in the entrance, because once you begin using an individual viewing station, your two hours will go quickly. The catalogue is on-line at the Forum's website (http://www.forum.vdp.fr). The admission price also entitles you to see the two feature films shown daily in one of the large auditoriums on the premises. Programmes can be found in *L'Officiel des spectacles* and

Pariscope, two inexpensive weekly entertainment guides sold at all news stands, which also list museum and gallery exhibitions, theatre, dance and music events. For more specialized film study, the Bibliothèque du Film (known as the BiFi), at 100 bd du Faubourg Saint-Antoine (13th arrondissement), has printed, video and archival materials, due to combine forces with the new Maison du Cinéma. For researching photographic images, the Maison de la Photo, rue de Fourcy, has an excellent photo library.

Bookstores: The biggest all-purpose bookstore is the FNAC, which has several branches in Paris and all over France. Gibert Jeune and Joseph Gibert on the boulevard Saint-Michel are good sources of both new and second-hand books (*livres d'occasion*) for students. Used and rare books are also sold by the *bouquinistes*, or booksellers who line the banks of the Seine in Paris. Many of the larger museums, such as the Musée d'Orsay, the Centre Pompidou, and the Cité de la Musique at the Parc de la Villette in Paris have excellent bookshops, which often sell books on a variety of subjects such as history, film, literature and music as well as art. The state-financed Documentation française has a shop at 29–31 quai Voltaire, selling official publications plus a range of reports and periodicals on all sorts of subjects, often illustrated or with slide sets (www. ladocfrançaise.gouv.fr).

In Paris, bookstores specializing in books about cinema include: Aux Films du Temps, at 8, rue Saint-Martin in the 4th arrondissement; Ciné-Images, at 68, rue de Babylone in the 7th arrondissement; Ciné-Reflet, at 3bis, rue Champollion, in the 5th arrondissement; and L'Arbre à lettres, at 62, rue du Faubourg Saint-Antoine, in the 12th arrondissement. Several more exist in provincial cities.

The Web as a resource for students

There is a large and growing amount of excellent material in French on the Web, but it is fair to say that France started off some four years behind the UK and rather further behind the US in this area. The present French government is well aware of this, but no-one would claim that the speed of progress has been rapid since François Fillon, then 'ministre des Technologies de l'information' said in November 1995 'Internet existe, la France doit être dessus.' The sub-text was clearly 'Frankly, we'd rather it didn't exist.' The French government's tentative steps on the Net were greeted by headlines such as 'Marianne flirte avec Internet' (*Le Monde*, 20 May 1996), and the symbol of 'la république' certainly did not fall into the (masculine?) arms of the new technology. A special issue on the web produced by *Le Monde diplomatique* in the same month was revealingly entitled, 'Internet, l'effroi et l'extase'.

There are two main reasons for a certain scepticism and reticence about the wonders of the Web in France. The first, which might at first appear paradoxical since it demonstrates an open-mindedness about technology (a characteristically French trait) and ease with the paraphernalia of screens and keyboards, was the existence of the Minitel, the freely-distributed terminal originally intended to make phone-books redundant but which swiftly spread to offer all kinds of services and information. Wonderful, cheap, forward-looking, but a closed system. 'Alors, il n'est pas beau, notre bon vieux Minitel?' seemed to be a common reaction. In a sense, France peaked too soon in this area; countries with no Minitel did not have the burden of huge investment in old home-grown but limited technology when the Internet came along. And both France Télécom and the providers of services over the Minitel were understandably reluctant to provide information for free on the Web if people were prepared to pay for it on their Minitel. What could the Web do which the Minitel could not? Communicate with the world outside France, basically. 'Le Minitel mondial' was the description of the Internet in the 1996 *Quid* encyclopaedia, underestimating the power and impact of the Internet. The second reason was prickly suspicion of all things American in some circles, seeing the Internet as yet another weapon of US cultural imperialism, an electronic Trojan horse. Perhaps even more than in the UK and the US, early media coverage of the Web in France focused disproportionately on vague fears that it would be used for forms of sexual or political extremism. More recently, lucid and intelligent commentators such as Ignacio Ramonet of *Le Monde diplomatique* have pointed out the twin dangers of the existence of 'inforiches' and 'infopauvres' (the 'information-rich and information-poor'), though this is not peculiarly French – ownership of home computers is still a largely young and middle-class phenomenon – and of speed and quantity becoming more important than content.

The absence of the first of these two factors (Minitel) made Canadian French-speakers adopt the Web with speed and enthusiasm as a weapon with which to defend the language. Their inventiveness and determination has been a delight. For example, Quebec's e-mailers had invented and were using the wonderful and totally French-sounding 'courriel', from 'courrier électronique', at a time when the French were still wondering what on earth to call an e-mail. The official line from the Académie and from the Délégation générale turned out to be the feeble and absurd 'mél', too late to prevent everyone saying 'e-mail' instead.

A couple of other points about the language itself help illustrate both how hesitant and how different from the anglophone one has been the French reaction to 'la Toile'. First, according to Pierre Merle ('Tire ta langue', *France Culture*, 4 June 1999) 'C'est le Web là-dedans' is current slang for 'C'est le bordel, la pagaille, le boxon...', i.e. 'It's a complete shambles'. Since the image of the Web in English-speaking countries is generally more positive, it is difficult to imagine an anglicised version of this one catching on in the UK, though '(w)orld (w)ide (w)aste of time' has gained a certain currency among Anglo-Saxon sceptics. Second, from the start there has been a great deal of variation, even within a single newspaper or article, about article use with the word 'Internet'. 'Doit-on dire: "Je suis branché sur l'Internet" ou "branché sur Internet"?' was the question raised by Claude Duneton in the literary supplement of *Le Figaro* in April 1997. At that stage the Académie française had recommended 'Internet' without the article, whereas the Délégation générale à la langue française was for 'l'internet'. Duneton found the capital 'I' and the absence of an article absurd and pretentious, every bit as silly as if we said 'Alors, mon cher, avez-vous essayé Téléphone?' Current usage would suggest that 'Internet' is winning, but the uncertainty and the debate about article use are revealing.

The key point about the francophone Web, as about the anglophone one, is that the best single source of information about the Web is the Web itself, despite the increasing number of books on the subject. If you know a certain number of good sites and search engines, they will provide the best possible gateway. Most of what I need comes from between thirty and forty sites, all fairly recent. The first key technique you need to acquire, to speed up searching and save time, is to use francophone search engines when looking for information in French. There is no point in searching millions of English-language pages in addition to the French ones. The second is to assume or hope that someone may well have done some of the hunting and categorizing for you, and may even have organized the sites under helpful thematic headings in a 'répertoire multi-liens'. One of the most comprehensive of these is the University of Tennessee site, at http://www.utm.edu/departments/french/french.html.

What follows is an annotated list of a manageable number of sites which should prove fruitful, either in what they contain or in where they can lead, together with some brief notes of guidance on how to consult them. By the way, the French version of Microsoft's 'Where will you go today?' slogan was 'Jusqu'où irez-vous?' Is this significant? Discuss...

1. To speed up your searches for francophone Web material, use a French-language search engine, such as http://www.nomade.fr (currently the best), http://www.lokace or http://www.voilà.fr. At http://www.culture.fr/culture/dglf/ressources.htm, you can click on 'Des moteurs de recherche en français'.

2. http://www.ncl.ac.uk/~nsml/links/french.htm
This is an invaluable and very clear multi-link site for general information about France, with sites grouped by theme and links to other multi-site pages, including that of the celebrated Tennessee 'Bob' (see above). This will lead you to everything from a site that allows you to plan a trip to Paris or to investigate Paris hotels to others that will test your French grammar. Usefully, there are links to Canadian francophone multi-link sites as well.

3. The 'French Press' sections of the Newcastle site (site no. 2 above, based at the University of Newcastle) or the Tennessee site offer a wide choice of

newspapers, both regional and national. For example, *Le Télégramme* caters for the Breton diaspora in much the same way as the *Irish Times* keeps a different family of Celts in touch with the old country.

4. If you want a totally free daily paper with superb archives, and are happy with a left-of-centre slant, *Libération* is the one to head for: http://www.liberation.fr/ is the 'page d'accueil', which lists all the features, http://www.liberation.fr/quotidien/index.html takes you straight to the paper of the day. This is possibly the best and most generous newspaper site. It contains many articles and the editorial in full every day, front page in pdf format (to read which you will need Adobe Acrobat Reader or a plug-in for your browser), articles from the entire current week, and an astonishing 'chapitre un' feature with archives with dozens of first chapters from recent books. It also offers an excellent 'cahier multimédia' on the Web itself, on CD-ROMs etc., as well as a huge number of 'portraits', with interviews with everyone from MC Solaar and Emmanuelle Béart to Julian Barnes. The multimedia supplement is at least as good as that of *Le Monde*, there are excellent archives, and it is also an invaluable source of links to sites which they have discovered. This site is worth a daily visit, even if the language is at times all too knowing and cool in a hyper-Parisian kind of way, and the sub-editors appear to be having a punning contest with those of *Le Canard Enchaîné* . . .

5. http://www.lemonde.fr/
Some of the daily paper *Le Monde* is free, and the Multimedia supplement with huge archives is always free, as are many fascinating dossiers. For example, there has been excellent material on the Front National and on Algeria. Complicated technical rigmarole is needed to be able to pay 5F to read *all* of the paper of the day. At one point only the front page was free, but in spring 1999 *Le Monde* yielded somewhat, perhaps because *Libération* is so generous, and there is now much more of the paper available free every day. Consultation of archives is possible, but payment is required.

6. http://www.ina.fr/CP/MondeDiplo/mondediplo.fr.html
Le Monde diplomatique; excellent archives grouped by theme (searches possible by topic, country or date of appearance of article), all current and many past articles translated into English, on 101 political and socio-economic themes. There are hundreds of articles, not easy reading, but with excellent, well-researched content.

7. Among the serious weeklies (known as 'les news' in heavily anglicized French) *Le Nouvel Observateur* has the most comprehensive site at http://www.nouvelobs.com as well as TV listings and a free personalised TV listings by e-mail service.

8. All French TV stations feel obliged to have some kind of presence on the Web. Some stations are clearly more enthusiastic or have more resources than others. Certain announcers gleefully present the www. address, others are more 'vieille France' or sceptical about this new-fangled gadget. http://www.france3.fr/ is the address of the huge and elaborate France 3 site. There are many excellent links, transcripts of programmes, summaries of the day's and the week's news, and good dossiers on topics of the moment (e.g., in 1998, *vache folle* and asbestosis.) There are word-for-word transcripts of the superb 'Un siècle d'écrivains' programmes, and, if you have the technology, the possibility of watching extracts from the news.

9. http://www.france2.fr/
Similar to and almost as good as the France 3 site. Again, transcripts or summaries of the news, but (infuriatingly) in block capitals because it's the same news as goes out on French teletext.

10. http://www.rfi.fr/
This is the excellent and constantly improving site of Radio France Internationale. Click on 'kiosque' and then on 'Revue de presse' and 'Revue de presse hebdomadaire' to see what the French press of the day (or the week) is saying. There are also English and Spanish versions of these press reviews, but they're different, not translations, as well as topical articles about the Web and language items aimed at 'la Francophonie'. Often there are brief bite-sized transcripts of radio features, such as 'Parler au quotidien', which takes a word and talks about it, its history and how it's used.

11. http://www.le-petit-bouquet.com/
Excellent daily press and news review; you can visit the site every day or click on 'abonnement' to receive it as a Monday–Friday e-mail, if you have *une adresse électronique.* Make sure you click on the right version, depending on (a) whether your e-mail can make sense of accents or not (b) whether you'll be reading it within Netscape / Explorer or not – if the latter, you'll need to opt for the html version so your browser can read it.

12. Just after each *baccalauréat* exam, from mid-June onwards, look for http://www.lettres.net/ Started in 1999, this is aimed at Francophone teachers preparing pupils for the bac, and has many useful features. To quote from the site, 'avec en particulier des conseils méthodologiques pour le Bac de français, des ressources sur les auteurs au programme ou encore un lexique des termes littéraires et des listes de diffusion. En outre, une équipe de professeurs de français bénévoles répond aux demandes de corrections personnalisées que peuvent envoyer les élèves par courrier électronique'. I wonder for how long that last service, of the 'unpaid volunteer teachers sending out individual corrections by e-mail', will be offered... Either this site or the

Libération one should carry questions and then possible answers and teachers' comments during the bac season. This site still carries bac material from 1998 and 1999.

13. As further proof of the rare generosity of Web users, you can find phonetics fonts for both the Mac and the PC, easy to download and install, at: http://babel.uoregon.edu/yamada/fonts/phonetic.html

14. Canada offers some of the finest and most comprehensive lexicons of Web-related jargon; the official Quebec site at http://w3.olf.gouv.qc.ca/banque, where you can enter the French or English for techno-babble you want to translate, is well worth a visit, as is that of the 'Délégation générale de la langue française' at http://www.culture.fr/culture/dglf/liens/lexique.htm, which will lead you to a variety of lexicon sites.

As the above list shows, France has managed to 'épouser son Internet' but there are still many signs that the French reaction to the Web is reluctant rather than enthusiastic, something of an arranged marriage. Jacques Chirac's alleged ignorance about the new technology, supposedly revealed by his question 'Qu'est-ce que c'est qu'une souris?' at the opening of the Bibliothèque Nationale de France in 1998, gave the satirical TV programme 'Guignols de l'info' of Canal Plus the opportunity to run a sketch in which the puppet of the President, enthusing about computers, said 'Pour écrire, y a qu'à cliquer sur un mulot et ouvrir des fenêtres.' 'Mulot' was immediately ironically adopted by many as the term for mouse. A *Nouvel Observateur* feature (18 April 1999, 4) was, however, noticeably more positive than previous articles which had presented the Web as a 'repaire de pédophiles et de Nazis'. And the public and media image of the Web is generally becoming much more positive, with regular spots on the France 3 news, for example, presenting worthwhile sites. La Cinquième, the educational TV channel which occupies the same spot as Arte but in the daytime, has the weekly and punningly-titled 'Net plus ultra' programme, with gimmicky presentation but sound content. Arte has twice shown an entire theme evening of programmes about the Web. The review *Le Français dans le monde* has, for some time now, been a champion and discoverer of sites offering teachers and students of French excellent teaching and learning material, with a 'Multimédia' section in every issue. *Le Monde* also has a daily article on interesting websites.

In summer 1999, after launching the 'Programme d'action gouvernemental pour la société de l'information' (PAGSI) there in 1997, Lionel Jospin chose the Hourtin conference on communication to make a bold speech (typically, available in full on the *Libération* site), this time promising a new bill on the 'information society' for the start of the year 2000, and saying that the use of new technology should strengthen, not reduce cultural diversity. This is in reaction to the common view that the Web is essentially an

English-speaking zone and yet another example of cultural imperialism, but Jospin's positive attitude and the existence of a great many fine French-language sites have proved that 'le tout-anglais n'est pas une fatalité', in the words of a May 1996 headline in *Le Monde diplomatique*. No, the Web is not inevitably 100 per cent English-speaking, and the increasing number of excellent French sites proves this.

THE BACKGROUND TO FRENCH CULTURAL EXCEPTIONALISM

|3|

How the French present is shaped by the past: the last hundred years in historical perspective

BY SIÂN REYNOLDS

This book is appearing at the start not only of a new century but of a new millennium. A new year is sometimes represented by a baby, unmarked by time, as the old year creeps away. But no baby is really unmarked by the past: he or she carries a set of genetic messages inherited from previous generations. The France of the twenty-first century too carries a set of messages from its past. To understand cultural messages, one needs at least some acquaintance with the past. As suggested elsewhere in this book, we need to look back at least two hundred years, to the French Revolution of 1789, to make sense of much in French culture today. One obvious example, the national anthem the Marseillaise, dates from 1792: it is one of the 'sites of memory' as Pierre Nora (1984) has called them, the *lieux de mémoire* embedded in French life. Such symbols of past events are part of the 'taken for granted' that every nation possesses, but which may seem unusual and distinctive to outsiders.

It is the purpose of this chapter however to look back over a shorter period: just the last hundred years or so, and to pick out some of the distinctive experiences which have contributed to the French identity for people living today. This is not a history book, and what follows is not a chronological account of events, but an attempt to make sense of the 'French twentieth century'.

France was of course a major centre of world culture in the twentieth century, whether one thinks of fine art, literature, philosophy, music, theatre or cinema – matters which will arise in later chapters. At this point though, we will be more concerned with the *French experience of the twentieth century:* a century which saw great technological, economic and social transformations, two World Wars and a changed global order. France experienced the century in the light of its own distinctive identity, different in many ways from the various cultures in the English-speaking world. Here we will single out some key differences, special to France, to offer a context for later chapters.

Let us start with a sweeping, simplified, and no doubt debatable generalization. Taking the long view, it could be argued that for roughly the first half of the twentieth century, French society was still dominated by a set of concerns and cultural phenomena arising from the nineteenth century, while the second half saw the emergence of a new kind of France. This second France, although still bearing traces of the past, is the one we would recognize today. As a working hypothesis – a starting point for discussion – this can be tested out by readers in different contexts; they may find that it works better for some than for others. It is based on the suggestion that the Dreyfus Affair (1894–1906) holds some of the keys to the 'first twentieth century', while the second half, post-1945, calls for a different set of keys.

France's first twentieth century

The Dreyfus Affair, which focused world attention on France at the turn of the century, was a trauma which laid bare the cultural conflicts within French society, for good or ill. The facts are briefly as follows. In December 1894, Captain Alfred Dreyfus, a Jewish officer in the French army, was accused of spying for Germany. He protested his innocence. The evidence against him later proved to be irrelevant or forged, but he was court-martialled and sentenced to deportation. The army long refused to reconsider the case, despite evidence pointing to another officer. But a passionate campaign for revision of the verdict, during which the novelist Emile Zola published his famous article 'J'accuse', led to Dreyfus's re-trial in 1899. When the army once more found him 'guilty with extenuating circumstances', the outcry was so great that the President offered him a pardon, which he accepted, to prevent further unrest. Dreyfus's name was finally cleared in 1906. Many outsiders, including the international press, seized the chance to criticize the French nation for allowing such a miscarriage of justice to occur in the first place (and the second). More Francophile and perhaps more thoughtful observers noted that in other countries the cover-up might have been total: it was after all the republican reflexes of a section of French opinion which had alerted their compatriots to the problem.

The novelist Roger Martin du Gard wrote in 1913 that 'in fifty years or so, the Dreyfus Affair will just be one little episode in the struggle of human reason against the passions which blind it: just one moment, no more, in the slow and wonderful progress of humanity towards a better world'. In fact, the cultural and political echoes of the Affair did not subside for many years. We might single out four major areas of ferment which were either

Figure 3.1 Soldier with broken sword: the victim of France's most celebrated miscarriage of justice stands vulnerable but erect in Tim's 'Hommage au capitaine Dreyfus' (Paris, 1994).

provoked or revealed by the Dreyfus case, and which would have some impact over the next fifty years or so.

Franco-German relations and France's world status, 1900–c.1950

France's antagonistic relations with Germany lay at the centre of the Dreyfus case. Thirty years earlier, the Franco-Prussian war of 1870–1871 had brought humiliating defeat for France, hitherto regarded as the leading nation of Continental Europe. Fear of Germany and regret for the two lost provinces, Alsace and Lorraine, marked the period that followed (1871–1914), sometimes called the Belle Epoque. In this context, espionage naturally took on added importance. But direct confrontation with a powerful Germany was to be avoided. Instead, partly to compensate for the stand-off in Europe, France set out to acquire an enlarged colonial empire. By 1914, it was the second colonial power in the world after Britain, with an overseas empire of over 10 million sq km, and almost 50 million inhabitants, at a time when the population of metropolitan France was about 40 million. The empire would bring some immediate benefits and some long-term problems.

Twentieth-century France was therefore likely to be drawn into diplomatic alliances designed to preserve the precarious balance of power in Europe, while at the same time creating a new identity as a colonial world power. The effects of these two kinds of foreign policy were far-reaching. France and Germany would eventually go to war twice more, in particularly deadly fashion, while the colonies would become the focus first of French pride and ambition, and later of bitter wars of decolonization.

The two World Wars, viewed from a French perspective, were Franco-German conflicts taking place partly on French soil. The first (1914–1918) brought massive bloodshed, with the loss of one and half million French lives. The second (1939–1945) led first to an unexpected defeat in 1940, then to the Nazi occupation and an internal conflict setting French against French. The Vichy government under Marshal Pétain collaborated with the invader, while the Resistance and General de Gaulle's Free French continued to fight alongside the Allies. Fall-out from the Occupation has been a traumatic matter in France, as the full extent of collaboration has been explored and confronted. Yet paradoxically, in retrospect, 1945 marks the beginning of the end of hostility between France and Germany. A defeated and divided Germany, with Nazism eliminated, was no longer the threat it had earlier been; relations between the two countries were to alter dramatically.

France's empire meanwhile had become a strong cultural presence during the 1920s and 1930s, with the Paris Colonial Exhibition of 1931 marking a high point of its visibility in France. 'The intention was to inculcate pride and commitment to the colonial project, producing a new national identity, intimately connected to empire' (Evans 1999, 403). The French army sent soldiers to Indochina and maintained bases all over North Africa, a presence romanticized in popular films of the 1930s. Schoolchildren learnt which countries of the globe were marked by the French 'civilizing mission'. But although the colonies were crucial to both Vichy and the Free French during World War II, and although France emerged from that war with the colonial empire broadly intact, the latter did not long survive the world-wide movement of decolonization in the 1950s and 1960s. With hindsight, early twentieth-century France could be seen as seeking a global identity to compensate for the shadows over Europe, whereas after 1945 it would more firmly embrace a European identity – while facing some of the consequences of the colonial era.

Church and state

The second critical area connected with the Dreyfus Affair was the relationship between the Catholic Church and the republican state. The Third Republic was established rather precariously in the 1870s. The restoration of a monarchy, a Bonapartist Empire or even a military dictatorship seemed by no means impossible in the early days. In the past, the Church had sided with monarchy or Empire, so it was viewed by republicans as politically and socially conservative. Its schools were identified as enemies of the independent and scientific thought inherited from the eighteenth-century Enlightenment.

The Prussian victory of 1871 was regarded as the result of superior education and technology, so the new French Republic made education a cornerstone of its policies – aiming to create a modern and literate nation and to reduce the power of the Church. The education laws of the 1880s, under the reformer Jules Ferry, gave every town and village in France a state primary school for boys and girls. Schooling was free, compulsory and non-religious between the ages of 6 and 13. Previously many country children (and most girls) had been taught in Church schools. By contrast, newly trained state teachers saw it as their mission to provide a 'non-superstitious' education. (For a vivid picture of one such *instituteur,* see Marcel Pagnol's *La Gloire de mon père.*) Private schools, mostly Catholic, became the minority, with pupils choosing them mainly on religious grounds (they are still part-underwritten by the state so the fees are low). This helps explains why, on the whole, the road to a good education in France still today runs through the public sector, rather than via exclusive private schools as in some countries (cf. chapter 5).

In this context the Church found itself on the 'wrong' side in the Dreyfus Affair. Republican values, such as the right of the individual to a fair trial, freedom of speech, belief and the press, were seen by pro-Dreyfusards as the key issue. And while republicans of the 1890s were no revolutionaries, most of them remained fiercely anticlerical. Why was the Church implicated at all? For one thing, bourgeois families from which army officers were recruited often sent their sons to Jesuit colleges. Second, while it would be quite wrong to see all Catholics as having been anti-Dreyfusards, some outspoken groups within the Church backed the army, often insulting the republic at the same time. (Protestants, a small minority in France, mostly took the republican side.) From the high feelings raised by the Affair, pressure built up for the Church to be separated from the state – until then the two had coexisted uneasily, with the state paying the clergy. Republican governments in the 1900s took the final step of formal Separation, completed in 1905 with some bitterness (the banning of religious orders, the taking of inventories of churches, etc.). The two have remained separate: there is no question of prayers being said in the French National Assembly, as they are at the opening of the British Parliament.

Hostility between Church and republic probably remained its fiercest in the fifty or so years after the Dreyfus Affair. Even in the 1940s, as older people can remember, state and Church school pupils could come to blows in the street. Political life reflected this too. Maurice Larkin has pointed out that when General de Gaulle became head of the provisional government in 1944, he was the first practising Catholic to be head of government for 70 years. And one reason why French politicians resisted women's suffrage during the inter-war years was the fear that women, believed to be more religious than men, would vote for pro-clerical parties. Some traces of this Church state hostility still remain – as late as 1984 when a socialist government tried to modify the status of Church schools, a widespread outcry prevented the changes, so it is not dead. And Catholicism remains a cultural presence in many subtle ways in French literature and the arts. But looking back from 2000, what seems most obvious is that with the decline of Catholic observance in France, anticlericalism too has waned. On the other hand the question of religious background and schooling has arisen in connection with Islam (see chapter 8).

Discrimination against the 'other': the problem of antisemitism

One of the key features of the Dreyfus Affair was the suggestion that because the army had identified a Jewish officer as a possible suspect, it decided to look no further. In other words, it was guilty of antisemitism. This term, meaning hostility to or discrimination against Jewish people, first became current at this time all over Europe. It is ironic that it should have become entangled with French history, since after the 1789 Revolution discrimination was uniquely *banned* in France, where Jews could be citizens – so Dreyfus was able to pursue a career in the higher ranks of the army. But when in the late nineteenth century Jews fleeing persecution in Eastern Europe began to arrive in France, stirrings of antisemitism appeared there too. Edouard Drumont, editor of the antisemitic newspaper *La Libre Parole*, played an energetic role in the Affair. Anti-Dreyfusards like him claimed that there was a Jewish 'syndicate' protecting Dreyfus: antisemitic invective reached levels that would appal people today.

Such propaganda was temporarily silenced after the Affair, and as Pierre Birnbaum has argued (cf. Caron 1999, 174), French Jews became strongly republican, rightly seeing the republic as defender of their rights. Under the pressure of Nazism during the 1930s, however, antisemitism revived, coinciding once more with a wave of refugees, and the growth of a home-grown version of fascism in France. Once more, newspaper articles which would be banned today for racism became fairly commonplace. Shortly before becoming prime minister, the Jewish leader of the socialist party Léon Blum was set upon in the street. France was certainly not alone in this:

antisemitism was also quite openly voiced by people in Britain at the time. But in France, the tragic circumstances of the German invasion of 1940 turned antisemitism into an affair of state. After the fall of France, the Vichy authorities introduced discriminatory measures against Jews, and cooperated when ordered by the Nazis to assist in deporting thousands of Jews, of both French and foreign origin, to concentration camps.

This aspect of Vichy policy has been revealed progressively since the war and is now fully recognized by French historians and politicians. In the 1990s, both Presidents Mitterrand and Chirac called for remembrance of the suffering of Jews in wartime France. But without underestimating the role this reappraisal has played in the psychic history of France since 1945, it seems true to say that the traumas of the war have effectively put an end to the kind of antisemitism seen in earlier days, except for its residual form in the right-wing party, the Front National.

The rise of the intellectuals

The fourth area of 'ferment' emerging from the Dreyfus Affair is the rise of the intellectuals – the very word first came into use around 1900, and has always been associated with France (see chapter 21). It may seem odd to connect it with ferment. But from the start, the term 'intellectuals' was explicitly linked to combat. When Zola wrote 'J'accuse' in January 1898, accusing the French army of a cover-up, scientists, academics and literary figures signed petitions on both sides of the debate, lending their names and reputations to a political cause – as many still do in France today. Julien Benda later (1928) called this 'La trahison des clercs', complaining that the educated were betraying their calling by descending into the political arena. During the 1930s, intellectuals were once more prominent, many joining anti-fascist groups, some supporting the fascist cause in their writings. If the right-wing journalist and polemicist Robert Brasillach was executed at the liberation, it was for what he had written, not for any military action.

Looking back from beyond 2000, 'French intellectuals' in this political sense might be viewed as having arisen from a particular historical context, between the Dreyfus Affair and the Algerian War. The concept arises out of the existence of a highly educated elite, before educational reforms had spread to the entire population. Meritocratic access to higher education was in theory open to all, but in practice before about 1945 it favoured boys (and a few girls) from well-off families. It produced several remarkable generations of gifted, well-trained and often world-famous philosophers, scientists and thinkers, whose exposure to the tormented politics of the century's first fifty or so years explained their *engagement* or 'commitment'. Jean-Paul Sartre, Albert Camus, Simone Weil and Simone de Beauvoir all belonged to one of these generations. Many of them took up some kind of position (favourable, hostile or ambiguous) in relation to the French Communist

Party, which was at its most influential in the years from 1936 to the mid 1950s – as described in Beauvoir's novel *Les Mandarins* (1954) – while Marxism more generally appealed to many intellectuals (unlike in Britain) until the last quarter of the twentieth century.

From this brief overview, we might suggest first that from about 1900 to about 1950 and perhaps beyond, these four features could be seen as specific forces in French history. It is true that some of them might be found in other European countries – but not in quite the same form. Second, after World War II, all of these factors either became less important or were modified, as France underwent far-reaching change, making it more like the country we recognize today.

France's second twentieth century

No doubt the seeds of change were already there by 1939. But the remarkable pace at which France was transformed from a country largely identified with farmers and small businesses to an advanced urban and technological nation, in the latter half of the twentieth century, makes the last fifty years a time of exceptional cultural change. To simplify a complex picture, let us concentrate on five major features.

Economic and demographic change, and the role of the state

After 1945, the French economy experienced the 'trente glorieuses', the 'thirty miracle years' which saw a population explosion, the dramatic 'rural exodus', and the expansion of industry.

The single most important change after 1945 was not immediate, and came as a surprise to contemporaries: population revival. Between the wars France had had a strikingly low birth rate, the despair of governments who feared military defeat if too few children were born to replace the losses of 1914–18. After 1945, there was a predictable baby boom: what was not so predictable was that it lasted until the 1960s, bringing all the benefits and some of the problems of a young nation. In Dreyfus's time the French population had been about 40 million and it was still at this level in 1945. Now the figure is nearer 60 million. The birth rate slowed from the 1960s however and is now once more low, hence the incentives in the French social security system for larger families. In the latter half of the twentieth century, these changes were mostly beneficial and seen as marking a new confidence: in the twenty-first century however, the baby boom generation may pose more of a problem as it reaches retirement (see chapter 6).

The population also changed its patterns of residence. At the time of the

Dreyfus Affair, about half the French population (18 out of about 40 million) depended on the land for a living. Not until 1931 did the 'urban' population (people living in *communes* of over 2000 people) overtake the rural population. The 1930s depression and the Occupation of 1940–44, when it was an advantage to live in the countryside, slowed down the move to the towns, but it took off dramatically after 1945, as peasant-farmers and their relations left the land. Today, although French farmers are still a noticeably vociferous pressure group, less than 6 or 7 per cent of the population depend on farming for a living. Agriculture is no longer the self-sufficient way of life it remained as recently as the 1950s, but is now an important and subsidized export sector of the French economy, linked to intensive food manufacture. 73 per cent of French people now live in large cities or their suburbs, perhaps keeping in touch with their rural origins through an inherited *résidence secondaire* used for summer holidays. Patterns of domestic consumption have changed too. France is still a country where good food matters, but French people now shop in supermarkets and buy labour-saving food – less than Americans or the British, but far more than previous generations. From the 1960s, French households acquired cars, TV sets, and other goods, developing living patterns quite different from those of their predecessors.

Last, France has also undergone a technological revolution, symbolized for many by the high-speed trains (the TGVs, *trains à grande vitesse*). The post-war modernization of the economy was achieved partly with the help of another feature particular to France, and one less obviously to the fore in the early twentieth century: the role of the centralized state in directing the economy and administration. After World War II, the state nationalized several key sectors of heavy industry, and introduced a form of indicative planning which was much admired elsewhere.

The French *étatiste* or 'statist' tradition goes back at least to Napoleonic times, if not to Colbert and the seventeenth century. It certainly played a part in the 'trente glorieuses', and post-war recovery. In the twentieth century, the modern heyday of *étatisme* was perhaps from 1945 to the early 1980s (when the socialist government under President Mitterrand further expanded the state sector.) Since then, there has been something of a retreat from state ownership and planning. The TGV may come to seem the last grand state enterprise, a prestigious success achieved by means of large-scale public investment. Today, politicians of both right and left have accepted modification of the state tradition, including privatizations and some decentralization of political power, not to mention the impact of Europe. But France still has a large public sector compared to its neighbours, and the state tradition is more ingrained into French everyday life than it may be in the reader's home country. French public employees for example have a particular conception of their service which carries certain rights and privileges. And in the realm of culture and language, the state plays a quite special role in France (see chapters 4, 5, 10 and 11).

France's relations with the wider world

All these changes have brought complex consequences. For example, in pre-war times, the 1930s depression hit France less immediately and less sharply than its more industrialized neighbours, Germany and Britain, because France was less connected to the European and American economies. Then too, it still had a colonial empire. Today's French economy – more outward-looking and export-led – is also more vulnerable to world competition. Unemployment is often the price that is paid for openness to the outside world and the thirty 'glorious years' were followed by another twenty or more (1970s–1990s) when France suffered high levels of unemployment.

One important kind of openness to the outside world came in both symbolic and material form with the creation of the European Community. It would have been hard to predict in 1945 how closely France and Germany would be cooperating, as first the Coal and Steel Community (1951) and then the Common Market (1958) were set up. The Community was devised by Jean Monnet and others precisely to reconcile these two continental nations. Even today differences of interest can arise. But whatever the issue, Germany is for France the key partner and interlocutor in the European context – much more so than Britain. Whereas in the first part of the century, France was a rather uneasy ally of Britain, and feared Germany, now it respects Germany and is in some ways fairly indifferent to Britain, a country which has been ambivalent about Europe. As the newspaper *Le Monde* put it in 1995, 'nothing could be further apart than the British Eurosceptics who openly ask whether their country ought to get out of a Europe they think of as "foreign", and the Eurosceptics on the continent who criticize the abuses of Brussels in order to promote a firmer union'. During World War II, the stained glass of Strasbourg Cathedral in Alsace was taken down and hidden for fear of German bombing. Now Strasbourg houses the European Parliament. With the creation of the Euro on 1 January 1999, France and Germany both joined something described in English as 'Euroland'. The new common currency joined world finance markets as an alternative to the US dollar. The cultural implications of this change, which will mean the disappearance of the franc, have yet to become clear, but it is the culmination of a very different trajectory for France from the history of 1895–1945.

If France has increasingly come to be identified as a European nation, that is in part because of the loss of empire. Many of France's colonies achieved independence in the early 1960s by agreement, but in the major cases of Indochina and Algeria, independence came after long and bitter struggles (1946–1954 and 1954–1962). The Indochina war was in part linked to geopolitics and great power struggles: France was replaced by the US after 1954, and after further conflict, the Vietnam war came to an end only in the 1970s. In the case of Algeria, administratively regarded as part of France, the effects of the war were more hard-felt in France itself. It was the cause of the fall of the Fourth Republic and the return to power of General de Gaulle in 1958. Four years later, his government concluded a peace treaty leading to Algerian independence, but not without some bitter legacies, at least in the short term.

Last, France's place in the world has also been affected by the collapse of communism (both inside and outside France) especially since 1989. Under de Gaulle and to a lesser extent under his successors, France operated a fairly independent foreign policy within the western alliance, having unilateral relations with some communist countries, notably the former USSR. The collapse of the Cold War world order and the growing hegemony – not least in cultural affairs – of the United States since 1989 in particular, has been the occasion for much debate about *la fin de l'exception française* (see the introduction to this book).

Political change

France's trajectory has been a different one politically as well as economically. France is still a republic, and republican sentiments run deep in a number of its cultural institutions (cf. chapter 12). But it is no longer the same republic. For one thing – and this is a pointer to a major cultural change – it now has a political system encompassing both sexes. When women voted for the first time in 1945, the event was noted, yet many did not sense it as the sign of major change. It has indeed taken a long time for women to be admitted to the centres of political power through election to councils and parliament. But in retrospect, the change points to a very striking difference from pre-war France. The republic is now truly based on universal suffrage and (despite the persistence of a distinctive Gallic 'vive la différence' culture that Anglo-Americans sometimes find hard to take) women play a very significant role in French society. The historian René Rémond, in conclusion to his history of twentieth-century France (1990), singled out the status of women as the greatest change in his lifetime. In the 1990s, 'parity of representation' for men and women in the Assembly became an issue (cf. chapter 7 for reflections on French attitudes to sex and gender).

Second, the republic has changed its constitution or formal rules. In 1958, fears for the republic's existence almost seemed justified, as the Fourth Republic collapsed in division over the traumatic Algerian War. The Fifth Republic, distinguished from its predecessors by the key role of the president and of presidential elections, was largely the creation of General de Gaulle. Born in 1890, he was exactly the same age as Dreyfus's young son during the Affair, but his impact on France was felt most in the later part of the twentieth century. In 1940, defying his superior officers, he launched the Free French, and became a national hero at the Liberation. In 1958, he was recalled to power by the army, 'to restore order' – ironically, precisely the kind of scenario republicans had feared during the Dreyfus Affair – as well as to hold on to Algeria. But the clock was not turned back. De Gaulle was no dictator and proceeded to decolonize France's overseas possessions, including Algeria, and to institute the Fifth Republic which, although not undisputed, is now compared favourably with its less stable predecessors. The socialist François Mitterrand, who originally opposed the whole presidential idea in a book called *Le coup d'Etat permanent*, eventually became President himself and served two terms (1981–1995), longer than de Gaulle (1958–1969), signalling the acceptance of the institutions by the political left as well as the right.

It is true that de Gaulle's paternalist and patriarchal approach to politics barely survived the explosion of youthful protest of May 1968, which is referred to in several chapters below. De Gaulle had encouraged France's modernization by saying that the nation should 'épouser son siècle', literally 'marry the [twentieth] century'. But he could not put himself in the shoes of the baby-boomer generation, who fought the police from behind barricades and shouted, in their desire for utopian liberty, 'Sous les pavés la plage' ('Under the cobblestones, the beach'). The regime he had created though, perhaps because it did after all coincide with visible modernization and the end of colonialism, survived the sharp shock it received. Serge Berstein, reflecting on the myth of the republic, has also suggested that the Fifth Republic indeed marks the end of the symbolic order associated with the Dreyfus Affair, drawing instead on the symbolism of Free France and Resistance, the source of a new kind of legitimacy. The founding myth of the Fifth Republic he says, is de Gaulle's broadcast from London on 18 June 1940.

Fewer intellectuals, more culture-shocks

If May 1968 did not in the short term cause a *crise de régime* – June elections restored de Gaulle's government to power, although he himself soon retired – it was certainly a profound cultural crisis, the coming of age of the post-war generation. The pre-war intellectuals mentioned earlier, a 'generation of intellectual turbo-compressors … working flat out', found themselves side-lined in 1968. Jean-Paul Sartre was enthusiastically on the side of the student revolution, but he found an unaccustomed note on the lectern when he went to speak at the Mutualité: 'Sartre, be brief and to the point'.

Several changes combined to reduce – though not to abolish – both the commitment of intellectuals and the respect which they had once been accorded. One was the decline – though not quite disappearance – of the French Communist Party, with which so many post-war intellectuals sympathized. The world decline of communism was not as predictable in 1968, despite the 'Prague Spring', as it seems now from the other side of 1989, but the dwindling of the Communist Party in France during the 1970s and 80s reduced the size of an important subculture. In retrospect it is possible to see that this partly explains the so-called silence of the intellectuals remarked on during those decades, before a certain revival in very recent years.

Another factor was the expansion of higher education, a root cause of the unrest of 1968. In 1900 and even in the 1940s, only a tiny minority of French school pupils thought in terms of a university education. It has now become the ambition of most people that their children have some form of higher education. There are still educationally privileged elites – in France's unique system of *grandes écoles* – but the ambitions of their graduates are often administrative or commercial rather than intellectual-political. Today there are large numbers of well-educated adults, and plenty of academics, scientists and teachers, not to mention students, all ready to contest received opinion, so the rarity value of the intellectuals has been diluted.

With these changes it might be argued, the place of the intellectual in the post-Sartrean years was for a while vacant and became divided among various categories who did not quite fit the 'freelance-philosopher' model. Professional academics for example – historians of the Annales School like Fernand Braudel and Emmanuel Le Roy Ladurie, or scientists like Laurent Schwarz – became celebrated figures without being firmly identified with political stances. Some became *maîtres à penser* or gurus – often accorded particular fame outside France: Jacques Derrida, Julia Kristeva and Roland Barthes are examples. (Cf. chapters 21 and 22 below: Martyn Cornick suggests that the French intellectual has re-emerged for the millennium, in a new context, while Jeremy Lane analyses examples of French influence on modern thought worldwide. The trajectory of Pierre Bourdieu, the academic sociologist who has developed a high profile as a committed intellectual, is doubly significant in this respect.)

Another challenge to the pre-eminence of the intellectual has been the expansion of the media, which has created a number of well-known and street credible personalities. France was naturally affected by the arrival of radio and television: it had an early version of the home computer in the Minitel, and has now (after a few wobbles, cf. chapter 2) enthusiastically embraced the Internet. The advertising image, the soap opera, the computer screen, the sound-bite and the mobile phone compete for the attention a previous generation would have given to reading books and newspapers. The cultural change symbolized by 1968 was in part a generational change. Youth culture, centred in part around music, in part around sport, in part around fashions of all kinds, has become pretty much world wide (cf. chapters 13, 14, 17, 19). Future role models will not necessarily be 'intellectuals' at all.

A different 'otherness'

The fifth great change to be mentioned here is not peculiar to France, but it could be argued that it has a particular resonance in France. In Dreyfus's day, Jews from Eastern Europe were among immigrants seeking asylum in France, traditionally a country of refuge. The twentieth century was to see much immigration into France, especially when adult male labour was needed. Young men from Poland, Belgium and Italy were drawn to France after World War I, while after World War II, with the massive expansion of the French economy, workers came from further afield, especially from France's colony Algeria, the protectorates of Tunisia and Morocco, and later from a wide range of Third World countries.

Immigration always causes stress for both sides, but in prosperous times these are less obvious. After the oil crises of the 1970s, the French economy began to move into recession; unemployment and racial tension grew, and economic immigration virtually stopped. But many immigrant workers had settled in France with their families and became a new feature in French society. Incomers of European origin, such as the many Portuguese who came to France in the 1950s, had a comparatively short cultural distance to travel. But North African Muslims formed a large percentage of incomers. Their cultural difference was greater and was exaggerated by effective, if unintentional segregation, families often being lodged in new housing schemes outside cities, *les banlieues*. School-leavers from these families were not well placed as high youth unemployment hit France in the 1980s and 1990s. Racial tensions were magnified by the rise of the Front National. In response, movements such as SOS Racisme were launched to combat discrimination.

As noted by several contributors, multiculturalism – allowing various cultural groups to maintain their identities in all circumstances – is regarded with suspicion by some people in France, as likely to create a society of ghettos. Others suggest that it is possible to combine a distinctive cultural identity with conformity to the legal limits of the state in which one lives, and that to suppress people's cultural identity is to practise intolerance. Similar questions have arisen in other European countries with large minorities of foreign residents of fairly recent arrival, but the French debate has taken on a particular form. Taking the long view, it is arguable that younger generations may be able to handle these issues with fewer preconceptions than their parents (cf. chapters 6 and 8).

This chapter has set out not to give a history of twentieth-century France, but to isolate – a little artificially, and with the aim of provoking questions – certain issues relating to the historical specificity of France, providing a context for what follows. France is a rewarding country to study and compare with other traditions. If one were to hazard a generalization to summarize the foregoing, it might be that in the first half of the century, France was mainly concerned to protect its territorial existence, and to export French culture, in particular to its empire, while in the second half, it has secured its existence firmly within the new Europe, but has become more concerned to defend French culture against competition from elsewhere, whether the United States or Islam. The reader may not necessarily agree with this or any other propositions suggested here; but enough has been said, I hope, to suggest that an ancient and complex culture such as France cannot be reduced to a single or stereotypical identity.

References and further reading on twentieth-century French history: recent books in English

ALEXANDER, Martin (ed.) 1999: *French history since Napoleon*. London: Arnold.
CARON, Vicki 1999: The 'Jewish question' from Dreyfus to Vichy. In ALEXANDER 1999, 172–202.
EVANS, Martin 1999: From colonialism to post-colonialism: the French empire since Napoleon. In ALEXANDER 1999, 391–415.
GILDEA, Robert 1996: *France since 1945*. Oxford: OUP.
LARKIN, Maurice 1988 2nd edition 1997: *France since the Popular Front 1936–1986*. Oxford: OUP.
McMILLAN, James F. 1992: *Twentieth-century France: politics and society 1898–1991*. London: Arnold.
REMOND, René 1990: *Notre siècle*. Paris: Fayard.
VINEN, Richard 1996: *France 1934–1970*. Basingstoke: Macmillan.
All these books have very full bibliographies, directing readers to works in French, and Rod Kedward and Charles Sowerwine are both completing new histories of France in the twentieth century.

A special mention should be made of a work which combines history and culture, Pierre Nora's monumental seven-volume collection *Les Lieux de mémoire* (1984–) which contains chapters on dozens of cultural topics. This was republished in paperback in three volumes by Gallimard in 1997; a selection in English has been translated by Arthur Goldhammer as *Realms of memory: the construction of the French past* (New York: Columbia University Press, 1998). For a thematic guide to this collection, see Appendix below, pp. 302–308.

|4|

French cultural policy: the special role of the state

BY SUSAN COLLARD

What does the word 'culture' mean to French people? Since the rest of this book will be introducing the reader to some varied aspects of French culture today, the purpose of this chapter is to look at the national context in which all these cultures and subcultures function. This means that we need to examine the role of the state (in the French sense of the word, *l'Etat*), since in France it is essentially the state that has set up the formal context within which most forms of cultural expression have been either encouraged or repressed.

By contrast with Britain and America, there is something very distinctive about the close relationship between French culture and political power. In France today, the state, represented mainly by the Ministry of Culture, plays a more influential and visible role than any other actor. It does this, not simply by funding the arts on the British model, 'at arm's length', but centrally, by developing and applying a highly interventionist cultural policy designed to reflect national objectives. Outside observers will find it impossible to understand French culture without having some idea of the political importance and impact of state-driven cultural policy. So this chapter will first give a brief but essential historical account of how and why current attitudes to cultural affairs have developed as they have, before going on to examine the cultural role of the state in France today. It will discuss its economic impact, and the extent to which cultural policy-making is still influenced by tradition.

Culture and the state: the historical tradition

It is true that in France, we have a special shared idea of what culture is. This does not just date from M. Mitterrand's presidency, nor even from the days of Malraux or Pompidou, but goes back centuries. Despite our troubled history, the idea of culture has always been a constant: we know it to be an irreplaceable component of our national identity and of our country's vocation to radiate (*rayonner*) beyond its borders, and we know that it implies a degree of responsibility on the part of the state. In this respect, for us in France 'cultural exceptionalism' [. . .] is a categorical imperative.

Rigaud 1995, 17

This quotation from Jacques Rigaud (a top civil servant and specialist on cultural policy) is a good example of how French policy-makers consider the roots of the distinctive French approach to culture to be deeply embedded in historical tradition, and part of their national identity. The tradition is generally said to have begun in the sixteenth century with the beginnings of absolute monarchy under François I (1515–1547), when the state began to use culture as a political tool to enhance French status and power (Poirrier 1996; Djian 1996; Burguière 1993). The kings of France set an early precedent for state intervention in cultural affairs in several ways: chiefly, by introducing the practice of state commissions to create art works and monuments intended to reflect and enhance the prestige or *grandeur* of the French monarchy. This practice, known as *le mécénat d'Etat*, is usually seen as the precursor of public funding for the arts as we know it today. All the best artists were working for the greater glory of the state, by channelling their creativity towards such things as ceremonial odes, statues of the king to decorate palace courtyards or symbolic public spaces, or portraits of monarchs in glorious circumstances. François Mitterrand's programme of monumental architectural projects in Paris in the 1980s and 1990s, known as the *grands projets culturels* or the *grands travaux*, has often been interpreted as a conscious revival of this tradition (Collard 1998). By affording the monarchy a controlling influence over cultural production, *le mécénat* went hand in hand with royal censorship, established by setting up a series of artistic academies endowed with authority over every aspect of cultural life: music, dance, architecture, painting and sculpture.

The first of these was the Académie Française, created in 1635 by Louis XIII under the authority of his minister Richelieu to exert control over the use of the French language, seen as the key to French culture (cf. chapter 10). In this way, writers, *les hommes de lettres,* were to be encouraged to celebrate royal grandeur. It has been pointed out by Roger Chartier that the Academy introduced into the French cultural system 'the very forceful and enduring idea that all aesthetic production must be judged on its degree of conformity to the rules set out by the legitimising institution' (Chartier 1993, 351). This was the foundation for what is referred to as *académisme*: a tendency to observe a set of rules laid down by the ruling elites, often linked to artistic conservatism. It is a feature which has constituted one of the most entrenched dimensions of French cultural life. The academies still exist today – though considerably modified and with less influence – under the auspices of the famous Institut de France (opposite the Louvre). So it is

not hard to see why the link is made so freely between the monarchy's intervention in cultural life, and the role played by today's cultural establishment, since members of the Institut are also chosen by representatives of the
state.

This royal legacy, perhaps surprisingly, was not repudiated under later
republican regimes in France after 1789. Initial impulses to destroy the symbols of autocratic power soon gave way to a realization that it was in the
state's interests to preserve and build on the cultural heritage of the newly
emerging French nation. Within France, the *patrimoine culturel* was used as
a vehicle for the construction of a national 'shared' memory of, and pride in,
French history, designed to have a unifying influence on the population.
Abroad, the monarchical preoccupation with grandeur was superseded by
the republic's universalist claims to a 'civilizing mission', providing ideological justification for the plundering of so-called 'uncivilized' territories
whose cultural artefacts could be brought back to the cradle of liberty. The
symbol of the First Republic's 'nationalization' of culture was the conversion of the Louvre palace (the traditional home of the French monarchy
until Versailles was built) into a national museum, opened to the public in
1793: it still contains many 'plundered' exhibits, such as Egyptian antiqui-
ties brought back by Napoleon's armies. The fact that Mitterrand made the
reorganization of the Louvre a key feature of his architectural projects can
be seen as a highly significant gesture towards renewing the link with this
revolutionary cultural tradition.

Later regimes of both right and left – empire, monarchy and republic – all
harnessed the use of culture for political purposes. There has been a surprising degree of elite consensus (given the troubled nature of French political history more generally) over the importance of culture in national
political life, and especially over making the 'pérennité de l'œuvre national',
the lasting values of national achievements, the basis of French national culture. This was particularly true under the Third Republic (1870–1940),
whose leaders were concerned to strengthen the republican system of government and its universalist values introduced by the Revolution, through a
range of nation-building measures applied through the education system.
Schools had the task of transmitting a universalist *culture générale* as the
necessary grounding for all future citizens (cf. chapter 5). Using state-
imposed textbooks, it involved the digestion of a considerable volume of
knowledge about French history, art and literature, plus a large measure of
classical philosophy – all of course taught through the medium of the French
language, not in any of the many regional dialects and languages in common
usage at the time. This general culture was in reality not so much 'universal'
as distinctively French, and was taught to all children throughout the French
empire, regardless of their ethnic origins; nor was there any attempt to
include any element of their own cultures, since these were not considered
part of the 'national' heritage.

The overwhelming impact of this policy was to generate the (perhaps illusory) sense of a unified, homogeneous notion of French culture, a central element in the formation of French identity, and still a defining influence today. The *culture générale* thus acquired has ever since been used as one of the formal ways of selecting the future civil servants (*les serviteurs de l'Etat*), by means of general cultural test-papers which are an essential ingredient not only in the *baccalauréat*, but also in the *concours* (competitive exams) opening the door to all the *grandes écoles* and many public sector jobs or training programmes. The continued importance of this testing process can be seen in the many publications on the shelves of bookshops and hyper-markets, helping students prepare for this sort of exam. (For foreigners too, these can be a good source of information about French culture.) The emphasis is on breadth of knowledge, but the Franco-centric focus of the questions in fact defines the kind of knowledge about their national cultural heritage that educated (*cultivé*) French people are expected to have absorbed. This is one of the less visible ways in which the state, through its highly centralized education system, has traditionally shaped French people's ideas about their own culture.

The fact that the state historically took such a leading role in deciding what French culture should be meant that it was inclined to be highbrow (museums, great writers, world-famous artists), with little input from popu-lar forms of culture, and hardly any influence from non-metropolitan France or French regional cultures. It was really accessible only to middle- and upper-class people in large cities, especially in Paris. Consequently, towards the end of the Third Republic, the left-wing government of the 1936 Popular Front, concerned by the exclusion from this culture of the working classes, was the first to try to popularize culture and broaden it to include 'mass culture' such as cinema, and popular festivals. But the brevity of the Popular Front experience, lack of funds, and the coming of the war limited the number of changes introduced.

The 'invention' of cultural policy

After World War II, pressure from renewed 'popular culture' movements led to the inclusion of *le droit à la culture*, both in the new French Constitution and in the Universal Declaration of Human Rights (1948), but it was not until the creation of the Fifth Republic that the French state really tackled what had become a major problem: how to democratize culture. This was the main task allocated to the well-known writer and Resistance figure, André Malraux, chosen by de Gaulle to be France's first Minister of Cultural Affairs in 1959, the date that technically marks the beginning of French cultural policy as we understand it today (Urfalino 1996). Malraux saw his main objectives as being 'to make the great works of art of human-ity, and in particular of France, accessible to as many French people as pos-sible; to ensure as much access as possible to the French cultural heritage and to encourage artistic creativity'. He thus maintained the traditional insistence on the idea that only 'high culture' was worthy of public subsidy, yet he also broke with the 'académisme' of the cultural establishment by openly embracing the avant-garde and by encouraging wider access to 'great art'. He had intended to set up a Maison de la culture in at least twenty *départements*. These centres, with exhibition and performance spaces, were often described as 'cultural cathedrals' because of Malraux's aim to turn them into beacons of cultural excellence, though less than a dozen were built in the end. This was partly because Malraux's ministry never had a budget large enough to underpin his ambitions, but also perhaps because he misjudged the ability and inclination of the wider population to respond positively to a package of culture defined in a rather classic way. Only the educated middle classes really benefited.

The other main objective of the ministry was to contribute to the glory and grandeur of the French state – de Gaulle's own overriding ambition. The renewal of a close relationship between political power and culture became a distinctive feature of the Fifth Republic. By showcasing the cultural role of the state, emphasizing the national character of French culture, encouraging the 'rayonnement culturel de la France' abroad, and using the apparent consensus to build a new sense of national identity, Malraux played a full part in the Gaullist political agenda. It was in fact this overt political association that brought an end to the Malraux ministry, when de Gaulle resigned in 1969. But the events of May 1968 also represented a much broader questioning of the definition and power of culture and its role in society, as a result of many new ideas that had informed intellectual debate in the 1950s and 1960s: in particular, the increasing influence of the relatively new and intellectually fashionable discipline of ethnology (anthropology), which saw culture not simply as Malraux's *culture noble*, but as a much broader concept, including the whole range of everyday activities that ordinary people engaged in, referred to as *le quotidien* (Lefèbvre 1968). Other intellectuals such as Michel de Certeau spoke up for forms of popular culture that had either been repressed or simply not recognized by the state (popular music for instance). The unified national culture traditionally encouraged and imposed by the state was giving some ground to cultural pluralism (de Certeau 1974). May 1968 had revealed the fissures in what the Fifth Republic had described as the national heritage, and the ministry was forced to reconsider its position. However, in the absence of a personality like Malraux to lead the way, the *entre-deux-mai* (Ory 1983) proved to be a period of hesitations for the ministry. Not until the nomination of Jack Lang as Minister of Culture after the election of François Mitterrand in May 1981 was a completely new approach to cultural policy adopted. Since 'the Lang years' have had such a massive impact on cultural life in France in the 1980s and 1990s, it is worth looking briefly at what people mean by this expression.

The Lang years

Jack Lang, a flamboyant and iconoclastic politician, was Minister for Culture under President Mitterrand from 1981 to 1986, and then again from 1988 to 1993, holding this post long enough to leave a very distinctive mark on French cultural policy. His greatest contribution was undoubtedly the striking way in which he brought cultural policy to the very forefront of the political agenda. Several reasons, not all of them disinterested, explain this politicization of cultural policy: first, the importance attached to culture by the Parti Socialiste in opposition in the 1970s (Urfalino 1996, 307–17, Looseley 1995, 56–65); second, Lang's use of his position for electoral manoeuvring (Urfalino 1996, 312–17; Rigaud 1995, 99–103); and third, the level of support given to Lang by the President, who wanted to leave a cultural stamp on his political legacy. As a result of the Lang-Mitterrand era, cultural policy has remained a high priority for all later governments, making this a field of politics where consensus has replaced conflict.

As soon as he was appointed minister, and in accordance with Mitterrand's expressed wish that 'partout en France, les talents s'éveillent' (author's interview with Lang, 1995), Lang began to put in place the elements of what was intended as 'une sorte de révolution culturelle'. The most significant change was the immediate government decision to double the budget of the Ministry of Culture, with the aim of raising it to the symbolic level of 1 per cent of the national budget. The second major innovation was to broaden the scope of the Ministry's intervention (and subsidy) to include a whole range of much more popular cultural practices previously not recognized, referred to as 'les arts mineurs': jazz, rock, rap, tag (i.e. graffiti art), cartoon strips, the circus, fashion, photography, gastronomy – and more. An effort was also made to increase access to cultural activity for disabled people, those in prison and hospital, and other disadvantaged or minority groups (Colin 1986). This aspect of Lang's policy was a departure from the Socialist Party's traditional stress on the working class as the chief excluded group. It indicated a controversial new acceptance by at least one arm of the state of le droit à la différence as the basis for the multicultural society that France had in reality become. To embrace cultural diversity as a matter of policy was to go some way towards the position of the 'pluralists' instead of insisting on one universal cultural diet. The much repeated formula used at the time was 'le tout culturel'. The third innovation of Lang's policy was the spectacular way in which it was communicated to the public; Lang's colourful personality, and his skilful use of the media, made for a potent combination that kept the ministry and his controversial policies in the public eye. Lang's use of la fête, a word which has the connotations both of festival and of partying, borrowed from intellectual debate in the 1960s and 1970s (Lefèbvre 1968; de Certeau 1974), was another strategy to harness both media attention and public enthusiasm. For example, la Fête de la Musique started in 1982 as an attempt to create a spontaneous and public celebration of musical talent at all levels by encouraging musicians literally to go out into the streets and play. It was followed by festivals focusing on books, the cinema, theatre, cartoon strips etc. and there is a thriving festival culture in France today (see chapter 17).

The minister's fourth major innovation was the least expected: a totally new approach to the relationship between culture and the economy, summed up in Lang's phrase: 'Economie et culture, même combat'. These two domains had traditionally been considered as belonging to quite separate logics. Now cultural creativity was seen as an important factor encouraging economic development: cultural industries (such as the cinema, book publishing, video, multimedia etc.) received a whole range of supportive state measures, but private business sponsorship was also encouraged. The cultural state was thus to develop a new type of relationship with the open market, which needs some explanation. Basically, the gradual worsening of the economic situation in the 1980s meant that to justify his plea for more public funding, Lang had to compromise by making cultural activities more financially viable. But it is also true that Lang's vision included the idea that cultural activity could be positively linked to the wider economy via private enterprise, not just state finance.

Lang's legacy as Minister of Culture has been highly original, even if in some respects he preserved continuity. But another important dimension of the Lang-Mitterrand legacy was the so-called presidentialization of cultural policy. The agreement by Lang and Mitterrand that an ambitious cultural policy should be driven by a number of major 'gestures' led them to initiate a major programme of architectural projects in Paris (and to a lesser extent in the provinces): the *grands travaux* or *grands projets culturels*. These included the Opéra-Bastille, the Arche de la Défense, the Grand Louvre, the Musée d'Orsay, the Institut du Monde Arabe, the Cité des Sciences at La Villette and the Bibliothèque Nationale de France – all in Paris (Collard 1992). The thinking behind these projects was that they would bring about a revival of creativity in France; put Paris back on the map as the centre of the cultural world (a position partly lost to other capital cities such as New York); provide better facilities for the culture-loving Parisians while embellishing the capital's reputation as a Mecca for cultural tourism, and finally, act as a motor to encourage similar projects outside Paris. The President took an active role in the preparations for designing and building these projects, effectively sidelining Lang and his ministry, though most of the finished products are now run under the auspices and the budget of the Ministry of Culture. This aspect of the works was controversial: Mitterrand's critics accused him of entertaining illusions of grandeur reminiscent of Louis XIV, and the *grands travaux* were seen by many as a revival of the old royal tradition of *mécénat* under a republican flag (Chaslin 1985).

So the Lang-Mitterrand era offered a curious combination of quite unexpected innovations in which history and modernity expressed themselves in often paradoxical ways. Socialist cultural policies generally proved popular with French people. However, a number of intellectuals launched a virulent critique of the way in which the ministry's increasingly tentacular and defining role, expressed in the idea of 'l'Etat culturel' (Fumaroli 1991), had led to the alleged dumbing down of 'true culture' in favour of an entertainment-driven cultural consumerism that no longer justified public subsidy or the existence of a ministry (Finkielkraut 1987; Schneider 1993). The echoes of this debate in the French media and its impact on the general public showed that questions of culture and cultural policy can still provoke passions in contemporary France. Although observers with no axe to grind also agree that the critics have identified real issues of concern for the future, the attacks on the ministry have not undermined its status or influence, as the following section will show.

Cultural policy in contemporary France

As we have seen, the idea that the state in France has a cultural mission is widely accepted. Despite the recent criticisms by intellectuals of 'l'Etat culturel', the state's intervention in cultural affairs is seen by most French people as legitimate and indeed necessary, even if the scope and manner of it can cause controversy. The Minister of Culture until March 2000, Catherine Trautmann, often said that the cost of cultural policy was justified because it could be considered as a public service. The aims of today's ministry in fact remain much the same as when it was created, notably: 'rendre accessibles au plus grand nombre les œuvres capitales de l'humanité, et en premier lieu les œuvres françaises; assurer la plus vaste audience à notre patrimoine culturel' (www.culture.gouv.fr: 'Les attributions de Madame la Ministre'). There is still an emphasis on admiring great works by French artists and writers, alongside an ongoing concern for 'cultural democratization'. But the latter does seem to have eluded successive ministries. Several surveys carried out by the ministry since the 1970s have shown that the extent to which French people engage in cultural activities is *still* determined largely by their social class and educational background, with the middle and professional classes still the great beneficiaries. For example, a 1997 survey shows that whereas only 4 per cent of *cadres supérieurs* had never visited a museum, the figure was 38 per cent for unskilled workers; similarly, only 13 per cent of *cadres supérieurs* had never been to the theatre, compared to 71 per cent of unskilled workers (Donnat 1998). Recent policies have attempted to reduce the social inequalities of access to culture in three ways: first, through pricing policies targeting a new public, aimed at reducing *la distance économique*. Second, by introducing policies designed to reduce what is called *la distance culturelle* by encouraging projects and visits within the education system. The aim here is to introduce children at a young age to habits with which their families may not be familiar, such as visiting exhibitions or theatres – and in this way breaking down some social distinctions. The Ministry of Education works in partnership with the Ministry of Culture to fund these projects, in and out of school hours, as well as trying to encourage more art and music teaching in French schools – where there has traditionally been little emphasis on creative arts.

The third strategic approach aims to tackle the uneven geographical distribution of cultural facilities across the country. Traditionally, Paris has been considered as the showcase for French culture, and Mitterrand's *grands travaux* aimed explicitly to restore the international cultural status of the capital city, putting Paris (and by extension, France) at the centre of the 'civilized' world. But this concentration of resources to the detriment of the rest of the country aroused criticism, so efforts have been made to refocus on cultural decentralization. First, back in the 1970s, the ministry itself established a network of offices called Directions Régionales des Affaires Culturelles (the acronym DRAC can mean the institution or its director, *directeur*) in each of the regions of France – a collection of mini-ministries. Since the 1992 law on 'déconcentration', the DRACs have been given more of the ministry's budget, along with more responsibilities. They basically carry out at regional level policies drawn up by the minister, adapting them to each region and seeking to reduce imbalances. But DRACs also have an advisory role, providing professional knowledge for local authorities and cultural groups (www.culture.gouv.fr: 'Rôles et missions des DRAC'). In this way, the state manages to keep a close eye on what is going on in the provinces, without always having to refer things back to Paris.

Second, also since the 1970s, the ministry has been encouraging local authorities to develop their own cultural policies, through a system of partnership contracts based on shared expenditure for specific programmes. The partnership model enables the ministry to be selective in handing out money, but some local authorities have pursued independent policies. It is the municipalities, i.e. towns, cities and even villages, rather than the regions or *départements*, that have taken on the most active role in cultural politics. This is because many mayors, acting as 'municipal monarchs', have emulated the national model of the Lang-Mitterrand years. What is most striking about French culture in recent years is the way local mayors, especially of large towns, have gone in for major cultural gestures such as supporting a new opera house or concert hall; or hosting annual exhibitions or festivals of, say, photography, as part of their broader strategy to improve the quality of living in their towns. Some large cities are said to spend as much as 14 per cent of their budget on culture. This local cultural policy is obviously driven partly by electoralism. A high profile can embellish the image and status of a town or city. But local politicians also see cultural policy as a means of dealing with social and economic issues: tourism, urban renewal, the fight against social exclusion or against rural 'désertification'. Local authorities collectively now spend about the same amount as the state (see tables showing public expenditure on culture on the Ministry's website under 'mini-chiffres clés: dépenses culturelles'). For all that, the ministry manages to maintain its guiding role (some would say its grip) across the country through the DRACs and partnership contracts.

It also operates beyond national frontiers, in order to carry out France's traditional cultural 'mission' in the world. It does this through a special Department of International Affairs whose policy is to promote French culture abroad and encourage international cultural cooperation. For example, it gives practical help and funding for French artists to exhibit or perform abroad, helps galleries to retain a presence at international contemporary art fairs, and actively promotes French cultural industries (music, video, publishing, multimedia and cinema) to the rest of the world, at big trade fairs and other international organizations and conferences.

It also works in partnership with the Ministry of Foreign Affairs (the equivalent of the UK Foreign Office, or US State Department) which has a special section (la Direction générale des relations culturelles, scientifiques et techniques: DGRCST) dedicated to the promotion of French culture abroad. This department runs 32 French cultural institutes across the world offering French language teaching and organizing cultural events. (You may be aware of your local Institut Français.) It also supports French-language schools and teaching establishments abroad, such as the Alliance Française, which has over 1000 centres spread across 140 countries. And it funds the Association Française d'Action Artistique (AFAA) (www.afaa.asso.fr), an association dating back to 1922, and now one of the main instruments of the diffusion of French culture abroad. This cultural affairs department accounts for an astonishing 35 per cent of the *foreign ministry*'s total expenditure (Djian 1996, 101). This indicates how seriously the French state takes its cultural mission worldwide, within the context of its foreign diplomacy.

One particular aim of the French cultural mission in the world is the promotion of the French language – traditionally a concern of the state since the creation of the Académie Française. A group of 52 French-speaking states now constitute the 'Organisation internationale de la Francophonie' (see the website of the Ministry of Foreign Affairs listed below: you get to 'la Francophonie' via the Espace culturel: Politique Etrangère, and also chapter 10). Originally an informal group in 1970, it has been meeting formally in 'le Sommet de la Francophonie' every year since 1986, reinforced since 1997 by the Secrétariat général de la Francophonie, led by Boutros Boutros-Ghali. It aims to strengthen cooperation between Francophone countries in the interests of cultural diversity within a common language, but there has been a recent move to make the organization more political, and to encourage its members to call for respect of human rights.

Finally, French cultural presence in the world has lately been expressed through the notion of 'l'exception culturelle', which was established during the Uruguay round of GATT (General Agreement on Tariffs and Trade, now superseded by the World Trade Organization) negotiations in 1993 between countries of the European Union and the US. The French government successfully argued that cultural products and services should not be treated in the same way as any other goods, and it was able to win the support of fellow EU members to support its case for maintaining subsidies to national audio-visual industries and especially the cinema – even though this is likely only to be a temporary respite from the encroaching logic of free trade. France was in this instance able to use to its advantage its membership of the EU. But the EU's regulation policies are in other ways increasingly being seen as a constraint on French cultural policy. It is not surprising therefore to note that at the Francophonie summit in Canada in September 1999, the French President called on this other arena to campaign for 'l'exception culturelle'. The attachment of the French to their argument in favour of cultural distinctiveness can be explained by the particular importance of the home-grown cinema industry both in terms of its economic impact and because of the significance attached to its survival (along with the French language) as one of the bulwarks against the increased threat of American cultural domination.

The cinema has a special place in France, both as an industry which is popular at home and as an export. France ranks third after the US and India in terms of the number of films made annually, and despite the competition, 35 per cent of ticket sales in 1997 were still for French films. French cinema is fully discussed in chapter 16, but the point to note here is that French filmmaking is still strongly subsidized by the state, via the Centre national de la cinématographie (CNC). France has also made sure that Paris has become the home of the Fondation européenne des métiers de l'image et du son (FEMIS), created in 1986 under Lang, and situated in the Palais de Tokyo; this is now considered Europe's most important institute for training future professionals in the cinema industry. The links between the cinema and television are also vital: the state has strict rules controlling the diffusion of films on television, and imposes a quota of 40 per cent of French films. One might add (see chapter 18 for more details) that cultural input to television was also closely regulated in the past. Privatization of TV channels in the 1980s has much reduced this, but France has supported the creation of the new-ish cultural TV channel, Arte, in cooperation with Germany, while the public channels continue to produce cultural programmes such as Bernard Pivot's popular 'Bouillon de Culture'.

Conclusions

Will France will be able to sustain its distinctive approach to cultural policy into the twenty-first century? It is hard to say. Governments will probably continue to emphasize claims to cultural exceptionalism, partly because of the economic and political implications, and partly because this is such an important aspect of the way in which France projects its national image abroad. But globalization and new technologies could force the French to some unwelcome compromises. The economic imperatives taken on board by Lang have set an irreversible pattern which could lead to increasing calls for private and business sponsorship to fund cultural projects, thus reducing the influence of the state. Some would argue that this might result in a more balanced model of support for the arts, since the traditional French model carries the inherent danger of producing a form of 'state art', which can threaten the principles of artistic freedom. Others claim that to allow market forces to take a greater part in the funding of cultural policy will lead to the 'uniformization' or Americanization of a global culture based on consumerism and entertainment rather than 'true' culture. Whatever the outcome, it is politically unlikely that France will abandon its Ministry of Culture in favour of a more 'hands off' approach, and the ministry will certainly continue to play an important role as 'manager' of the national cultural heritage. Figures indicate that there is a growing public for cultural tourism linked to recently renewed public interest in history and memory, and there is currently a thriving 'memorial culture' in France, with new museums celebrating all kinds of things from cheese to sailing-ships.

Finally, it seems inevitable (cf. other chapters in this book) that the notion of French culture will increasingly evolve to be more inclusive of other cultures, in particular those with which France has strong historical links, or those linked to communities living in France. Since the Lang years, the ministry's international policy has been to encourage the opening up of French culture to external influences by supporting the reception of other cultures in France through a range of different measures. And given the very multi-cultural composition of the French population today, the absorption of some influence of those cultures that would in Britain be called 'ethnic' is long overdue. In recent years though, the breakthrough of new forms of expression such as 'raï' (a form of music originating in Morocco) are an indicator that some things are moving in this direction. Nevertheless, there are still important pockets of resistance to the embracing of cultural diversity, most notably at the level of local, departmental or regional councils where there is a Front National presence: a number of incidents involving the withdrawal of funding for certain types of cultural activity considered politically unacceptable have shown how cultural policy in France today remains potentially explosive. The French state will continue to have a delicate role to play in balancing the many opposing forces and tensions at work, and in trying to navigate a path for the future that will make French culture reflect more accurately the nature of its population whilst maintaining its claim to being distinctively French.

References

BURGUIÈRE, André, et al. 1993: *Histoire de la France. Les formes de la culture.* Paris: Editions du Seuil.

CHARTIER, Roger 1993: Trajectoires et tensions de l'Ancien Régime. In BURGUIÈRE, André, et al. *Histoire de la France. Les formes de la culture.* Paris: Editions du Seuil.

CHASLIN, François 1985: *Les Paris de François Mitterrand.* Paris: Gallimard.

COLIN, Jean-Pierre 1986: *La Beauté du manchot: culture et différence*. Paris: Publisud.
COLLARD, Susan 1998: Architectural gestures and political patronage: the case of the Grands Travaux. *European Journal of Cultural Policy*, 5.1, 33–47.
COLLARD, Susan 1992: Mission impossible: les chantiers du président. In *French Cultural Studies*, ii, 97–132.
DE CERTEAU, Michel 1974: *La Culture au pluriel*. Paris: Christian Bourgeois.
DJIAN, Jean-Michel 1996: *La Politique culturelle*. Paris: Le Monde Editions/Marabout.
DONNAT, Olivier 1998: *Les Pratiques culturelles des Français*. Paris: La Documentation Française.
LEFÈBVRE, Henri 1968: *La Vie quotidienne dans le monde moderne*. Paris: Gallimard.
FINKIELKRAUT, Alain 1987: *La Défaite de la pensée*. Paris: Gallimard.
FUMAROLI, Marc 1991: *L'Etat culturel*. Paris: Editions de Fallois.
LOOSELEY, David 1995: *The politics of fun. Cultural policy and debate in contemporary France*. Oxford: Berg Publishers.
ORY, Pascal 1983: *L'entre-deux-mai: histoire culturelle de la France, mai 1968–mai 1981*. Paris: Seuil.
POIRRIER, Philippe 1996: *Histoire des politiques culturelles de la France contemporaine*. Dijon: Université de Bourgogne/Bibliest.
RIGAUD, Jacques 1995: *L'Exception culturelle. Culture et pouvoirs sous la Ve République*. Paris: Grasset.
SCHNEIDER, Michel 1993: *La Comédie de la culture*. Paris: Editions du Seuil.
URFALINO, Philippe 1996: *L'Invention de la politique culturelle*. Paris: La Documentation Française.

Further reading

DONNAT, Olivier 1994: *Les Français face à la culture. De l'exclusion à l'éclectisme*. Paris: La Découverte.
GOETSCHEL, Pascale et LOYER, Emmanuelle 1994: *Histoire culturelle et intellectuelle de la France au XXe siècle*. Paris: Armand Colin.
RIOUX, Jean-Pierre et SIRINELLI, Jean-François 1997: *Pour une histoire culturelle*. Paris: Seuil.
SAEZ, Guy (dir.) 1996: *Institutions et vie culturelles*. Collection 'Les Notices'. Paris: La Documentation Française.
strode, louise 2000: france, cultural policy and identity in the *fin de siécle*: the opportunities of European union. In CHADWICK, K. and UNWIN, T. (eds), *France: fin(s) de siécle(s)*. Lampeter and New York: Mellen Publications.

Websites

www.culture.gouv.fr
Has a brief history of the Ministry to celebrate its 40th anniversary and many links to other sites of cultural interest (museums, galleries etc.) and specialized search engines.

www.france.diplomatie.gouv.fr
Has details of French institutes around the world, including ideas and resources for learning French on the Internet.

|5|

French education: equal or elitist?

BY LUCY MITCHELL

The French place a high value on educational achievement, and are proud of their national tradition. At the same time they are conscious of inequalities in the system, which have generated much debate and attempts at reform, particularly since 1958.

No-one who pays attention to French discussions of the educational system can fail to be struck by the deep symbolic significance of two essential features, rooted in a tradition going back to the 1880s, when the foundations of the modern state system were laid. A basic understanding of these concepts is vital to any account of the forces that shape French educational culture.

The first is reflected in recurrent references to *l'école laïque et républicaine*. 'Lay schooling in accordance with the ideals of the French Republic' gives only a weak idea of the symbolic power of this phrase. It encapsulates the democratic ideal of equal access to educational opportunity for all, the opposite of the practices inherited by the Third Republic in the 1870s, whereby secondary education was the privilege of male elites and primary schooling was largely in the hands of the Church. 'Dans toute sa pratique, le lycée doit veiller à ce que l'égalité des chances pour tous soit respectée car c'est le socle de l'école républicaine' ('On every level of activity, the secondary school system must safeguard equal opportunity for all, since this is the cornerstone of Republican schooling' – French Ministry of Education website magazine, April 1999). The accompanying notion of *laïcité* has its origins in the separation between Church and state in educational matters which was established in the school legislation of the 1880s and which continues to have important connotations, not only for relations between the state sector and the smaller private sector (95 per cent of French private schools are linked to the Catholic Church) but also for the integration of the children of the Muslim community into the school system (see chapter 8). This goes with a stress on the school's role in teaching *la citoyenneté* – good citizenship – a notion which goes beyond the civic education classes attended by all French schoolchildren, to embrace the ideal of the school as a force for social integration.

The second feature, equally rooted in cultural tradition and history, is the aspiration to educational excellence as a means of forming a meritocratic elite at the service of the state: *le savoir libérateur* ('knowledge, the key to freedom') gives access to *l'ascenseur social* ('mechanisms of social promotion') leading to success in life through achievement in education. This principle lies behind the system of competitive entry (*concours*) to every area of employment in France's vast public sector, from postmen to higher civil servants. It also underlies the peculiarly French system of shaping its national leadership (in all spheres, from government and management to education, engineering and technology) through a highly competitive system (the élite university-level *grandes écoles*). Entry to these is in theory accessible to all, and largely non fee-paying; in practice, access is largely limited to children whose parents have the financial and intellectual resources to guide and support them through the arduous selection process. The republican ideal of the *ascenseur social* of achievement through education continues in reality to be heavily skewed towards the higher socio-economic classes who are so equipped (see Prost 1997, and Baudelot and Establet 1990).

Thus the French educational system has had constantly to grapple with the tensions generated by two different and not easily reconcilable sets of principles: the democratic aspirations of the *école républicaine*; and the elitist pressures generated by 'meritocratic' competitive selection. The latter works admirably for those who succeed within it, but adds to the sense of failure and social disadvantage of those who do not.

Historical overview

The basic system of state education for all was initiated in the 1880s by the Minister of Education, Jules Ferry. The laws bearing his name decreed that a school with a trained teacher should be provided in every town and village in France to dispense free, compulsory primary school education for all: this education was to be under the control of the recently-restored Republic rather than the Church. By the mid-1920s, the vast majority of French people were at least basically literate, and 50 per cent attained the *certificat d'études* awarded at the end of primary education at the age of 12.

As for secondary schooling, the *lycée*, for boys only, was created in the time of Napoleon I, along with a school-leaving examination, the *baccalauréat*. But these schools were fee-paying, so were open only to the privileged few and scholarship holders. Girls' *lycées* were created in the 1880s, but fees remained until the 1930s. Only about 3 per cent of the population benefited from secondary education until 1914. Most children still left school at 12 or 13 after receiving their basic education at primary school, and the two systems were quite separate. In the 1930s, the minimum school leaving age was raised to 14, and secondary schooling became progressively free of charge. The system remained very stratified however, according to class, income and cultural capital, until well after World War II. During the decades of expansion after 1945 known as the *trente glorieuses*, it is true that intellectually gifted pupils could benefit greatly from the selective *lycée* system, but the kind of training and qualifications given to those in the *collège*, the extension of the primary school, was more and more clearly perceived as inadequate.

The 1960s and 1970s, however, saw major changes. Following the population explosion of the post-war years, the *écoles maternelles* (kindergartens) were greatly expanded. Compulsory education was extended to age 16. During a series of reforms in the 1970s, after the cultural explosion of 1968, the two systems, *collège* and *lycée*, were merged, to fulfil the aspiration towards the *école unique*. Today, 11-year-olds all enter the *collège*, whose four-year syllabus takes them up to age 14–15, and the term *lycée* refers to the last three years of schooling culminating in the *baccalauréat*. The late 1970s and 1980s saw the abandonment of streaming at *collège* level but its replacement by three main streams at the *lycée* level. These are: *général* (the traditional academic system intended to lead to university); *technologique* (based on technological skills, normally leading to shorter post-secondary training); and *professionnel* (for training skilled workers in specific crafts). Each stream has its own *baccalauréat*, the intention being to make the diploma accessible to all school-leavers in a form appropriate to their talents and capacities. By the end of the 1990s, over 60 per cent of French school-leavers were passing the *baccalauréat* each year: the declared national objective for the next century is for 80 per cent to do so.

The most striking feature of the last hundred-odd years is the steep upward curve in the school-leaving age in recent decades, plus a sharply increased level of qualification in one's final year. The vast majority of pupils, whatever their grades, stay on past 16. Students in difficulties are kept in school by the system of *redoublement* – repeating a failed year – which helps them progress at their own pace. The overall effect is to raise the average age of school leavers. Those who reach the *baccalauréat* in a 'normal' length of time, without repeating, will sit the examination between 17 and 18: but *redoublement* has led to a situation in which the average age of *baccalauréat* candidates is now 19. The level of qualification at which the majority of pupils leave education has also risen very significantly, and is continuing to rise (cf. Auduc 1998). In 1960, the most commonly-held qualification was the *brevet d'études primaires* (primary school-leaving certificate). A decade later, it was the *brevet des collèges* (diploma taken at the end of *collège*), and by 1990 the *baccalauréat* (matriculation examination at end of secondary school). In the year 2000, it is expected that this will have been displaced by 'Bac + 2' (*baccalauréat* plus 2 years of further study).

Present-day French education – a thumbnail sketch

Ecole maternelle (nursery school: 3- or 4-year cycle: age 2–5)

For practically all French children, education starts with the excellent nursery school or *maternelle* system. Their school day is long, with classes and activities from 8.30–11.30 and 1.30–4.30, but usually with Wednesdays off. By the age of three, 80 per cent of French children are attending full time, partly because facilities are very good, partly because both parents are probably working and partly because of their conviction that the earlier a child's education starts, the better.

Ecole primaire (primary school: 5-year cycle: age 6–10)

Things become much more serious with the start of *l'école primaire*. As soon as they enter and learn to read, children are expected to work hard in a disciplined way, with homework and revision of classwork every evening after six hours of lessons. Class numbers in the first year are kept low (around 25 where possible). By the end of the primary school cycle children are expected to have fulfilled the requirements of the national curriculum by reaching a certain level of competence in French and maths, and also to have followed the *programme* in history, geography and *l'éducation civique* (civics). There is a strong emphasis on acquiring correct French grammar at primary level.

Organized sports and other extra-curricular activities generally happen outside the school. Traditionally they take place on Wednesdays, a school-free day in primary school and a half-day for secondary pupils. This structure of a hard-working week with long hours spent at school, but broken up by a relatively restful day in the middle, finds a parallel in the overall shape of the school year. This falls into a pattern of half-terms of six to eight weeks of studies, interspersed with relatively long breaks of up to two weeks, crowned by the long summer holidays (two months or more). The outside observer may be forgiven for the irreverent impression that the French school year progresses in spasmodic, kangaroo-like leaps from intensive study periods to spells of relaxation and back again!

The observer is also struck by the emphasis on the sheer absorption of information in class, at the expense of creative and/or project work, which is signally absent from the timetable. But there are often visits to museums and art galleries for primary school children, though here again the emphasis tends to be on information gathering rather than on creative involvement. An equally striking feature is the importance of marks and tests throughout the year, so that every child knows not only its own marks in each subject but also its place within the class hierarchy. This grading system, even at primary level, is no empty ritual: teachers and parents are highly aware of how important these performance indicators, recorded in the termly report, will be for what happens next.

Collège (first stage of secondary education: 4-year cycle: 11–14)

Collège is, by general agreement, the weakest link in the French school system. The 1980s experiment of the *collège unique*, unstreamed schooling with a more or less unified national curriculum for the age group, has not been an unqualified success. The current system turns out too many young people inadequately prepared to make an informed choice of *lycée*. The basic education offered at *collège* is nonetheless very good. Literacy and numeracy skills are strongly stressed, and pupils are expected to follow classes in both arts and sciences. There is limited choice over foreign languages or optional extras. Artistic and technological subjects get scant space on the timetable (and computing skills are not yet fully integrated into the curriculum). As in *primaire*, substantial amounts of homework are set and assessed. Systematically recorded in the termly report, homework assessment and tests are a crucial factor in pupils' grades.

In theory, all classes are mixed-ability; in practice, a good deal of behind-the-scenes orientation takes place, the result of tacit collusion between ambitious parents and the school establishment. One standard sorting device is the choice of German (reputed to be difficult and intellectually demanding) rather than English (the most popular choice) as the first foreign language for a pupil, coupled with Latin or Greek as an optional extra. The group of pupils taking German plus ancient languages will often become a beacon class which will tend to remain together throughout *collège* and to which the best teachers will be assigned.

Lycée (second stage of secondary education: 2-, 3- or 4-year cycle: 15–17+)

On leaving *collège*, pupils are streamed either into *lycée professionnel* for vocational training, or into a combined year during which they are oriented to either the *bac général* or the *bac technologique*.

The *lycée professionnel* trains its pupils in skills offering direct entry into employment. Rather under half leave after two years with a *certificat* or a *brevet* in a particular skill or area of services; the rest go on for two more years to the *bac professionnel* in their chosen skill. Work experience is an important feature of the '*bac pro*': about a third of the training time is spent on work placements.

Pupils taking either the *bac général* or the *bac technologique* have to keep up a wide range of subjects, whichever option they choose. All will be expected to study at least one foreign language, and to take papers in French, history and philosophy in the *baccalauréat*, so school-leavers are equipped with a good level of general culture of a largely Franco-centred kind though it does not include music or the visual arts (cf. chapter 4). The *bac technologique* offers four main options: industrial, laboratory, medico-social or tertiary science and technology, to prepare pupils for careers as qualified technicians. It is designed to lead to two further years of training, though many pupils switch to mainstream university studies, with mixed results.

In the *bac général*, three main options are available: scientific, literary or economic studies. The 'S' (scientific) option is considered the most prestigious, as it paves the way to the widest variety of good career openings, whether in engineering school, medical studies, computer science, or whatever. Good pupils will almost certainly find themselves steered towards a *bac 'S'* (if their maths and physics are up to a high standard) as this is viewed as the *voie royale*, the 'royal road' to success. The 'L' (literary) option is seen as intellectually admirable but limited in job prospects: teaching, journalism or publishing. The *bac 'ES'* (economic studies option) is a recent creation intended as an alternative route into business or administration and similar careers, but has not yet dented the pre-eminence of the 'S' option.

The *bac général* traditionally leads to university studies and beyond. Within the hierarchical French career structure, where socio-economic success and educational qualifications are directly related, this stream remains much the most sought-after of the three, to the detriment of the technological and vocational. Everyone agrees that it is a pity that the latter are undervalued, but this reflects high parental ambitions for their children. One consequence of this bias towards the academic stream is a marked distortion of the job market. There were 180 000 job vacancies for blue-collar workers in French industry in 1999: see the editorial comments of Jean-Michel Djian (*Le Monde de l'Education* No. 271, June 1999, 3), introducing a special dossier on 'La Course aux diplômes' ('The Rush for Qualifications'), which provides revealing insights into the imbalance between school-leaving qualifications and the available job openings in 1990s France.

Post-baccalauréat study strategies

After the bac, most *général* and *technologique* students go on to further study: entry into '*la fac*' (*faculté*), the mainstream university system, or into a selective-entry establishment of some kind. The continuous assessment system at school becomes important here: good reports rank even higher than getting a good grade in the bac. Since the late nineteenth century, when not more than 1 or 2 per cent of the population passed the bac, it has given automatic entry to a French university. Mass access to the examination in the modern era, plus the importance attached to university degrees in France, has meant that the number of potential students has far outstripped the capacity of the universities to cope with their intake.

Three striking features of university life in France, to an outside observer (apart from the sheer numbers of students), are the broad choice of subjects on offer; the low cost of living, helping offset the lack of student grants; and the local character of many French universities. In the late 1990s, nearly half of all French people aged between 18 and 22 (46 per cent) were students, about a million and a half of them at university. The resultant overcrowding in the first year can be a problem: the smallest teaching unit may be the *travaux dirigés* (seminar) groups, typically about 30. Efforts to make the system more user-friendly have recently brought down the drop-out rate in the first two years, but it is still about 40 per cent. The French university system is however in many ways very open and democratic. The wide choice of subjects available to students on entry is one aspect of this. Following the *bac*'s broad-based curriculum, students can enrol more or less in the subject of their choice: a student from the 'ES' (Economic Science) stream might take languages, or a student from the 'S' (Maths and Science) stream opt for law. But while prospective students may change stream, subsequent movement from one university to another is still unusual; it is assumed that that you will stay at your original university at least up to *licence* (BA), and probably for your *maîtrise* (MA) as well, if you take one.

Life as a student is pretty cheap. Only the lowest income groups have grants, but the cost of living is kept down by indirect subsidies. University fees are remarkably low: at the end of the 1990s, it cost about 750 francs a year to enrol at the Université de Paris-4, for example. Student health insurance is inexpensive, and the CROUS, the state-run network of university canteens, provides substantial (if unexciting) three- or four-course midday and evening meals for about 15 francs. There are also accommodation grants, and tax breaks for home owners renting out a room to a student. Add reduced rates for museums, cinemas and many other cultural venues, plus often excellent student sporting facilities with low fees, and few sectors of the student budget are unprovided for.

One last noteworthy feature of French university life is that most campuses remain rooted within the local community and its culture – counterbalancing the otherwise centralised university system. It is still common for French students to attend the local university, and to remain at home throughout, partly because it is cheaper, partly because it is accepted practice. Many French universities give priority to candidates from their regional catchment area over 'outsiders'. University teaching staff too will often be local products, having received their training and spent much of their career within the same region if not the same institution.

An undergraduate course at a mainstream university can become a real endurance test, without necessarily offering any obvious job prospects. And yet successive attempts at making university entrance more selective have been systematically blocked by massive demonstrations by students (supported by their parents) against what they see as a threat to their democratic right. Paradoxically however, this has increased the popularity of those institutions which *are* selective on entry right across the board: whether it is an ambitious *bac général* student aiming to get into a *classe préparatoire*, a course preparing for the entry examinations to the prestigious *grandes écoles* (see below), or a student from the technological stream trying to get into an IUT (*Instituts universitaires de technologie*), relatively recent creations which protect teaching quality by limiting intake, in all cases, entry will be decided primarily on the basis of the students' reports from their last years of school, even before their *bac* result is known.

Bac technologique students can do a two-year diploma course, either in one of the technological institutes attached to the university system (the IUTs) or in sections for further study attached to the *lycée* system (the STS – *sections de techniciens supérieurs*). The more ambitious opt for mainstream university entrance, because the IUT/STS system is seen as less prestigious than university, but paradoxically, the weaker students also try their luck at *fac* because at least they can get a place there, whereas entry to the IUTs and to the better STS courses is limited.

Bac général students can go to mainstream university or, if they have a sufficiently good school 'dossier', they will try for a *classe préparatoire*. These offer studies over two or three years leading to the entry examinations to the *grandes écoles*. The *classes préparatoires* are in many ways more like a prolongation of school, with long classroom hours, like university courses, but the high-quality teaching dispensed there gives the students the equivalent of two years of undergraduate study at university. Even if a student fails to get into a *grande école* from *classe préparatoire*, he or she will still have been steered through the first two years of a first degree in exceptionally good conditions and with a broad range of subjects.

Finally, at the very tip of the post-*baccalauréat* educational pyramid are the *grandes écoles* such as Polytechnique, the Ecole Normale Supérieure, the Ecole des Mines, the Institut d'Etudes Politiques or the Ecole Nationale d'Administration. Founded for the express purpose of forming the nation's leadership in all sectors, they offer extremely privileged conditions of study to their students (several pay them a salary), and a guarantee of very high-quality career prospects. But even these institutions have become the subject of criticism and debate in recent times. In theory, any sufficiently bright student can get into *classe préparatoire* (non-fee-paying if attached to state schools) to prepare for the examinations. But in practice the demanding conditions of study and the high level of educational culture required of candidates means that most successful entrants come from privileged homes. As a result, the *écoles* are perceived as being largely the preserve of a self-perpetuating elite which has become too closed in on itself and too insulated against outside influences for the rapidly-changing conditions of the modern world (see Prost, 1997).

Democracy versus meritocracy

The above sketch of the options and choices open to school leavers shows how modern French schoolgoers find themselves caught between conflicting educational models: the principle of equality of opportunity (hence the reluctance to abandon the ideal of open-access, low-cost university education) versus the culture of excellence via selection.

'Le Marché scolaire'

In accordance with the first principle, education in general is relatively inexpensive. The best schools in France are non-fee-paying, public-sector schools. Even the private school sector is regulated and subsidized by the state, so fees are relatively low. As a result, in both sectors, while practically all pupils will start their careers in a neighbourhood school, the one deciding factor that will determine their educational future will be their record of academic achievement.

The result is a highly competitive system within a theoretically egalitarian framework. A tacit 'market' in schools has sprung up, and there are now *palmarès*, league tables of *lycées*, widening the gap between 'good' and 'bad' establishments. The better *lycées* can pick and choose among the ablest candidates; the best, at the top of the market, are ruthless about weeding out the weaker elements from their associated *collège* to make room for a high-potential intake from elsewhere. The worst-regarded *lycées*, particularly in disadvantaged *banlieue* areas, have to watch their brightest pupils go off to successful inner-city schools. The total population of Parisian inner-city *lycées* is artificially boosted to a level one-third higher than it would be if they took in only Parisian students.

This pressure for academic achievement certainly produces hard-working, well-informed, highly motivated pupils. But even those who succeed within the system feel that success has been achieved at the expense of personal initiative and creativity. Here is part of an exasperated outburst against the gap between the democratic ideals and the market-biased realities of the system taken from a broadsheet published by pupils at one of the 'better' Parisian *lycées*, in December 1998:

> L'Education Nationale, cet emblème de la démocratie hexagonale, ce socle de la société française ... est en parfaite opposition vis-à-vis des valeurs du système auquel elle appartient: la République. ... Peut-être serait-il bon de rappeler ... que l'école de la Liberté suppose ... l'au-

togestion du savoir, et non pas la distribution mécanique de marchan-
dises – oups! Excusez-moi, je voulais dire de connaissances – éculées
qui n'ont au final pas d'autre effet que celui de bourrer un peu plus des
crânes déjà fort futilement encombrés.

[The state system of education, that emblem of national democracy,
that cornerstone of French society ... works directly against the values
of the system of which it is a part: the Republic ... Perhaps we ought
to remember ... that training for Liberty should entail ... a learner-
centred approach to knowledge, and not the mechanical distribution
of clapped-out merchandise – oops! Sorry, I should have said information – which only results in stuffing a little more into skulls that are
already quite uselessly overloaded.]

La Bombe. Lycée Victor Duruy, December 1998

What emerges from these lines, alongside the ironic use of the Ministry's
own rhetoric (cf. reference to its website above) is not only one young man's
indignation with the educational system but also the high quality of the
intellectual equipment that it has given him. The expressive, vigorous prose
style is a credit both to the writer and to what he has been taught in French
class. The knowledge with which he and his fellow-students are 'stuffing'
their heads, plus their training in organizing that knowledge, means that
they will leave school with the high level of general culture that is one of the
most attractive fruits of the French educational tradition.

'Le lycée, c'est la galère!'

For those who get to the top of the pile, the hard work needed to get there
is worth the sacrifice. For those who do less well, the state of mind of many
lycéens is pungently summed up by the term *la galère* (slave galley). In
young people's slang it has become a catch-all term for the general state of
struggling to cope with *lycée* and not managing very well (see Dubet 1987).

For the moderate achievers who nevertheless will manage to get their
bac and make it to the crowded benches of the university lecture theatres,
la galère is still more or less worth the effort. A more fundamental problem faces those who cannot succeed within the system, or see no point in
trying, for social and/or intellectual reasons. The *galère* is at its worst in
socially deprived areas, including poor rural areas, and perhaps most
acutely of all in the *banlieues*, the suburban estates of Paris, Lyon and
Marseille (see chapter 6), where high concentrations of poverty, unemployment, and less assimilated immigrant communities are to be found.
Efforts have certainly been made, in particular by the classification of particularly deprived areas as ZEPs or *zones d'éducation prioritaire*, where
extra teaching resources should be made available and local children given

schooling appropriate to their real needs. The cruel fact nevertheless remains that these schools are victims of the pressures of the *marché scolaire*, so that pupils with a capacity to get on and parents socially skilled enough to help them will get out of their ZEP and into the better schools in more favoured locations, while the others are left behind. It is almost inevitable that such schools should be stigmatised as the dustbins of the educational system – pupils and teachers all too often regard them precisely in this light – where young people are simply parked until they reach school-leaving age. It is hardly surprising that these schools suffer from problems of indiscipline and violence.

It would be quite wrong, though, to suggest that the French educational system fails completely in its ideal of providing educational opportunity for all. Plenty of success stories do occur. The children of North African immigrant families, for example, frequently do very well in the French educational system in spite of coming from a relatively disadvantaged socio-economic

Figure 5.1 A state 'lycée technique' on the Left Bank with the ubiquitous signature of the graffiti artist, and an earlier *collage* evoking the post-May '68 empowerment of the imagination.

group. Their families place an especially high value on education as the route to integration, and the academic achievements of both boys and girls are noticeably higher than those of the children of other immigrant communities, and contribute to a higher degree of socio-economic success: by 1990, 29 per cent of 'Beurs' – the children born in France of North African immigrants – were achieving higher socio-economic status than their parents, as opposed to an average of 23 per cent for the children of immigrant families in general (Borkowski 1990; Bosc 1993; Dubet and Lapeyronnie 1992). During the *Mouvement des lycéens*, the wave of demonstrations against learning conditions in French *lycées* in autumn 1998, the voice of these young, ambitious 'Beurs' was clearly heard, particularly that of the girls, whose dynamism and confidence in their democratic right to a place within the system brought several of them to the forefront of the movement. When *Le Monde* devoted an editorial and two pages of comment to the leaders of the *lycéens* (24 October 1998), it focused on six girls, two of them daughters of immigrant North African families at *banlieue* schools in Dijon and Paris; a third also had a North African family background.

Two case histories

The case histories which follow outline the real-life school careers of two intelligent young people of the same age but different backgrounds, who started off in the same neighbourhood primary school together but whose educational paths diverged as time went on: I shall call them Fernando and Anaïs. They have been chosen as complementary examples of how present-day French education can work in practice.

Fernando

Fernando is the son of Portuguese immigrants who entered France as unskilled labourers: his mother is a caretaker in an apartment building, his father works (intermittently) as a house painter. He did not do well in school to start with, particularly in French, and had to repeat a couple of years, though he was always very good at maths. He is good with his hands, so his parents put him into *lycée professionnel* to train as a car mechanic. He ended up doing so well, in maths as well as in mechanical skills, that his teachers suggested that he was 'too good' to waste himself in a garage. Perhaps he should train as a maths teacher – or try to qualify as a bank clerk? The banking idea was attractive, for its respectable salary and status, but he finally decided to carry on with what he was good at, working with cars. This was fortunate for him – nobody had told him that employment in banking is rapidly shrinking because of computerisation.

So he completed his mechanic's *brevet* and went on to the *bac profession-nel*, specialising in car maintenance. By now he was already 19 and went on living at home in his parents' two–room flat until he was 21. It is one of the injustices of the highly stratified French system – again, nobody told him this – that statistically, Fernando has little chance of getting a better job with his *bac pro* than he would have done after his *brevet*. So in a small way he is still the victim of the pressure towards over-qualification, though he will have gained in his own self-esteem by his achievement.

In June 1999, he took his *bac pro*, and found a job (not as good as he was hoping for, but far more easily than if he had trained as a bank clerk) – and married his girlfriend of the previous two years. In educational terms, his story is a very positive one. He has managed to steer a successful course among the varied and occasionally misleading choices opened to him by his hard work and ability, and to make what is clearly a good choice of career, within a fairly limited set of options, helped by his own good sense and the moral and financial support of his family.

Anaïs

Anaïs comes from a prosperous and cultured background: her father is a university professor, her mother a librarian. She did well at school, and had no difficulty in gaining admission to one of the best State schools in France, the Lycée Henri IV in Paris. Her main difficulty, as a good all-rounder, was in choosing which option to take in the *baccalauréat*. She allowed herself to be influenced by the climate that pushes good students towards Maths and Science, and took a *bac 'S'*, followed by a year's *classe préparatoire* for entrance to the scientific *grandes écoles*. But she realised that she really wanted to study literature. So, after much soul-searching, she transferred into a literary *classe préparatoire* – a difficult but not impossible move after years in the scientific stream, as the broad-based French school curriculum meant that she had never completely lost touch with the Arts side.

Anaïs continued in the *classe préparatoire* for two years of very hard work, living at home like Fernando (it is common for young French people to go on living at home even when they get to university, as there is no sys-tem of maintenance grants). Having gained entry to a *grande école* at the age of 20, she has at last been able to leave school behind and choose for herself her personal academic interests. There is the problem of finding a specific line of literary research, but she is enjoying her new-found intellec-tual and financial independence (her *école* is one of those which pay a small salary to their members).

In their different ways, Fernando and Anaïs are success stories, and exem-plify much of the culture of French education today, with its virtues and aspirations as well as its inequalities and inconsistencies. Both have had to work long and hard, and to overcome obstacles, to reach their goals. Both had to go on putting up with the constraints of school and of living at home with their families, when they were already young adults. In both cases, their personal successes are also successes for the French educational system. Their future incomes will be very different, but they are well on the way to becoming just the kind of useful and well-integrated citizens that the *école républicaine* aspires to produce. Not everyone is so fortunate.

References and further reading

AUDUC, Jean-Louis 1998: *Les institutions scolaires et universitaires*. Série Education. Paris: Nathan.

BAUDELOT, Christian, and ESTABLET, Roger 1990: *Le Niveau monte*. Paris: Seuil.

BORKOWSKI, J.-L. 1990: L'Insertion sociale des immigrés et de leurs enfants. *Données sociales*. Paris: INSEE.

BOSC, Serge 1993: *Stratification et transformations sociales: La Société française en mutation*. Paris: Nathan.

DUBET, François 1987: *La galère: jeunes en survie*. Paris: Fayard.

DUBET, François and LAPEYRONNIE, Didier 1992: Immigrés et minorités. *Les Quartiers d'exil*. Paris: Seuil.

LEQUIN, Yves 1998: *La mosaïque France: histoire des étrangers et de l'immigration*. Paris: Larousse.

PROST, Antoine 1997: *Education, société et politique: une histoire de l'enseignement en France, de 1945 à nos jours*. Paris: Seuil.

Films

Zéro de conduite Jean Vigo, 1932. A satire of some of the more fustian aspects of Republican schooling.

La Gloire de mon père Yves Robert, 1989. Affectionate depiction of traditional French school culture before the First World War.

L'Argent de poche François Truffaut, 1975. Sympathetic portrayal of school life in a small provincial town.

Ça commence aujourd'hui Bernard Tavernier, 1999. The problems of running an *école maternelle* in a very deprived area of Northern France.

Magazines and websites

Le Monde de l'Education, de la Culture et de la Formation is a really excellent monthly magazine published by *Le Monde* newspaper. Its website is well worth a visit: http://www.lemondefr/educ/

The website of the French Ministry of Education naturally presents the Establishment point of view but it is a very handy source for all kinds of information about French education: http://www.education.gouv.fr

CULTURAL DIFFERENCES AND IDENTITY POLITICS IN FRANCE TODAY

|6|

Social difference: age and place

BY MARION DEMOSSIER AND SUSAN MILNER

During the last twenty years, French culture has become an arena where social issues are played out and identities are challenged. As elsewhere in Europe, culture has been employed as a political tool, and the idea of a universal French culture has been challenged by major socio-economic changes. The last census (1999) strikingly confirmed the decline of rural society and the predominance of an urban way of life today incorporating 80 per cent of French people (*Le Monde* 1999, 1). It is also apparent that the French population has aged. While several indicators, especially economic ones, show real convergence between the European countries, cultural and social differentiation has increased at national or regional level (Mendras 1996, 21). The *exception française* has changed its form.

This new fragmented French society still offers an original landscape in which differences related to age and place dominate. Older people now represent an important part of the French population and, compared to previous generations, have seen their social and economic position improve significantly. Meanwhile, young people, despite a massive influx into higher education, have been confronted by labour market insecurity. A new generational division has emerged and broadening patterns of cultural consumption have become an important means of exploring new social identities. Society is now defined as much in terms of age as in terms of class and although youth values and generational solidarities remain, the contrast between younger and older people has grown sharper.

The aim of this chapter is to examine the differences in French culture from a perspective related to age and place. Our main questions are as follows: How can we define culture in contemporary France? What is the relationship between society and the process of culture? What does it mean to be French today? And, finally, what is the influence of the generational factor in cultural production?

When it sought to address these questions, the French Ministry of Culture declared its mission to be:

de permettre à tous les Français de cultiver leur capacité d'inventer et de créer, d'examiner librement leurs talents et de recevoir la formation artistique de leur choix; de préserver le patrimoine culturel national, régional ou des divers groupes sociaux pour le profit commun de la collectivité tout entière; de favoriser la création des œuvres d'art et de l'esprit et de leur donner la plus vaste audience; de contribuer au rayonnement de la culture et de l'art français dans le libre dialogue des cultures du monde.

to enable French people to develop their inventive and creative capacity to examine freely their talent and to receive the artistic education of their choice; to preserve France's cultural heritage, whether national, regional or social, for the benefit of society as a whole; to encourage and promote the creation of artistic and intellectual works for a wide audience; to contribute to the influence of French culture and art in the free dialogue of cultures in the world.

Decree of 10 May 1982

Cultural changes are now one of the essential factors for understanding social behaviour (Dirn 1998). However, despite large-scale financial investment by public authorities, significant media interest in culture, increasing acquisition of audiovisual goods and broader access to higher education, the relationship of French people to culture has not changed radically (Mucchielli 1996). To some extent, social cleavages have been eased by the development of a *minimum culturel* (Donnat 1994), that is, a common cultural birthright and sense of national belonging. Yet cultural attitudes remain closely related to social positions and trajectories, notably to cultural capital (the stock of educational and cultural knowledge and networks possessed by individuals). However, in this approach to culture, the main elements of disparity are still age, generation and socio-economic category.

Age, generation and social differentiation

France today is an increasingly fragmented society, with multiple fault-lines and new social divisions. In one sense, society has opened up, generating new opportunities for self-expression. But this also means that those unable to take advantage of new opportunities are left even further behind, creating new categories of 'excluded'. In particular, the gap between generations has changed, with some groups of young people increasingly dependent on family ties and others alienated from all social institutions. Rather than the old spectre of class conflict and social revolution pitting workers against bosses and the upper classes, urban youth has come to represent the face of social discontent. Perhaps one film, above all others, served to illustrate the new fears of social polarisation in the 1990s: Matthieu Kassovitz's *La*

Haine, with its streetwise but vulnerable trio of young men of Jewish, North African and West African descent, pitted against a merciless concrete jungle, unemployment, boredom and racist authorities.

Old class divisions mean less as consumerism promotes increasingly similar lifestyles. In 1995, 58 per cent of French people pronounced themselves middle class, indicating a huge cultural shift away from the social divisions which marked the major part of the twentieth century and informed cultural and intellectual attitudes, in particular, the decline of Marxist-inspired analysis based on class struggle (see chapters 21 and 22). Advertising tends both to assume and to promote a standard middle-class lifestyle. Yet what is perhaps surprising is the limited extent of real social mobility. If 40 per cent of men were to be found in the same occupational category as their fathers in 1970, by 1993 the proportion had fallen only slightly to 35.1 per cent (Vallet 1999). The majority of men were socially mobile in the 1990s, but over a third remained immobile and the proportion had hardly changed in twenty years despite the massive restructuring of the French economy in the same period. With new jobs opening up in the service sector, the main beneficiaries of increased social mobility have been women. But although social categories may have changed, the shift from manual to white-collar status may hide similarities in terms of routine work and low pay and status.

Alongside the persistence of social rigidities, the labour market has sometimes functioned in an exclusionary way. One effect of the employment crisis in France was that as those in work sought to protect themselves from redundancy, new entrants to the labour market in the 1980s and 1990s were effectively 'locked out'. Young people especially found it difficult to enter the labour market, partly because of problems in France's vocational training system which left large numbers of them unqualified, but also because of a general 'qualifications inflation' which forced graduates to seek low-grade jobs, squeezing out jobs for those less qualified. Youth unemployment reached alarming rates in the late 1980s and early 1990s; by 1996 young people represented around 20 per cent of the unemployed, although they accounted for less than 15 per cent of the total population (Ambassade de France 1997). At its peak in 1985, unemployment struck 30.5 per cent of young men (between the ages of 15 and 24), and 21.6 per cent of young women (*Le Monde*, 14 May 1991). The state sought to encourage integration of young people through training schemes or fixed-term contracts, with wage subsidies as an incentive to employers (the state paid the employers' social security contributions, for example, as well as allowing employers to pay young people less than the statutory minimum wage). However, the evidence suggests that wage subsidies do not have a positive effect on youth employment, as they do for older people (Charpail et al. 1999); rather, youth employment schemes often represent a kind of social 'car park' with few chances of real employment at the end. Nevertheless, a combination of active labour market policies and contractions in the labour market (due to demographic trends) caused youth unemployment to fall, as elsewhere in Europe, in the second half of the 1990s.

Educational policy in the 1980s and 1990s also aimed at raising educational standards (with targets set in particular for the proportion of young people obtaining the *baccalauréat* seen as the 'gold standard' for secondary-level achievement). Since the *baccalauréat* is the key to university entry in France's non-selective system, a knock-on effect was to increase numbers in the higher education sector. Among OECD countries, France has the second highest proportion of 21-year-olds in higher education (35.3 per cent in 1993–4). In 1950, only 5.1 per cent of the relevant age cohort obtained the *baccalauréat*; by 1970 the proportion had reached just over 20 per cent. The rise in the 1990s was astonishing: from 25.9 per cent in 1980 to 43.5 per cent in 1990 and 62.7 per cent in 1995. This has raised the general educational standard of the population as a whole, so that France today stands in the top league and has gone a long way towards catching up with Germany, Britain and the United States at the top of the secondary level and higher education level. France now spends almost as much, proportionally, on education as the United States (6.4 per cent of GDP), although this lags far behind the efforts of the Scandinavian countries. However, increased numbers in higher education have not been matched by increases in spending, with the result that universities remain potential social flashpoints, as was demonstrated by the 1995 strike movement which was launched in university lecture theatres, recalling the heady days of May–June 1968.

Together with prolonged study, the effect of France's peculiar employment structure has been to concentrate paid employment in the middle years. In the 1990s, the proportion of the active population aged between 25 and 49 increased from 69 per cent to nearly 71 per cent. Young people's share of labour market activity dropped four points from 12.3 per cent to just 8.3 per cent (Marchand 1999, 104). For young people, this means fierce competition for jobs alongside a general devaluation (through dilution) of qualifications. In this context, it is not surprising that *lycéens* evince anxiety about their own future and that of their peers, as shown for example in Cédric Klapisch's award-winning film *Le Péril Jeune* (1993). Strike and protest movements by *lycéens* have become as much a regular feature of French social life as rail transport strikes in Paris. A further consequence of educational and labour market change has been increased dependence on parents and grandparents: in 1992, 72 per cent of 20-year-olds were still living with their parents, compared to only 59 per cent in 1982. Kinship relations play a crucial role in France today and recent studies have confirmed their role as job-providers or financial helpers. Although for young people family represents a source of comfort, security and relaxation, delayed independence can create tensions between generations. It also means that those who cannot rely on their family (because of family breakdown, bereavement, or parental unemployment, for example) either depend increasingly on the state for support or have no support system whatsoever.

It is perhaps equally unsurprising that young people have turned away in droves from traditional politics. They are less likely to vote in elections, and more likely to vote for protest or anti-system parties (far right, far left, or ecologist). In 1993, Prime Minister Edouard Balladur was so concerned about young people that he commissioned a massive opinion survey of young people under 24, asking them to list their concerns and priorities. The survey showed French youth to be worried by a wide range of social issues, with unemployment at the centre, together with the quality of education and training. A committee of experts set up to consult with young people in the wake of the report noted the weighty impact of unemployment: 'anxiety, conflict with adults effectively competing for the same jobs, job insecurity, problems with finding accommodation, resorting to higher education as a refuge against unemployment, which is one of the reasons for university overcrowding' (*Le Monde*, 23 December 1994). Generational conflict was also sparked by another of the survey's main findings, which revealed the prevalence of soft drug use (cannabis) among young people and a strong desire for decriminalization.

A further study carried out in 1996 by *Le Figaro-Magazine*/SOFRES both confirmed and nuanced the Balladur survey (Witkowski 1997). Overwhelmingly, young people felt that they lived in a particularly bad time for youth (78 per cent). Nearly half of them chose the adjective 'anguished' (*angoissé*) to describe their generation. Wider society was seen as dishonest and corrupt, and hostile to young people. Established institutions such as the army, organized religion and politics were singled out for particular criticism. However, although young people saw adults in general as selfish and hostile to them, almost half of them felt optimistic about their own chances of success, and most placed great store by private happiness (in family, friendship and love).

Perhaps the most striking finding of the 1996 survey was the difference between young respondents according to social class and educational achievement. Interest in politics ranged from 25 per cent among working-class respondents to 45 per cent among children of managers and professionals, reflecting wide divergence in individuals' perceptions of their own life-chances. Commenting on the survey results, political scientist Denis Witkowski (1997, 171) classified the young people in three main categories: 'marginals', representing about 15 per cent of youths; 'worriers', adding up to around 41 per cent of the cohort; and 'optimists', representing a majority of around 44 per cent. In other words, young people could be divided in two, winners and losers, with children of middle-class parents torn between the two depending on precise family circumstances. A similar poll in 1999 found that, although a majority of young people expressed confidence in their own future, 75 per cent felt that society did not offer much chance of upward mobility to children from working-class or underprivileged backgrounds (Gurrey and Subtil 1999).

Differentiation between young people according to family background and level of educational achievement also emerges strongly from surveys of cultural practices. In general, young people are more interested in active and outdoor pursuits than their elders, preferring sport, meetings with friends and cultural outings to indoor activities such as reading, listening to the radio or watching television (Bozon 1990). However, sporting and cultural activities remained differentiated according to social class, with children of managerial/professional parents considerably more likely to ski or attend classical music concerts than their working-class peers. Young people from working-class backgrounds, on the other hand, pursued no specific cultural practices apart from football, which remains a male working-class sport. They tended to go out less for organized activities (shows, concerts) and were more likely to say they got bored on Sundays. However, social differences tend to be less pronounced than among adults (Ambassade de France 1997), probably because of relatively greater similarities in spending power at the level of cultural outings. In addition, the French government has actively sponsored youth participation in the arts, sports and leisure, providing many free activities particularly during the school holidays and actively promoting 'youth' values in order to modernize its own image.

Whilst in many ways young people's attitudes and practices tend to reflect wider changes in society rather than determine them, in some ways they can be seen as harbingers of change, particularly as regards attitudes on sexuality which became much more open and tolerant in the 1980s and 1990s. In December 1999, Education Minister Ségolène Royal allowed the 'morning after' pill to be issued in French schools. Shifts in society towards greater individualization of behaviour are more strongly identified with the young, as well as other trends affecting French culture such as microcomputing or rock, rap and techno music, which was given a central place in France's cultural output by Jack Lang.

At the other end of the age span, older people may therefore feel excluded by the pace of social change. Like young people, the over-50s too have increasingly been squeezed out of the labour market. The retirement age was lowered to 60 in 1981, a move seen by Mitterrand as the major social achievement of his first presidency – but in most cases it is effectively lowered to 55 because of the combination of unemployment, early retirement and voluntary leaving (Dirn 1998, 4). As elsewhere in Europe, early retirement has become a major plank of government unemployment policy, so that over-50s represent today only around 20 per cent of the active population, although their share of the overall population is increasing steadily (nearly 30 per cent in 1990, up from 25 per cent in 1962, and it is expected to exceed 41 per cent by 2020). As life expectancy increases, the proportion of older people has risen: 16 per cent of the total population was aged over 60 in 1946, and by 1998 the proportion had reached 20 per cent. France stands somewhere in the middle among its European partners as regards the proportion of people past the retirement age: its population grows relatively fast for an advanced Western economy but the net birth rate is not particularly high due to long life expectancy. Whereas until the 1980s poverty was primarily associated with old age, generous early retirement packages and pensions give today's older populations an unprecedented power in the market. Just as previous older generations sought to empower themselves by 'universities of the third age', marketing hype has it that today's older people (labelled 'séniors') can stake their place in society through greater spending power as targeted in new marketing campaigns by the SNCF, FNAC, RATP and car industry. According to the incomes analysts CREDOC, purchasing power among the over-50s is 30 per cent greater than that of the younger population (Belot 1999). Seventy-five per cent of share-holding is concentrated in the hands of the over-50s. If a society is to be judged according to the way it treats its eldest citizens, France fares much better than the United Kingdom, in material terms at least.

Older people spend more time watching television than young people, and they also read more books. But as well as enjoying these non-energetic and solitary activities, they seem to enjoy better social relations than in the past. They spend more time in voluntary activities and are more likely to be members of voluntary associations of virtually all types, including sporting associations: 10 per cent of over-60s said they were members of sports associations in 1997, as opposed to only 4 per cent in 1980. Almost a third of retired people declared themselves members of cultural/leisure associations in 1997 (22.9 per cent in 1980) (Hatchuel and Loisel 1999). These features differentiate them from younger generations. In cultural as well as economic terms then, older people represent an increasingly powerful and vocal section of the population. They participate more in cultural activities and their lifestyle more resembles that of the middle class.

However, fears have frequently been expressed about the wider consequences of an ageing society, not only in terms of the burden on the state, taxpayers and social security contributors, but also in broad cultural terms. Many of today's older people have a lower socio-cultural capital and lower levels of education; proportionally fewer of the past generations pursued higher education. Some observers argue that an ageing society is less likely to take risks, innovate or experiment. In cultural terms, the greater purchasing power of older people could lead to producers sticking to tried and tested formulae, 'heritage'-style values and to more traditional styles based on French 'grandeur' in the arts. The need to balance increasingly divergent tastes and lifestyles therefore constitutes a major challenge for French cultural policy at the end of the 1990s, the more so as younger and older people tend to define their cultural identity in explicit opposition to each other.

Place: the quest for identity, social space and representation

The 1999 census confirmed the trend, already visible in 1990, towards the decline of traditional rural communities and the dominance of urban or 'peri-urban' lifestyles: around 85 per cent of French people live in or in close proximity to urban centres, and very few – even those living in deepest countryside – escape urban life in their work or daily social contacts. Rural living has changed as a result of broad changes in employment structures which mean that, if urban employment is mainly in the tertiary (service) sector, rural employment is no longer agricultural (only 13 per cent of rural dwellers are farmers) but largely industrial. Thanks to widespread car use, networks have developed around large cities which act as the focus of cultural life; at the same time, collaboration between regional, departmental and municipal government ensures some sharing-out of cultural production between the major urban centres and surrounding smaller towns and villages. Generally, regions or departments which are more dynamic are organized around a leading metropolis; those with two or more competing cities tend to fare less well, and rural areas with weaker major urban centres tend to trail behind in terms of economic performance and ability to attract residents (in particular, a large swathe of territory around Paris and the north into Champagne and Berry, as well as the Massif Central).

According to some commentators (Hervieu and Viard 1996; Dirn 1998), the development of broad urban catchment areas and the decline of traditional rural communities means that there is no longer any difference, in cultural terms, between urban and rural lifestyles: 94 per cent of French homes have television sets and television viewing is the main leisure activity across the territory. 20 per cent of French homes have two or more television sets, and five million people subscribe to Canal Plus and/or cable TV (Gentil and Rotman 1995). Time spent in front of the small screen is increasing for all social categories, although viewing habits differ.

Those living in or near urban centres have access to other forms of visual culture, notably cinema, which apart from some rural areas in the south-west and south-east remains a predominantly urban activity (Vigoureux 1997, 84). Nevertheless, cinema-going is less popular than it used to be, except in Paris and in some areas of western France. Indeed, the main difference in cultural behaviour seems to lie between Paris, with its exceptionally rich cultural provision, and the rest of France, rather than at a more general level between urban and rural areas. Paris's long-standing dominance of France's social, political and economic life is well documented, although the 1999 census suggested that its power to attract ever greater numbers of residents may have begun to diminish.

In some other respects, however, traditional rural life has managed not only to survive but to use cultural production as a means of knitting together communities through local voluntary associations. Local village festivals, often boosted by tourism, experienced an upsurge in the 1990s and indeed are seen by many local political leaders as a major part of strategies to keep young people in the rapidly-depopulating villages. Significantly, large cities have emulated the traditional village festival in seeking to build an urban cultural identity: as well as the more traditional drama festival of

Avignon, Paris and Lyon have built up an international reputation for local dance companies through the organization of annual festivals. Musically, France offers a vast variety of international festivals, from the 'Eurorockéennes' near Belfort to Montpellier's techno festival which it promotes as part of its marketing image as a forward-looking, high-technology city, or from Paris's big-name music festival, first set up by Jack Lang in 1982, to the eclectic 'transmusical encounters' which take place annually in Rennes and the 'interceltic' festival held in Lorient (also in Brittany). Such festivals accentuate France's local diversity but also provide a common cultural thread, the more so as they are actively promoted by the Ministry of Culture as a specifically French product (see Dae 1999, and chapters 17 and 19).

Sporting practices remain highly regional in character. Football teams provide a major focus for local identity and social practices not only in the big-club cities like Marseille or Bordeaux, but also in Saint-Etienne and many of the northern industrial towns, particularly Lens or Valenciennes. In these latter cases, football forms part of a local male working-class subculture which has been weakened as a result of deindustrialization and new social divisions due to immigration from developing countries, but which has not died out completely. However, football has become an increasingly international business, whilst the 'quintessential French sporting spectacle', the Tour de France, is now sponsored by a state-owned French bank, an Italian car manufacturer and Coca-Cola (Dine 1999, 253).

New spatial divisions have emerged, not so much between urban and rural areas but within urban areas. In particular, the 'outer cities' or 'banlieues' have come to represent the 'dangerous' face of city living, and to be associated in the popular imagination (and in its cultural representations) with unemployment, crime and violence. These new divisions reflect new forms of spatial segregation which have, very rapidly, found expression in cultural production. Alongside *La Haine*, mentioned above, a series of films appeared in France in the early to mid-1990s, to be greeted collectively as a new genre of 'banlieue' films. Perhaps above all, urban culture is associated with youth lifestyle, particularly music (rap and hip-hop). In this context, urban life is equated with youth (not surprisingly, since run-down outer city areas have a disproportionately large youth population; conversely, people under the age of 35 are significantly under-represented in rural areas) and more specifically with young people of immigrant descent. Not only do rap and hip-hop artists define their music primarily as urban, many of them proudly assert their local origins (for example IAM from Marseille, or 93 NTM from Seine-St-Denis) (Warne forthcoming). Urban culture is at the same time marginal, representing the socially excluded, and increasingly mainstream, in terms of youth consumption at least. It has strongly influenced modern dance in France, and its influence is increasingly seen in theatre and cinema. But many mainstream cultural media still have difficulty handling urban youth culture: for example, young people complain that it is very rarely showcased on television, and documentaries dealing with rap and hip-hop tend to treat it with condescension.

What seems to bewilder many French people is the 'foreign' aspect of new urban subcultures, whether this foreignness designates African origins or North American influences. Urban lifestyles have become increasingly globalized (which means in practice that they draw heavily on US cultural mores, from pizza delivery to cult TV series like *Ally McBeal*). However, French specificities persist thanks to the strength of local identities, sociological factors (such as the ethnic mix of the cities, which is different from that of the US or France's European neighbours) as well as the political framework. Political decentralization, with the cooperative networks it creates between local municipal, departmental and regional authorities on one hand, and between local authorities and central government on the other, acts as a powerful agent promoting both innovation and tradition.

In fact, attachment to local customs and cultures may be seen as a response to globalization. Although the cultural values and norms of urban and rural residents are no longer fundamentally opposed to each other, rural resistance to what is perceived as a process of cultural standardization finds political expression (Dupoirier 1999). European integration and world trade issues have provoked demonstrations, road blocks, attacks on McDonald's restaurants and the celebrated appearance of farmers' leader José Bové at the World Trade Organization discussions in Seattle in November 1999. European Parliament elections have seen the reemergence of the cleavage between urban and rural interests (long presumed dead by many political scientists), with the spectacular success of the Hunters, Fishers and Defenders of Local Traditions party in June 1999, when it won six seats. Widespread public support for Bové's actions and for farmers generally suggests that French attachment to particularistic values and local traditions remains strong.

Conclusions

As we have argued, French culture is about a particular set of responses to economic, social and cultural globalization. Traditional communities – rural or industrial – have not died out completely; they have had to adapt to massive structural change. In many ways this has led to a standardization of lifestyles and values. But resistance to change is also expressed in political behaviour and in the maintenance or revival of cultural particularisms, particularly in celebrations of local or regional identity. The old urban–rural divide no longer seems salient in an overwhelmingly urbanized country; yet it still manages to capture the public imagination and acts as a mobilizing force for political discontent. At the same time, new forms of spatial differentiation and segregation have emerged as a result of socio-economic change and political decisions (urban planning), which have proved their explosive potential in a series of youth riots from the early 1980s onwards.

Although at first sight age and place may appear to be unrelated, we have seen that they overlap in some respects. Young people are concentrated in the problematic 'outer city' estates which appear dangerous to outsiders, and their culture expresses defiance towards the outside world. Mainstream culture has to some extent appropriated urban youth culture (think of the rap background to a 1999 advertisement campaign for Kronenbourg 1666 beer) but on the whole tends to reinforce its marginalization. Young people assert their difference but also express a desire for social integration.

New forms of social division and fragmentation, particularly according to age and level of education, have been created by socio-economic change. Rather than simply replacing the old class cleavages, they run alongside them. This greater social differentiation means an opening-up of life-chances for many French people, but it tends to condemn those with multiple disadvantages (young people from working-class backgrounds with poor educational and cultural capital) to a life on the margins. Culturally, there are more opportunities than ever before for innovation and increased consumption, yet powerful constraints continue to limit access and to maintain clear distinctions between the ways different people relate to cultural activity. Individual expression – one's own way of being French – is still based on collective identity (town or district or housing project, age group, social group, ethnic background), but the overlap between these identities allows more room for self-identification than in the past. French society at the threshold of the twenty-first century may be arguably more at ease with itself than at the end of the 1980s, and certainly than at the end of the 1960s. Like other advanced economies, but in its own way, it is still however trying to resolve contradictions between individual freedom and universality.

References

Ambassade de France à Londres 1997: Young people in France. *France Reports*, R/97/2.
BELOT, L. 1999: Quinquagénaires et riches, des clients à conquérir . . . avec tact. *Le Monde Dossiers et Documents* 280, October, 3.
BOZON, M. 1990: Les loisirs forment la jeunesse. In INSEE, *Données Sociales*. Paris, 217–22.
CHARPAIL, C., GÉLOT, D., GUBIAN, A. and ZILBERMAN, S. 1999: L'évaluation des politiques de l'emploi. *Données Sociales*. Paris: INSEE, 117–27.
DAE, V. 1999: La musique en fête, *Label France*, no. 7 (also available at http://www.france.diplomatie.fr/label_f).
DINE, P. 1999: Leisure and consumption. In COOK, M. and DAVIE, G. (eds) *Modern France. Society in transition*. London and New York: Routledge, 235–56.
DIRN, Louis 1998: *La société française en tendances 1975–1995*. Paris: PUF.
DONNAT, Olivier 1994: *Les Français face à la culture*. Paris: La Découverte.
DUPOIRIER, E. 1999: Villes-campagnes: pas de fractures mais des opinions distinctes. *Le Monde*, 19 November, 18.

GENTIL, B. and ROTMAN, G. 1995: La dépense des ménages en programmes audiovisuels. In INSEE *Première*, 355.

GURREY, B. and SUBTIL, M.-P. 1999: Les jeunes critiquent la société mais ne souhaitent pas la bouleverser. *Le Monde*, 21 November, 8.

HATCHUEL, G. and LOISEL, J.-P. 1999: La vie associative: participer, mais pas militer. In INSEE, *Données Sociales*. Paris, 359–65.

HERVIEU, B. and VIARD, J. 1996: *Au bonheur des campagnes (et des provinces)*. Paris: Editions de l'Aube.

MARCHAND, O. 1999: Population active, emploi et chômage au cours des années quatre-vingt-dix. In INSEE, *Données Sociales*. Paris, 100–7.

MENDRAS, Henri 1996: *La seconde Révolution française*. Paris: Gallimard.

Le Monde 1999: Une société française morcelée. *Dossiers et documents*, October.

MUCCHIELLI, L. 1996: Les désillusions du progrès culturel. In DIRN, L., Chroniques des tendances de la société francaise. *Revue de l'OFCE*, 57.

VALLET, L.-A. 1999: Quarante ans de mobilité sociale en France, 1953–1993. *Revue Française de Sociologie*, 40/1, 5–64.

VIGOUREUX, M. 1997: Société et culture *Atlas de France*, vol. 5. Paris: Reclus, La Documentation Française.

WARNE, C. (forthcoming): The meaning of the streets: reading urban cultures in contemporary France. In BLOWEN, S., DEMOSSIER, M. and PICARD, J. (eds) *Recollections of France: memories, identities and heritage*. Oxford and New York: Berghahn.

WITKOWSKI, D. 1997: Les jeunes en 1996: le bonheur est dans le privé. In SOFRES, *L'état de l'opinion 1997*. Paris: Seuil, 161–92.

|7|

Sexual fault lines: sex and gender in the cultural context

BY LUCILLE CAIRNS

This chapter examines how gender and sexual orientation may inflect the structures of French society and culture. In other words, it is about the cultural politics of sexual and gender differences (rather than the specifics of cultural production or consumption). It will question the tenacious but idealistic belief that no particular category of citizen, whether 'women' or 'gays', is disadvantaged by the institutions of the French Republic, and it will touch on two debates which were taking place as the millennium ended. One concerned *la parité*: equal representation between men and women in parliament; the other the PACS, the *pacte civil de solidarité* granting rights to cohabiting (including same-sex) couples.

Gender differences

French people's experience of their national culture is closely bound up with their gender. As in other countries, men and women's tastes and consumer habits in France diverge rather obviously in the domain of leisure. The magazine, fashion and sport industries market their products to gendered consumers, by appealing to and shoring up established notions of masculinity and femininity. Does this really matter? Your answer will depend on how much you regard gender as a political issue: that is, as related both to power and to the absence of power. The importance of politicizing gender becomes even more apparent when we examine more central areas of French people's experience. What we find is that in almost every sphere – the domestic arena, education, employment, and politics – French women consistently fare differently from French men, in ways that arguably still set them at a disadvantage.

To set this in context, it should be pointed out that in many symbolic and practical respects, French women's lives have greatly changed in the last 50 years or so. Equality between men and women was written into the 1946 and 1958 Constitutions. Working parents in other countries sometimes look enviously at the very good state-provided arrangements France has for childcare, including crèches, nursery schools for all, after-school and holiday clubs and so on, which make it possible for parents, whatever their family situation, to work full-time. It is true that childcare provision has been promoted more because of France's historical concern to boost the birthrate than in response to feminist demands, but it is a measure of the strongly-expressed intention of French women to work outside the home that governments have seen childcare as a necessity. And France was the first country to create a Ministry of Women's Rights, with modest aims in the 1970s but a high reforming profile in the 1980s.

All the more striking therefore that asymmetries should appear, as figures from July 1998 *(Le Point*, 4 July) illustrate. In the domestic sphere, it was found that, on average, women devoted three hours per day to childcare, shopping and housework, whereas men spent less than one hour per day on such activities (with 93 per cent escaping the ironing!). In education, although differences between girls and boys have narrowed hugely in the post-1945 period, with girls receiving the same opportunities and performing at least as well as boys, the higher educational qualifications of women still do not lead to employment on the same terms as men. Three years after obtaining a postgraduate qualification, 83 per cent of men had attained executive status, as against only 69 per cent of women. In the job market, despite a massive influx of women especially after the 1960s, more men continue to be employed than women. As a national average, 68 per cent of men are in paid work, as against 47.6 per cent of women. And importantly, the kind of work women do is often lower-status than that performed by men, with traditional division of labour seeming to operate: 60 per cent of working women are relatively unskilled; only 13 per cent of engineers and technical executives are female. This imbalance is, predictably, reflected in wage differences. On average, French men earn 22.5 per cent more than women; and male executives earn 30 per cent more than their female colleagues, despite legislation aimed at ensuring equal pay for equal work.

Finally, the world of politics is more androcentric in France than in any other European country: French women only got the vote in 1945, and in 1997, only 10.9 per cent of deputies elected to parliament were female, the lowest proportion of female MPs in any European country, except Greece. Not only is it more difficult for French women to succeed in politics beyond local level; the few French women who do make it further, whether from the right, centre or the left wing, complain frequently about the machismo of national political life. 'Before I went into politics, I didn't realize how archaic this milieu is' – Anne-Marie Idrac. This cri de coeur from the UDF *députée* for Yvelines, a former woman minister in the Juppé government, echoes that of many women in politics. They see it as a bastion of macho behaviour, where men see women, according to the Gaullist *députée* for

Paris, Françoise de Panafieu, simply as a 'splash of colour in their assemblies' (*Le Point*, 19 December 1998).

Of course, apart from the scale of under-representation in politics, these gender inequalities are hardly peculiar to France. Arguably, however, there is a cultural specificity about the French 'take' on gender inequalities. This can be illustrated first by the debate over one particular dimension of gender inequality which, while not unique to France, certainly distinguishes France from anglophone countries: language.

As learners of the language will know, French marks every noun by gender: all words are either feminine or masculine. Traditionally, possible discrepancy between the gender of the word and the sex of the person it refers to has not been thought important. Thus, the referent of words like 'le médecin' or 'le professeur' may be a female human being, but the words remain masculine. More recently, as women have begun to occupy important posts, this can lead to such self-contradictory expressions as 'Madame le ministre'.

Arguments in defence of continuing such usage take various forms. Some insist that the grammatical gender of words is arbitrary, so need not reflect the biological sex of the human being in question. For others, there is an obvious hole in this argument, since 'the feminine refers almost exclusively to female human beings, but the masculine does not only denote males [. . .] The masculine overrides the feminine: to express a general term, the masculine singular is used' (Comparat 1998). In other words, the masculine is used as the norm, while the feminine designates peculiarity – hardly a value-free convention. Maurice Druon, Perpetual Secretary of the Académie Française (which legislates on linguistic usage, and numbers only 2 women out of 40 academicians), argued in 1998 against any change – such as 'la ministre' – claiming that 'the appropriation of a post by the person exercising it' was contrary to the principles of equality contained in the Constitution (*International Herald Tribune*, 1 July 1998). Is it simply a coincidence then that most words designating prestigious posts have been masculine, implying the absence of women from positions of power? We quickly realize that this linguistic orthodoxy had its origins in the socio-political reality of women's exclusion from such positions. Why has linguistic usage not moved with the times, to reflect the post-1945 increase of women in higher-level jobs and posts?

This is the question asked by those who advocate the 'féminisation' – or, more accurately, the 'sexuation' – of the French language. These included Lionel Jospin's socialist administration, which issued a circular on 8 March 1998 calling on all branches of government to 'use the feminine term [where appropriate] for descriptions of profession, function, grade or title'. Significantly, the prime minister himself in March 1998 asserted the need for the French language to reflect the gendered evolution of society, with more women than ever active in the public domain: 'I respect the French language, but it seems to be time to correct some grammatical inequalities which are remnants of a past form of society' (*Libération*, 9 March 1998). Christine Bouchara put the case more bluntly: 'To take action so that professions and functions can be expressed in the feminine when necessary – whether the words exist yet or have to be created – simply means making sure women are visible in the world of work and civil society' (Bouchara 1998).

On the wider question of French cultural specificity relating to gender, it is often thought abroad that French representatives of second-wave feminism from the 1960s focused more on the importance of language and subjectivity in the formation of gendered identities, while Anglo-American feminists concentrated more on women's material oppression and on practical strategies for combating it. Put simply, French feminists are regarded as more inclined to theory and abstraction, Anglo-American feminists to social and political practice. While containing some truth, this does not reveal the whole picture. Through selective translation, publication, and promotion of certain writers (Julia Kristeva, Luce Irigaray, Hélène Cixous in particular) French feminist thought has been represented abroad as either an arcane form of intellectual discourse, linked to leading lights in French philosophy (Lacan, Foucault, Deleuze, Derrida), or as abstruse 'différencialisme' stressing the essential difference of women and men. This concentration on a particular rarefied group, however interesting their work, has had the distorting effect of sidelining other varieties of French feminism, such as materialist feminism, for example, represented by writers like Christine Delphy, who engage in dialogue with their counterparts abroad (cf. chapter 22). And it gives a rather partial view of women's cultural presence in France over the last thirty years.

The culture inspired by the French women's movement from the early 1970s – as distinct from that of the fashion world and the classic women's magazines, which remain of course both popular and very gender-specific – was at least for a while both eclectic in range and highly visible. In particular, books published by and about women increased greatly in number. More than one publishing house specialised in feminist books: les éditions des femmes was one of the best known and still has a bookshop on the Left Bank. A number of feminist magazines rose and fell in the 1970s and 1980s (cf. Duchen 1986). The Bibliothèque Marguerite Durand, a library devoted to works on and by women, was visited by far more readers than ever before, and is still the best place to consult reference works, journals, books and manuscripts about French women. The multi-volume *History of Women in the West*, written mostly by French historians, was an international publishing success in the 1990s; and every Easter the Créteil festival of films by women directors brings in many foreign visitors. Many of these activities were encouraged by the Ministry of Women's Rights under Yvette Roudy from 1981 to 1986: its increased budget allowed it to offer subsidies, although not all feminists entirely liked the 'official' patronage.

Feminism in France has never had an easy time however and during the 1990s – partly, it is true, because of its own success in removing discrimination – it was often presented by the media as outdated and no longer needed, while the same media continued both to wonder at women's achievement and to use what might be viewed abroad as sexist language and images (cf. chapter 14). The debate over *la parité*, which will be discussed below, did however bring the feminist agenda into the public gaze again, while at the same time proving a source of disagreement among both men and women.

First it should be mentioned that there is a particular strand of feminism, sometimes called 'universalist' feminism, which is perhaps unique to France, and certainly given prominence in the domestic French press. The French historian Mona Ozouf has argued that 'true' French feminism is necessarily universalist. Human rights to such things as equal treatment and equal opportunities are universal rights, and not gender-specific, so French women claim their rights not as women but as individuals (Ozouf 1995, 391–2). Elisabeth Badinter, a writer often perceived as a champion of the women's cause, agrees: 'French feminists are in the main universalists, even if they don't know it' (Baczko et al. 1995).

Paradoxically, this tendency in France has led to a certain demonization of 'Anglo-Saxon' feminism. The influential journalist Françoise Giroud, who was in the 1970s a junior minister for women's affairs, recently penned a caricature of American feminism, presenting it as a fundamentalist movement aiming at emasculating men. She described French women, by contrast, as admirably free from such separatist violence, aiming rather at 'taming' men, whom, on the whole, they loved: 'globalement, les Françaises aiment les hommes' (*Le Nouvel Observateur*, March 1999). Ozouf has similarly depicted American feminism as the paranoid matrix of 'the war of the sexes', and French feminism as uncontaminated by this alleged 'systematic hostility' – due, she argues, to France's 'long tradition of sensible relations between the sexes', originating in pre-Revolutionary, mixed aristocratic society (Ozouf 1995). Badinter, using the same military vocabulary, sees American feminism as separatist warfare which has failed to achieve anything, and as the origin of a policy of quotas and affirmative action in women's favour which she disdains (*Le Nouvel Observateur*, 23–9 January 1999). In their robust attachment to French universalism, both Ozouf and Badinter, who belong to a certain generation, are perhaps saying something that many French men want to hear. But it must be stressed that by no means all French feminists agree with them. Historian Michelle Perrot for example contests Ozouf's view: 'One does not have to be a radical feminist to point out the mystification which can accompany the "universal". Almost all the various currents [in French feminism] agree about this' (Baczko et al. 1995, 125). But the praise of universalism does raise a question which is in some ways peculiar to France, and which crops up throughout this book. It is particularly strikingly illustrated by the debate over 'la parité'. After a period in which French feminism seemed to have lost some impetus, this question – the equal representation of the sexes in politics – became one of the more hotly debated issues of the 1990s.

Badinter went on record as disliking positive discrimination, and in particular the proposal for complete parity between men and women in French politics. She claimed to share the same aim as supporters of parity – equitable representation of women in political life at the highest levels – but disapproved of proposals to amend the Constitution making parity (i.e. equal numbers of representatives) obligatory.

> Women are not the only 'victims' of society, and other groups will demand their rights, destroying our cohesiveness. If we let the citizen be defined by his/her particularism, we will end up with a sinister set of separate ghettos. I do not want to see *communautarisme* [approximately: 'multiculturalism']. The Republic is based on the abstract rule, the general application of the law, not on the specificity of individuals or groups. France's magnificent specificity is that French people are in solidarity as citizens, not as women, blacks, Muslims etc.
>
> *Le Nouvel Observateur*, 23–9 January 1999

In short, Badinter assumes the capacity of the French Republic to cater for the rights of all its citizens, without the need for special treatment for any community. Indeed, she sees 'communautarisme' as a dangerously divisive trend, threatening social harmony.

Significantly, Badinter's opposition to 'communautarisme' is shared even by a leading supporter of obligatory parity. When asked whether the measure might lead to 'une dérive communautaire', Gisèle Halimi, a long-standing fighter for the women's cause, replied 'L'engrenage communautaire est exclu' (roughly: 'This will not take us into the spiral of multiculturalism'). Her argument was that women do not make up a special category like immigrants or gays, but are half of humankind and indispensable to its survival, in a way that other particular categories are not. What is interesting is that by her choice of words ('the spiral') she too shows an allergy to 'communautarisme'. Such opposition is arguably the most distinctively French feature of attitudes to gender and gender inequalities. Where the American feminist historian Joan Scott argues that 'human universalism has been appropriated by men for themselves', writers like Ozouf defend a French view of the individual as neutral in gender, class, race, seeing anything else as 'communautarisme'. Their stance derives from something British readers certainly, and American readers too perhaps, may find foreign to their cultural experience: faith in the Republic, and a particular type of republic, inextricably linked to France's revolutionary past and its enduring ideal of universalism. Many people in present-day France are suspicious of the multicultural models adopted, with varying degrees of success, by Britain and America (see Baczko et al. 1995).

It seems then that the very notion of gender politics is itself problematic in France, where there is some wariness of any form of identity politics, whether based on gender, ethnicity, or sexual orientation. The interesting thing is that these debates are conducted very openly. During 1999, parity was debated in the National Assembly. After some opposition, largely from the Senate, the Constitution was formally amended in a special session on 28 June to contain a form of words proposing 'equal access' for men and women to the exercise of political functions (the term 'parité' was avoided). At the time of writing, it is not yet clear how this will be enacted – perhaps through the financing of political parties. The construction of dichotomies between republicanism and 'communautarisme', universalism and particularism, which surfaced in this debate, will also be a feature of the second part of this chapter, focusing on gay cultures in France.

Sexual differences

For those who think of the French as having always been a nation of 'libertins', pretty much free from sexual hang-ups, especially compared to the repressed British, the following facts may come as a surprise. As recently as 1960, an amendment to a French law classed homosexuality as a social scourge ('fléau social'), on a par with tuberculosis, alcoholism and prostitution. And if we go back another fifteen years, we discover further inconsistencies. Just as France was reaffirming its citizens' rights to *liberté*, *égalité*, and *fraternité*, after the Liberation, General de Gaulle on 8 February 1945 endorsed a law introduced in 1942 under the Vichy regime, criminalizing homosexual acts in which one of the partners was under 21 years of age, whereas no such punishment was incurred for equivalent heterosexual acts. This may be contextualized by the little-known fact that Vichy France implemented what has been described as a 'gay Holocaust' during World War II, deporting homosexual men as well as Jews, gypsies, communists and other such 'undesirables'. Even today, associations of former French deportees have been reluctant to allow gays to commemorate the deported homosexuals at official memorial ceremonies (cf. Seel 1994; Le Bitoux 1995).

On the other hand, to describe the French as a nation of homophobes, hypocritically excluding gay men and women from revolutionary and republican values, would be going too far the other way. There is, in fact, a strong case for saying that, with the exception of the period from 1942 to 1982, French homosexuals have, since the Revolution of 1789, been subject to *less* discrimination and persecution than, say, their British counterparts. After the downfall of the *ancien régime*, no mention of irregular sexual practices was made in the new penal code, approved by the Constituent Assembly in 1791. (Until the late nineteenth century, homosexuality as a category of identity did not of course exist; while it was recognized that such sexual acts as sodomy and tribadism existed, there was no social concept of the 'homosexual' of either sex. Cf. Foucault 1976.) This did not mean that homosexual acts outside the domain of the private went uncensored, for under the Napoleonic penal code they could be construed as acts of public indecency and severely punished as such. Yet the fact remains that, from 1791 to 1942, homosexual acts performed in private were not forbidden by French law, although they would of course have incurred the condemnation of the Church. The last vestiges of Vichy-inspired discrimination were removed from French legislation in 1982. With the liberalization of French society inaugurated by the Socialist administration of 1981, the gay age of consent was equalized with the heterosexual age of consent (it is now fixed at 15 for all) in August 1982. By contrast, British law still maintains a differential, though recently reduced.

Pressure groups on behalf of French gay men and women had been campaigning for change well before 1981. Arcadie was France's first organized homosexual association. The magazine of that name, founded in 1955, lasted until 1982. By the end of the 1960s, the somewhat conservative agenda of Arcadie (assimilation, respectability) was being overtaken by a new, more revolutionary mood. Radicalization of the movement was fostered by various factors, including the influence of Gay Liberation in America following the famous Stonewall riots in New York. But the new context in which issues of sex and sexuality were viewed was also, of course, a product of the general *contestation* of established moral order triggered by the events of May 1968.

If gay activism subsided after the major legislative conquest of 1982, it resurfaced vigorously later in the 1980s – with new actors and new imperatives – in response to the AIDS crisis, for the stakes here were literally those of life or death. After the AIDS-related death of his long-term partner, the celebrated philosopher Michel Foucault, Daniel Defert set up Aides in 1984, an association aimed at fighting AIDS with the help of the medical establishment. Early members included writer Hervé Guibert and philosopher Gilles Deleuze. 1989 saw Didier Lestrade's launch of Act Up-Paris, whose style and strategies (including direct action and 'zapping' – graffiti campaigns) contrasted sharply with those of the pragmatic and relatively respectable Aides. Act Up-Paris was from the start radical, provocative, and accusatory rather than co-operative vis-à-vis the state institutions which it saw as largely responsible for the gravity of the AIDS crisis in France. While divergent in many respects, Aides and Act Up-Paris are linked not only by their obvious common aim of combating AIDS, but by the participation of both gay men and gay women (and a not negligible number of heterosexual women). While lesbians are a low risk group compared to gay men, the gender divisions plaguing the early days of the movement in the 1970s were to some extent suspended in the face of this life-and-death issue, in order to resist homophobic public discourses on AIDS.

After this brief historical sketch, one might ask what it is like to be a French gay person now, at the end of the millennium. In responding to this question, it is important not to fall into the trap of homogenizing gay life-experience, for that may vary enormously from individual to individual. Is the question even answerable? Same-sex orientation may be the only common factor amongst persons whose identity is made up of many other elements: sex, ethnicity, class, age, being able-bodied or disabled, and so on. As gay writer Guillaume Dustan put it in an interview: 'If you are Jewish, homosexual, S/M, HIV-positive and take drugs, you are the minority of a minority of a minority, which makes you a bit paranoid' (Trieulet 1997). Even so, it is still possible to point to a number of cultural, social and political factors which affect the majority of French gays in the 1990s.

In terms of text-based cultural forms such as literature, film, and art, gay sexuality is more visible than ever before. From the 1970s, textual productivity has flourished, signifying a clear break with the largely coded and/or censorious inscriptions of homosexual desire in earlier French literature. A number of writers depicting gay male desire in particular have been lionized by the critical establishment, for example, Hervé Guibert, Guy Hocquenghem, Michel Tournier, some receiving literary prizes, for example Dominique Fernandez and Yves Navarre (cf. Heathcote in Hughes and Reader 1998, 264–7). Writers whose work foregrounds lesbianism are fewer in number (in metropolitan France, as opposed to, say, Quebec), but have been granted critical respect. Among such writers are Mireille Best; Jocelyne François (who dislikes the word 'lesbienne' and its cognates, but writes overtly about love and sexual desire between women, and was awarded the prestigious 'Prix Femina' in 1980); Hélène de Monferrand (awarded the 'Prix Goncourt du premier roman' in 1990); and, in the domain of more self-consciously experimental writing and of theory, Monique Wittig and Luce Irigaray. Elula Perrin is is less well known but has produced a colourful, uncompromising, and stylistically accessible account of lesbian existence in post-war France.

French cinema, though at first less rich than French literature in this respect, has recently produced some memorable representations of same-sex desire – even if French films have rarely taken homosexuality as their central focus, and even if, as Guy Austin observes, 'Films made by gays and lesbians about their own sexuality have generally existed only on the margins of French mainstream cinema' (Austin 1996 and Marshall in Hughes and Reader 1998, 262–3). Firmly within that mainstream, however, were Cyril Collard's *Les Nuits fauves* (1992) and Josiane Balasko's *Gazon maudit* (1995), both huge box-office successes. *Les Nuits fauves* is an example of another recent cinematic genre obviously relevant to gay male culture: the AIDS film. French films treating AIDS include Léos Carax's *Mauvais sang* (1986), Paul Vecchiali's *Encore* (1988), Bertrand Blier's *Merci la vie* (1992), François Margolin's *Mensonge* (1993), Xavier Beauvois's *N'oublie pas que tu vas mourir* (1995), and Olivier Langlois's *Histoire d'hommes* (1996). However, it should be noted that French AIDS films generally do not treat the subject from an exclusively gay perspective.

Among the new magazines and journals which produced a shared sense of identity, the best-known was perhaps *Gai Pied*, aimed at gay men, which ran from 1979 to 1992. *Masques: revue des homosexualités,* a more intellectual and arts-based publication, addressing gay women as well as gay men, ran from 1979 to 1986. The pressure-group CUARH had a monthly journal *Homophonies*, from 1980 to 1985. The 1990s saw the launch of several new titles, some of them distributed free in gay bars and clubs: *3 Keller, Androzine, Exit le journal, La Grimoire, Homosphère, Illico, La Revue H* and *Têtu.* Surprisingly, given the relative cultural invisibility of lesbians in France, the most successful gay magazine in terms of longevity is *Lesbia Magazine*, launched in 1982 and still going strong. Lastly, modern technological developments have given rise to a particularly effervescent form of communication: lesbian and gay web-sites.

As for cultural activity in a wider sense, the male gay scene is at least as visible in Paris as in any other Western capital, despite the ravages of AIDS. The Marais in the 4th arrondissement of Paris is noted for its gay bars and clubs, contains a well-stocked bookshop *Les Mots à la bouche*, and hosts Gay Pride celebrations each summer. The lesbian scene is small in comparison, and far less commercialized, but embraces a number of financially viable bars and night-clubs (the French-language *Dyke Guide 1997–98* listed no fewer than 18 Parisian establishments either exclusively for lesbians or with a lesbian-friendly profile). Some French provincial cities also now have their own gay culture, albeit on a smaller scale.

Despite the existence of these subcultures, everyday life within a predominantly heterosexual society may not be one of straightforward acceptance. While French society and media are certainly less 'puritan' than their equivalents elsewhere, they tend by the same token to give more prominence to heterosexuality. Does this affect the way gay people are treated by the mainstream? What of their freedom and rights, or lack thereof, in terms of kinship formations, an issue which has been raised in several countries?

With the exception of AIDS, perhaps the single most important social issue for gay men and women in 1990s France was legal recognition of same-sex couples, and access to the rights and benefits accorded heterosexual (in particular married) couples. Support for these demands grew from the early 1990s, with campaigns being mounted for a variously named form of state-endorsed contract, or pact, to legitimate and empower the gay couple. The contract was also to improve the rights of cohabiting heterosexual couples, of whom there are now very many. The title changed several times from the original term, the *contrat d'union civile* to the final formula, the *pacte civil de solidarité* or PACS, but the broad ambition remained constant: to achieve legal standing and social benefits for gay couples relative to straight couples. A 1997 poll of French gay men and women showed that 91 per cent of them were in favour of such a reform, with 55 per cent of them viewing it as the most justified of all their political demands (*Têtu*, January 1997). Predictably, enthusiasm was rather more tepid amongst the general

French population, with an element of backlash occurring. A survey conducted in 1998 by the mainstream magazine *L'Evénement du jeudi* revealed that 54 per cent of French people were opposed to gay marriage. About 49 per cent had no objections to the PACS, which was to grant gay couples welfare benefits; but this still left a majority (51 per cent) who were either opposed to or not prepared actively to support such a pact. And if the simple idea of granting the gay couple recognition and rights is problematic for roughly half the French population, the notion of according gay couples access to parenthood has proved frankly unpalatable: 59 per cent of those polled disapproved granting adoption rights to a lesbian couple, 63 per cent disapproved of granting such rights to gay male couples, and 67 per cent disapproved of the idea of a lesbian couple having recourse to artificial means of procreation.

One survey is not the last word on the subject, but these figures suggest the persistence of what might undoubtedly be described as a guarded attitude towards lesbian and gay kinship, within the French population at large. It should be noted however that following this debate, France has moved further than other countries towards legal change. On 13 October 1999, a bill allowing the PACS was approved by the French National Assembly. The text of the bill permits 'cohabiting couples, whatever their sex', to register their union and, after a transitional period, to benefit from tax and welfare rights equal to those of married couples. At the time of writing, the bill had still to complete its transit through the usual channels, but the critical step had been taken.

Some French town councils had independently taken this first step towards recognizing the legitimate existence of same-sex couples: on 13 September 1995, the town council of Saint-Nazaire announced that it would provide a *certificat de vie commune* for same-sex couples wishing to acquire one; and in the following months, 280 further town halls followed suit. Such measures are indicative of change, though they do fall short of many gay people's aspirations.

The media coverage of such campaigns and demands has fuelled a growing polemic within French public discourse (journalistic, televised, political and intellectual) on the very concept of a gay community, or gay communities, distinct from the rest of society. In what has come to be known as the debate on 'républicanisme-communautarisme' or, sometimes, 'universalisme-communautarisme' (concepts already mentioned in relation to the problematic model of women as a particular group or category), two mutually antagonistic models of society emerge.

The republican model idealizes the French Republic as catering for all citizens, who are deemed to have equality before the law and in terms of personal dignity, and not to need to form communities based on their alleged differences (ethnic, sexual, etc.): to do so would threaten social unity. Some gays accept this model: for instance sociologist Frédéric Martel, who mistrusts identity politics, and stresses the need to 'refuse a concept of the State as the juxtaposition of a set of communities, since that assumes such communities are homogeneous and reduces individuals to a fixed identity' (*L'Evénement du jeudi,* 11–17 April 1996).

The communitarian model, by contrast, heavily influenced by the American example, claims that certain groups of people are not treated equally by the state, that their difference needs to be acknowledged and accommodated, but not used as a pretext for negative discrimination. Thus many French gays describe the republican model as hypocritical, since it has resisted granting them the same rights as heterosexual citizens in terms of kinship, access to parenthood, inheritance rights, welfare benefits, and so on. As the sociologist Pierre Bourdieu noted in 1998, 'it is indeed, paradoxically, just as they are mobilizing to demand universal rights which are effectively refused them, that symbolic minorities are called back to the order of the universal; thus the particularism and "communautarisme" of the gay and lesbian movement is condemned, precisely when that movement is asking for the common law to be applied to gays and lesbians, notably with the *contrat d'union sociale*' (Eribon 1998). Perhaps the last word of this brief introduction to the biggest issue (bar AIDS) for present-day French gay men and women should go to Didier Lestrade, co-founder of Act Up-Paris, the most militant gay group of the decade, and editor of *Têtu*. Instead of promoting the gay community as an end in itself, Lestrade presents it as a necessary, and perhaps only provisional, political strategy: 'like every sub-group in society which is not recognized by the public authorities and market strategy, gays have been obliged to regroup under the banner of community to claim their rights [. . .] In fact, if the state had been quicker to recognize the rights of gays and lesbians, they wouldn't have needed to organize in groups' (*L'Evénement du jeudi,* 11–17 April 1996). For most of the (hypothetical?) gay community of 1990s France, the main objective was hardly glorification of a ghetto; rather, it was acquisition of the rights already enjoyed by heterosexual citizens; or, in the case of many seropositive gay men, simply survival, in the face of what many fear to be an indifferent state.

References

AUSTIN, Guy 1996: *Contemporary French cinema: an introduction.* Manchester: Manchester University Press.
BACZKO, Bronislaw et al. 1995: Femmes: une singularité française? *Le Débat,* 87, November–December, 117–46.
BOUCHARA, Christine 1998: La féminisation des titres et fonctions. *Lesbia Magazine,* November, 18–19.
COMPARAT, Françoise 1998: [untitled]. *Lesbia Magazine,* November, 20–22.
DUBY, Georges and PERROT, Michelle 1995–8: *A history of women in the West.* Tr. A Goldhammer. Harvard: Belknap, 5 vols., esp. vol 5.

DUCHEN, Claire 1986: *Feminism in France from May 1968 to Mitterrand*. London: Routledge.

ERIBON, Didier 1998: *Les Etudes gay et lesbiennes*. Paris: Editions du Centre Pompidou.

FOUCAULT, Michel 1976: *La Volonté de savoir*. Paris: Gallimard.

HEATHCOTE, Owen: see Hughes and Reader.

HUGHES, Alex and READER, Keith (eds) 1998: *Encyclopedia of contemporary French culture*. London: Routledge. See esp. articles by Owen Heathcote and Bill Marshall (on gay writing and gay cinema).

LE BITOUX, Jean 1995: Il y a 50 ans les camps s'ouvraient. *3 Keller*, 11, 31–5.

MARSHALL, Bill: see Hughes and Reader.

OZOUF, Mona 1995: *Les Mots des femmes: essai sur la singularité française*. Paris: Fayard.

SEEL, Pierre 1994: *Moi, Pierre Seel, déporté homosexuel*. Paris: Calmann-Lévy.

TRIEULET, Stéphane 1997: Entretien Guillaume Dustan. *Têtu*, 18.

Further reading

On women, gender, feminism, women's writing, the parity campaign

NB This chapter has not sought to deal with the immense body of literature by women, nor with the secondary literature on women's writing. See references below for initial guidance. See also chapter 22 for feminism within contemporary French thought.

ALLWOOD, Gill 1995: The campaign for parity in political institutions. In KNIGHT, D. and STILL, J. (eds) *Women and representation*. Nottingham: WIF Publications.

ATACK, Margaret and POWRIE, Philip (eds) 1990: *Contemporary French fiction by women: feminist perspectives*. Manchester: Manchester University Press.

DUCHEN, Claire (ed.) 1987: *French connections, voices from the women's movement in France*. London: Hutchinson (translations).

FALLAIZE, Elizabeth 1993: *French women's writing*. Basingstoke: Macmillan.

GASPARD, Françoise, SERVAN-SCHREIBER, C. and LE GALL, A. 1992: *Aux Urnes, Citoyennes!* Paris: Seuil (the original campaign for parity).

GREGORY, Abigail and WINDEBANK, Jan: *Women's work in Britain and France. Practice, theory and policy*. Basingstoke: Macmillan.

HOLMES, Diana 1996: *French women's writing 1848–1994*. London: Athlone.

HUGHES, Alex and READER, Keith (eds) 1998: *Encyclopedia of contemporary French culture*. London: Routledge, relevant articles (see classified contents).

MANASSEIN, M. de (ed.) 1995: *De l'égalité des sexes*. Paris: Centre National de Documentation Pédagogique.

MOSSUZ-LAVAU, Janine 1998: *Hommes/Femmes, pour la Parité*. Paris: Presses de Sciences Po.

MOI, Toril (ed.) 1987: *French feminist thought: a reader*. Oxford: Blackwell (translations).

PICQ, Françoise 1993: *Libération des femmes, les années-mouvement*. Paris: Seuil (history of the movement).

On sexuality, gay writing, etc.

COPLEY, Antony 1989: *Sexual moralities in France 1780–1980*. London: Routledge.

MOSSUZ-LAVAU, Janine 1991: *Les Lois de l'Amour: les politiques de la sexualité en France de 1950 à nos jours*. Paris: Payot.

HEATHCOTE, O., HUGHES, A. and WILLIAMS, J. (eds) 1998: *Gay signatures: gay and lesbian theory, fiction and film in France 1945–1995*. Oxford: Berg (essays on cultural creators).

ROBINSON, Christopher 1995: *Scandal in the ink: male and female homosexuality in twentieth-century French literature*. London: Cassell (general overview).

|8|

The challenges of multiculturalism: regional and religious differences in France today

BY ALEC G. HARGREAVES

This chapter will take us to the heart of the debate over French *national* culture. How you view the questions raised here may depend on your own experience of regional and/or religious diversity. With its long history of centralization, the French state has traditionally been unsupportive and often positively hostile towards both regional and religious diversity. Only in recent decades have regional cultures had significant but still limited state support. Meanwhile religious minorities, particularly those of recent immigrant origin, are still faced with a system of *laïcité* (i.e. the formal separation of church and state) which in principle guarantees the neutrality of the state towards different religious faiths, while in practice tending to favour the Catholic Church. Yet *laïcité*, as will be seen, is not an empty formula.

The reappraisal of regional cultures has been fostered by at least three factors: first, the anti-centralizing spirit which emerged from the events of May 1968 and helped to shape the political agenda of the left when it came to power in the 1980s; second, fear of Americanization – regional diversity has come to be seen as a valuable element contributing to the uniqueness of French culture; and third, the growth of tourist industries trading on picturesque and folkloric traditions which offer holiday-makers a respite from the sort of global culture they can get at home.

By contrast with the improved fortunes of long-established regional minorities, immigrant groups – particularly those originating in Islamic countries – have yet to find among the majority ethnic population in France a comparable degree of openness towards their cultural traditions. These inhibitions are linked partly with still painful memories of French decolonization and also with the recent revival of Islam as a major force in world politics, seen in heavy media coverage of anti-western states and terrorist organizations. While few Muslims in France have any connection with violent movements of that kind, this is not always understood by the majority ethnic population.

To review these issues, this chapter is divided into two main parts, the first tackling regional cultures while the second focuses on religious differences, with particular reference to minorities of recent immigrant origin.

Regional cultures

France is a country with striking regional variations in the physical and human landscape. It is the only country looking out on to both the Mediterranean and the North Sea as well as the Atlantic Ocean. The building materials and architectural styles of northern France have more in common with those of neighbouring Belgium and Germany than with the urban and rural landscapes of southern France. The 'Midi' more closely resembles other Mediterranean countries such as Italy or Spain. Culinary traditions are no less diverse, reflecting different patterns of farming. These and other local traditions such as variations in folklore and costumes are commonly highlighted in tourist brochures. Regional identities have also been foregrounded by a number of prominent film-makers. The films of Marcel Pagnol and those inspired by his stories, with their strong emphasis on the regional heritage of southern France, have helped create an appealing image of Provence. Using powers and resources devolved to them by the socialist-led government of the early 1980s, many regional councils now offer subsidies to film-makers with the aim of gaining publicity for their regions among cinema-goers (Guyotat 1999). An unlikely beneficiary of so-called 'heritage cinema' has been the former coal-producing area in the Nord-Pas-de-Calais region. Claude Berri's block-buster screen adaptation (1993) of Emile Zola's nineteenth-century novel *Germinal*, set amid the coal-tips of northern France, was made with regional council support and helped to attract visitors to an area suffering from industrial dereliction.

De Gaulle is reputed to have joked about the difficulty of governing a country with 246 different varieties of cheese. Despite the centralist tradition, centrifugal forces are undoubtedly present in France, but where regional cultures acquire a political profile this seldom depends on the local cuisine or folklore. The most potent cultural forces around which regionalist movements now mobilize people are minority languages and dialects.

Distribution of regional languages

According to a government-commissioned report by Bernard Cerquiglini (1999), as many as 75 regional and other minority languages are spoken in territories currently administered by France. This headline figure needs to be treated with some caution. Two-thirds of these minority tongues are spoken solely in the Départements et Territoires d'Outre-Mer (DOM-TOM), remnants of the French colonial empire now officially known as Overseas Departments and Territories. Dotted around the globe, the DOM-TOM are characterized by a long and complex history of inter-continental population movements. As the total population of these overseas areas is relatively small – about two million compared with 58 million in metropolitan France – many of the minority tongues identified by Cerquiglini overseas are spoken by very small numbers of people. Within metropolitan France, around half of the 25 minority tongues listed by Cerquiglini would probably be classified by most linguists as dialects, i.e. sub-forms, of two broadly scattered regional languages – *la langue d'oïl* and *la langue d'oc* – rather than as a dozen separate tongues in their own right.

For a long period, the early form of what is today recognized as standard French was spoken by only a small minority of the population living in the territorial area that is modern France (cf. chapter 10). What was to become modern French gained its ascendancy because of the privileged status accorded to it by the unifying power of the state, rather than by simple weight of numbers. For many centuries, as the power of the central state grew, other dialects and languages were spurned or repressed. But as they remained widely used, their minority status was political rather than numerical in nature.

Before the French Revolution, the monarchy imposed a standardized form of French as the sole language recognized for administrative, legal and other official purposes while allowing other languages and dialects (often dismissively referred to as 'patois') to be used in other, more lowly social contexts. In France's Caribbean and Indian Ocean colonies, new dialects of low social standing known as *créoles*, mixing French with elements drawn from other languages, were developed by slaves of African origin. During the French Revolution, regional languages and dialects were regarded as reactionary by the centralizing faction known as the Jacobins, who wanted standard French to be spoken everywhere. While French was by then firmly established as the dominant language in towns, throughout most of the nineteenth century, regional dialects and languages continued to flourish in rural areas, especially in outlying regions around the borders of France.

By introducing a nationwide system of compulsory, non-religious schooling conducted solely in French, the Third Republic (1870–1940) set out both to tame the cultural influence of the Catholic Church and to marginalize or eradicate regional languages, which were forbidden altogether on school premises. This marked a turning point, greatly increasing the use of standard French among the general population. Other dialects and languages now became minority tongues not only politically but also numerically (Weber 1976).

During World War II, certain regionalist movements, in areas such as

Brittany, were badly compromised by collaborating with the Nazis, who played on cultural differences in the hope of weakening resistance to the Occupation of France. By contrast, regionalist movements in south-west France, where Catalan and Basque are spoken, are unusual in having relatively long traditions of left-wing leanings. It was not until the events of 1968 ushered in a wave of new thinking that regionalist movements elsewhere began to lose their reactionary image, with a shift to the left in Brittany for example.

Autonomist and separatist movements tend to gain support where cultural demands are linked with regional economic grievances. At present, the most explosive cocktail of this kind is in Corsica, where the cultural and economic demands of autonomist and independence movements are further complicated by the activities of mafia-style groups which have helped to create a climate of intermittent violence and lawlessness. There has also been sporadic violence in Brittany and the French Basque country, but nothing on the scale of the paramilitary operations carried out by Basque separatists in Spain. In the DOM-TOM, autonomist and separatist movements fuelled by cultural and economic grievances have gained varying levels of support. The overseas territory which has been most deeply marked in recent years by independence movements is the Pacific island of New Caledonia, where bands of guerrilla fighters challenged French security forces as recently as the 1980s.

The number of people resident in France today who are able to speak or understand regional dialects and languages is not known with certainty. No data on this subject are collected in national censuses, a fact that reflects the traditional reluctance of the state to grant official recognition to these languages. Créoles are known to be spoken by most people in overseas *départements* such as Martinique. Within metropolitan France, the best available estimates suggest that regional dialects or languages are known by around 10 per cent of the total population, or about 30 per cent if the highest (but doubtful) estimates of Occitan-speakers are accepted (Ager 1990, 29). Many have only a passive understanding of a regional language; those who can really speak one are far fewer in number. Their age profile is older than that of the general population. Virtually all also speak French, which predominates everywhere for official purposes such as administration, education and legal transactions. Most regional languages are spoken in less formal contexts such as in the family home or in rural workplaces. The name given by linguists to this co-existence of different languages or dialects serving hierarchically distinct functions is 'diglossia'.

Even when regional languages are spoken by elected representatives during local or regional council meetings – as sometimes happens in Brittany and Corsica, for example – the official minutes are kept solely in French. When the Regional Council in Corsica voted in 1983 in favour of bilingualism, which would have given equal status to Corsican and French, this was ruled out by the socialist-led central government in spite of its commitment to administrative decentralization and limited support for regional cultures (Laroussi and Marcellesi, 1993, 89).

Occitan, the name given to a group of dialects spoken across a wide area of southern France, is spoken or understood by a larger number of people (variously estimated at between three and 12 million) than any of France's other regional dialects or languages. Like standard French – derived from one of the group of northern dialects known as *la langue d'oïl*, as distinct from *la langue d'oc* in the south – Occitan is a variant of the Gallo-Roman language, which developed from Latin during and after the Roman occupation. A third group of Gallo-Roman dialects, known as Franco-Provençal, is spoken in south-east central France. The other regional languages spoken in France are all confined to narrower and more peripheral areas. In clockwise order, starting from the north-west, they are Breton, Flemish, Alsatian, Corsican, Catalan, and Basque.

Alsatian dialects, variants of the German language, are spoken or understood by about a million people, who make up a majority of the population in the Alsace region. Breton, spoken by about 1.5 million people early in the twentieth century, is now spoken by only about half a million. There are perhaps 180 000 Catalan-speakers and 80 000 Basque-speakers in France, with larger communities of both language groups across the border in Spain. Most of the population in the *département* of Pyrénées Orientales speak or understand Catalan, while probably less than half of the population in the Pyrénées Atlantiques know Basque. In Corsica, out of a total population of 250 000 more than half are able to speak Corsican. There are probably only about 40 000 Flemish-speakers in France, concentrated in the area around Dunkirk, close to the border with Belgium (Ager 1990, 18–81; Laroussi and Marcellesi 1993).

Although the precise number of people able to speak these languages is unknown, there is no doubt that the overall trend is one of steady decline. A survey conducted in 1992 jointly by the Institut National de la Statistique et des Etudes Economiques (INSEE) and the Institut National d'Etudes Démographiques (INED) found that only a minority of parents able to speak these languages used them regularly with their children (Héran 1993). With declining family usage, minority languages face a difficult future unless more is done to promote them through the educational system and the mass media.

Public policy towards regional languages

The 1951 Deixonne Law permitted a small amount of optional teaching of certain regional languages within French state schools. The dividing line between approved and unapproved languages revolved around the unwillingness of the authorities to support any language that might enjoy a power base distinct from that of the central state in France. Four languages were approved: Breton and Occitan, which are not spoken to any significant degree outside France, and Basque and Catalan, which at that time were prohibited by the Franco regime in Spain. Alsatian (a variant of German), Corsican (a form of Italian) and Flemish (more widely spoken in Belgium) were excluded on the grounds that the languages of which they were variants were recognized by states other than France. Corsican eventually gained approval in 1974, and during the 1980s and early 1990s socialist-led governments further widened the approved list of languages in both metropolitan France and the DOM-TOM (Laroussi and Marcellesi 1993, 87; Aub-Buscher 1993, 204).

In spite of this official recognition, lessons in regional languages remain optional and the public funds committed to them are still very limited. In 1996–97, in state and private schools across the whole of metropolitan France a total of 320 000 children were receiving at least some of their lessons in regional languages. They represented 2 per cent of France's total school population. With only a few hours tuition each week, few were likely to achieve a significant degree of proficiency. Corsica was the only area where most children (as many as 85 per cent) received at least some schooling in the regional language. In other regions, Catalan lessons were being given to 13.5 per cent of local schoolchildren, while the figure for Breton and Occitan was just 5 per cent. A fully bilingual education was being given to 5 per cent of schoolchildren in the Basque country and to a mere 1 per cent of those in Brittany (Andreani 1998; Andreani and Dupont 1998).

These figures include not only state schools but also language programmes run by private and voluntary organizations, such as the Diwan schools in Brittany, which since 1977 have catered for children of kindergarten age. Ikastola schools, launched in 1969, play a similar role in the Basque country. In both regions, these privately-run schools now receive public subsidies and have extended their activities to older groups of children. It is usually possible to study regional languages in one or more local universities, and CAPES (teacher training) qualifications can be taken in Breton and Corsican.

Regional languages enjoy at best patchy access to the mass media. F3 is the only one of France's six terrestrially-based television channels to have been created with a regional structure. Much of its programming is in fact national, and very few of its regional broadcasts are in languages other than French. In regions such as Alsace, Brittany and Corsica, there are now short daily news bulletins in the regional language and somewhat longer programmes at the weekend. This is still a minimalist approach compared with that of S4C in Wales, where Britain's fourth television channel devotes most of its prime-time broadcasts to Welsh-language programmes.

Regional languages have fared somewhat better on radio, particularly since the liberalization of the airwaves in the early 1980s brought a huge expansion in the number of local radio stations. In most areas where regional languages are spoken, listeners now have access to local stations broadcasting at least some of their programmes in the regional language. Examples include Radio Bretagne Ouest and Radio Corsa Frequenza Mora. There are varying amounts of literary production in most regional languages, which are also used in a range of magazines and newssheets, but none of these languages is spoken sufficiently widely to sustain a full-scale daily press.

Looking to the future, French governments of both the left and the right initially refused to sign the Council of Europe's 1992 Charter on Regional and Minority Languages, which would require increased support to be given to languages other than French. Then in 1996, centre-right President Jacques Chirac spoke in favour of signing the Charter, comparing the plight of regional languages with that of French in the face of the international domination of English. Two years later, Socialist Prime Minister Lionel Jospin made a similar commitment. The Charter was eventually signed in May 1999, but shortly afterwards, France's Constitutional Council ruled that it was incompatible with the French Constitution, which would therefore have to be amended if the Charter were to be ratified and implemented. In support of its ruling, the Constitutional Council pointed to Article 1 of the Constitution, proclaiming the 'indivisibility' of the French Republic and to Article 2, where French alone is enshrined as the language of the republic. Weakened in the 1999 European elections by the strong showing of parties on both the left and the right opposed to any dilution of national sovereignty, President Chirac reneged on his commitment to the Charter by refusing to propose the necessary constitutional amendment. Ratification and implementation were thus effectively blocked for the time being.

The moral panic surrounding the Charter rested on grossly exaggerated interpretations of the provisions to which France had signed up. Many important details – including the list of minority languages to which official recognition would be accorded and the nature of the support which they would receive— had been left vague. While recognized regional languages would probably have improved access to the media and other rights, French would undoubtedly have remained the sole official language for most if not all administrative purposes, and minority languages which are not regionally based appeared likely to be excluded from this process altogether (Jérôme 1999).

These other minority tongues are sometimes referred to as 'non-territorial' or 'immigrant' languages. Most were introduced into France by peoples originating in relatively distant countries, and they tend to be fairly dispersed rather than concentrated in a single region. Some of these languages are regarded with considerable suspicion by political elites who fear they may threaten the cultural integration of immigrants and their families. The main languages to suffer in this way are Arabic and Berber, which are spoken by minorities originating in the Maghreb (i.e. the former French colonies of Algeria, Morocco and Tunisia). Far more politically sensitive than the language issue, however, are the religious differences associated with Maghrebi immigrants, the vast majority of whom are Muslims. In recent years, the status of Muslims has become by far the most controversial issue in the negotiation of religious differences within France.

Religious differences

At the end of the sixth century, the Frankish King Clovis became the first monarch in the area now known as France to convert to Christianity. Today, despite the official separation of Church and state (1905), Clovis's baptism remains widely regarded as the founding act of the French nation-state. Significantly, in 1996 President Chirac personally welcomed the Pope to France on the occasion of ceremonies marking the 1500th anniversary of Clovis's baptism. In so doing, Chirac reminded his compatriots of the long tradition of Christian, and more especially Catholic, belief shared by the majority of the nation's population.

In the past, bloody wars were sometimes fought between rival Christian sects, with regional concentrations playing a significant role. The so-called Albigensian heresy, which led to the Cathars of southern France being savagely repressed by northern barons acting on the orders of the Pope during the early thirteenth century, is now no more than a dim historical memory. The sixteenth century saw a long series of wars between Catholics and Protestants, at the end of which the latter gained official toleration, though this was withdrawn a century later and not fully restored until the French Revolution. During the Revolution, the Catholic Church was branded as an enemy of republicanism, a reputation strengthened by its support for the counter-revolutionary insurrection which took place in the western region known as the Vendée. Today, Catholicism remains relatively strong in certain rural areas where regional movements have gained momentum. But the Catholic faith still retains at least the loose adherence of most of the national population, and is seldom a major rallying point for regionally-based cultural movements. Surveys regularly report that as many as 80 per cent of the national population say they are Catholic – attending baptisms, church weddings and funerals for instance – though only about 10 per cent are regular church-goers (*Etat de la France* 1995, 202–5). The cultural tradition of Catholicism has thus formed a context for much French literature in the past.

During the twentieth century, new forms of religious difference have come to the fore, though since no census data are collected on religious beliefs (an example of official state blindness towards cultural differences, seen as belonging to the private sphere), the number of adherents to different faiths cannot be accurately determined. There is no doubt, however, that while Catholicism remains by far the main faith, Islam is now the second largest religion in France. Most estimates put the number of Muslims at around four million or more. There are generally estimated to be about 800 000

Protestants, 600 000 Jews and 400 000 Buddhists (*Hommes et migrations* 1993; *Etat de la France* 1994; Boyer 1999).

In practice, some publicly-regulated aspects of everyday life in France continue to favour Christian traditions over other faiths. Many of the main public holidays, such as Christmas, Easter, Whitsun and All Saints' Day (la Toussaint) have their origins in Christian festivals. There are no comparable public holidays on days of special significance to other faiths. Sunday, the main official day of rest, is convenient for Christian church-goers, but less so for orthodox Jews, for whom Saturday is the main day of rest and of worship, or practising Muslims, for whom Friday has similar significance. The officially-sanctioned practice of closing state schools on Wednesday afternoons was introduced to permit children to attend catechism classes run by the Catholic Church. In such schools, the 'lost' half-day is traditionally made up on Saturday mornings. While convenient for Catholics, this arrangement can pose problems for children brought up in orthodox Jewish families (see below).

The educational system is in fact crucial to the long-term future of different religious traditions, since it plays a key role in transmitting knowledge, values and beliefs to the younger generation. Although religious organizations are banned from exercising any official role within the French state, the system of *laïcité* does not prevent the state subsidising religious schools, provided they teach the national curriculum while making religious classes technically optional. Some two million children attend state-supported Catholic schools, and there are around 10 000 pupils in subsidised Jewish schools, but so far not a single Islamic school has been awarded public support (Morin 1994). The dice are loaded against religions that are relatively new to France, particularly Islam, since new schools have to operate successfully on their own resources for at least five years before they are eligible to be considered for state support. This is not easy for ethnic groups which are relatively poor.

Non-Christian religions:

Judaism

The longest established non-Christian religion in France is Judaism. As in many other predominantly Christian countries, France's small Jewish minority was subject to residence and other restrictions before the 1789 Revolution. During the Revolution, Jews were granted full citizenship, but were regarded with suspicion by much of the population. At the end of the nineteenth century, the Dreyfus Affair revealed widespread anti-semitism (cf. chapter 3). During this period, France's Jewish population was expanding with the arrival of Jewish immigrants fleeing persecution in Russia and eastern Europe. At the same time, a tense international climate and increased economic insecurity resulting from a slow-down in industrial growth led to heightened suspicion of those perceived as 'foreign' elements within France, prominent amongst whom were Jews. A similar combination of factors helped to provoke fresh outbreaks of anti-semitism during the economic slump of the 1930s, when tens of thousands of Jewish refugees from Nazi Germany sought asylum in France. During World War II, the collaborationist Vichy regime passed anti-Jewish laws and helped to round up Jewish residents for deportation by the Nazis, at whose hands six million of Europe's Jews were to die. After the war, when the horrors of the Holocaust became widely known, antisemitism became very largely discredited in France, though it is still present in a submerged form and is regularly played upon, for example, by the extreme right-wing Front National (FN).

Just as the small historical core of long-established Jews was outnumbered during the first half of the twentieth century by newcomers from Eastern Europe, so these in turn were subsequently overtaken by Jews originating in former French North Africa, who settled in France with the advent of decolonization in the late 1950s and early 1960s. Today, the Jewish population in France – at 600 000 the largest in any west European country – is traversed by many internal differences. While French is the main language in dealings with non-Jews, there are internal speech differences separating Ashkenaze Jews, who brought Yiddish with them from Eastern Europe, from Sephardic Jews originating in North Africa, among whom a number of Arabic dialects are spoken. There are also growing differences between secular and non-practising Jews and those who favour the more orthodox observance of religious practices. In addition, political divergences may arise over Israel and its relations with Palestinians and the wider Arab world (Becker and Wieviorka 1998).

Until recently, Jews generally adhered punctiliously to the French system of *laïcité*, confining their religious practices to the private sphere and avoiding any challenge to established public conventions. The influx of Sephardic Jews has helped to strengthen the hand of those who favour greater religious orthodoxy. This has been especially visible in the field of education, with a rapid expansion in the number of Jewish schools, greater emphasis on religious teachings within such schools, and an (unsuccessful) court case seeking exemption from Saturday morning classes for Jewish children attending state schools. In 1994 the Chief Rabbi of France, Joseph Sitruk, created a stir when he asked for Jews to be allowed to vote in French cantonal elections on a different date from the rest of the population because polling day clashed with a Jewish religious festival. When this was refused, Sitruk took the unprecedented step of calling on Jews not to vote (Tincq 1994).

Islam

The Muslim population in France is composed primarily of Maghrebis, people originally from Morocco, Algeria and Tunisia, together with smaller numbers of other ethnic groups, such as Turks and certain West Africans. It is only since the 1960s that immigration and permanent family settlement by these groups has become a significant feature of French society. Before then, most immigrants were Europeans. Now Maghrebis make up the largest single group of recent immigrant origin. Most Maghrebi immigrants received little formal education in their home countries. As the unskilled job vacancies which they filled in France were poorly paid, they and their families have generally had to manage with low incomes. That was an unpromising skills and resource base on which to build the infrastructure necessary to support the religious beliefs and practices of the Muslim minority in France (Boyer 1999).

Islam also has to battle against strong prejudices at both elite and popular levels among the majority ethnic population. These were seen in massive media coverage of the *affaire du foulard* (Islamic headscarf affair), which first erupted in 1989. The affair became widely regarded as emblematic of an unwillingness or incapacity on the part of the Muslim population in France to respect the rules of *laïcité*. This is however a very misleading interpretation. Seen in context, the headscarf affair actually demonstrates both the compliance of most Muslims with the code of *laïcité* and the discriminatory attitudes towards Islam found among many members of the majority ethnic population (Gaspard and Khosrokhavar 1995).

In the original headscarf affair, three girls – two of Moroccan origin, and one of Tunisian origin – were excluded from a *collège* in the town of Creil, 50 kilometres north of Paris, because they insisted on wearing headscarves for religious reasons while on school premises. The headmaster argued that the wearing of headscarves was incompatible with the laws governing *laïcité*. Asked to pronounce on the case, the Conseil d'Etat, France's highest administrative court, ruled that exactly the opposite was true. The girls were perfectly entitled to wear headscarves in state schools, just as it has long been commonplace for Catholics to wear crucifixes and for Jewish boys to wear yarmulkas, without any complaints from the authorities. The person judged to have broken the law was the headteacher in Creil, who had failed to respect the right of every individual to hold and express religious beliefs of their own choosing.

The Conseil d'Etat confirmed that it was illegal to proselytise (i.e. to preach or try to persuade others to accept particular religious beliefs) within state schools, but did not regard the wearing of religious insignia as an act of proselytism. Nevertheless, in 1994 the centre-right Education Minister, François Bayrou, tried to ban the headscarf by issuing a circular instructing schools to exclude any pupil wearing religious insignia judged to be 'ostentatious', on the grounds that this amounted to proselytism. According to Bayrou, Islamic headscarves were ostentatious and therefore illegal, whereas Catholic crucifixes and Jewish yarmulkas were unobtrusive and therefore acceptable. This distinction was both nonsensical and discriminatory, and numerous court rulings have since confirmed the right of Muslim girls to wear headscarves if they wish.

Opinion polls have however shown overwhelming public support among the majority ethnic population for Bayrou's anti-headscarf stance. Less widely appreciated is the fact that opinion surveys among Muslims show that a majority of them, too, support a ban on headscarves in state schools. Most Muslims in France clearly accept the principle of *laïcité* and, in opposing the wearing of headscarves at school, favour a stricter interpretation of this principle than is required by the law. Even at the height of the second headscarf affair, when Bayrou's circular appears to have provoked hundreds of girls into wearing headscarves as an act of defiance, the total number involved – 2000 at the very most – was insignificant when compared with the 350 000 Muslim girls attending state schools without wearing any such apparel.

Majority ethnic hostility towards Muslims has often been explained or justified on the grounds that Muslims do not want to integrate into French society. This is part of a wider argument advanced by opponents of multiculturalism, according to whom the so-called French model of integration, designed fully to incorporate immigrant minorities into mainstream society through the educational system and other institutions, has in recent years broken down in the face of resistance by minorities originating in the Islamic world. Yet the headscarf affair does not, in my view, justify such a belief. Schools and other institutions, including the mass media, are clearly functioning very effectively in transmitting to young members of Muslim families values and aspirations shared by majority ethnic youths.

Numerous surveys have shown that second-generation members of minorities originating in Islamic countries are far less religious than their immigrant parents. Rates of agnosticism and atheism among second-generation Maghrebis are in fact slightly higher than among young people from majority ethnic Catholic families. While most young people of Maghrebi origin continue to regard themselves as Muslims, this is in many cases a sentimental attachment bound up with feelings of loyalty to their parents rather than a whole-hearted commitment to Islamic doctrines. The proportion of the total nominally Muslim population who actively practise their religion by praying and going to the mosque is probably smaller than the proportion of church-goers among Catholics (Hargreaves and Stenhouse 1991; Cesari 1998; Boyer 1999).

How, in these circumstances, are we to explain the fears and hostility surrounding Muslims in France? At least three sets of factors are involved: the unhappy legacy of decolonization in North Africa, the heightened visibility of anti-western Islamic states in international politics, and feelings of personal insecurity linked to the processes of globalization and economic restructuring with which France and other industrial countries have been grappling since the 1970s.

As in earlier periods of economic difficulty, when Jewish and other minorities were scape-goated by members of the majority ethnic population, so today the most visible minorities of recent immigrant origin – those originating in North Africa and other Islamic countries – are the prime targets of prejudice and discrimination. Maghrebis are particularly unpopular in some quarters because of the Algerian war of 1954–62, at the end of which France was forced to concede independence to nationalists who had highlighted the Islamic heritage of Algerians as an emblem of their national identity.

The Iranian revolution of 1979 brought a new prominence in international politics to anti-western Islamists, i.e. Muslims committed to maximizing the political role of Islam. Although very few Muslims in France have any connections with Iranian or other Islamists, this distinction has often been blurred in the mass media. During the 1990s, many atrocities were committed in Algeria in a guerrilla war between Islamist insurgents and the military-backed government. In 1995, a small number of terrorist attacks were also carried out in France by a handful of second-generation Maghrebis working in league with Islamists from Algeria. Again, media coverage of these events helped to create the widespread and unfounded belief that religious fanaticism was rife among Muslims in France.

Buddhism

Not surprisingly, perhaps, Islam has made relatively few converts in France. Only about 1 per cent of Muslims are converts, whereas about half of France's Buddhists are converts. Compared with Islam, Buddhism has a much more peace-loving image. While media coverage of Islam has tended to make it appear menacing, Buddhism is more often seen as a welcome antidote to the stresses of Western materialism. Most foreign-born Buddhists in France come from former French colonies in Indochina, where Buddhism mingles with Taoist beliefs drawn from neighbouring China. Although Indochina, like Algeria, was the scene of a bloody war of decolonization, the independence movement there was perceived in France primarily as communist rather than religious in nature. Following France's withdrawal in 1954, a renewed anti-communist war was waged by the United States in Vietnam, where Buddhists were often seen playing a prominent role in peace movements. Most Vietnamese living in France today fled Indochina following the communist victory in 1975 (the so-called 'boat people'), bringing with them Buddhist and Taoist beliefs that are relatively unmarked in French eyes by the kinds of antagonistic images sometimes associated with Islam.

Laïcité and multiculturalism

Multiculturalism is often regarded in France as a dangerous 'Anglo-Saxon' idea from which the French are mercifully protected by their system of *laïc-*

ité. This kind of reasoning rests in many ways on a faulty understanding of the situation in both Britain and the US, as well as on a failure to appreciate entirely the principles of *laïcité* itself (Hargreaves 1997). Although Britain and the US *are* in some respects more open than France to public expressions of cultural diversity, these differences should not be exaggerated. Meanwhile, far from systematically repressing minority religions, *laïcité* does in fact afford important elements of protection by requiring the state to maintain a neutral position in relation to different faiths – although as noted earlier, this obligation is not always fully observed.

The 1789 Declaration of the Rights of Man and of the Citizen, which among French republicans enjoys a secular status equivalent to that of a sacred text, guarantees freedom of religious belief and expression to everyone in France. This freedom is unrestricted in the private sphere (including places of worship such as churches, temples or mosques), while in the public sphere it is limited only by the requirements of state neutrality and the maintenance of public order, in the interests of which religious groups are barred from preaching or other kinds of ostentatious behaviour in places such as public highways or state schools.

Although there are in practice many inequalities in the treatment of different religious faiths by the state as well as by private individuals and the mass media, it must be recognized that the French Constitution does guarantee basic rights to all believers. Court rulings in cases such as those thrown up by the Islamic headscarf affair have shown that these constitutional principles *can* be successfully invoked on behalf of religious minorities even in the face of marked hostility among the majority ethnic population. In the field of religious differences, as in relation to regional languages, public policy in France is often less than fully even-handed, yet the French legal and republican tradition does allow for a real and in some respects expanding space within which minorities of both kinds are able to assert their rights.

References

AGER, D. 1990: *Sociolinguistics and contemporary French*. Cambridge: Cambridge University Press.

ANDREANI, J.-L. 1998: Le gouvernement veut valoriser les langues régionales. *Le Monde*, 4 February.

ANDREANI, J.-L. and DUPONT, G. 1998: La France devrait ratifier la Charte européenne des langues régionales en 1999. *Le Monde*, 9 October.

AUB-BUSCHER, G. 1993: French and French-based creoles: the case of the Caribbean. In Sanders, C. (ed.), *French today: language in its social context*. Cambridge: Cambridge University Press, 199–214.

BECKER, Jean-Jacques and WIEVIORKA, Annette (eds) 1998: *Les Juifs de France de la révolution française à nos jours*. Paris: Liana Levi.

BOYER, A. 1999: *L'Islam en France*. Paris: Presses Universitaires de France.

CERQUIGLINI, B. 1999: *Les Langues de la France. Rapport au Ministre de l'Education Nationale, de la Recherche et de la Technologie.* URL: http://www.culture.fr/culture/dglf/lang-reg/rapport_cerquiglini-france.html.

CESARI, J. 1998: *Musulmans et républicains: les jeunes, l'Islam et la France.* Brussels: Complexe.

Etat de la France. 1994: Edition 1994–1995. Paris: La Découverte.

Etat de la France. 1995: Edition 1995–1996. Paris: La Découverte.

GASPARD, F. and KHOSROKHAVAR, F. 1995: *Le Foulard et la République.* Paris: La Découverte.

GUYOTAT, R. 1999: Les régions participent de plus en plus au financement des films. *Le Monde,* 4 March.

HARGREAVES, A.G. 1997: Multiculturalism. In FLOOD, C. and BELL, L (eds), *Political ideologies in contemporary France.* London and Washington: Pinter, 180–99.

HARGREAVES, A.G. and STENHOUSE, T.G. 1991: Islamic beliefs among youths of North African origin in France. *Modern and contemporary France* 45, April, 27–35.

HERAN, F. 1993: L'Unification linguistique de la France. *Population et sociétés* 285, December, 1–4.

Hommes et migrations 1993: Le bouddhisme en France, 1171, December.

JEROME, B. 1999: La France signe la Charte européenne des languages régionales. *Le Monde,* 8 May.

LAROUSSI, F. and MARCELLESI, J.-B. 1993: The other languages of France: towards a multilingual policy. In SANDERS, C. (ed.), *French today: language in its social context.* Cambridge: Cambridge University Press, 85–104.

MORIN, H. 1994: La crise de croissance des écoles juives. *Le Monde,* 30 June.

TINCQ, H. 1994: Les crispations du judaïsme français. *Le Monde,* 19 March.

WEBER, E. 1976: *Peasants into Frenchmen: the modernization of rural France 1870–1914.* Stanford: Stanford University Press.

Further reading

G. Vermes (ed.), *Vingt-cinq communautés linguistiques de la France,* 2 vols (Paris: L'Harmattan, 1988) and C. Sanders (ed.), *French today: language in its social context* (Cambridge: Cambridge University Press, 1993) offer rich panoramas of linguistic diversity within France, while D. Ager, *Identity, insecurity and image: France and language* (Clevedon: Multilingual Matters, 1999) provides an up-to-date survey of French public policy in this field. H. Giordan, *Démocratie culturelle et droit à la différence* (Paris: La Documentation française, 1982) has been influential in the debate surrounding minority languages, though many of its recommendations remain unimplemented.

A basic reference book on religion is G. Cholvy and Y.-M. Hilaire, *Histoire religieuse de la France contemporaine,* 3 vols (Toulouse: Privat, 1985–8). A very readable collection of short articles on religious diversity within France is available in a special issue of the magazine *L'Histoire,* 135, July–August 1990: Chrétiens, juifs et musulmans en France. In English, see M. Larkin, 'The Catholic church and politics in twentieth-century France' in M. Alexander (ed.) *French history since Napoleon* (London: Arnold, 1999), 147–71. Semi-official thinking in relation to immigrant minorities is typified by the work of the Haut Conseil à l'Intégration, whose report on religious and linguistic issues was published as *Liens culturels et intégration*

(Paris: La Documentation française, 1995). The principles and practice of *laïcité* are discussed by J. Bauberot, Le débat sur la laïcité, *Regards sur l'actualité*, 209–10, March–April 1995, 51–62. Revealing insights into the Islamic headscarf affair are contained in F. Gaspard and F. Khosrokhavar, *Le Foulard et la République* (Paris: La Découverte, 1995).

|9|

French political culture: homogeneous or fragmented?

BY BRIAN JENKINS

What does it mean to talk about a country's 'political culture'? This concept allows us to identify key features of a particular political community – such as France – and offers a useful historical shorthand for what is distinctive about symbols and practices, institutions and patterns of behaviour inherited from the past. These special features may reflect peculiarities of social and economic development, decisive formative moments, wider cultural influences such as language and religion, the impact of external events, and the international environment. Insofar as this legacy has left its mark on popular attitudes and perceptions, it finds expression in a 'political culture'.

How do we define the boundaries of a given community (and thus its culture)? Here the key reference-point is the division between nations (and often the physical frontiers between nation-states). This chapter will examine the notion of a specifically French political culture. But it should be recognized at the outset that the boundaries might be drawn differently. For example, regions, minority ethnic groups, social classes, rival ideological traditions, and even transnational groups can all be depicted as relatively autonomous political communities with distinctive 'political cultures' of their own, thus challenging the notion of a homogenizing 'national' culture.

Still there is no doubt that the nation-state, having become the dominant model of state organization worldwide over the last 200 years, is a powerful agent in the shaping of political culture. Where it does not reflect a pre-existing sense of community, it sets out to create one. As the main focus of political sovereignty and legitimacy, it makes sub-national political communities/cultures adapt and enter into relationship with one another. And while in an age of globalization, national differences are undoubtedly being eroded, any given history of nation-building will leave traces that cannot lightly be dismissed.

In this respect, France can legitimately claim to be one of the world's oldest 'nations'. Geographically it had already begun to assume its modern hexagonal shape in the mid-sixteenth century. Under the centralized absolutist monarchies of the seventeenth and eighteenth centuries, it achieved a degree of administrative unity and developed some of the trappings of modern statehood. The Revolution drew the masses on to the political stage, and laid the foundations for genuine nationhood by invoking the concept of citizenship. From now on, the legitimacy of the state would depend on its capacity to represent the political community of the 'nation'. After 1870, the Third Republic provided the institutional framework for the attainment of that ideal, and actively promoted a sense of nationhood through the agencies of compulsory education and military service (Weber 1976).

So political culture in the 'hexagon' has been shaped by this distinctly 'national' context for several centuries. A history punctuated by revolution, war and foreign occupation has provided a powerful shared experience, and though the effect has often been to create domestic conflict rather than consensus and cohesion, it has helped to forge a profound sense of difference and distinctiveness, and to reinforce the notion of French exceptionalism.

French exceptionalism

The idea that France is somehow unique is deeply embedded in the nation's self-image. This is not just the routine rhetoric common to all nationalisms, nor even the inflated vanity typical of most great powers. It reflects the conviction that France has an exemplary, universal role as a civilizing force, that its aspirations are those of humanity at large.

This notion builds, of course, on a long history of French intellectual and artistic, as well as military and diplomatic, pre-eminence on the continent of Europe. Above all, the period of the Enlightenment and the Revolution gave it popular resonance. Whether as champion of the oppressed and liberator of mankind, or in the imperialistic guise of the 'mission civilisatrice', France was seen as having a privileged historical destiny. When de Gaulle claimed that France could not be herself 'sans la grandeur', he was appealing to sentiments cultivated over several generations, not least through the primary school history textbooks of Lavisse (Citron 1987).

While some outsiders have found this claim to pre-eminence arrogant, others (especially on the left) have looked to France as an inspirational example, a spiritual second home. As for those who study France from abroad, whatever their political sympathies, they are often captivated by a special fascination with their subject. The richness and drama of France's history, its special role in the development of ideas and movements that have shaped modern societies, may be reason enough. But there is perhaps an added ingredient, especially for students from across the Channel or the Atlantic ('les Anglo-Saxons' as de Gaulle called them), namely that France does not conform in a number of respects to the norms of capitalist liberal democracy laid down by mainstream Western political analysis in the Cold War era.

A cautionary note is in order here. Scholars who study a particular foreign country are often drawn to what is distinctive or unusual about their subject, rather than to features shared with other comparable societies. The absence of comparative references may lead them to treat as specific what are actually local expressions of more general phenomena. In other words, the focus of what we call 'area studies' has a natural bias towards the 'exceptional'.

We also have to contend with the many kinds of analysis produced from within the society under observation. While outsiders may believe they have the advantage of detachment, they may also recognize the insider's privileged knowledge and 'feel' for the subject and so be drawn into the 'mindset' of the domestic commentator. In the case of France this matters, since many French historians and social scientists writing about their own country tend to employ a largely domestic frame of reference rather than a comparative one. That is, they adopt a 'Franco-centric' approach seeking explanations from inside the national community. The idea that France is indeed exceptional, not amenable to comparison, understandable only in terms of its own special history, has arguably influenced academic as well as political discourse.

These opening remarks are intended to clear the ground for discussion in two ways. First, we should recognize that the notion of *l'exception française* cannot simply be taken at face value. A comparative approach can help lead to a more realistic appraisal of what is genuinely distinctive. Second, a wider-ranging approach may be more appropriate in the present context, where some have argued that globalization and 'normalization' are putting an end to French exceptionalism (Furet et al. 1988). This debate, which calls into question the whole concept of French 'national identity', can be over-dramatized if it is based on an exaggerated portrait of what made France unique in the first place.

Any appraisal of the distinctiveness of French political culture needs, however, to take account of how it is transmitted and how it remains salient in everday experience. The emphasis in French state schools on civic instruction, on an early familiarization with French history, on the acquisition of a 'culture générale', and at later stages on formal intellectual training through subjects like philosophy, literature, mathematics and physics, has an impact on generations of young people which is difficult to measure but which certainly cannot be dismissed. Equally difficult to calculate, but nonetheless tangible, is the effect of a symbolic environment where history is omnipresent in street names, monuments, museums, public holidays, anniversaries (a veritable 'industry' nowadays) and diverse other sites of remembrance (Nora 1984–93). In similar vein, the institutional iconography of the Republic, evident on every public building and given a strong local focus in the office of mayor and the apparatus of city hall, is intended to serve as a constant reminder of the rights and obligations associated with 'citizenship'.

A more significant indicator today is perhaps the mediatization of this political culture (Debray 1979). In this area of programming, French television has often been derided as elitist and didactic, but such criticisms from abroad may also reflect ignorance of what appeals to many French viewers. The allocation of prime-time slots to intellectual celebrities, to historical controversies and dramatized history, to the psycho-drama of political life, would seem to indicate that hard-headed market researchers are happy enough with the recorded audience figures. How far this interest permeates French society at large is a different matter, but even if the target group is primarily that sizeable proportion of French people who have had access to higher education, it would seem that their taste for history and politics is more resilient than elsewhere. The high press and television profile of debates on the Revolution during the bicentenary, on the legacy of the occupation during the Mitterrand revelations (Péan 1994) and the Touvier and Papon trials, confirms this continuing fascination.

As we shall see, this political culture is also expressed through continuing traditions of political activism, which for example still mark out the school and the university as natural breeding-grounds for radical ideas. *Lycéens*, students and teachers have thus been associated with many of the 'social movements' of the 1980s and 1990s, mobilizing around issues like anti-racism, unemployment and defence of public services. Equally striking, however, is the continuing success of the annual communist Fête de l'Humanité, which despite the Party's electoral decline continues to attract half a million participants, testifying perhaps to a residual culture of solidarity and sociability in an increasingly individualistic society.

Numerous examples could, of course, also be invoked to show how these distinctive national traditions and reference points are being eroded and displaced by the new images and symbols of a global economy and culture. The rearguard actions to defend the French language, French cinema and even French popular cuisine against such inroads are easily represented as Canute-like in their vanity. But while such processes may undermine some of the traditional symbols of cultural autonomy, the emerging polycultural synthesis will no doubt continue to display many features that will be regarded as distinctly French.

The French state

Few would deny that the nature of the French state, and its relationship with the rest of society, are central to the distinctiveness of French political culture. Its proverbial centralization, its tentacular reach, its claim to incarnate the general will and to act as the agent of the national interest, the whole mystique surrounding public service, are all seen as different from the usual pattern of state–society relations elsewhere in the west. Built on foundations laid by the absolute monarchy in the seventeenth century, the centralized interventionist state apparatus has been one of the most stable features of French political life, surviving revolution, war, foreign occupation and changes of regime. Over the last 100 years, the state has extended its scope to include education, welfare provision, the ownership of public utilities and other strategically important enterprises.

Recent history underlines the continued vigour of this tradition. The programme on which the Socialists were elected in 1981 widened the state's intervention by nationalizing a swathe of major industrial enterprises, against the prevailing international mood in favour of deregulation and market liberalism. While this interventionist approach was soon reversed, later French versions of economic liberalism have been less thorough-going than in comparable countries: the re-privatization programme, though radical in scope, allowed the state to retain strategic shareholdings to forestall any foreign control. And despite the decentralizing reforms launched in 1982 (quite far-reaching on paper), specialists argue that informal channels of central control have largely survived (Wright 1994; Mazey 1994; Stevens 1992, 118–64).

At a deeper cultural level, this reflects a technocratic ethos at top levels of the French state apparatus, with special prestige accorded to senior civil servants trained in the country's most influential *grande école*, the Ecole Nationale d'Administration (ENA). Graduates of ENA (*énarques*) not only dominate the administration, but can move sideways, both into the political arena (Giscard, Chirac, Seguin, Chevènement, Rocard, Fabius, Jospin) and into key executive posts in the private sector (*pantouflage*) (Birnbaum 1980; Suleiman 1979). Belief in the special competence and responsibility of the state therefore goes beyond the civil service, effectively braking any moves to reduce state regulation of the economy.

The ENA was founded in 1945 under a provisional government led by Charles de Gaulle. This underlines another unusual feature of French political culture, namely that the commitment to state economic intervention has never been confined to the left. Gaullism provides the most striking example of a movement based primarily on conservative support yet favouring state-led macro-economic and industrial policies – harnessed of course to the pursuit of national grandeur. Centre-right parties in other Western countries may have supported the post-war commitment to social welfare, full employment and a mixed economy (the 'social-democratic consensus') during the prosperous 1950s and 1960s, but this was seen by conservatives as a necessary compromise, at odds with their normal inclinations. In France the Gaullists positively endorsed the notion of the heroic State as an agent of national revival (Cerny 1980).

It is true that this aspect of the Gaullist legacy was substantially diluted by the General's successors in the 1980s and 1990s. But their conversion to economic liberalism was nothing like as wholehearted and dramatic as that of the British Conservative Party under Margaret Thatcher in the same period. Jacques Chirac's 1995 presidential campaign combined a liberal commitment to the Maastricht criteria with populist pledges to deal with unemployment and social exclusion, an uneasy combination which rebounded on him only months later: his Prime Minister Juppé's proposed measures – seeking to reduce the social welfare budget and reform the public sector – raised a storm of popular protest and led to parliamentary defeat for the right in 1997. These events confirmed that the notion of public service is deep-rooted in French political culture: challenging the interests of state employees, for example, affects so many people that it resonates throughout the population.

The Socialist Prime Minister, Lionel Jospin, caught the mood precisely with his formulation 'yes to the market economy, no to the market society'. Although it has abandoned policies that once placed it far to the left of other European social-democratic parties, the Parti Socialiste still remains qualitatively distinct from Blair's New Labour or Schroeder's SDP: the latter would make far more concessions to economic liberalism in welfare reform and labour market deregulation. If the 'cohabitation' between Prime Minister Jospin and President Chirac has reflected a degree of convergence between left and right, this 'consensus' offers a more positive view of the state than that held in Britain or Germany.

State and civil society

While the state remains then a resilient feature of the French attitude to the economy, the debate over its power has always extended well beyond its economic role. Critics hold it responsible not only for inhibiting the 'enterprise culture', but also for stifling the energies of civil society as a whole. By concentrating too much power at the centre, by intervening bureaucratically in the professional and cultural spheres, by seeking to impose uniformity, it has allegedly weakened the bases of democracy itself. Writers like Michel Crozier and Stanley Hoffmann have argued that the powerful and meddlesome central state undermines the intermediate institutions and *vie associative* on which a healthy functioning democracy depends (Crozier 1970; Hoffmann 1974).

It does so in a number of ways. First, its bureaucracy provides avenues of personal advancement which 'drain' civil society of its most dynamic and talented people. Second, its own fear of rival interests makes it intolerant of pluralism and diversity. Finally, it creates a culture of over-reliance on the state which discourages active citizenship. And when (as *la République*) the state claims the democratic legitimacy conferred by universal suffrage, these trends are exacerbated.

The revolutionary concept of the 'general will' underlying the creation of the modern French state saw intermediate bodies between the citizen and the state as vehicles for selfish, partial interests, subversive of the common good and the principles of equality on which true democracy must be based.

This so-called 'Jacobin' doctrine has since influenced both left and right, and has been used to limit the powers of local or regional government, and to devalue trade unions, professional associations and other pressure groups. De Gaulle even despised the role of political parties and the parliamentary process itself. The presidential system he established in 1958 arguably reinforced France's traditional administrative centralization with an unprecedented degree of political centralization.

Anyone familiar with the Third and Fourth Republics – weak governments at the mercy of shifting parliamentary alliances and powerful lobbies – might find this insistence on the weakness of French civil society somewhat unconvincing. But it can be argued that sectional interests were mobilized precisely to resist the action of the state rather than to engage in constructive dialogue. Some observers have pointed to France as a 'stalemate society' (*la société bloquée*). In the absence of effective intermediate channels of communication between the state and the citizen, issues were left unresolved leading to *immobilisme* or revolt. Overburdened with conflicting demands from the periphery, the central state simply 'administered' on the basis of well-established routines, while dissatisfied interest groups were sustained by a culture of protest punctuated by occasional piecemeal concessions.

This picture has gradually been altered since the war, first by a more dynamic and technocratic state apparatus, and second by more stable political leadership under the Fifth Republic. Economic and social modernization has weakened the lobbying power of certain interest groups resistant to change (farmers, small business, and now workers' unions), though new causes (ecology, anti-racism, women's rights) and new social movements with more sophisticated techniques of communication have appeared. Since the upheaval of May 1968, pressures for greater social and cultural pluralism have been released, hence a more vigorous *vie associative*.

The older pattern of state–society relations has not entirely disappeared, though. Against a background of greater personalization of power, but still with comparatively weak parliament, parties and unions, governments are still apt to misread the public mood, to take action without enough consultation, and to reap the whirlwind of popular protest. While May 1968 remains the classic reference point for this type of analysis, there have been plenty of occasions in the last 30 years when governments have had to back down on their proposals in the face of (sometimes violent) direct action and mass mobilization.

The revolutionary tradition

Not surprisingly, this state–society axis has also been one of the frameworks for explaining France's revolutionary tradition. The absence of intermediate institutions to negotiate demands means that relatively minor issues can quickly escalate out of control; localized protest can assume violent symbolic form to attract the attention of the central state. The metaphor of the pressure cooker is sometimes quoted: when the legacy of unresolved grievances across society has built up sufficient head of steam, a broader revolutionary explosion may be triggered. But since revolutions breed disorder and insecurity, citizens may soon opt to return to the stability provided by the strong centralized state, and the cycle begins again (Aron 1968).

According to this perspective, change in France has come about via alternating revolutionary upheavals and periods of consolidation, rather than by the more gradual evolutionary process which is supposed to characterize Britain and the United States, for example. This kind of analysis, while not entirely the work of 'Anglo-Saxon' commentators, is nonetheless based on mainstream liberal political science, for which American-style democracy is the norm, and revolutionary politics an aberration (Almond and Verba 1963). Rather than exploring the nature of revolutionary movements, this approach sees them as exceptional forms of political behaviour produced by a dysfunctional political system.

This perspective provides valuable insights, but an incomplete picture. For the revolutionary tradition also reflects the intense conflicts that emerged in nineteenth-century French society, above all around class and religion. France is far from unique in this respect, of course, but the decade of the 1789 Revolution not only left a legacy of bitter rivalry, it also channelled these antagonisms into political ideologies and movements – conservative and liberal monarchists, Bonapartists, moderate and radical republicans, socialists and anarchists – each with their own preferred form of regime and views on social and religious issues. What has been called 'la guerre franco-française' has been as much a battle of ideas as of 'interests', hence the prominent role of intellectuals in politics. While on occasions this conflict has crystallized into the opposition of 'deux France' – Order versus Movement, Reaction versus Progress, Catholicism versus Anti-clericalism, Right versus Left – more often an uneasy government coalition of the centre has struggled to hold the line against the 'extremes' on each side.

Consensus-building has thus been a difficult task in France, as evidenced by around 20 different constitutions since 1789. Regimes have been toppled by revolutions (1830 and 1848), by military defeats (1815, 1870 and 1940), and by coups d'état (1799, 1851 and, some would argue, 1958). Even the apparently stable Fifth Republic had to cross the revolutionary hurdle of May 1968 before assuming a greater degree of permanence and stability. Perhaps the most dramatic example in the twentieth century of *la guerre franco-française* was the period of the Nazi Occupation during World War II and the country is only now beginning to come to terms with the complex legacy left by collaboration and resistance. But the cycle did not end there, as shown by the bitter strikes of 1947, the fears of army insurrection in the extended Algerian crisis of 1958–62, or the only recently acknowledged massacre of up to 200 Algerian demonstrators on the streets of Paris in

October 1961. While May 1968 has been dismissed by some as a 'psychodrama' rather than a true revolution, de Gaulle's trip to Germany to check that the French army would support him indicates that events could have taken a very different turn.

In other words, dramatic, confrontational politics has been part of the French collective experience, and while violent, direct action may be a minority phenomenon, it is perhaps regarded with greater equanimity in France than in neighbouring countries where political life is more humdrum. In this respect, it may be seen as part of French 'political culture'. More recently commentators have begun to argue that 'la guerre franco-française' is over, that 'la Révolution est terminée', that the historic divisions between those supporting the egalitarian ideals of the Revolution and those who regarded these ideals as a threat to public order and individual freedom have finally been healed. The decline of class struggle, of the Communist Party and industrial unionism, and the new moderation of the Socialist Party, are seen as evidence that free-enterprise capitalism and liberal democracy are now largely accepted as the only viable model, and that French politics has been 'normalized' by the pressures of the global market economy. *L'exception française* has had its day.

Such predictions may seem a little premature in the light of recent popular protests in defence of hard-won rights. But few would see a left-wing revolution as likely today. On the other hand, ever since the late nineteenth century, there has been a recurrent radical politics of the extreme right, and the influence of the Front National does not fit easily with the image of the supposedly consensual character of French political life. Some argue that behind the movement's quest for political respectability lies a fundamentally anti-democratic fascist-style agenda appealing to undercurrents of authoritarianism and intolerance in the French electorate (Fysh and Wolfreys 1998). Those who have written off the FN in the wake of the 1999 split would be wise to look beyond short-term electoral performance before they start to compose obituaries.

Nationalism

Nationalism is often seen as an ideological device for uniting a political community. The French state worked hard to build a homogeneous national community, especially under the Third Republic between 1870 and 1914, turning 'peasants into Frenchmen' in Eugen Weber's famous phrase (Weber 1976). At the same time, as already noted, France equipped itself with the collective enterprise of the 'civilizing mission', and has frequently used the notion of an external threat to great effect. The identification of Germany as the hereditary enemy after defeat in the 1870 Franco-Prussian war successfully united the nation for the traumas of the 1914–18 conflict. In more muted vein, de Gaulle's anti-Americanism in the 1960s struck a chord across the political spectrum and won him sympathy and even electoral support well into the ranks of the left.

But today the end of the Cold War has removed the space between the two global blocs which Gaullist-style foreign policy once exploited to provide the illusion of French independence. And the days of heroic national economic strategies appear to be numbered. Nationalism is now a more muted affair for the mainstream government parties, hinging on the capacity of France to play an influential and distinctive role within the European Union. Arguably, however, this has opened the way for the Front National to exploit nationalist nostalgia for lost status and influence, and certainly Euroscepticism and anti-globalism may yet provide the movement with a populist bridgehead to a wider audience.

So far, however, the nationalism of the FN has a largely internal focus, and its principal theme, rejection of France's non-European ethnic minorities, builds on the racist traditions of the extreme right. Ironically, this has revealed flaws in the Republic's own more liberal nationality code, which opens access to French citizenship on the principle that immigrants will be 'assimilated' into a supposedly homogeneous national culture. In as far as they may be unwilling to abandon elements of their own cultural identity, they may be deemed 'non-assimilable' in the Republic's own terms (Brubaker 1992; Silverman 1992). Thus the celebrated Muslim headscarf affair was seen by sections of the left as a challenge both to the secular principles of the Republican school system, and to the principles of gender equality, while others argued that the notion of the 'one and indivisible French Republic' was no longer appropriate to an increasingly multicultural French society. A country that has been so permeated, and divided, by nationalist discourses for the last 200 years will not find it easy to resolve these conflicts.

Consensus and 'la République'

In many respects, the issues that historically divided the French political community have waned in importance. Catholicism and anti-clericalism no longer define the boundaries between right and left. Distinctive class cultures (peasant, bourgeois, proletarian) have given way to more diffuse and pluralistic forms of social identity (Mendras and Cole 1991). The Fifth Republic has provided a broadly acceptable constitutional framework for political activity. Civil society has asserted itself, and somewhat less is expected of the central state. Finally, French endorsement of European integration and a degree of internal decentralization has reduced the appeal of nationalism as an aspect of French exceptionalism.

It might therefore seem that the foundations have been laid for the sort of social and political consensus that previous Republics failed to achieve. The republican ideal of popular sovereignty rests on the notion of the people as a socially undifferentiated citizenry, equal in their common exercise of civil and political rights. In a society deeply divided by class, religion and ideology, such as the Third Republic, this failed to convince. The situation as the Fifth Republic enters the twenty-first century is very different. Inequalities of course remain; indeed, contemporary analysis is more sensitive than ever to their complexities – gender, ethnicity, regional imbalances, the new roots of urban poverty and social exclusion such as permanent unemployment, family breakdown and homelessness. Gone however are the former solidarities (including class) which provided a framework for the articulation of social discontent, and which mobilized calls for social change.

Some people welcome this as symptomatic of a new political maturity in a France with more pragmatic and managerial political parties, citizens more realistic in their expectations, political activity more electoral than militant, a France where single-issue campaigns have more mileage than attempts to revolutionize society. Much is made today of the concept of 'citizenship', but this no longer carries the radical edge of what David Held has called 'developmental democracy', the active involvement of citizens (Held 1987, 72–104). Rather it is based on the liberal view of a sharp separation between the private and public spheres, the former expanding under the impact of mass consumerism and the privatization of social life, the latter a shrinking domain where external pressures limit the range of political options and where citizens must learn to work within the system. In this view, lack of activity, e.g. electoral abstentionism, may simply indicate high levels of social contentment and widespread political acquiescence.

While such a view might be tempting for politicians, it now has less credibility among seasoned observers who have watched rosy depictions of consensus politics fade somewhat in the last ten years (Hewlett 1998). Divisions over Europe, strike movements, the realignment of the left under Jospin, the persistent vote for 'outsider' parties, all reflect a more vigorous and conflictual political climate than that suggested by the 'normalization' thesis. France may have become less 'exceptional', but it nonetheless remains pretty 'distinctive'.

A fragmented political culture?

This chapter has suggested that many of the key features of French 'exceptionalism' have faded under the Fifth Republic, though they are still detectable. But while mainstream politics increasingly resembles that of other similar countries in the age of 'globalism', this more consensual pattern does not characterize the political community as a whole. The notion of a fragmented political culture might be a useful device for examining some of these contradictions.

France's class structure has certainly been transformed since the war, as distinctive cultures have been eroded by individualism and social diversification. Older patterns of behaviour shaped by class solidarities may persist, however, despite the decline of the organizations that once represented them. Thus the tradition of spontaneous direct action has been continued in the last 15 years, in strike movements where improvised 'coordinations' filled the vacuum left by increasingly weak trade unions.

But the decline of the PCF, and Socialist pursuit of the electoral middle ground, means that French industrial workers are now neglected as a specific class community. The Front National has been able to exploit their entrenched mistrust of bourgeois politicians, their instinctive anti-system reflex, and indeed the racist and xenophobic tendencies which the Communist Party (in its post-war patriotic/nationalist guise) did very little to correct. The 1995 presidential elections indicated a wide dispersion of the working-class vote across the political spectrum, with the FN (through Le Pen's candidacy) emerging as the most proletarian party of all with 27 per cent of all such voters. The left vote meanwhile had a larger proportion of voters with higher educational qualifications, and of people employed in public service rather than in the (largely private) manufacturing sector. The days when Renault Billancourt car workers were the vanguard of the organized industrial working class have clearly gone: many of the major strike waves since the mid-1980s have concerned public sector employees in white-collar rather than blue-collar jobs. The state still employs a larger proportion of the working population than in other developed capitalist economies, and this sustains a specific mindset in which notions of public service, professional status, job security and social protection are deeply implanted.

The rise of the new professional middle strata, the massive expansion of higher education, the special importance attached in France to formal educational qualifications, have meanwhile affected another traditional feature of French political culture, namely the role played by intellectuals in French political life. Politically engaged thinkers of the stature of Camus, Sartre and Beauvoir are rare today; on the other hand there are larger numbers of highly educated people than ever before, often working in the media and in para-intellectual occupations. Politics still attracts figures of measurable intellectual calibre, as indicated by the high number of 'énarques' in key positions. Indeed, their presence provides a target for the anti-intellectual populism of the FN.

However, this 'cultural capital' is not mobilized exclusively in service of the 'system'. May 1968 has been seen as the political coming of age of the radical educated middle classes, and though idealistic projects like 'le socialisme autogestionnaire' which so excited left intellectuals in the 1970s have since faded, other causes have arisen related to civil liberties, anti-racism and humanitarianism, feminism and ecology – which could provide the bases for a radical and comprehensive critique of modern societies.

These movements are arguably more highly developed and have a longer ancestry in some other countries, but what makes them distinctive in France is the level of ideological debate, and their concern to locate themselves within specifically French intellectual and historical traditions. Thus French feminism (like anti-racism) has to address the ambiguities of the revolutionary tradition, while ecologists are preoccupied with the question of whether their values belong on the left or imply a break with classical political rivalries – *ni droite ni gauche*. Some would argue that these ideological preoccupations have been an obstacle to the achievement of a wider audience, that a more pragmatic approach would have built a wider grass-roots base. However, the status enjoyed by French intellectuals and the continuing importance of 'ideas' in French political life is certainly one of the features that makes France such an attractive subject for foreign academics and students.

It has also been the function of outside observers, however, to challenge some of the orthodoxies established by French historians. The 'revisionist' critique of the Marxian approach to the French Revolution was largely pioneered by British and American specialists (Cobban 1968; Doyle 1980). Another example is the French historiography of the extreme right, which has tended to insist on what is specifically French about this tradition, rather than on historical parallels with comparable developments elsewhere. Under the influence of René Rémond's classic study of 'les droites en France' (Rémond 1982), emphasis has been on the ideological continuities of the extreme right within France, thus treating for example fascism as an alien import which was unable to take root because of France's strong democratic political culture. Writers like Robert Paxton were the first to challenge this perspective by revealing the full complicity of the Vichy regime in the oppression of Jews under the Nazi Occupation (Paxton and Marrus 1981; Paxton 1982).

Similarly, French studies of the Front National continue to emphasize its historical antecedents at the expense of its contemporary rationale in a wider European context (Milza 1992; Taguieff 1986; Winock 1990). A more illuminating explanatory framework might consider the impact of mass migration throughout Europe in the 'post-colonial' context, the social dislocations of an increasingly 'post-industrial' society, the crisis of socialism and nationalism in the global market economy, and the decline of traditional class and religious solidarities in an increasingly atomized and individualized society. The FN may display locally distinctive characteristics, and feed on locally distinctive political circumstances, but developments in other countries (Germany, Austria, Belgium, the Netherlands, Italy) suggest that it is far from unique, and recommend a less parochial approach.

The same recommendation might apply to some other features of the society that has emerged in France and elsewhere over the last 20 years, namely the emergence of an 'under-class' of the long-term unemployed, those in precarious temporary jobs (often in the so-called 'black' economy), the homeless and other victims of 'social exclusion'. By definition such categories, barely integrated into French society let alone into mainstream political life, are difficult to characterize in terms of 'political culture'. The permanence and growing size of such groups has undermined the notion of an industrial 'working class', defined by its place in the system of production. The lines of social division now seem to fall between those with relatively secure employment and those without. How members of this under-class relate to a party political system which neglects their aspirations remains unclear.

Similar uncertainty surrounds the political complexion of France's ethnic minority communities, many of whom fall within the contours of this under-class, and have no voting rights unless they were born in France. Anti-racist movements like SOS Racisme have often lost impetus because of their links with the established parties of the left, and their failure to reflect the authentic voice of those they claim to represent. The vigour of ethnic sub-cultures is reflected in a flourishing *vie associative* and a growing influence on youth lifestyles, but they have yet to take distinctive political shape. This in itself is a salutary reminder that political culture is not a fixed inheritance from the past, but a constantly changing mosaic reflecting the emergence of new social identities. Similarly, new patterns of territorial government in France may produce new solidarities based on cities and urban cultures, as well as sustaining the older historical consciousness of regions like Brittany and Corsica. 'Doing' creates a sense of 'being' rather than the other way round, as those who envisage a future 'European' identity would also insist.

The notion of a 'fragmented' political culture is perhaps an excessively negative view of what could be celebrated as pluralism and diversity. But it also implies that we are witnessing the breakdown of a previously more homogeneous political culture, currently being exposed as something of a myth. If the past is increasingly being 'demythologized', and some of the forgotten historical corners of French political culture explored, the present perhaps also needs to be freed from the intellectual straitjacket of French 'exceptionalism', so that its problems can be analysed and addressed in a less introspective and parochial way.

References and further reading

ALMOND, G. and VERBA, S. 1963: *The civic culture: political attitudes and democracy in five nations*. Princeton: Princeton University Press.

ARON, R. 1968: *La révolution introuvable: réflexions sur les événements de mai*. Paris: Fayard.

BIRNBAUM, P. 1980: *Les sommets de l'état: essai sur l'élite du pouvoir en France*. Paris: Editions du Seuil.

BRUBAKER, R. 1992: *Citizenship and nationhood in France and Germany*. Cambridge, MA: Harvard University Press.

CERNY, P. 1980: *The politics of grandeur: ideological aspects of de Gaulle's foreign policy*. Cambridge: Cambridge University Press.

CITRON, S. 1987: *Le mythe national: l'histoire de France en question.* Paris: Les Editions ouvrières.

COBBAN, A. 1968: *Aspects of the French Revolution.* London: Cape.

CROZIER, M. 1970: *La société bloquée.* Paris: Editions du Seuil.

DEBRAY, R. 1979: *Le pouvoir intellectuel en France.* Paris: Ramsay.

DOYLE, W. 1980: *Origins of the French Revolution.* Oxford: Oxford University Press.

FURET, F., JULLIARD, J. and ROSANVALLON, P. 1988: *La République du centre: la fin de l'exception française.* Paris: Calmann-Lévy.

FYSH, P. and WOLFREYS, J. 1998: *The politics of racism in France.* London: Macmillan.

HELD, D. 1987: *Models of democracy.* Cambridge: Polity Press.

HEWLETT, N. 1998: *Modern French politics: analysing conflict and consensus since 1945.* Cambridge: Polity Press.

HOFFMANN, S. 1974: *Essais sur la France: déclin ou renouveau?* Paris: Editions du Seuil.

MAZEY, S. 1994: Power outside Paris. In HALL, P., HAYWARD, J. and MACHIN, H. (eds), *Developments in French politics.* Basingstoke: Macmillan.

MENDRAS, H. and COLE, A. 1991: *Social change in modern France.* Cambridge: Cambridge University Press.

MILZA, P. 1992: Le Front National: droite extrême ou national-populisme? In SIRINELLI, J.-F. (ed.) *Histoire des droites en France.* Paris: Gallimard.

NORA, P. (ed.) 1984–93: *Les lieux de mémoire.* 7 vols. Paris: Gallimard.

PAXTON, R. and MARRUS, M. 1981: *Vichy France and the Jews.* New York: Basic Books.

PAXTON, R. 1982: *Vichy France: old guard and new order 1940–44.* Columbia: Columbia University Press.

PÉAN, P. 1994: *Une jeunesse française: François Mitterrand 1934–47.* Paris: Fayard.

RÉMOND, R. 1982: *Les droites en France.* 4th edition. Paris: Aubier-Montaigne.

SILVERMAN, M. 1992: *Deconstructing the nation: immigration, racism and citizenship in modern France.* London: Routledge.

STEVENS, A. 1992: *The government and politics of France.* London: Macmillan.

SULEIMAN, E. 1979: *Les élites en France: grands corps et Grandes Ecoles.* Paris: Editions du Seuil.

TAGUIEFF, P.-A. 1986: La doctrine du national-populisme en France. *Etudes* 364, January.

WEBER, E. 1976: *Peasants into Frenchmen: the modernization of rural France 1870–1914.* Stanford: Stanford University Press.

WINOCK, M. 1990: *Nationalisme, anti-sémitisme et fascisme en France.* Paris: Editions du Seuil.

WRIGHT, V. 1994: The administrative machine: old problems and new dilemmas. In HALL, P., HAYWARD, J. and MACHIN, H. (eds), *Developments in French politics.* Basingstoke: Macmillan.

FRENCHNESS REVISITED: FORCES FOR CULTURAL UNITY

|10|

If it isn't clear, it isn't French: language and identity

BY JAMES MUNRO

Introduction: French and the challenge of English

To start with a truism: language is closely bound up with identity – of nations as well as individuals. Historically, the French language has been one of the main forces shaping the French sense of nationhood; over the years, national pride has constantly been linked to pride in the language. From the eighteenth century onwards, French dominated as the international language of diplomacy, and its prestige was reinforced by France's brilliant intellectual heritage: the classical dramatists, the eighteenth-century *philosophes,* and the democratic ideals of the French Revolution as expressed in the *Déclaration des droits de l'homme.* In the nineteenth century, French spread beyond Europe, mainly into Africa, as a result of colonization; within Europe it became not only a literary language but a scientific one, the language of such major figures as Pasteur, Poincaré and the Curies. Since then, however, pride in the French language has been seriously challenged by the prominence of English, which is well on the way to becoming an international *lingua franca*, rather like Latin in the Middle Ages. Given the historical importance of French in creating a sense of national identity, it is not surprising that the challenge to the language is widely perceived as constituting a challenge to Frenchness itself.

The threat posed by English is seen not only as a threat to the dominance of French, but also to its integrity and even to its survival. Predictably, this has provoked a very vigorous defensive reaction in France. Since the 1950s, there has been a chorus of protest against the 'invasion' or 'contamination' of French by borrowings from English. The scale of these borrowings is such that French is felt to be in danger of becoming a kind of mid-Atlantic hotch-potch of the two languages – 'franglais', to use the term popularized by Etiemble (1964). It has more recently been suggested that the term *franglais* (**français** + **anglais**) should be replaced by *franricain* (**français** + **américain**) (Hagège 1987). The current pre-eminence of English as a world language is due to the status of the United States as a world power, particularly in science and technology. English has to all intents and purposes become the language of the scientific community, and is also carried far and wide by the Internet, and by American films and TV shows which can be seen the world over. Through its audio-visual industry, the US exports *spoken* English, the English of everyday interaction; the spread of French, on the other hand, was almost entirely print based: what was transmitted was the *written* language, which almost by definition is less widespread and popular in its appeal.

Broadly speaking, then, the French language may be said to have a glorious past and an endangered present, with the watershed situated some time around the middle of the twentieth century. According to the humorist Pierre Daninos, this see-sawing of fortunes is a defining characteristic not simply of the language but beyond that of Frenchness itself. He writes that there are two situations for France: *rayonnement* (French influence spreading round the world) and *relèvement* (France finding the strength to fight back when invaded and conquered). Both of these states are heroic in their different ways. The first satisfies French pride and need for greatness, and this is the 'côté Napoléon' of the French character; the second is the 'côté Jeanne d'Arc' (Daninos 1954, 30). This analysis of contradictions in the French self-image is a light-hearted one, but it nevertheless provides a useful framework in which to consider French attitudes to language: in the earlier period it is the 'côté Napoléon' which predominates, while the modern period has seen a resurgence of the spirit of Joan of Arc.

Napoleon is an appropriate symbol of the French language for two reasons: at home he was associated with a strong centralizing tendency (the legacy of which can still be felt), and he used French (military) superiority to carry French influence abroad. Similarly, centralization and control (the forging of French into a unified national language) and colonization (the spread of French abroad and the demonstration of its superiority) are prominent features of French language development in the earlier of the two periods we have identified. We shall look at each of these characteristics in turn.

Centralization and control (1): the universalizing of the language

The process of turning French into a truly national language was a surprisingly lengthy one, and it is not until the last quarter of the nineteenth century that it can be said to be reasonably complete. At the Revolution, what we call 'French' was little more than one dialect among many, that of the Ile-de-France and Orléans region, spoken by a minority of the population. It was in competition not only with a profusion of local dialects which had developed in parallel with it but also with what were languages in their own right – Breton or Basque, for instance – or were dialects of other European languages (of German in Alsace, Spanish in the Pyrénées-Orientales, Italian in Corsica). But there is an old joke that a language is simply a dialect with an army, and the Ile-de-France was of course the seat of power. Just as importantly, its dialect had become a *written* language, the vehicle for a brilliant literary and cultural tradition.

It was above all Revolutionary ideals and values which provided the impetus to make French the standard national language. There was an obvious practical need for linguistic uniformity throughout France; government officials sent from Paris to distant parts of the country had to be able to communicate effectively with the local inhabitants. Beyond that, there was a political motive: dialects and non-French languages were potential sources of counter-revolutionary plotting, and therefore posed a threat to the fledgling republic. Beyond that again, there was a compelling ideological reason for the imposition of French: a republic which proclaims itself 'une et indivisible' needs a language to match. If all citizens are to have equal chances to accede to the highest positions in the land, then no-one must be excluded on linguistic grounds. The language question, then, is built into the very foundations of republicanism itself, inseparable from the three republican core values: only through what the Abbé Grégoire in 1794 calls 'l'usage unique et invariable de la langue de liberté' (Brunot 1967, 207), can there be true *égalité* and *fraternité*.

In order to spread French within France, the revolutionaries created a state school system which largely persists to this day. A decree of 1794 provided for 'un instituteur de langue française' to be appointed to each *commune* in a number of different *départements* where different languages (Breton, Italian, Basque, German and Catalan) were spoken. Interestingly, the duties of the *instituteurs* were not simply to teach the language but also to instruct the population in the founding principles and laws of the republic: they were to teach French language and the *Déclaration des droits de l'homme* on alternate days (Brunot 1967, 184). The purpose of education is to equip the population linguistically to approach texts which are religious not in the conventional sense but in the original sense of the word 'religion' ('binding together'), texts which somehow define and constitute the group identity in which all share.

The legacy of the Revolution, then, was to place the French language at the very core of the national identity; language became inextricably linked both to the values on which the republic was founded and to one of the key institutions of the republic, *l'école*. Tight though it was, however, this link was not finally cemented irrevocably until almost a century later, when the educational reforms of the 1880s, associated with the name of Jules Ferry, finally made primary schooling free, universal and compulsory. Crucially, education also became *laïque*, with religion resolutely banned from the classroom. A sign of this secularization was that moral education, which until then still retained links with religion, was replaced by *cours de civisme*, the training of pupils in the duties and privileges of citizenship. In other words, the Jules Ferry reform removed the last vestiges of pre-revolutionary values from the school system and thus completed the process of setting the language at the heart of republicanism.

Centralization and control (2): the standardizing of the language

In the language education begun at the Revolution the emphasis was on providing access above all to the *written* word, so that all citizens should be able to read for themselves the laws and declarations of the new republic. The veneration of the written language continues in our own time and is perpetuated largely through the school system, where the emphasis is very much on grammar. Balibar (1985) gives a fascinating glimpse of materials introduced to teach French in the post-Ferry period; primary school pupils were expected to be able to recognize parts of speech, analyse sentences, and so on. The grammatical tradition has remained strong in French education and has given the average French person a much greater awareness of grammar than the average Briton. The rules transmitted by *l'école* are rigorously enforced in the written form of the language, but spoken French freely departs from them; an obvious example is the dropping, in speech, of the *ne* in negatives. As a result, it is probably true to say that written and spoken French diverge more widely than is the case with English.

French preoccupation with the rules of language has a long history. In the seventeenth century, there were a number of prominent grammarians whose authority was such that even the major authors of the time deferred to their judgment. Institutions were set up as guardians of correct usage, the most important of these being the Académie française, founded in 1635. The purpose of the Académie was to codify and regulate the language, a function which it still carries out today. Interestingly, it is one of the few institutions from the *ancien régime* to have survived the Revolution; the need to standardize language was even more pressing in the republic than it had been in the monarchy, and in modern times it has an important role to play in countering the threat of English.

The existence of a body of clearly defined language rules, backed up by the authority and prestige of the Académie, has the effect of imposing an ideal of elegance and polish of style. French is therefore seen as a cultivated, élite language, one which is particularly suited for expressing the profoundest values of civilization; it is not simply a language like other languages, but has certain intrinsic qualities which make it superior to others. In the 1780s, the prestige of French was such that the reasons for its superiority formed the subject of an essay competition; the winner was Rivarol, one of whose statements ('ce qui n'est pas clair n'est pas français') has shaped the way in which generations of French people have seen their own language. The quality of *clarté* is claimed for French on the grounds that the language allows finer discriminations than others and thus is less prone to ambiguities. Among the seventeenth-century grammarians, for instance, Malherbe insists on the differences between such pairs as *neuf* and *nouveau, contraire* and *différent*.

Discriminations or not, however, French has its ambiguities like any other language, and its alleged *clarté* is largely a myth (Swiggers 1990). The myth is taking a long time to die, however, which suggests how deep language goes in individual and national consciousness. This is of course true of any language, but in the case of French, the bonds between language and national identity have been tightened still further by the linking of the language to the ideology on which the nation is founded, to the key concepts of republicanism and *laïcité*. This has not happened in the case of English, which ideologically speaking seems much more neutral, equally able to underpin a constitutional monarchy such as the UK and a federal republic such as the US. Equally, the French language, much more so than English, has been linked to the prestige of the nation abroad, associated with the perception of France as the torchbearer of civilization. The language, then, is a focus for the sense of what France is and its place in the world. This goes some way towards explaining the violence of the reaction to the perceived 'threat' of American English; an attack on the language is an attack on what de Gaulle called *une certaine idée de la France*.

The defence of French

If Napoleon symbolizes grandeur, Joan of Arc's achievement was to inspire her compatriots to make a firm stand against an apparently unstoppable English invasion. The Joan of Arc spirit is not dead; in modern times it manifests itself in a spirited defence of the French language against the inroads of Anglo-American.

This threat from the outside has been largely responsible for forcing some re-evaluation of the concept of the *langue une et indivisible*. There is a growing realization that defending French may in fact involve defending linguistic diversity; only by working towards a world which is not dominated by a single universal language but which accepts linguistic differences can French be protected against the Anglo-American threat. It is of course inconsistent to work for linguistic diversity in the world at large while not tolerating it at home, and so there are some signs of a (limited) softening of attitude towards both minority languages and non-standard varieties of French; the latter are coming to be seen not as threats to the national identity but as possible sources of renewal.

From the time of the Fifth Republic onwards, the policy of the French government in linguistic matters has been increasingly interventionist. Since 1966, various governmental bodies have been set up to promote and defend the French language, most recently the *Conseil supérieur de la langue française* (1989). Government action to combat the threat of English has taken two main forms. One is that of legislation designed to ensure the survival of French in various key areas of national life. The chief landmarks here are the so-called *loi Bas-Lauriol* (1975) and the *loi Toubon* (1994) which replaced it. Essentially, these laws aim to protect the French speaker from the sometimes dangerous misunderstandings which would arise if certain texts were written in languages other than French: instructions for the use of products and machines, offers and contracts of employment, public notices and so on. These laws also affirm the right of francophones to speak French at any conferences or colloquia held in France, and stipulate that scientific papers published in France in a foreign language must be accompanied at least by a summary in French; such measures guarantee at least some role for French in scientific meetings, which tend to be dominated by English.

The 1994 law is complemented by various provisions that deal specifically with the use of French in the media, obviously a key centre of operations in the linguistic war. The effect of these provisions has been to fix quotas, both for pop music and for television programmes in general. Since 1996 a minimum of 40 per cent of songs broadcast must be in French; similarly, various national and European directives limit the number of non-European and non-French programmes on TV. Such measures appear to have had a certain degree of success; it is claimed that the proportion of American series broadcast fell from more than 50 per cent in 1992–5 to 46.5 per cent in 1996.

A second strand of government action has been an attempt to influence the shape of the language itself. The key issue here is vocabulary, the number of loanwords that have passed from English into French. Since Etiemble (1964) it has become almost obligatory to illustrate the extent of the problem by satire, by writing texts artificially full of Americanisms or simply by grouping those that relate to a particular area of life. A more objective approach is adopted by Hagège (1987, 79), who lists the areas of activity which are particularly vulnerable to the invasion of English: science and technology, advertising, the media. If French has imported terms such as *baby-sitter, unisex, hamburger, hot-dog, interview, junkie, leader* or *look,* this is simply a reflection of how everyday life has changed. The widespread acceptance of such terms is largely due to the influence exerted by young people, who are particularly receptive both to new habits and ideas, and to the linguistic forms in which these habits and ideas are clothed.

The official response to this lexical invasion has been to set up a number of *commissions de terminologie* charged with creating French equivalents for Anglo-American loanwords. A number of these bodies were set up in the 1970s and 1980s, covering lexical areas as widely different as tourism, telecommunications, defence and the oil industry (Judge 1993, 19); in the rapidly expanding field of information technology, word lists were published both in 1981 and 1987. The purpose of these commissions is both to coin new words and to plug lexical gaps by extending the meaning of existing French words; *le présentateur* for instance is proposed as an alternative for *le speaker* (in the sense of 'announcer'). Some, though not all, of the terminology put forward in this way has the force of law, which makes its use obligatory in official texts and documents.

These official attempts to defend the vocabulary of French raise a number of questions. Concerning the *rationale* of the defence (to use a French loanword), it is perhaps permissible to wonder why new words coined from Latin or Greek roots should be allowed into French while English loanwords are perceived as parasites which will eventually destroy their host. When the Normans invaded England, they created not only a political but a linguistic upheaval, resulting in the massive importation of French loanwords into English; and this, far from causing English to wither on the vine, enriched it immeasurably. Concerning the effectiveness of the defence, direct intervention at the level of vocabulary has had some effect. By no means all of the new coinages become a standard part of the language, but a number of grafts have taken: terms such as *l'ordinateur, l'oléoduc, le baladeur,* have met with widespread acceptance as replacements for *le computer, le pipeline* and *le walkman* respectively. It is sometimes argued that one cannot change a language by legislation, and of course it is true that the final verdict lies not with the legislators but with the speech community as a whole. The French experience however shows that language behaviour can be changed to a limited extent – not sufficient perhaps to halt the American invasion altogether but at least able to slow down its progress.

Pluralism (1): Francophonie

Even in a defensive ('Joan of Arc') situation, then, the French 'Napoleonic' reflex towards standardization and control remains intact. At the same time, however, there has been a movement in the opposite direction: the increasing realization that the linguistic threat posed by English is not an exclusively French problem, but is even more pressing elsewhere – notably in Quebec, where the issue is whether French can survive at all. The common peril has heightened the importance of the concept of *Francophonie,* the sense that France is part of a world-wide community of French speakers. This in turn has led to an increasing respect for the varieties of French spoken in these countries; the language is no longer seen as the private property of France alone.

The concept of *Francophonie* was born in the 1960s, not in France itself but rather surprisingly in its former colonies, where influential figures such as Senghor and Bourguiba, the presidents of Senegal and Tunisia respectively, were insisting on the importance of French as a means of access to universal values, and on the need for cooperation between French-speaking countries. At first, Francophone cooperation was limited to special interest groups (universities, members of parliament and so on); the government was understandably reluctant to involve itself, for fear of being accused of neo-colonialism. Momentum increased however in the 1970s and 1980s, and in 1984 resulted in the creation of the Haut Conseil de la francophonie, chaired by the French President and including representatives from a variety of French speaking countries. Since 1986 this body has organized a series of biennial summits to discuss matters of common concern.

One concrete result of francophone cooperation is the satellite TV channel, TV5, set up, like the Haut Conseil, in 1984. The intention behind TV5 was to promote the French language, both by making French-speaking programmes generally available to an international audience, and by focusing on language teaching as a priority. The channel can justify its claim to be international in two ways. It now broadcasts to all five continents, with programme schedules tailored to each area; and the schedules themselves contain material not only from France, but also from other French-speaking countries, notably Belgium, Switzerland, and Quebec. In this way, TV5 physically symbolizes a move to pluralism in matters linguistic; the French language is no longer seen as the exclusive possession of French people, but the common ground on which people of various cultures can meet.

What is important to stress is the perceived role of *Francophonie* as a *contre-pouvoir,* perhaps the only way of saving the planet from linguistic domination by American English. In a speech made in Hungary in 1997, President Chirac is quoted as saying:

> The calling of *Francophonie* is to bring together all the other languages of the world in order to ensure the survival of cultural diversity, which springs from linguistic diversity. [...] It is our duty to be militants for multiculturalism in the world in order to prevent one single language from stifling the various cultures which constitute the wealth and dignity of humanity.

In other words, the French language still has a world mission – no longer to conquer and dominate, but to beat off the invader (which although not specifically identified is obviously English). Clearly, the Joan of Arc spirit lives on.

Pluralism (2): Varieties of French

Within France, enthusiasm for linguistic diversity is less obvious. The status of minority languages such as Breton and Basque has not improved much (see chapter 8 in this volume). Indeed, the movement has been largely in the opposite direction. In 1992 an additional sentence was inserted in Clause 2 of the Constitution, specifying that the language of the Republic is French. The implication is that while minority languages are tolerated for private use, all public affairs are to be conducted in French. This provision conflicts with the European Charter (also of 1992) which seeks to protect the right of individuals to use their mother tongue in dealings with officialdom. The European Charter has reinforced the aspirations of speakers of minority languages in France, but has also led to a passionate defence of French based on the kind of arguments advanced during the French Revolution: the French language is so intimately bound up with republicanism that any threat to its supremacy is seen as a threat to the values that define the nation itself.

The situation is slightly better with respect to the varieties within French itself. Attitudes to these differ, but there is a school of thought which sees in them a reservoir of linguistic creativity which if properly exploited will enable the language to evolve and adapt to the modern world. Local dialects for instance are seen (by Hagège 1987) as a rich vocabulary source from which new terms (of impeccably 'French' origins) can be minted to replace parasitical Americanisms, and even wider possibilities of this kind are offered by varieties of French spoken abroad (notably in Quebec and Francophone Africa). As yet, however, it has to be said that there are few signs of this happening in practice.

The driving force behind the evolution of 'mainstream' French appears to be coming not from geographical dialects but social ones, that is, varieties of French which depend not so much on where one lives but on the social class to which one belongs. There are always groups in society who create a slang of their own, a distortion of the standard language, in order to communicate secretly with each other; the use of slang marks off insiders from outsiders, and creates a sense of exclusiveness and belonging, of being special and of being different. In France as elsewhere, *argot* is associated particularly with the underworld, with different occupations (military or medical slang, for instance), and perhaps most importantly with the young, who use it to distinguish themselves from their elders. An important phenomenon of recent times has been what is sometimes called *la langue des cités,* the *argot* spoken in the large housing estates (*cités*) found on the edge of towns. The inhabitants of these are often young, unemployed and immigrant – all potentially factors contributing to social exclusion.

The outstanding characteristic of *argot* is its linguistic playfulness and inventiveness, its constant capacity to renew itself (which of course is why slang dates so quickly). Ironically, perhaps, one factor in this creativity is the readiness to borrow from other languages; Goudailler (1998) has shown that *la langue des cités* for instance draws not only on Anglo-American, but also on Arabic, African languages and gypsy language as well as traditional French *argot* and local dialects. As well as drawing on other languages, *argot* resorts to a whole range of procedures to create to new words (or to give new meanings to existing words). Noteworthy among these is *verlan,* the practice of reversing the order of syllables in a word; *tomber* for instance becomes *béton, faucher* (in the sense of 'steal') becomes *chéfo, roman*

policier becomes *polar* and so on (the term *verlan* itself results from applying this process to the syllables of *l'envers*). In monosyllables, it is the con-
sonants fore and aft of the central vowel which are reversed, and the vowel
itself usually becomes an *-eu-* sound. So *femme* becomes *meuf, faire*
becomes *reuf,* and *beur* (i.e. a second generation immigrant from North
Africa) is a verlanization of *l'arabe.*

Some *argot* terms have always fed into *spoken* French, becoming part of
the colloquial everyday language. There are however increasing signs that
argot is beginning to penetrate the *written* language (Ball 1997). It has
become quite acceptable for instance to make extensive use of *argot* not simply in crime fiction but in mainstream novel writing; a particularly delight-
ful example is Anne Bragance's *Anibal* (1991), where *argot* is used to record
the thoughts of the child narrator. It seems then that if French is to renew
itself to meet the challenge of English, forces for renewal will well up from
below – Joan of Arc rising from among the people to resist the invader.

Conclusion

The symbols of Napoleon and Joan of Arc serve as convenient shorthand
notation for clusters of ideas about language: Napoleon for uniformity,
standardization, control, centralization, universality, spread, language
approached from above as an expression of political power; Joan of Arc for
diversity, difference, rootedness, spontaneity, language approached from
below. Both of these tendencies have helped to shape the situation the
French language is in today, and are in evidence in the French reaction to the
threat of English domination. On the one hand, French remains a highly
standardized language, giving primacy to written forms and to rules of good
writing legitimized by institutions such as the Académie française and transmitted by the school system; this has led to a strongly interventionist policy
over such issues as the penetration of French by English loanwords. The
association between language and republican values, forged at the
Revolution, reappears in the privileged position currently afforded to
French by the Constitution; possession of the same language is necessary to
guarantee all citizens equality of opportunity and of rights. On the other
hand, cracks in this monolithic view of language are now beginning to
appear, and it is possible to argue, as leading French academic Françoise
Gadet has done, that the notion of a uniform language which all must adopt
is part of a *mentalité archaïque* (C. Genin, *Le Monde,* 18 January 1996).
The perceived need to protect French from the challenge of English has led
to a championing of cultural (and therefore linguistic) diversity, to a defensive grouping of French-speaking nations, and to a realization, in some
quarters at least, that the existence of non-standard varieties of French is to
be welcomed as a possible source of renewal of the language.

What of the future? In the short term at least, it seems inconceivable that

France will completely abandon the concept of a *langue unique et indivisible*, inherited from the Revolution. Yet pressure for a softening, if not for an overthrow, of the concept seems set to intensify. In the past, the way in which the French have seen their own language has closely mirrored the way in which they have seen France itself. At the end of the twentieth century, the perception of the state is changing rapidly; France is no longer a self-contained expansionist power, but, like Britain, a member of a *community* of nations. The constitutive principle of a community is not unity through uniformity, but unity in diversity – a principle which increasingly will have an impact on how French people view both themselves and their language.

References

ANTOINE, G. and MARTIN, R. (eds) 1985: *Histoire de la langue française 1880–1914*. Paris: Editions du CNRS.

BALIBAR, R. 1985: L'Ecole de 1880. Le français national: républicain, scolaire, grammatical, primaire. In: ANTOINE and MARTIN (eds) 1985.

BALL, R. 1997: *The French speaking world: a practical introduction to sociolinguistic issues*. London: Routledge.

BRUNOT, F. 1967: *Histoire de la langue française des origines à nos jours. Tome IX: La Révolution et l'Empire*. Paris: Colin.

DANINOS, P. 1954: *Les Carnets du Major Thompson*. Paris: Hachette.

ETIEMBLE, R. 1964: *Parlez-vous franglais?* Paris: Gallimard.

GOUDAILLER, J.-L. 1998: *Comment tu tchatches!* Paris: Maisonneuve et Larose.

HAGÈGE, C. 1987. *Le Français et les siècles*. Paris: Odile Jacob.

JOSEPH, J. and TAYLOR, T. (eds) 1990: *Ideologies of language*. London and New York: Routledge.

JUDGE, A. 1993: French, a planned language. In SANDERS (ed.) 1993.

SANDERS, C. (ed.) 1993: *French today: language in its social context*. Cambridge: CUP.

SWIGGERS, P. 1990: Ideology and the 'clarity' of French. In JOSEPH and TAYLOR (eds) 1990.

|11|

French public culture: places and spaces

BY HELEN BEALE

'Public culture' in this chapter does not mean collective cultural activities such as concert-going, gallery-gazing, football playing or taking part in political demonstrations, all of which crop up in other chapters, but rather the public spaces and places where such activities might be carried out. Nor am I concerned with the physical characteristics of specially designed venues such as the new 'Stade de France': my focus is not primarily on architecture, but on topography, the disposition of buildings and sculpture and its interface with mental and imaginative 'space'. Physical place and imaginative space are, of course, closely related, and Pierre Nora's concept of 'sites of memory' neatly encapsulates their proximity. Place de la Bastille and Place de la République, to take an obvious double-example, are clearly more than just the starting and finishing points of left-wing marches in Paris since the Popular Front and before. They also belong to the urban geography of Paris, to a historical landscape reaching back to 1789, and to internalized commonplaces of working-class culture of which they serve as iconic images, 'sites' whose importance is often belied by their everyday familiarity: the passer-by is not constantly conscious of their historic associations any more than the 'joueurs de boules' in the left-bank Arènes de Lutèce are constantly aware of the Roman associations of their venue, whose architecture is in one sense 'invisible', in another defining.

Architecture is what the Scottish TV presenter Kirsty Wark recently called the 'unavoidable art', not simply because of its physical presence, but because of its integral significance to our sense of place, local and national, and hence a certain type of identity. The same could be said of other social spaces, which are also forms of social and cultural organization, such as cafés. These are open to a variety of clienteles and show that while expressions such as 'having one's own space' and 'giving people enough space' are quite recent expressions, the ideas behind them are not. Architecture expresses and shapes, mediates between past and present, and defines social relationships. On another level, so too does public sculpture: 'public art serves many purposes, but none can have more point and dignity than investing a public space with a renewed vitality, extending its availability as a place to be, in which a sense of identity and of the possibilities of the civil life, are enhanced' (Gooding 1997, 13). Like other public symbols of identity such as the 'iconography' found on bank notes, sculpture and statuary, space creates links between the individual and the collective. This chapter will examine a number of distinctively *French* expressions of place and space, using these 'sites' to illuminate cultural practices which help define the evolving nature of the national identity. It does so in the acknowledgement, however, that France's urban topography shares problems common to most developed industrial and and post-industrial societies: it has depressing inner-city areas, over-densely built HLMs, sprawling satellite towns (a condition nicknamed 'Sarcellitis', after Sarcelles, one of the first), and 'sink estates' where deprivation and social tensions periodically erupt into vandalism and violence. Like those in other countries, French planners dealing with complex social issues do not always get it right.

Place and geometric space

The observant visitor to any fairly large French town is quickly aware of signs identifying different kinds of 'espace' (lit., space), from the familiar 'espace public, espace privé, espace vert, espace loisirs' to the less familiar 'espace-livres' (more than just a bookshop...?), 'espace-voyages' (more than just a travel agency?), 'espace-coiffure', and so on. Such innovations arise from the nature of the French language and its capacity for creating neologisms, arresting new definitions for old activities, but they are also a function of historical, geographical and cultural forces which determine a specifically French conceptualization of space.

By comparison with countries of similar size, France is famously geometrical in shape: its coastline and land frontiers describe a hexagon whose points in turn describe a circle of 1000 km diameter. This configuration not only influenced the development of its communications, of roads and thereafter railways radiating like the spokes of a wheel from the Parisian hub. It also contributed an internalized sense of national identity as spatial as well as geographical in concept, reinforced by the administrative division of the country into *départements* of roughly equal size. Moreover, if modern commentators refer to 'L'Hexagone' as a convenient term to distinguish metropolitan France from its neighbours and from its overseas territories and dependencies, it is partly because successive generations of children were familiarized with its periphery by *Le Tour de la France par Deux Enfants*, written after the loss of Alsace-Lorraine in 1870 and still in use in French primary schools until World War II. Those children also learned the geographical/geometric centre of the Hexagon (near Bourges), the courses and lengths of the principal rivers and the 'partage des eaux' in the Morvan massif between the Seine, the Saône and the Loire river-systems, with their Channel, Atlantic and Mediterranean outfalls.

If the land-mass is hexagonal, its capital, by comparison with other European cities, is strikingly circular: from the medieval Ile de la Cité and Notre-Dame, via the eighteenth-century *mur des fermiers généraux* and the nineteenth-century fortifications to the post-war outer cordon of the 'boulevard périphérique', the urban expansion of Paris has followed a process of widening concentric circles. Twelve avenues radiate geometrically from the Place de l'Etoile (Place Charles de Gaulle), including the Champs-Elysées whose 1800-metre trajectory to the obelisk at Place de la Concorde, recalled from a pre-war guide-book, proved vital to a young Free French gunner at the Liberation (Lapierre and Collins 1964, 352–3). That axis also bisects the Carousel Arch in an almost mathematically straight line and was prolonged further westwards to La Défense in 1989. Other major thoroughfares (*les grands boulevards*, notably) run north-south and east-west, though there is nothing like the grid-iron street pattern of Glasgow or New York. Paris is also unusual among northern cities in that since the Haussmann modernization of the 1850s and 1860s, it has changed remarkably little. It has grown organically, a process of continuity and historical accretion, unlike Berlin, where the destruction of 1945 erased much of the past, or even London, damaged in the Blitz. Despite the depredations of planners and developers and the demise of old districts lamented by historians such as Richard Cobb (1998), it retains distinct 'quartiers', some with a village atmosphere. It has also retained its unmistakable sky-line, much wider in compass than the 'illustrious valley' described by Balzac in *Le Père Goriot* (1834) marked out by the Pantheon, the Val de Grâce, the Vendôme Column and Les Invalides, but recognizable still with its 'buttes', the Eiffel Tower and Sacré-Cœur, the Pompidou Centre (Beaubourg), the Tour Maine-Montparnasse and the Grande Arche de la Défense.

The complex interaction of space, place and cultural association is strikingly illustrated by the map of the Paris Metro system, which in one respect appears curiously less 'conceptual' than its London counterpart. Henry Beck's celebrated map of the Underground (1933) has long been considered a model of design in its diagrammatic abstraction (Hollis 1994, 18), since it does not seek to reproduce spatially the above-ground topography of London; and the names of Tube stations are always precisely that, names of places. By contrast, the Paris Metro map is more realistically configured. However, in a major difference with London, many station names evoke historic events, places, people or values. You can travel to Liberté and Convention as well as Nation or Bastille, alight at philosophers and scientists from Voltaire to Pasteur and Curie, choose a route including politicians and freedom fighters, national and international (Louise Michel, Gambetta, Simon Bolivar, Garibaldi, Marx Dormoy, Franklin D. Roosevelt). Other station names recall defining battles of the fight against Nazism during World War II (Stalingrad, Bir-Hakeim), and artists who espoused the revolutionary

or communist cause (Picasso, Aragon). Naturally, the ideological significance of these names does not constantly impinge on the thoughts of ordinary Parisian commuters, urban man and woman in thrall to the tyranny of
métro-boulot-dodo (tube-job-kip). But in a more subtle, contemporary and
complex way than is the case in London (Tower Hill, Waterloo, Trafalgar
Square, Westminster), they describe a parallel universe, a mental map capa-
ble of being resurrected, a 'lieu de mémoire' or 'espace mémoriel' not co-
terminous with physical place (*endroit, lieu*), where topography and history
(memory) interact.

Topography and history: the traditional image

Each French city, town and village has basic topographical features which
are also cultural sites: church, town hall, war memorial, public park or garden, etc. Such landmarks are not of course peculiar to France, but they have
an identifiably French form and configuration, usually though not always
derived from their relationship with national as well as local history. Elected
mayors were established in every commune in 1884, not long after the
enactment of the 'lois scolaires' (cf. chapter 5). The arrangement of boys'
and girls' primary schools to either side of the town hall was an abiding spatial as well as moral construct for generations of French children, part of a
democratic as well as a national identity, which is also expressed in street
names: there is invariably a Place or an Avenue de la République, sometimes
a Rue du 4 Septembre, and so on. The Great War (1914–18) added a Place
de la Victoire and often a boulevard named after Marshals Joffre or Foch,
sometimes a Clemenceau or a Jean Jaurès, the pre-war Socialist leader assassinated in 1914. The Avenue des Champs-Elysées was first used for ceremonial purposes in 1840 (the return of Napoleon's remains from
Saint-Helena), and thereafter for Victor Hugo's state funeral in 1885. It was
however victory in November 1918 and the creation of the unknown soldier's tomb at the Arc de Triomphe which established it as the major site of
national memory and the route of preference for the annual Bastille day celebrations and state parades, including the 1989 bi-centennial procession.
Events and personalities of World War II are recalled in Place du Général de
Gaulle or Place du 18 Juin, common all over France, along with a lycée or
'groupe scolaire' Jean Moulin, and streets named after local resistance mar-
tyrs and victims of deportation. Victory in Europe (VE Day), in 1945, and
the ending of France's longest colonial conflict, the Algerian War, are
marked in many communes by characteristic blue and white street name
plaques bearing the dates 8 mai 1945 and 19 mars 1962 respectively.

The historical referents embedded in topography are reinforced in public
monuments: many towns have statues of the Republic, of Liberty and
Marianne, the latter often simple Phrygian-capped busts, the former more
grandiose edifices. Allegorical incarnations of the Republic tend to echo

Delacroix's celebrated 'Liberty leading the people' (1833) or Rude's influential relief, the 'Departure of the Volunteers' (1833–36), nicknamed 'la Marseillaise', on the Arc de Triomphe. Scrolls bearing the Declaration of the Rights of Man or the republican constitution are important sculptural motifs. So too is the 'torch' of progress, of education and enlightenment, also symbolic of the transmission of the 'flame' of civilization (and Frenchness, the incarnation of universal humanist values) from generation to generation. Local war memorials, which identify the 'commune' with France itself and often with the Republic, sometimes have two 'faces', a public one turned towards the school as an example of sacrifice, virtue and vigilance, and a more private face, often opening on to a garden or green *espace aménagé*, for adult recollection and contemplation. Important, too, for the ideological defining of space is the inscription of the Republican motto 'Liberty, Equality, Fraternity' on the façade of local town halls (the *Hôtel de Ville* or less grand *Mairie*). Symbols are also found on schools, post offices, and other public buildings such as libraries, museums and even railway stations – part of the railway network was nationalized before World War I, the remainder in 1938.

Inherited in the main from the pre-1940 Republican régime, such spatial constructs reflect its centralizing, unifying imperatives ('la France une et indivisible'). But it would be an error, even from the perspective of the year 2000, to regard this architecture as in some senses 'top down' and therefore imposing values alien to the mass of the population. Civic architecture in secular societies, unless of course they are one-party states, is usually a reflection of a certain democratic negotiation. Popular culture imposes its own definitions from epoch to epoch and though architecture may be an 'aristocratic' art, its values on the whole reflect the nature of the social consensus of the day: 1914–18 war memorials which reflect the academicism of the previous century epitomize in other respects a certain popular culture. Which is not to say that the image constructed has always been inclusive: the Third Republic made widespread use of 'woman' as allegorical symbol while denying real women political and legal rights. Like her British and German equivalents (Britannia and Germania) but much more ubiquitously, Marianne functioned as an allegory which was meant to unite and rally the nation, though in the volatile ideological climate of the pre-1914 period, she could also be a figure of discord. As is argued in chapter 12, the task of art and iconography today is to devise new forms of representation for a less homogeneous, more diverse, society.

Site and memory have an obvious relationship with age: older Parisians will remember General de Gaulle's triumphant progress down the Champs-Elysées in August 1944, overlaying but not fully erasing the humiliation of the German victory parade four years earlier which had begun the occupation of the city and the country. Brassaï's photograph of young Parisians crowded onto the 'Lion of Belfort' on the Place Denfert-Rochereau on the morning of 26 August 1944, to greet General Leclerc's Liberating Second

Armoured Division (la deuxième DB) with its Sherman tanks, is in its way as important as the better-known film footage of de Gaulle on the Champs-Elysées, but the latter has become iconic. For a younger generation, Denfert-Rochereau was the starting point of student protest marches in May 1968, and those who remember these events will recall the strangely anachronistic counter-demonstration by Malraux and other ministers, against the tide of history, so to speak, marching *up* the Champs-Elysées. In November 1994, to mark the eightieth anniversary of the outbreak of World War I (August 1914), huge photographs of the victorious armies and their leaders were erected alongside Rude's familiar sculpted reliefs, asserting a historical continuum with the national mobilization of 1792, uncovering another layer of the composite past and illustrating the investment of public spaces with the 'renewed vitality' recommended by Gooding (1997).

The development of new forms of public space

New ideas began to emerge in the 1970s, with changing aesthetic conventions, new concepts of place and space, and growing public awareness of local as well as national 'patrimoine'. Briefly, the older, ideologically-driven definitions of public space, and the statuary which occupied it, gave way to less explicitly 'republican' but perhaps more accessibly civic concepts. In France as elsewhere, a major part of the stimulus to fresh thinking was provided by the increasingly intractable problem of urban traffic. Communities that had for a long time tried to accommodate the car, creating additional parking, proliferating traffic controls and building new freeways – in Paris, a major stretch of the right-bank *quais* was sacrificed to the 'voie express' – began to reclaim their public spaces for pedestrians, leading to changes in the physical landscape. Underground parking allows the planners to open up public space in important and historic squares, and may also lead to new emblems and icons.

A major example outside Paris illustrates this well. The city of Nîmes in Provence was long embodied in its Roman past and in two of the most remarkably preserved Roman buildings in the world: the first-century AD Arènes or Arena (still seating 23 000, now used for spectacles from bullfights to opera) and the fifth-century AD Corinthian temple, now museum, known as the Maison Carrée. In 1989, the adjacent Place d'Assas was revitalized by underground parking and reconfigured by Martial Raysse, using a complex scheme of fountains. How one of these, 'Day and Night', whose bronze figures and columns surmounted by a pediment are all in modern idiom, interacts with the more classical aspects of the site was captured in a special supplement to *Paris-Match* ('Vu dans Match', 13 July 1989), where a subtly edited cover photograph created an interplay between what is now seen and what is remembered. That a widely-disseminated magazine made this emblematic use of Place d'Assas, under a banner headline 'Nîmes', is all

Figure 11.1   Martial
Raysse's 'Day and Night',
modern idiom columns in
the reconfigured Place
d'Assas, Nîmes.

the more remarkable when the complex, indeed arcane symbolism of
Raysse's work is recalled, a reminder that new public art has ceased to be
primarily didactic, ideological or exemplary. It can indeed present a real
challenge to a general public more comfortable with the classical (or with
Raysse's crocodile in the Place du Marché in Nîmes, so recognizably taken
from the arms of the city), and who have been slow to espouse more enig-
matic styles. This is in distinct contrast to the media, on the one hand, and
the galleries and museums, on the other hand, which are alive to the importance of the new, and its power to 'displace' the traditional icons. Nîmes's
renewal received further national attention with the 'Expo Expérience
Nîmes' held at the Centre Georges Pompidou in February 1993. And the
city continued to court the new, with the Carré d'Art complex (1993), the
work of British architect Sir Norman Foster, which includes the Museum of
Modern Art and the Library with its high-tech echoes of the Centre
Pompidou. Part of this complex lies underground, to maximize use of the
site opposite the Maison Carrée.

Figure 11.2 Liberation anniversary, 1989: Marianne joins the spectators at La Cadière d'Azur (Var).

In the decade 1980–90, Nîmes benefited from decentralization and the Ministry of Culture's lavish policy for attracting artists of international standing, but the city was also sensible enough to choose artists of calibre with southern connections. It thereby avoided accusations of bland internationalism or remote elitism, and provided further evidence of core principles in what is a discernibly French 'policy for people': a concern for the quality of life and a recognition of changing patterns of public space use which has been endorsed by government. This need not be writ large – it extends to informal spaces too, as even cycle tracks and viewing bays on new pedestrian bridges demonstrate, enabling the improved infrastructure to serve as a link, not a means of separation.

In April 1999, the urbanist Jean-Pierre Charbonneau, whose work includes responsibility as a *Conseiller technique* for implementing a policy of public space development in a number of major cities (Grand [Greater] Lyon, Lyon, Saint Etienne, Grenoble), addressed the annual conference of the Royal Society of Architects in Scotland on such matters. The RIAS conference took place in Glasgow, districts of which Charbonneau had himself analysed in 1994–5, along with Manchester, London, Rotterdam and Hamburg, as part of a French fact-finding project on economic development and employment. Charbonneau is not working with regional 'Grands projets': starting from written and sketched profiles which aim to capture the spirit of the place, he is essentially a decorator who re-shapes and embellishes, who screens a chemical valley near Lyon with trees, who humanizes and renews urban environments. His materials – such as vegetation – are low cost but renewable and a 5-year budget makes him the envy of his British counterparts limited to annual funding. His work is an indication of the policy pursued by France's Ministry of Culture to enhance quality in architecture, town planning and landscaping. Although high-profile light shows have been staged (in Lyon, for instance), to make a promotional splash for the policy, urban spaces are not so aggressively modernized or sanitized that they lose life and colour. For Charbonneau, the key word in the policy for people is 'proximité', with its user-friendly connotations of neighbourhood facilities (a 'magasin de proximité' is a 'corner shop'): spaces are returned to the people who mark the occasion by holding festivals, largely spontaneous in nature, when the space is first reclaimed, thereafter consciously restaged for performance in the city where Charbonneau works next.

An important influence here is the increasing reversal of the relationship/sequence between site and the object it receives. It used to be the case, as Buren observes (1998, 20) that the work of art had primacy: works were created as important objects in themselves, without relation to a space; then public space was found for them, and some were even moved from site to site. Nowadays, Buren contends, the space or the site comes first: an artist is asked to 'do' something for a particular space, which might involve creation in the traditional sense, or perhaps installation, or temporary transformation. Christo's 'wrapped' Pont-Neuf (1985) became 'the' fashionable place to meet in Paris; Klein's Blue illumination of the Concorde obelisk (1996) gave the hieroglyphs improved clarity and contrast. Familiar landmarks and sites became strange, acquired new meaning (Lovell, in press).

In other words, public art and public spaces can be fun. Statues which used to be raised above the hoi polloi have gradually come down off their pedestals and are much closer to ground level, and to the spectator. Notable examples include Kern's *Mauriac* (1990), Peignot's *Mendès-France* (1984), and Granet's *Sartre* (1987). The Colonnes Buren at Palais Royal may be variously interpreted as stepping-stones, ornamental pieces on a draughts board, tree trunks in a petrified forest, a low seat from which to sketch or for children to jump off: ludic, abstract space has been born. The desacralization of artistic space is neatly encapsulated by Picasso's request that his bronze 'L'Homme au mouton', a piece of museum art bequeathed to Vallauris (Alpes Maritimes) as public art, should be 'set up outdoors in a square where the children could climb over it and the dogs water it unhindered' (Penrose 1971, 383). The alternative cultural practices encouraged by Mitterrand's Minister of Culture, Jack Lang, the officially-tolerated graffiti of 'les taggeurs' which have displaced the once sacrosanct 'défense d'afficher – loi du 29 juillet 1881' on public buildings, and whose expanses accompany the RER traveller from Roissy airport into the Gare du Nord, 'le look', with its Nike and Adidas fashion icons, rollerblading (a transatlantic import) in streets and pedestrian zones, are equally symptomatic of a more diverse concept of the spatial-cultural environment.

Certain distinctively French features in the urban environment such as cafés have been replaced by fast-food outlets, not even uniformly American-owned (Flunch, Quikburger, etc). The differences in pace and atmosphere are quite as radical as the differences in fare, and in some cases perpetrated by French companies. The roller-blader listening to his or her *baladeur* and consuming fast food on the move is the acme of this spatial-cultural shift, zooming through les Halles instead of, as in the old days before the markets moved to Rungis, lingering there for onion soup and a first glance at the morning papers. For the roller-blader, such a lifestyle is dead, and infrastructure, architecture and public art are for him or her a blur, barely registering even as something to feel indifferent to – for in moving they carve in the air around them their own space which is protean and hence exhilarating. Little wonder that a recent number of the Newsletter of National Museums in Provence Alpes-Côte d'Azur (November 1997), devoted to dialogue on museum education services, boldly asks whether, despite all the innovative programmes of guided visits and drawing sessions to attract children into museums, the children are given enough personal space to experience the shock of art, the power of a work of art to speak to the uninitiated without mediation. Even today's adult museum-goers, accustomed to choose contemplation and a concomitant measure of stasis, are being coaxed into ambulatory experience of art, for instance in Antibes on the Côte d'Azur, at the Musée Picasso. Here, exhibition rooms open to a small sculpture garden of olfactory appeal too (*la Terrasse du Château et le Jardin de Sculptures et de Parfums*), with a highly photographic Mediterranean backdrop, against which figure sculptures are disposed along the retaining walls. Museum-conditioned body language loosens up: people relax, circulate, glance at the art objects, snap, compose and recompose the world.

In April 1992, a sell-out performance by Pavarotti at Opera-Bastille was simultaneously relayed on to a huge screen outside, where it was attended free of charge by 20 000 Parisians and tourists who occupied Place de la Bastille, transforming the physical space from historical site, traffic interchange, Metro station, into a virtual opera-house and behaving with a curious mixture of conventionality (alternating hushed attention and applause) and élan engendered by the appropriation of that space (some perched on the column). The experience of *délocalisation* was replicated in other towns and cities: Toulouse (8000), Aubagne (5000) and Lyon (3000). Another example of people 'constructing' a public space socially is provided by Carpentras, to the east of Avignon, where Michèle de la Pradelle (1993) observed how private individuals, shopping in the street market, construct a 'community' inside which class and social differences are temporarily set aside, where a local identity is affirmed (even by visiting tourists) and information given in a way that would be unthinkable in the alienating environment of the hypermarket. Common affinities are explored – children, weather, recipes – while differentiating status and identity markers are set aside. Familiarity is engendered both by the patter of the stall-holders who manage the space as if it were a theatre, and the fact that all (believe they) can barter, and therefore enjoy a kind of egalitarianism. During the 45th anniversary celebrations of the Liberation in La Cadière d'Azur (Var) in 1989, the 'Marianne mobile' was taken from its usual place in the Mairie and positioned across the street, by an open window above the bar of Le Cercle des Travailleurs, as though watching the procession below. This witty placing, part-symbolic statement, part-caricature of a nosy woman on a balcony, reveals a popular touch: the familiar symbols are re-invested with an admixture of the ludic and the respectful. Public space may also be appropriated as informal sites for spontaneous displays of collective grieving which now commonly occur in Britain and the United States as well as France, in the wake of disasters, massacres or the tragic deaths of iconic individuals such as Princess Diana who died in Paris (flowers were placed at the Place de l'Alma by her admirers). By placing flowers, token objects or regalia, often with personal messages, outside football grounds, schools and at kerbsides, sympathizers have a sense of participating in the creation of new rituals and in the consecration of that space as something sacred to memory.

If some new forms of commemorative practice suggest that France is not immune to the development of media-driven cultural globalization, the use of space to create dialogue between past and present ensures the continuation of a certain French distinctiveness. As part of the modernization of the square behind and above the new Montparnasse TGV station, a children's play area and a Resistance shrine were imaginatively combined to create an alternative form of memorial site, more traditional examples of which exist in numerous locations across France. In Apt (Vaucluse), a children's games area is adjacent to a columned nineteeth-century 'Republic' with quotations from Victor Hugo on each face of the plinth. Iconography linking the war dead and a present generation of children echoes a dominant theme of the 1920s, a time of demographic decline. To take an English example by a French sculptor, Paul de Monchaux's Wilfred Owen memorial at Shrewsbury (1994), a ground-level stone frame bearing the words 'I am the enemy you killed, my friend', offers a bench and a place to play. Jochen Gerz's update of the 1914–1918 war memorial at Biron (Dordogne) is inscribed with the thoughts of the village's present-day inhabitants, who thereby contribute to the memorial and the space it occupies. Gerz has suggested that major European cities, one-time enemies now reconciled, should exchange their war memorials. Too radical to meet universal approval, the proposal does however conjure up imaginative dislocations and re-orderings of the links between sculpture and context, throwing the underlying social and ideological agendas into relief.

Text as subject-matter is a feature of Schein's work in the Paris Metro, for Concorde station (1989–1991), using tiles as individual letter squares to compose the text of the *Déclaration des droits de l'homme et du citoyen* of 1789 (see *Monument & Modernité* catalogue, 1996, 144–5). In this work of art, the text itself has primacy, and it surrounds and frames the passengers, composing their cocoon world. Letters and text are also used imaginatively by Patrick Raynaud in les Halles, passage Mondétour, in his lacquered steel and neon Sonnet de voyelles, 1988 (*Monument & Modernité* 1996, 148–50) . Raynaud colours the vowels AEIOU according to the prescription of the poet Rimbaud, and he tumbles them over a bridge, parallel to a covered pedestrian walkway, in such a manner as to evoke plurality of response: a young child's desire to run and re-assemble the letters physically, like building blocks; an adult's prompting to mental and imaginative dexterity.

Museum space and virtual space

A significant incidental benefit of the 'grands projets' has been to give older buildings a new lease of life. The new Finance Ministry at Bercy returned a wing of the Louvre to its artistic function; the Musée d'Orsay now groups collections previously housed elsewhere whose coverage – from 1848 to 1914 – coincides with the heroic age of the railways, and revalidates the architecture of the old mainline station as starting point of an imaginative 'journey'. Thanks to the Museum's website (www.smartweb.fr/fr/orsay/index.html) and CD-ROM technology, it is also accessible now as 'virtual space'. Science and architecture, museum and environment, past and present converge in new and exciting synergies (the Cité des Sciences with its Géode, the Pyramide du Louvre, the inversion of above and below ground at the Forum des Halles, or the Nationale Bibliothèque de France). Conversely, the Louvre sculpture halls (les cours Marly et Puget, off Passage Richelieu) put public art in the museum by bringing the outside inside, isolating it from urban 'pollution visuelle' which Daniel Buren (1998, 70) credits museum space with hermetically excluding. The sculpture halls occupy a space the equivalent of at least three floors' height, with glass ceilings. These sculpture halls were not universally well received: Jean Pierrard writes somewhat disparagingly of the 'aquariums' and of Marly as a 'cratère sans ombres', altogether reminiscent of vast hotel lobbies or soulless airport space (*Le Point*, 20 novembre 1993, 59–65). Marc Fumaroli (1991, 202) reminds us that the Mona Lisa has a new rival under the Pyramid at the Louvre: *un espace*, where ever-increasing numbers of tourists see more of the cafeteria and postcard shop than of the works of art themselves! Yet, isolated from the urban paraphernalia which usually surrounds them – as Pierrard conceded – the sculptures are now afforded that exclusive attention which is the preserve of the cocooned museum-goer if not of the pedestrian. And Pierrard, among many other plaudits, acknowledges the elegant discretion of the new signs and escalators, allowing visitors to circulate in spaces where 'Seules les œuvres ont le droit de briller'. These new projects, and the upgrading and cleaning of older buildings or the *aménagement* of their sites and surroundings, may make Beaubourg look simply old-fashioned, but it will doubtless retain its claim to have re-created a kind of pre-modern public space, its forecourt where fire-eaters and mime-artists congregate making it reminiscent of a medieval 'foire aux miracles' in a twentieth-century décor.

Significant among new museum or exhibition spaces is IMA, the Institut du monde arabe, which houses exhibitions of both French and Middle East art. The IMA building is a delicate equilibrium of high-tech and traditional Arabic design, created by one of the leading Mitterrand-generation architects, Jean Nouvel, who pursued 'l'épure, la transparence, l'immatériel' (Marjorie Alessandrini, *Le Nouvel Observateur*, 17–21 mars 1996, 15, in Spécial Culture, Que reste-t-il de notre rayonnement à l'étranger?).

Besides formal museum-going, there is now official cognisance of what is called *lèche-vitrines patrimonial*, heritage window-shopping 'pour l'amour des vieilles pierres' (Maryvonne de Saint Pulgent, *Le Point*, 1357, 19 sept 1998, 108–9), the informal strolling around churches, parks and historic parts of towns: statistics say that Notre-Dame is as much visited as Disneyland Paris. This is not just a feature of the Open Door Days (Journées du Patrimoine). When due allowance is made for the number of foreign tourists in the figures, there are still many French people between 18–55 whose pride in 'la merveille du coin' (the local sights/site) impels them to go to see elements of their heritage and show them off to visiting friends. Interest in the past is not a dated pastime; it looks towards future generations, for whom the National Inventory catalogues and preserves France's inheritance.

References

BEKOUCHE-DEMAILLY, Marie-Claude 1996: *Les Monuments publics de Nîmes, 1900–1990, Inventaire de la sculpture dans l'espace urbain. Mémoire de Maîtrise en Histoire de l'Art: Art Contemporain.* Sous la direction de Luce Barlangue. Nîmes: Lacour, 150. Pièces justificatives 23.
BUREN, D. 1998: *A force de descendre dans la rue, l'art peut-il enfin y monter?* Coll. Dits et contredits. Paris: Sens et Tonka.

COBB, Richard 1998: *Paris and elsewhere.* Selected writings edited and introduced by David Gilmour. London: John Murray.

DE LA PRADELLE, Michèle 1993: Market exchange and the social 'construction' of a public space. In *French cultural studies* 6, October, 359–71.

FUMAROLI, Marc 1991: *L'Etat culturel.* Paris: Editions de Fallois.

GOODING, M. 1997: *Public : art : space, a decade of public art commissions agency, 1987–1997.* London: Merrell Holberton.

Monument & Modernité à Paris: art, espace public et enjeux de mémoire 1891–1996. Paris: Electra (1996 exhibition catalogue).

HOLLIS, R. 1994: *Graphic design, a concise history.* London: Thames and Hudson.

LAPIERRE, Dominique and COLLINS, Larry 1964: *Paris brûle-t-il? (25 août 1944). Histoire de la Libération de Paris.* Paris: Robert Laffont.

LOVELL, Vivien. In press: Contemporary monuments of the millennial kind. In Jeanne Marie Teutonico (ed.) *Monuments and the millennium. The Victoria and Albert Museum, London, 20–22 May 1998.*

PENROSE, R. 1971: *Picasso, his life and work.* Harmondsworth: Penguin Books.

PIERRARD, Jean 1993: Musée du Louvre, Grandissime! *Le Point* 1105, 20 November, 59–65.

DE SAINT-PULGENT, Maryvonne 1998: Pour l'amour des vieilles pierres. *Le Point* 1357, 19 September, 108–9.

Suggested reading

AGULHON, Maurice 1981: *Marianne into battle. Republican imagery and symbolism in France, 1798–1880.* Trans. by Janet Lloyd. Cambridge and Paris: CUP and Editions de la Maison des Sciences de l'Homme.

CURTIS, Penelope 1999: *Sculpture 1900–1945. After Rodin.* Oxford: OUP.

HARGROVE, June 1989: *The statues of Paris: an open-air Pantheon.* New York, Paris: The Vendome Press.

NORA, Pierre 1984–93: *Les Lieux de mémoire.* Paris: Gallimard.

On the modernization of Nîmes, see the city's website www.ville-nîmes.fr

|12|

Frenchness: constructed and reconstructed

BY WILLIAM KIDD

'Chaque homme a deux pays: la France et le sien'. There are few more his-torically self-assured (or unconsciously sexist) assertions of 'l'exception française' than the semi-proverbial dictum, variously attributed to recent and not-so-recent authors, and endorsed by a variety of commentators, not all of them men, in the nineteenth and twentieth centuries. European and Anglo-American expatriates from Friederich Sieburg and Ernst Junger to Ernest Hemingway and J.D. Fergusson, from Sylvia Beach and Gertrude Stein to Scott Fitzgerald and Samuel Beckett, are just some of those who found a second country, temporarily or permanently, in France. Though the phenomenon probably reached its modern high-water mark just after World War II, its foundations were laid during the previous century. They included a stimulating intellectual atmosphere in which art and literature were informed by a sharp, at times irreverent Gallic intelligence; the liberating quality of an environment, mainly though not exclusively Parisian, whose ethos and values, whose 'savoir faire' and 'savoir vivre' were also associated with a natural and 'authentic' pace of life with its roots in a still vital rural tradition. There was, finally, the diversity and abundance which made France a 'pays de cocagne' for the well-off foreigner if not for all of its own citizens and generated the German expression, to live 'like God in France'. These and other factors contributed to the perception that there existed a definably French identity, a sense of Frenchness which sat unproblematically with its official, republican institutions, and the overarching historical expe-riences which both cemented and validated it.

Now we know, of course, that 'national identities', and many of the socio-cultural 'traditions' which express those identities, are characteristi-cally *constructed*, products of evolving economic forces and manipulation by powerful interest-groups and parties. Just as British national identity was progressively woven from diverse strands: anti-Catholicism, industrial expansion, economic imperialism and monarchism (with a monarchy suc-cessfully reinvented during Victoria's reign and again after the abdication crisis of 1936), so the concept of French national identity has meant something different in the seventeenth, eighteenth and nineteenth centuries. Its contemporary (twentieth-century) emergence is usefully encapsulated in Eugen Weber's famous title *Peasants into Frenchmen* (1976), not, note, peasants into industrial workers, as was the case in Britain and to a lesser extent Germany. As previous chapters (on the French language, on the school system, etc.) have shown, the creation of Frenchness was inseparable from the creation of citizens in a democracy of republican, 'universal' values. Underpinned by the Ferry educational laws of the 1880s and the melting-pot of national military service, this received concrete and symbolic expression in universal male suffrage, including elected mayors in the smallest villages, and was buttressed overseas by France's so-called civilizing mission in the colonies. Disseminated in school curricula and reinforced in collective rituals (the holiday on le Quatorze juillet, the Tour de France and so on), the essential themes and constituents of that identity were deliberately enshrined in symbols designed to crystallize and when necessary mobilize national feeling: the iconic image of the fall of the Bastille, the Declaration of the Rights of Man and of the Citizen, Delacroix's revolutionary 'Liberty leading the People towards the barricades', Marianne and her Phrygian cap, the tricolore and the Marseillaise, definitively adopted in 1879–1880, etc.

It is true that the Weberian paradigm did not extend to the progress of peasants into French*women*, whose attainment of full democratic status would take quite a bit longer; nor was democracy extended to the colonies themselves. In neither case, admittedly, was the pre-1914 Third Republic (an essentially conservative, bourgeois regime founded in revolutionary rhetoric) manifestly out of step with other constitutional regimes of the day. It is also true that acceptance of the republic was fitful, partial and in some areas never realized, as the series of political crises of the 1880s, 1890s and early 1900s amply confirm. But the traumatic experience of World War I (1914–1918) helped to reconcile some of the old political and religious tensions and generated unifying dates and rituals which, like their UK equivalents, have formed part of the French national commemorative repertoire ever since. 11 November (Armistice Day) at the tomb of the unknown soldier at the Arc de Triomphe is replicated in 36 000 communes all over France at the local war memorial ('monument aux morts'), where alongside ex-servicemen children have taken an active part, becoming ex-servicemen in their turn in further conflicts in 1939–1945, 1946–1954 and 1954–1962 (Indochina and Algeria).

To the effect of state-led paradigms of Frenchness must be added the impact of popular culture and social customs, the local *bal de quartier* or *kermesse*, as well as homogenizing sentimental stereotypes and 'images d'Epinal': Victor Hugo's revolutionary Gavroche in *Les Misérables* (1862) belongs to a tradition of Parisian street urchins, the 'titi de Paris', while the Republic's master narratives and symbols were ironically troped in the post-

Figure 12.1 1792 meets 1914 in 1994 at the Arc de Triomphe. Photomontage juxtaposing troops leaving for the front with Rude's 'Departure of the Volunteers' (aka the *Marseillaise*).

cards announcing one's status as an 'ancien élève des écoles communales de Paris', or the *clochard*'s begging pitch as the apocryphal 'fils du soldat inconnu'. Collective identity was reinforced by the social transformations effected by the Front Populaire in the 1930s, when paid holidays and cheap mass travel initiated the annual August exodus to the seaside or the mountains, supplementing the culture of the *colonie de vacances*, and making household names of good quality camping equipment such as Trigano and Lafuma. France and Frenchness were further emphasized in popular song: Trenet's 'Douce France' is an obvious case in point; the French *paras* adoption of Piaf's 'Je ne regrette rien' during the Algerian War offers a more aggressively nationalist variant of the same impulse. Despite real social change, and the spectacular economic progress realized after 1945 by the Fourth Republic, other factors contributed towards the maintenance of a long period of stasis. In his Parisian 'lycée de quartier' in the late 1950s, François Truffaut's young filmic protagonist Antoine Doinel (in *Les 400 coups*) belonged to a universe not so very different from his predecessors half a century earlier, unproblematically and recognizably French.

National identity and official culture since 1958

Historically, the state's role in shaping the national collective consciousness has been more conspicuous and more direct in France than in Britain, where voluntary bodies and organizations play a larger role and where there is a less centralist approach to the dissemination of art and culture. As we saw in chapter 4, a sustained programme of central cultural intervention was undertaken under de Gaulle's presidency by Culture Minister André Malraux, whose twin aims of 'democratizing' culture while asserting national grandeur and historic continuity were symbolized in the creation of the 'maisons de la Culture' and in the Pantheonization of the resistance hero and martyr Jean Moulin in 1964. That year also saw the Beatles visit Paris, a sure harbinger of more seismic cultural shifts, while the Ex-Servicemen's Ministry enjoined councils and elected representatives in every commune in France to devote special attention to the condition of local war memorials 'dans le courant de la présente année au cours de laquelle sera célébré le double anniversaire des événements de 1914 et 1944' (in Kidd 1999, 118). Circulated on the symbolic date of 8 May (VE Day, end of World War II in Europe), this instruction received particular emphasis in the Moselle *département*, where memories of the German annexation (1940–1944) were still strong, as in Alsace-Lorraine in general. Even there, however, anti-German feeling has gradually abated: in 1976, the construction of a resistance memorial at Bambiderstroff involved transporting to it a fortified Maginot line cupola where none existed previously, to create a composite 'lieu de mémoire'. Carefully preserved on the same site is a small calvary erected there by its German defenders in 1916. Chancellor Kohl and President Mitterrand's handshake on the battlefield of Verdun in 1984 was the symbolic proof that a chapter had finally been closed and that a historic enmity is no longer a major factor in the definition of a certain concept of Frenchness.

Paradoxically but unsurprisingly, the trend of anniversary commemoration has continued unabated and increased, as the ranks of those old enough to remember the historic events being commemorated have thinned and older generations disappear. As well as the bi-centennial of the revolution (see below), the end of the Great War was recalled in 1988, and its outbreak in 1994, fortuitously but usefully combined with celebrations to mark the fiftieth anniversary of the 'D-Day' landings. The 50th anniversary of the founding event of Gaullism in 1940 was marked by the addition to war memorials of a plaque bearing the 'Appel du 18 juin 1940' framed in blue, white and red. By 1990, however, this was a commemoration of the past, an appeal to memory, not to present themes and energies. As societies evolve, their invented traditions and symbols gradually lose their mobilizing capacity, while continuing to emit residual signals. Like dead metaphors around us in language, like statues of Lenin rendered redundant – *insignificant* – by the collapse of the former Soviet Union, they mean something to us but we no longer respond to them. Not all crises of identity are so sudden or total, but they are no less real: post-war Britain, it is often observed, lost an empire and has not yet found a mission. Post-May 1968, France has witnessed the more progressive weakening of the overarching institutions and organizations upon which its identity was based over a period of some 120 years. The concept of *laïcité* – secular education for all – has been eroded. Military service, sometimes now referred to by a variant of former English terminology as 'le service national', has also been eroded, partly because in an era of hi-tech warfare, non-specialist conscript armies have long outlived their usefulness. Progressively reduced in length to ten months, it now includes community service options for which women are eligible. However, it is unlikely much longer to constitute a decisive formative experience for the totality of the nations's young adults, still divided by educational attainment but united in behavioural codes, like the 1990s 'taggeur' evoked in this portrait in *Le Monde*:

> Gavroche de grande banlieue ou collégien des faubourgs, Parisien 'branché' ou étudiant facétieux, il a entre douze et vingt-cinq ans, raffole de rap, rêve des Etats-Unis mais ne déteste pas Paris. Il est en quête d'identité et de sensations.

> A streetwise adolescent from inner-city or outer-urban sprawl, or a schoolkid from the suburbs, a trendy Parisian or a student with 'attitude', he's between 12 and 25 years old, crazy about rap, fantasizes about the US but basically quite likes Paris. He's into identity and experimenting.

> Forbes and Hewlett 1994, 486–7

Identity-creating structures such as social class are also eroding. Like many of the traditional industries from which it drew its support, the French Communist Party, which literally schooled a previous generation of immigrants (in its evening classes and language groups, replicated in its wartime resistance structures) has declined as a serious political force for integration. Its ethos and ideology are uncongenial to a present generation of immigrants from Afro-Caribbean or Arab-speaking countries, Muslim in the main, who appear less amenable to industrial 'blue-collar', class-based action than their 1920s and 1930s Belgian, Italian or Eastern European predecessors (cf. chapter 9). The process of erosion and fragmentation has been compounded by the continuing *remise en question* of once sacrosanct myths about wartime France, with the revelations about former President Mitterrand's role under Vichy and the recent Papon trial prolonging a 'passé qui ne passe pas' which sits ill with Gaullist and Resistance nostalgia and collective, i.e. selective, memory of the period.

New torches for old? Contemporary cultural and iconographical signifiers

There have, however, been some attempts to react positively to the changing situation, and to develop more diverse and pluralist forms of French identity which, without surrendering the central role of state institutions, would afford greater freedom of cultural practice. Mitterrand's first Culture Minister, Jack Lang, recognized and worked hard to establish a cultural 'droit à la différence'. Despite its imperfections, misjudgements in application and wilder manifestations, this idea has made considerable progress, though one commentator has argued that the policy has merely changed the French from inheritors of a culture into commercial consumers of a market-segmented and necessarily ephemeral product (Fumaroli 1991, 33). In a market-led world in which France's younger generation is probably as aware of Coca-Cola and Adidas as of Chambourcy and the Renault Twingo, Fumaroli may have a point. Marketing of a different kind, combining images of plurality with a distinctly homogenizing spin, was central to the remarkable video-clip compilation devised for Mitterrand's presidential campaign in 1981. This evoked iconic 'French' citizens from Afro-Caribbean or Afro-American roots (such as Toussaint l'Ouverture and Josephine Baker), as well as French dynamism and ingenuity (its exploits in engineering and space exploration, from the pre-war Citroën 'traction avant' to today's Ariane and the TGV, etc.). And in celebrating national know-how, flair, style and sexiness, the Mitterrand video sought to celebrate unity in diversity, to foster a sense of *collective because cumulative* belonging from which no-one could feel – or would wish to feel – omitted, a kind of identifying 'feel French, feel good' factor. This was also part of the inspiration of Jean Paul Goude's elaborately choreographed bi-centenary parade on the Champs-Elysées in 1989, which brought together groups from other countries and France's former colonies; flowingly draped in the three colours, the black American singer Jessye Norman sang the Marseillaise at the obelisk on Place de la Concorde.

Whether such events mean that the 'génération Mitterrand' feels more French or simply, to borrow a British political expression, more 'at ease with itself', remains a moot point. It is true that in France as in other modern societies, inclusiveness is an ideal as yet unrealized for the poor, the underprivileged, those of low educational attainment and skills, those 'marginaux' against whom right-wing xenophobia often finds a ready public. And national identity as expressed in citizenship has had its ups and downs, with successive tightening, loosening and re-tightening of the criteria for French nationality in 1986 (the 'lois Pasqua'), 1988 and 1993. But women are more equal, more wholly citizens than ever before, as legal reforms in the 1970s and 1980s consolidated the bridgehead achieved in the medico-legal and human rights sphere by the 1967 and 1975 liberalization of contraception and abortion. There is always some mismatch between reality and the ideal self-image(s) encoded in iconography, and Mitterrand's successors of centre-left and centre-right have by and large followed the same route with policies designed where possible to encourage social inclusion and foster a sense of unity.

An important part of that process is coming to terms with the past and repairing the 'broken mirror' (Rousso 1987, 118–54) essential to the articulation of a renewed sense of national identity. In 1993, the first Sunday after 16 July was designated a 'Journée nationale à la mémoire des victimes des persécutions racistes et antisémites commises sous l'autorité de fait dite "gouvernement de l'Etat français" 1940–44' (Barcellini and Wieviorka 1995, 452) and a poignant group memorial was inaugurated on the Quai de Grenelle to the victims of the 'rafle du Vel d'Hiv'. (The Vel d'Hiv [Vélodrome d'Hiver] was an indoor cycle track: on 16–17 July 1942, with the co-operation of the Vichy authorities and the Paris police, the Germans rounded up some 13 000 French Jews, including some 4000 children, who were imprisoned there for five days prior to deportation.) In 1995, President Chirac said that France as a whole had to assume responsibility for her history and no longer blame Holocaust complicity on the Vichy regime. During the same period, a commemorative line was drawn under a more recent national wound, the Algerian war, with a memorial in the 19th *arrondissement*. At the other end of the country, on the seafront at Fréjus-Saint-Raphael, a memorial was erected in 1994 to the colonial Armée Noire d'Afrique whose members fought for France in both world wars. It was inaugurated by the then mayor of Fréjus and Defence Minister François Léotard, a longstanding local campaigner against the extreme right in an area where the Front National continues to harbour political ambitions. In this context, the unambiguous negritude of the bronze figures and Léopold Sedar Senghor's engraved reminder to the passer-by that 'ils sont tombés fraternellement unis pour que tu restes Français' is ironic as well as eloquent.

Old symbols remain potent. It is inconceivable that France would ever abandon the tricolour flag or the republican imagery on the stamps and the currency, though it is going to lose the franc to the euro. In fashion model Laetitia Casta, Marianne, previously represented by screen actresses Bardot and Deneuve, has acquired a more contemporary 'look' and incurred the disapproval of iconographical historian Maurice Agulhon, who found the republican effigy 'travestie par le système médiatique et commercial' (*Le Nouvel Observateur*, 14–20 October, 1999). Since 'Marianne' is usually chosen by France's 30 000-plus mayors, the overwhelming majority of whom are male, her commercial exploitation also has more traditional roots: as Trouillas has shown (1988, 201–75), Marianne as sexual fantasy has a long pedigree. Casta received further national consecration in being chosen to play the lead role in the television adaptation of Régine Desforges's rather sentimental Resistance novel, *La Bicyclette bleue* (1973). But if one commune (Fremainville, Val d'Oise) has adopted a black

Marianne as a means of promoting racial integration, there is as yet little concession to ethnic diversity in these socio-cultural representations: and while a recent film about immigrant culture and family life is entitled *Hexagone* (Malik Chibane, 1994), by rights Gavroche should by now have metamorphosed into a 'beur' from one of France's *cités* or at the very least have acquired an Afro hairstyle. Displaced from the 100 franc note after a long reign, Delacroix's 'Liberty' continues to enjoy favour as a template for cartoonists on both sides of the channel, but that itself suggests that a certain image of Frenchness is an object of cultural consumption (for the record, Manet's *Le Déjeuner sur l'Herbe* comes a close second in Britain).

Institutions and organizations with a relationship with the state or historic 'national' traditions such as the SNCF and Air France (created in the 1930s) remain distinctively French, though the latter, like many other national 'flag carriers' (the once dominant British Airways is no exception), has proved vulnerable to high costs and overheads in a competitive market and has had to retrench. Re-branding, the attempt to identify change of substance with change of style, is however more readily espoused in Britain than in France. As it decelerates from the Channel Tunnel and runs over old-fashioned, overcrowded English tracks to Waterloo, Eurostar merely showcases the best of French and the worst of 'Cool Britannia'. The very success

Figure 12.2   Military service rebadged: new-look Marianne and SN logo at the garrison offices in Metz.

of the TGV, which has put a number of major towns and cities within two hours of Paris and will shortly link Paris-Lyon and Turin, has shrunk the 'Hexagon', profoundly transforming 'the individual's relationship to, and perception of, space' (Forbes and Hewlett 1994, 375). As European region-alization increases and new transnational groupings appear (l'espace Saar-Lorr-Lux) in an increasingly global market exploding into the frontier-free zone of cyberspace and electronic commerce, it may be that totalizing national identities – like old-fashioned gender ones – will outlive their use-fulness. But that such identities continue to exercise a powerful fascination for many of France's citizens and politicians, advertisers and media people, parties and groups of diverse ages and interests, was underlined by France's victory in the 1998 World Cup (cf. chapter 13) under the inspirational lead-ership of Zinedine Zidane, son of an immigrant grocer, which enabled the national team to redefine 'les trois couleurs' as 'black, blanc, beur'. France may no longer be an 'exception' in many ways; its capacity for creating new forms of 'exceptionalness', for re-aligning the national and the interna-tional, the central and the local, and for directing diversity towards identity, continues nonetheless to surprise.

References

BARCELLINI, Serge and WIEVIORKA, Annette 1995: *Passant, souviens-toi! Les Lieux du Souvenir de la Seconde Guerre Mondiale en France*. Paris: Plon.

FORBES, Jill and HEWLETT, Nick 1994: *Contemporary France. Essays on politics, economics and society*. London and New York: Longman.

FUMAROLI, Marc 1991: *L'Etat culturel. Essai sur une religion moderne*. Paris: Editions de Fallois.

KIDD, William 1998: Iconography. In HUGHES, Alex and READER, Keith (eds), *Encyclopedia of contemporary French culture*. London: Routledge, 290–92.

KIDD, William 1999: *Les Monuments aux morts mosellans de 1870 à nos jours*. Metz: Editions Serpenoise.

ROUSSO, Henry 1987: *Le Syndrome de Vichy de 1944 à nos jours*. Paris: Editions du Seuil.

TROUILLAS, Paul 1988: *Le Complexe de Marianne*. Paris: Seuil, l'Histoire immé-diate.

PART

V

*FRENCH CULTURAL
PRODUCTION AT THE
TURN OF THE
TWENTY-FIRST CENTURY*

|13|

Sport and identity in the new France

BY PHILIP DINE

Introduction: French sport in its cultural context

The historic French victory in the football World Cup on 12 July 1998 was achieved in the magnificent setting of the new, purpose-built 'Stade de France' at Saint-Denis in the Paris suburbs. A monument to the technical expertise, the aesthetic vision and the political self-belief of the modern Fifth Republic, it sits well beside such iconic edifices as the Arc de Triomphe and the Tour Eiffel, as well as more recent examples of *grands travaux* (major public works). Also significant was the ease of France's 3–0 win. Although a French team had never previously been involved in a World Cup final, and in spite of the fact that *les Bleus* (the Blues) had effectively been written off before the competition had even begun by the national sports daily *L'Equipe*, manager Aimé Jacquet's side ran out convincing winners over the reigning champions and hot favourites, Brazil.

Football was in fact a fairly late arrival in France, where historically certain sports have developed a very specific cultural resonance. While traditional pursuits such as hunting, shooting and fishing still maintain their age-old appeal, particularly in rural areas, more recently introduced games now dominate French leisure, both as participant activities and, ever more importantly, as televised spectacles. While many such sports were imported from Britain in the later nineteenth century (such as athletics, or association and rugby football), others were indigenous creations. Thus, the annual Tour de France cycle race is a genuinely French invention, and, moreover, constitutes the nation's greatest sporting celebration of unity in diversity. France has also played a particularly significant role in the development of tennis, winter sports, and Alpine mountaineering. The ranks of France's officially licensed leisure sportsmen and sportswomen – some 2 million footballers, 1.3 million tennis-players, 625 000 skiers, 140 000 athletes, and 140 000 mountain sports enthusiasts, among other *licenciés* (Frémy and Frémy 1995, 1730b) – are swollen by the much greater numbers of walkers, joggers, swimmers, cyclists and the like who prefer to take their exercise outside formal associations and federations. More numerous still are the millions of armchair followers of the country's sporting heroes; for all of the sports cited here have, at various times, served as a focus for the expression of pride in the French nation. The social significance attributed to the achievements of such star performers will provide the principal focus for the following discussion of French sport in its cultural context at the turn of the twenty-first century.

This chapter adopts as its basic premise the view that 'sport, whether it be through nostalgia, mythology, invented or selected traditions, contributes to a quest for identity be it local, regional, cultural or global' (Jarvie and Walker 1994, 7). Modern games thus play a significant role in the construction and reconstruction of a variety of personal and collective identities. From the individual player or spectator to national and transnational communities, sport is instrumental in shaping the way we imagine ourselves and our relationships with the world in which we live. The specific psychological and sociological mechanisms at work in this continuous process of identity-negotiation are beyond the scope of this study, which will examine aspects of the complex relationship between sport and what Lincoln Allison (1998) has called 'civil society', including particularly ethnicity and gender. Rejecting the still-widespread belief that sport is 'independent' of politics, or that it merely 'reflects' the structures of the wider society in which it occurs, my discussion proceeds from the altogether more productive thesis that 'sport creates interests, principles and meanings which do not exist if there is no sport and which have an effect on other aspects of society' (Allison 1998, 709–10). The most dramatic example of competitive sport's wide-ranging social significance – and thus its distinctive contribution to the national culture – is also the most recent. To return to the home nation's victory in the 1998 World Cup competition, this provides a powerful illustration of the way in which the performances of elite athletes may be appropriated as vehicles of broader communal aspirations.

France '98: the 'rainbow nation' *à la française*

A major part of the cultural significance of France '98 lay in the wave of popular enthusiasm which followed the victory, and which was itself actively encouraged by leading members of the French government. (Gaullist) President Jacques Chirac, (Socialist) Prime Minister Lionel Jospin, and (Communist) Minister for Youth and Sport Marie-George Buffet, although from rival political parties, joined together to support the national side by attending the match. The government shrewdly declared the day following the victory a public holiday, effectively linking the celebrations to the annual national festivities on *le 14 juillet*. In this, as in the organization of France '98 as a whole, the French government demonstrated the continuing moral and material investment made by the state in sport. It thus followed a pattern set by the wartime Vichy regime, which established France's first Ministry of Sport, while General de Gaulle's modernizing administration of the later 1950s and 1960s thoroughly overhauled the national sports infrastructure and its systems of management (Dine 1998). Success in major international competitions was always to be welcomed, as the General, that pragmatic promoter of *la France qui gagne* (triumphant France) in all available domains, realized only too well. However, in 1998 there was a very specific reason for the enthusiasm with which the politicians associated themselves with the national team's victory: the success of the Blues was 'read' as a victory for social inclusion and ethnic integration. The British newspaper *The Guardian* caught the mood of the country very effectively, drawing attention to the deeper social significance of the victory and the national partying which followed it: 'The success of France's multi-racial team on the field, and their unprecedented support off it, have sparked a sense of unity in a country that has grappled with recession and unemployment, racial and social divides, and the loss of old world certainties that it did much to shape' (Henley 1998).

Much of the political and journalistic rhetoric surrounding France's victory was reminiscent of the 'rainbow nation' discourse which had been generated in response to the victory of the host nation, South Africa, in the 1995 rugby union World Cup. At that time, the very visible support given to the overwhelmingly white home side by the country's first post-apartheid president, Nelson Mandela, was seen as a vote of confidence in a genuinely multi-racial future (Riordan and Krüger 1999, 244). In a similar way, even the most politically conservative of France's national daily newspapers, *Le Figaro*, joined in the general celebration of the victorious French team's ethnic diversity, thereby distancing itself from the extreme-right Front National. Although normally an astute populist, the party's leader Jean-Marie Le Pen had conspicuously failed to appreciate the public mood, going so far as to criticize the racial constitution of the national side earlier in the competition. For its part, the morning after the famous victory (13 July), *Le Figaro* hailed the varied origins of the French side, which included Breton and Basque Frenchmen among its 'metropolitan' contingent, alongside players whose family roots lay in Armenia, Guadeloupe, New Caledonia, West Africa, or even further afield (cf. O'Donnell and Blain 1999).

The cross-party consensus behind this rhetoric of sporting and social integration may also usefully be contrasted with the racism which continues to be associated with some French football clubs, and most obviously Paris Saint-Germain, based in the former national stadium at the Parc des Princes (Dine 1994, 253–55). Intriguingly, very few of the victorious 1998 French team were actually based in France, with most contracted to clubs involved in the (far stronger) domestic league competitions in Italy, Spain, Germany, and Great Britain. They thus reflected the considerable personal mobility characteristic of modern sports stars, itself a product of the commercially driven globalization of leisure. However, the foreign-based players had acquired valuable international experience on which to draw when they represented the nation in France '98. A key figure in this respect was the team's play-maker and 1998 World Footballer of the Year, the Juventus player of Algerian Kabyle origin, Zinedine Zidane. Brought up in Marseille, Zidane, or 'Zizou', as he is more popularly known, played the leading role both in France's World Cup victory and, crucially, in its cultural inflection. He not only guided the team to the final and then scored the first two of the three goals which ensured victory, he represented the most disaffected of France's ethnic minority populations, the so-called *beurs*: young North Africans of the second or subsequent generations, the great majority of whom are French citizens and were, like Zidane, actually born in France. It is this group primarily that 'indigenous' French people have in mind when talking about 'immigrants', particularly when they evoke the problems of unemployment and criminality habitually associated with non-European immigration. Against this background, Zidane has provided a positive role model and an iconic figure with whom all but the most extreme sections of French political opinion can identify. He was the star performer *Le Figaro* had in mind on 14 July 1998: 'Thank you France's overseas territories, thank you Africa. And thank you twice over Kabylia'. By the same token, it is the wholly positive figure of Zidane which underpins the optimistic editorial statement in the same issue that 'France is multiracial and will remain so'. Noëlle Chesnais, a 32-year-old (female) social worker interviewed by *The Guardian*, underlines the widespread view that 'For all France to come together like this, around a team of so many colours that represents our future – you have to celebrate it' (Henley 1998).

It is interesting to note that French football has long been regarded as a significant vector for the 'integration' (variously defined) of immigrant communities. The great Raymond Kopa, the star of Reims, Real Madrid, and the French national side in the 1950s, and perhaps the greatest ever French footballer, was the son of a family of Polish immigrant mineworkers (Lanfranchi and Wahl 1996). More recently, Michel Platini, who led France to a European Championship win in 1984 and a World Cup semi-final in 1986, and who was a key figure in the organization of the France '98 competition, represents the French game's long-standing Italian connection. The great difference with Zidane is that he comes from the ethnic minority most often held to be 'unassimilable' by commentators on French society, largely as a result of the North Africans' Muslim religion and culture. Whether or not Zidane's achievements on the field will help to deliver the social inclusion currently lacked by many other members of his ethnic community remains to be seen. However, some pioneering research in the underprivileged districts of the Lyon conurbation gives grounds for believing that sport may, indeed, have a concrete and positive impact on the evolution of French society. More specifically, the independent organization of sports such as street-football and street-basketball by youth of ethnic minority origin has been shown to be an important stage in the development of an awareness of citizenship and thus a sense of belonging to the wider community. In a recent project funded by the Ministry of Social Affairs, Health, and Urban Planning, the researchers came to the following conclusion:

> Contrary to what traditional views might lead one to think, young people playing self-organized sports in DSUs [underprivileged urban districts] do not form groups on the basis of ethnic origin... Such activities are not, in fact, a sign of social disorganization or lawlessness, but rather of social reintegration.
>
> Chantelat et al. 1996, 151–6

In fact, it would appear from this innovative research that street sports-players of ethnic minority origin regard themselves as young, first and foremost – rather than black or brown or, for that matter, white – and that their self-organized sporting activities do, consequently, contribute to the emergence of forms of citizenship, in so far as they offer both a motive for and a means of negotiating rights and responsibilities with the wider local community (for instance, access to municipal facilities or involvement in formalized competitions). This would seem to offer grounds for real hope at the 'micro' level, just as the example of Zinedine Zidane bodes well for the future on the 'macro' level of the French nation-state.

Les Françaises qui gagnent: the representation of French sportswomen

As stated above, in founding the Fifth Republic, General de Gaulle made it his mission to restore French grandeur and influence in all available spheres: military, diplomatic, economic, technological, and, indeed, sporting. France's poor showing at the 1960 (Rome) Olympics triggered a state-managed and publicly-funded promotion of both mass-participatory and elite sport. Through the newly established High Commission for Youth, Sport, and Leisure – headed by the conqueror of Annapurna, the celebrated mountaineer Maurice Herzog – de Gaulle launched a programme of building, coaching, and teaching which was intended to turn France into a world force in competitive sport. The conspicuous success of French athletes at the 1996 (Atlanta) Olympic Games (where they won 37 medals, including no less than 15 golds, to take fifth place overall) may be regarded as the slowly maturing fruit of this ambitious programme, after steady progress from Seoul in 1988 and Barcelona in 1992; hopes are high of similar success at Sydney in 2000.

France's star competitor at Atlanta and, with the American sprinter Michael Johnson, one of the two outstanding athletes of the 1996 Games was the double gold medal winner Marie-José Pérec. In Pérec, issues of gender and ethnicity come together, and we shall return to her case as one of a group of iconic sportswomen (with Suzanne Lenglen, Marielle and Christine Goitschel, 'Kiki' Caron and Catherine Destivelle) who cast useful light on the evolving role of sport in the 'negotiation' of female identities in France.

It will be apparent from the foregoing discussion that the focus in French sport, both in terms of participation and, even more obviously, cultural representation, is more often on male rather than female performers. The chronic failure of the Tour (de France) féminin to attract significant spectator or sponsor interest, in spite of the sustained success over two decades of the leading French cyclist Jeannie Longo-Ciprelli, bears this out particularly clearly. In this sporting gender bias, 'sport as male hegemony' (Horrocks 1995, 151–2), France is typical of western Europe and, indeed, much of the 'developed' world. Jennifer Hargreaves argues that sport may be regarded as 'a repository for dominant ideology in its celebration of ruthless nationalism, racism, militarism, imperialism and sexism' (1990, 295; cited in Horrocks 1995, 147). This does not mean, however, that sport is inherently incapable of serving as a vehicle for more positive ideological messages, as the celebration of France's ethnic diversity in the summer of 1998 shows. If sport is a 'site of struggle', both real and symbolic, it is also a place where victories can, from time to time, be achieved by the forces of social progress, victories whose impact may transcend the specific location and moment of the sporting event. In what follows, we shall focus on the social exclusion historically experienced by French sportswomen, and will identify a number of cases where female stars have provided positive role models comparable to that offered to male youth of ethnic minority origin by the iconic Zinedine Zidane.

It is interesting to note that French women were particularly privileged by journalists in their reporting of the social impact of the success in France '98 of 'Zizou' and his team-mates. In the build-up to the final, Françoise Inizan reflected a broader tendency in the French media when she hailed 'our mums, our sisters, and our cousins: they didn't have a clue what Marcel Desailly or Didier Deschamps even looked like a month ago, but they're now mad about tactics and footballing jargon, and can't wait to get stuck in front of the television screen and wildly supporting their beloved boys' (*L'Equipe Magazine*, 1998). That an estimated 30 per cent of the French television audience for France '98 were women seems to suggest that there was at least a grain of truth in this view, although one should be wary of assuming that the mere fact of viewing bears out the media stereotype of female 'fandom' articulated by Inizan and her (overwhelmingly male) colleagues.

We have already referred to the 'supporting role' played by Marie-George Buffet as Minister of Youth and Sport at the time of France's World Cup victory. She was thus following in the footsteps of other senior female politicians and administrators, including the only other woman incumbent of her post, Edwige Avice. A striking example of the successful conversion of an elite performer into an influential manager is provided by Monique Berlioux, a semi-finalist in the 100-metres backstroke at the 1948 (London) Olympic Games who subsequently combined a very successful career as a coach (notably of 'Kiki' Caron, see below) with her work as a journalist on *Le Figaro*, before becoming an outstanding administrator. She became Maurice Herzog's press officer in the early 1960s and played a similar role for the International Olympic Committee in Lausanne from 1967. Rising rapidly within the organization, she was effectively responsible for its running by the early 1970s, and continued to play this role under successive presidents of the IOC – Avery Brundage, Lord Killanin, and Juan-Antonio Samaranch – until 1988. This career at the highest level and across three decades has led to her being compared with the senior politician Simone Veil as one of the rare French women to play a leading role on the international political stage (Laget, Laget and Mazot 1982, 6).

When we consider French women as iconic performers, the obvious first reference must be to Suzanne Lenglen, the champion tennis player, and France's first internationally renowned sports star, irrespective of gender. As Richard Holt has pointed out, citing Simone de Beauvoir, 'tennis was really the only form of exercise permissible to well-bred young women in the early twentieth century' (1981, 178). Even then, doubts were expressed about the compatibility of Lenglen's achievements with femininity as conventionally conceived. French national champion for the first of six times in 1914 at the age of fifteen, Lenglen 'went on to win Wimbledon each year from 1919 to 1925, when she dropped only four games in the entire championship, after which she turned professional for a fee rumoured to be over a hundred thousand dollars' (Holt 1981, 178). Lenglen's international stardom – nowadays, 'superstardom' – earned her regular appearances on the front covers of French, British, and American newspapers and magazines (Clerici 1984, *passim*). However, this conspicuous success had a price in terms of social approval:

> Lenglen was ... labelled as a rebel. ... Whereas athleticism has always been a popular symbol of masculinity, sportswomen have had to deal with the constant tension between freer uses of the body and acceptable images of femininity. The focus of opposition to Suzanne Lenglen was her sexuality – opposition to her tennis dresses which made possible an image of the 'real' body underneath and which allowed her to move energetically so that people caught glimpses of parts that 'respectable' ladies never made visible in public. Some Wimbledon spectators were excited by her radical image; others walked out on account of her 'indecency'.
>
> Hargreaves 1994, 116–7

In time, of course, Lenglen's innovations as regards styles of both dress and play – she was considerably more mobile and athletic than her opponents –

would be accepted as the norm, and the prevailing male-defined image of sporting femininity would be effectively renegotiated in women's favour. For, as Jennifer Hargreaves points out, male hegemony has never been absolute in sports: 'In spite of the historic subordination of women, it has always been possible for outstanding female athletes to assert themselves and to disrupt conventional images of femininity' (1994, 116). However, the struggle for gender redefinition has always been a hard one, and has had to be waged anew by each generation of sportswomen. This will be seen as we conclude our survey by looking at two examples from the state-managed development of French sport in the 1960s and two examples from the overtly commodified and globalized sports market of the end of the twentieth century.

As France gradually became the 'civilisation du loisir' described by Joffre Dumazedier in 1962 and the 'société de consommation' identified by Jean Baudrillard in 1970, sport became an integral part of the aspirations of many of its citizens as well as an affair of state whose social significance is nicely brought out by a collection of illustrated books for children published in Hachette's 'Bibliothèque verte' series. *Huit champions français* (1964) and *Nos champions* (1969) provide a series of exciting narratives of youthful sporting achievement, with the emphasis placed firmly on national pride and the desirability of emulation: 'Five boys and five girls [*sic*] have made the colours of France shine out in the peaceful battles of sport. . . . This book tells their story: why and how they, although still very young, have become stars that we admire and wish to imitate'. Alongside such still well known sportsmen as the cyclist Jacques Anquetil and the footballer Raymond Kopa, we find a number of French sportswomen, all of whom have, perhaps symptomatically, been less well treated by posterity. However, the Goitschel sisters, Marielle and Christine, are worthy of commemoration as the teenage stars of the 1964 Winter Olympics at Innsbruck. Their success as the first French women ever to win an Olympic skiing title (they each won a gold and a silver) was duly marked by the French media and by that champion of *la France qui gagne*, General de Gaulle, who sent the pair a telegram of congratulation (Baudouin 1964, 65–66).

However, Marielle's relations with the French sporting press were often strained, and particularly by the emphasis it placed on her allegedly 'unfeminine' appearance and behaviour. This included her habit of addressing journalists and senior French sports administrators by the familiar 'tu' rather than the polite 'vous' form – including, famously, the High Commissioner for Sport himself, Maurice Herzog – as well, once again, as her dress sense. In *Huit champions français*, Marielle is given the opportunity to 'set the record straight':

> People have often described me as an unrefined mountain girl, lacking in femininity, and always in trousers. [. . .] But that's not true . . . like all young girls, I like pretty things . . . I've got dresses and I wear them

all summer long. I know how to knit and to cook ... I often help
Mum, I do it all the time when I'm at home.

Baudouin 1964, 69–70

Like Suzanne Lenglen, Marielle Goitschel thus felt obliged to conform to the
familiar stereotype of dutiful and submissive femininity in order to counter
the almost equally common image of the 'unfeminine' female sports star. In
comparison, Christine Caron, dubbed *l'enfant sage* (the good little girl) of
French swimming (Baudouin 1964, 109–42) appears to have been relatively
gently treated by the sporting press. Nicknamed 'Kiki', Caron was not yet
fifteen years old when she broke her first European record (for the 100-
metres backstroke) in 1963. Encouraged by her mother and her elder sister
Annie, who was also a national swimming champion, and trained by
Monique Berlioux, Caron became the focus of intense media interest with a
series of European records and, aged sixteen, a silver medal at the 1964
(Tokyo) Olympic Games. However, as with Marielle Goitschel, press coverage seemed less concerned to publicize her dazzling performances than to
make her conform to a preconceived model of youthful femininity. Having
confessed to a liking for the pop singers Claude François and Richard
Anthony and to knowing how to dance the twist and the hully-gully, she
was subjected to speculation that she was a dedicated rocker and night-
clubber, much to the chagrin of her mother (Baudouin 1964, 131). Whether
the elite sportswoman is depicted as a tomboy or as (potentially, at least) a
rebellious teenager, we are still in a symbolic realm which would be familiar
to Suzanne Lenglen.

In the second volume in the collection, such familiar male stars as the
round-the-world yachtsman Eric Tabarly, the much-loved cyclist Raymond
Poulidor and the monumental rugby player Walter Spanghero are joined by
'the two "gazelles" of French sport', Colette Besson and Roger Bambuck
(Baudouin 1969, 7–19). Besson, the surprise winner of the 400-metres
sprint at the 1968 (Mexico) Olympic Games, later became a friend and
adviser to Marie-José Pérec, who would thus benefit from the experience of
this first French female track star. Like Pérec, Bambuck is a black athlete
from the wholly assimilated French Caribbean territory of Guadeloupe, and
a product of the National Institute of Sport and Physical Education
(INSEP). Though his performances in Mexico City were less spectacular –
fifth place in both the 100 and 200 metres, with a bronze medal as the
anchorman of the 4 × 100 metres relay team – he later became Minister of
Sport on the strength of his track achievements, following the trail blazed by
his predecessors Borotra, Herzog and Guy Drut, winner of the 1964
(Tokyo) 110-metres hurdles. Bambuck's subsequent itinerary is all the more
remarkable in that this was the Olympic Games, and his was the specific
event (the 200-metres sprint), in which the American athletes Tommy Smith
and John Carlos made their famous 'Black Power' salutes on the winners'
podium (Riordan and Krüger 1999, 20 and 169), an episode to which, pre-

dictably, our children's volume makes no reference. Nonetheless, the alternative visions of the routes to ethnic minority empowerment at this watershed in post-war French and world history provided by these very different black athletes is striking.

Marie-José Pérec: sexualization, fragmentation, trivialization

By coincidence, Marie-José Pérec was born in 1968, the year of Bambuck's and Besson's Olympics. It was also, of course, the year of the quasi-revolutionary 'events' in the Latin Quarter of Paris which marked the end of the social consensus generated by the post-war economic boom, and the establishment of radically different political agendas, including particularly those of the women's movement and ethnic minority groups. Brought up by her single mother and maternal grandmother in a poor district of Basse-Terre, Guadeloupe, Pérec moved to France at the age of sixteen to pursue her career in athletics. Her first major success came in the 400 metres at the world championships in Tokyo in 1991, when she became the first French winner of such a prize. This was followed by her victory over the same distance at the 1992 (Barcelona) Olympics, and by her double victory in the 200 and 400 metres, the latter in a new Olympic record time (48.25s) at Atlanta in 1998. This outstanding record has made her the highest paid French athlete in history, with her appearance fee estimated at 200 000 francs (£20 000) per meeting in 1996 (Frémy and Frémy 1996, 2166).

However, Pérec's case demonstrates once again that elite sportswomen still need to struggle for the social recognition that would be granted automatically to their male counterparts. More specifically, her high profile has demonstrated the ease with which female sport in particular is subsumed by a media-led cult of glamour:

> The emergent meaning of sport is glamour. Since capital really moved to dominate the realm of leisure once post-war reconstruction was done, sport has become the vehicle of glamour, and sporting stars the essential bearers of the imagery whose dazzling accomplishments are cut out and reproduced as the flashing icon of the ads.
>
> Inglis 1988, 138

Thus *L'Equipe*'s front-page splash about Pérec's victory in the 1991 world championships in Tokyo was accompanied not by an action shot or a standard image of the triumphant victor, but by a close-up photograph of the athlete's buttocks clad in tight-fitting lycra. This was a particularly flagrant example of the fragmentation and sexualization of the female athlete's body, common in France and elsewhere, which tends to trivialize sportswomen and their achievements and reflects 'the power of media representations to

contain and naturalize women's sport and women athletes within the permissible spaces of sexual difference, female heterosexuality, and consumer
culture' (Hall 1996, 42; cf. Hargreaves 1994, 160). So angered was Pérec by
this representation that she devoted the press conference which followed her
1992 Olympic victory to an attack on the attitude of the French press to the
nation's female sports stars, stating that her pride as an athlete had been too
badly wounded to allow her to do otherwise, asking 'Is there a woman in
the world who would not have understood my position?' (1993, 176–7). It
is true that Pérec has, at times, agreed to do what would be regarded as
'glamour' work, such as modelling, but only on her own terms, insisting on
a strict separation of genres and refusing to engage in any such activity if her
sporting career is directly referred to or otherwise implied. She has thus
managed to find her personal solution to a dilemma that would seem to face
every elite sportswoman to a greater or lesser extent, and particularly such
an obviously glamorous black athlete in the France of the 1990s. Against
this backdrop, Pérec may instructively be compared with another French
sporting icon, Catherine Destivelle. An elite exponent of what Paul Yonnet
has identified as the move towards the 'extreme' in French sport (Yonnet
1998, 221–46), she is also an expert player of the complex game with the
media and marketing executives which characterizes the life of the modern
sports star.

The rise and rise of a 'rock queen'

Arguably the world's leading female climber, Catherine Destivelle was World
Indoor Climbing Champion four years in succession, and has made winter
solo ascents of the North Faces of the Eiger and the Matterhorn, as well as
having a distinguished record of achievement in the Himalayas. She also scaled
'The Old Man of Hoy', a celebrated pillar of rock off the Scottish coast, solo,
whilst three months pregnant. Like Pérec, Destivelle combines outstanding
achievement with obvious good looks. However, where the runner is a star in
one of the most traditionally codified and conventionally hierarchical of sports,
the 'rock queen' – as Destivelle is familiarly known – dominates a discipline
where the emphasis is on individual organization and initiative. This is part
of the appeal of 'extreme' sporting practices, which in addition to a range of
mountain sports include ocean yacht-racing, in which the French sailor
Florence Arthaud excels. The growth of such activities is probably a response
by the sporting elite to the rapid popularization in the 1980s and 1990s of
'sports that yield a heady sensation of speed and mastery of the elements'
(Prost and Vincent 1991, 91), such as off-piste skiing, snowboarding and wind-
surfing. Elite performers constantly seek to extend the bounds of the possible, often at considerable personal risk, as we are reminded by the death in
1995 of the British climber Alison Hargreaves, the first woman to climb Mount
Everest unaided and without oxygen. The criticisms which surfaced in the UK

press following the death of this 'British mother of two' are a reminder also of the social pressures faced by elite female performers.

Destivelle's climbing adventures have been sponsored not only by the sort of companies one might expect, such as the outdoor equipment manufacturer Lafuma, but also by Poivre Blanc (women's fashion), Whirlpool (washing-machines), and Neutrogena (hand-cream). Technical achievement is thus associated not only with the familiar female sporting glamour, but also a rather more mundane model of femininity. Destivelle's account (Destivelle and Decamp 1994, 80) of Whirlpool's motivations is particularly revealing: 'Whirlpool uses my image for the "successful woman" [*la femme qui gagne*], the woman who is on the way up. The brand is hoping to reach housewives by giving a new value to their position.'

Whether or not such marketing strategies actually improve the lot of female homemakers, their very existence tells us something about the perceived linkage between elite performers and their audiences. However wide the objective gap between the sports star and his or her public, an affective link is established between the supposedly self-creating actions of the housewife as consumer, and those of the star performer. Splashing out on a new washing-machine (or, presumably, if money is tight, opting for a different brand of hand-cream) thus becomes a more or less conscious act of identity-construction, containing at least a trace of '[the] "purposefulness without purpose" by which Kant defined the aesthetic [and which] is as readily found in games as in art' (Inglis 1988, 132). While this conception of the post-modern 'game' or 'art' of shopping may not convince all observers of modern French culture, there can be little doubt that both Destivelle's exploits and the marketing campaigns which help to pay for them are justified in terms of the prevailing post-war ethic of consumerist individualism, in that they are presented as valid expressions of rational personal choices made by conscious and confident individuals. We are here at the heart of the paradoxical world of the elite sportsman or sportswoman, the 'star system' where 'the sporting and entertainment worlds intersect' (Inglis 1977, 189):

> The stars make fortunes inasmuch as other people make fortunes out of them. And stars have become the success heroes of their time. The sporting stars sit easily beside the film and pop stars. They are all young, and they are all classless. [...] The stars are like a combination of travelling gunslinger and the people's hero. The vast payments instil not envy or resentment, but hope. The stars look down, and many others look up and say, this man, this woman, is ours.
>
> Inglis 1988, 134–5

Conclusion

Perhaps the most striking feature of French sporting culture at the turn of the twenty-first century is the increasing disjunction between mass sporting participation and elite competition: the post-war vision of 'sport for all' – or, at least, all who wish – may have become a reality, but the worlds of the star practitioner and the non-elite participant are further removed than ever. Yet, paradoxically, the moral and material investment made by millions of 'ordinary' French citizens in Zidane, Pérec, Destivelle and other elite performers may have a positive impact as regards their individual and collective quests for identity in the new millennium. The achievements of the superstars do, after all, provide examples of outstanding French success in a cultural domain which has not always been properly valued as part of the national heritage or *patrimoine*. If Zizou's mass-produced image helps to convince a generation of the merits of physical culture – in the face of the intense competition for leisure time of both 'high' cultural forms and, increasingly, electronic and/or 'virtual' media – then the gap between superstar and street-player may have been significantly narrowed.

References

ALLISON, L. 1998: Sport and civil society. *Political Studies* XLVI, 709–726.

BAUDOUIN, L. 1964: *Huit champions français.* Paris: Hachette.

BAUDOUIN, L. 1969: *Nos champions.* Paris: Hachette.

BAUDRILLARD, J. 1970: *La Société de consommation.* Paris: Denoël.

CHANTELAT, P., FODIMBI, M. and CAMY, J. 1996: *Sports de la Cité: Anthropologie de la jeunesse sportive.* Paris: L'Harmattan.

CLERICI, G. 1984: *Suzanne Lenglen: La diva du tennis.* Paris: Eds Rochevignes.

DESTIVELLE, C. and DECAMP, E. 1994: *Annapurna: Duo pour un 8 000.* Paris: Arthaud.

DINE, P. 1994: The tradition of violence in French sport. In GÜNTHER, R. and WINDEBANK, J. (eds), *Violence and conflict in modern French culture.* Sheffield: Sheffield Academic Press.

DINE, P. 1998: Sport and the state in contemporary France: from *la Charte des Sports* to decentralisation. *Modern and Contemporary France* 6/3, 301–11.

DUMAZEDIER, J. 1962: *Vers une civilisation du loisir.* Paris: Seuil.

FRÉMY, D. and FRÉMY, M. (eds) 1995: *Quid 1996.* Paris: Robert Laffont.

FRÉMY, D. and FRÉMY, M. (eds) 1996: *Quid 1997.* Paris: Robert Laffont.

HALL, M. 1996: *Feminism and sporting bodies: essays on theory and practice.* Champaigne, IL: Human Kinetics.

HARGREAVES, J. 1990: Gender on the sports agenda. *International Review for the Sociology of Sport* 25/4, 295.

HARGREAVES, J. 1994: *Sporting females: critical issues in the history and sociology of women's sports.* London: Routledge.

HENLEY, J. 1998: On top of the world: French flair leaves Brazil stunned. *The Guardian*, 13 July, 1.

HOLT, R. 1981: *Sport and society in modern France.* London: Macmillan.

HORROCKS, R. 1995: *Male myths and icons: masculinity in popular culture.* London: Macmillan.

INGLIS, F. 1977: *The name of the game: sport and society.* London: Heinemann.

INGLIS, F. 1988: *Popular culture and political power.* Brighton: Wheatsheaf Books.

INIZAN, F. 1998: Elle est à vous, cette finale. *L'Equipe Magazine*, 11 July, 18–19.

JARVIE, G. and WALKER, G. (eds) 1994: *Scottish sport in the making of the nation: ninety-minute patriots?* Leicester: Leicester University Press.

LAGET, F., LAGET, S. and MAZOT, J.-P. 1982: *Le Grand Livre du sport féminin.* Lyon: FMT Editions.

LANFRANCHI, P. and WAHL, A. 1996: The immigrant as hero: Kopa, Mekloufi and French football. In HOLT, R., MANGAN, J. and LANFRANCHI, P. (eds), *European heroes: myth, identity, sport.* London: Frank Cass, 114–27.

O'DONNELL, H. and BLAIN, N. 1999: Performing the Carmagnole: negotiating French national identity during France '98. *Journal of European Area Studies* 7.2, 211–25.

PÉREC, M.-J. 1993 (with Roland Brival): *400 mètres pour gagner.* Paris: Edition° 1.

PROST, A. and VINCENT, G. (eds) 1991: *A history of private life: 5. Riddles of identity in modern times.* Cambridge, Mass. and London: Belknap Press. (Originally published as *Histoire de la vie privée: 5. De la Première Guerre mondiale à nos jours.* Paris: Seuil.)

RIORDAN, J. and KRÜGER, A. (eds) 1999: *The international politics of sport in the 20th century.* London: Spon.

YONNET, P. 1998: *Systèmes des sports.* Paris: NRF/Gallimard.

|14|

Advertising culture in France: no Coca-Cola please, we're French!

BY ALASTAIR DUNCAN

Does advertising differ from country to country? Multinational companies are more and more standardizing their products and brand names, employing, world-wide, a single advertising agency: Levi's, Tag Heuer or Coca-Cola use the same or modified versions of the same ads in many countries. Even in France the language of the advertising industry bears strong traces of its predominantly American origin: 'les créatifs' work from 'le brief' to develop 'la copy stratégie'. American origin also explains the use of similar formulas in different countries, for instance the soap powder ad which shows a neighbour explaining to a baffled mother how she can get her washing whiter than white. Even so, an hour or two watching television from different countries will demonstrate that national styles of ads continue to differ. The settings, the way people dress, walk and gesticulate, not to mention the range of products: all these are signs waiting to be decoded by students of a foreign culture. When you go abroad you meet sets of images in the streets, in every newspaper or magazine. At home, you can beam them down from satellite, find them on the internet and compare these images with those present in your own culture. How, then, do the ads in a French number of *Marie Claire* differ from the ads in a British edition of the same magazine? What is distinctively French about French advertising and what can it tell us about French society and its values? This chapter will provide some facts about advertising in France, and then use a variety of products, mainly fashion and food, as a basis for exploring questions to do with style, values and taste.

The advertising industry

What media are used by French advertisers? How strictly is advertising in France controlled?

A comparison between the UK and France shows a broadly constant pattern of expenditure by advertisers on the different media through the 1990s. In 1997 for example, spending on television advertising was proportionately very similar in the two countries: 32.5 per cent in the UK, 34 per cent in France. French spending on television slowly climbed to that level following the creation of new commercial channels, for example Canal Plus, and the privatization of TF1 in the 1980s. Spending on magazines shows France in the lead: 18.4 per cent in the UK and 23.1 per cent in France. The French are a nation of magazine readers: television magazines, like *Télérama*, sell best, but there are also strong specialist titles, like the long-running *Le Chasseur français*; and France, like the United States, has news magazines: *Le Point, L'Express, Le Nouvel Observateur.* One reason for the relative strength of magazine advertising in France lies in the weakness of daily newspapers. British spending on newspaper advertising far exceeds French: 40.5 per cent in the UK compared with 24 per cent in France. France has no national tabloids comparable to the *Sun* or the *Star.* Only three national dailies correspond more or less to the British quality press: *Le Monde, Le Figaro,* and *Libération*; but their circulation is low compared to *The Times* or *Daily Telegraph.* The largest-selling daily in France is a regional newspaper, *Ouest France,* which sells in many locally-varied editions throughout north-western France. The relative weakness of the French national press means that national advertising tends to gravitate towards television or magazines. Radio advertising, on the other hand, is relatively strong in France: 6.6 per cent in France, 3.7 per cent in the UK. There are historical reasons for this. The so-called 'stations périphériques', broadcasting from just beyond the frontiers of France – Radio Luxembourg and Europe 1 – have a national audience and carry advertising. In addition, local private radio stations have mushroomed since being legalized in the 1980s.

Finally, special mention needs to be made of cinema and outdoor advertising. The figures for cinema are comparable and small: 0.6 per cent in France, 0.8 per cent in the UK (*European Marketing Pocketbook* 1999). But cinema advertising in France is not insignificant. For one thing, it reaches a crucial market, young people between the ages of 15 and 35. For another, cinema ads are relatively big budget: over the last twenty years a number of French film directors have either begun by making cinema or television ads or have done so to make money. Thus artistic values spill into commercial art and vice versa. The same overlap partly helps explain the relative importance of outdoor and transport advertising in France: only 4.2 per cent in the UK but 11.7 per cent in France – the highest in any other European country with the exception of Switzerland. French poster art flowered first in the nineteenth century: in the 1880s, Toulouse-Lautrec exploited advances in printing technology to produce posters advertising cabaret stars and venues – Aristide Bruant, le Divan japonais – of which copies are still sold today. The tradition continued into the first half of the twentieth century. Poster artists like Cassandre and Paul Colin signed their work and became well known in their own right. You may still see the faint outline on a gable or the wall of a metro tunnel of the famous punning slogan for an apéritif: 'Dubo ... Dubon ... Dubonnet'. In the second half of the century photography progressively displaced painting as the medium for printed advertising, and creative teams in advertising agencies took over from individual artists. Yet the tradition has left a legacy distinctive to France.

A first aspect of that legacy is the prestige attached not to the advertising industry, but to advertisements themselves. Cinema adverts from around the world are judged annually at the International Advertising Film Festival in Cannes. *Libération* has a regular column on ads, and the television channel M6 has a weekly programme, *Culture Pub*. The 'nuit des publivores' in Paris is an annual all-night marathon showing of televison and cinema ads. In all these cases the emphasis is at least as much on the entertainment or aesthetic value of ads as on their economic effectiveness. Second, French visual advertisements have a strong sense of history. They refer not just to other aspects of French culture, but also to previous advertisements. Very often this is a question of style and medium. For example, a number of magazine advertising campaigns of the 1990s – for Badoit table water and Nestlé's Sveltesse yoghurt – rejected photography in favour of coloured sketches in the style of ads of the 1950s. Third, French advertising has sometimes been accused, both from abroad and by its French business customers, of self-indulgence, of being more concerned with the creative excellence of the ad than with selling the product. Certainly, studies have shown that French television ads tend to be less centrally focused on the product, more inclined to fantasy, their messages more implicit than is the case with German TV ads (Schroeder 1991; Walliser and Moreau 1998).

The accusation of self-indulgence may say something about the style of French ads; but in the 1990s their creators have not been indifferent as to whether they work. Indeed, in the final decade of the century the French advertising industry became progressively leaner and stronger. Before 1993, French advertising agencies were traditionally paid a commission based on a percentage of what the advertiser paid to the media for space or time. It was therefore in the interest of the agency that the price should be high; and as the price was negotiated between the agency and the media, the advertiser might not even know how much was being paid. The Loi Sapin of 1993 directed that the media bill should go straight to the advertiser and that the advertiser should pay the agency. This not only made the financing of advertising campaigns more transparent, but also gave advertisers much more direct control over the work of agencies. It also favoured the large agencies who could negotiate bargain prices by buying large amounts of space (in the print media) and time (on television and radio). France and Britain are the only countries in Europe in which indigenous advertising agencies are large enough to compete with their

American-owned rivals. During the 1990s, some of the largest French agencies became ambitiously expansive. By 1998 Publicis-FCB and Euro-RSCG were respectively the first and third largest advertising agency networks in Europe (*Le Monde*, 14 July, 1999).

Despite this success, a long-standing suspicion of advertising persists in some quarters of French society, not least amongst politicians. For example, political advertising is itself strictly controlled by a law passed by the Socialist government under Prime Minister Michel Rocard in the late 1980s but not repealed by subsequent right-wing administrations. No electoral advertising in any media is allowed in the three months preceding a Presidential election or elections to the European Parliament, or in the six months prior to legislative or regional elections (Séguéla 1999, 26). This law, passed by a government fearful that it would be outspent by the opposition, also limited the amount of money to be spent on election campaigns. Officially, advertising during elections is now restricted to the posters displayed on temporary stands set up outside town halls and at other strategic sites, with equal space reserved for each political party.

In many other areas of life, too, advertising in France is more strictly controlled than in Britain or in the United States. When adverts were first introduced on French television in 1968, only four kinds of product were permitted to be advertised: foodstuffs, textiles, household electrical goods and cleansers. The reins were progressively loosened. By 1969, washing powder, cosmetics, photographic equipment and motor vehicles had been added to the list (Michel 1995, 53; Martin 1992, 335). Yet for many years it would remain true that what was not permitted was banned. Not until 1987 was this logic turned on its head: a decree (26 January) set out a list specifying which products and services were banned, implying that those not banned were permitted (Bourdon and Grunblatt 1986, 64–65). Even so, the defence of the written press, dressed up as pluralism of expression, has remained a consistent concern of French law-makers. Partly at French insistence, the European Transfrontier Broadcasting Directive of 1989 (revised in 1997) allowed member states to impose stricter limitations on what may be advertised on television than those defined in the Directive, in order to protect 'pluralism of information and of the media' (Article 19). The same theme was recapitulated in Prime Minister Jospin's general policy statement of June 1997 (Jospin 1997). Three sectors are still banned from television for reasons associated with defence of the press: first, the big supermarkets – Carrefour, Leclerc, etc. – whose nation-wide networks might tempt them to use television rather than the regional press; second, the written press itself, in case some title with strong financial backing should aim to crush its competitors; third, literary publishers, to protect the advertising revenue of the few remaining literary weeklies and periodicals.

Legal control of TV advertising and sponsorship has its basis in a decree of 27 March 1992. This lays down general requirements concerning truthfulness, decency, respect for human dignity and the protection of minors. It also stipulates that advertising may not undermine respect for the state and must not offend the religious, philosophical or political views of television viewers. Article 4 lists other prohibitions. Advertising must be free of all discrimination on grounds of race, gender or nationality, must not contain scenes of violence, and must not incite behaviour prejudicial to health, to the safety of people or property, or to the protection of the environment (BVP 1992).

The last of these prohibitions was introduced into this paragraph for the first time in 1992, bringing French law into conformity with the Transfrontier Directive. It conveyed in general terms a concern for the environment already expressed in a law passed the year before (Loi 91–2 of 3 January 1991) which made it an offence not merely to drive a motor vehicle in natural sites off the road but also to show any such scene in an advertisement.

France is particularly strict in controlling advertising on the grounds of health. Tobacco advertising was banned from television and from the other main media by the so-called Loi Veil as early as 1976; alcoholic drinks were blacklisted from television and from publications aimed at young people in 1987. Both these bans were tightened – beyond the requirements of the Transfrontier Directive – by the Loi Evin which came into effect on 1 January 1993. The main difference, as far as television was concerned, was that the new law banned 'toute propagande ou publicité, directe ou indirecte' for alcohol or tobacco products (Articles 3 I and 10 IV). In practice – and sometimes after test cases have gone through the courts – this has meant: no generic advertising; no sponsorship; no appearance of alcohol or tobacco products in advertisements for other products; no advertising of products or services using the name, logo or graphics reminiscent of tobacco or alcoholic products, for instance Peter Stuyvesant Travel or Camel Boots (Greffe and Greffe 1995, 585–86). Alcohol ads can appear on hoardings and in the press, but neither text nor image may do other than illustrate the origin of the product and describe how it should be drunk; such ads cannot show people enjoying the product. These new alcohol regulations have had a profound effect on the way alcoholic drinks are advertised on billboards and in the written press.

Advertising is also regulated for cultural reasons. The Loi Toubon of 1994 reinforced restrictions on the use of languages other than French. The main perceived threat is that of English. Foreign languages are not banned from adverts, but a translation into French must also be provided and this must be as 'legible, audible or intelligible' as the foreign language. The rule is not strictly applied in the case of slogans where they form part of the brand-image of the company (Greffe 1995, 501–07; BVP 1997). The regional languages of France appear only rarely in ads. An ad for the supermarket chain Super U, featuring on billboards in Brittany in summer 1999, illustrated both the existence and the timidity of regionalism. It used French and Breton, but 'Bienvenue en Bretagne' appeared in much larger letters than 'Deger mat Breiz'. Two forms of control protect feature films on television. On the commercial channels, from 1996, only six minutes of advertising were allowed to interrupt feature films (as opposed to nine minutes advocated by the Transfrontier Directive); on the public channels, no interruptions were allowed (CSA 1995, 81; Cluzel 1996–97, 75–76). Advertising for recent films is not allowed on television until a year after they are licensed to be shown in France (BVP 1992). This cultural measure with strong economic overtones is designed to protect the French film industry from the financial muscle and box-office appeal of American blockbusters.

As well as these legal constraints, the advertising industry in France runs its own self-regulatory system. The Bureau de Vérification de la Publicité, funded by advertisers and advertising agencies but independently run (and largely staffed by lawyers), formulates guidelines on what is acceptable, offers pre-publication advice on ads in all media and adjudicates complaints from the public and from one firm against another. Although ultimate responsibility for television ads lies with the Conseil Supérieur de l'Audiovisuel, since 1993 day-to-day authority has been delegated to the BVP: all TV ads have to be viewed and approved by the BVP before they can be screened (Franceschini 1996, 452–55; BVP 1996). The BVP's 'Recommandations', updated regularly, are revealing for what they tell about French public opinion. They are particularly firm with regard to ads aimed at children: these must not, for example, 'discredit the authority, judgement or preferences of parents'. On the other hand, they are silent on the use or abuse of animals in ads, except to require the presence of a water receptacle in ads for dry dog or cat food (BVP 1998).

Style, values and taste

Dior, Givenchy, Chanel: these and other newer names such as Jean-Paul Gaultier and Paco Rabanne give France world-wide pre-eminence in luxury products designed to enhance female beauty. Paris has had a predominant role in setting fashions in dress since the seventeenth century. The early centralization of power and wealth in Paris and the association of clothes with status at the court of Louis XIV first attracted the skills of design and craftsmanship which make fashion and its accessories possible. Above all, perhaps, fashion depends on a delight in seeing and being seen in public which the spaces of Paris provided, first in the gardens of the Palais Royal, later in opera, theatres and at racecourses. It is more surprising that Paris should have maintained its role and prestige into the later twentieth century, despite the intermittent challenges of Milan, London and New York. It has done so in part by attracting talent from elsewhere: Karl Lagerfeld at Chanel, John Galliano at Dior and Alexander McQueen at Givenchy (Steele 1998).

Advertising is scarcely necessary for *haute couture*: newspapers and magazines round the world publicize the Paris collections, their creators and top models, in text and photo. In any case there are reputed to be fewer than 2000 women who regularly buy the original creations of the couturiers. But there is advertising for the accessories of beauty and fashion, those luxury products and services which enable the many to taste by proxy the life-style of the few: scarves by Hermès, luggage by Louis Vuitton, above all perfumes, many of them produced by the same fashion houses which dominate the catwalks.

The image of France which has traditionally been projected abroad is that of sophistication. The ad for Chanel's Allure reproduced on page 190 shows some of the typical features of the artful simplicity used at the top end of the market: black and white photography, with a single splash of colour, gold, reserved for the bottle of perfume; no setting, all attention concentrated on the upper part of a woman's body, her gaze directed at the viewer; text limited to a simple slogan, the name of the perfume and the brand-name. This is luxury by understatement. Yet despite the suggested informality of pose and dress, the model's face conveys sophistication. The allure of smile and gaze is discreet, as is the curve of the bust: sensuality is hinted at, not forced on the viewer. The same message of self-conscious, almost self-contained beauty emanates from the glistening yet severely controlled hair, the shaped eyebrows, the made-up lips and eyes.

Chanel promoted this fictive ideal of French womanhood – refined elegance and rarefied sensuality – by using versions of the same ad in other countries. Variants of the same format were also used abroad by Guerlain and even by non-French firms bent on trading up by looking French, among them Giorgio Armani's Acqua di Gio. But Calvin Klein's Escape, while adopting the black, white and gold and the simplicity of text and context, showed a young woman barefoot and locked in a tango hold with her long-haired partner. Similarly, French perfumes aimed at a younger market were more overtly sensual, used colour and movement; an ad for Cacharel's Eau d'Eden, for example, showed a pert Venus, dressed scantily in roses, arising from a pink and green sea. Perhaps, in a shrinking market for perfume, classic images of French sophistication have now had their day.

Change is also affecting the French love affair with food and drink. Sales of wine have steadily decreased over the last 20 years. Fast food chains and convenience foods have altered eating habits. No longer is a two-hour lunch-break standard practice in the business community. Yet the attachment to eating together as a family remains, whether for the final meal of the working day at about 8 pm or at the traditional Sunday lunch and other festive occasions. On such occasions the French do not eat continuously. They eat, they talk about what they are eating and drinking, what they have eaten and drunk on other occasions, where the food was bought and how the wine compares to other vintages from the same or neighbouring vineyards; the children leave the table, go off to play and return when they are hungry or when a new course arrives: once, in a playpark near a restaurant in central Brittany, around 6 pm on a Sunday afternoon, I heard a female voice shouting 'Venez les enfants, c'est le dessert'.

Food advertising to some extent reflects this shifting scene, sometimes with a hint of embarrassment. A print ad for Marie's tinned ready-to-serve dishes in 1998 had the slogan 'Ce n'est pas parce que c'est déjà fait qu'il ne faut rien faire' – 'Just because it's ready made, doesn't mean there's nothing to be done'. This suggests that it is still the French housewife's role to prepare meals; the slogan aims to relieve her of the 'guilt' of letting her family down by resorting to convenience foods. Some French food ads show an appeal to values which seem common to readers of women's magazines throughout the western world, values of health, fitness, youth and shapeliness. But there are also some distinctively French things about food ads. First, their number: there are more ads for foods in France than in Britain. For example, the issue of *Marie Claire* for July 1997 had seven food ads in the British edition and 20 in the French (as well as a 24-page regular feature on 'la cuisine', absent from the British edition). Another significant difference between these two groups of ads was that of the seven British ads, six were for products which were either of foreign origin – apples, cheese, salad dressing, ice cream – or which made foreignness part of their appeal. A slogan for Highland spring water revealingly confirmed the prestige which French taste enjoys abroad: 'The Scottish water the French drink'. By contrast, all but three of the French ads were for products with French names.

The French, then, prefer to eat – and drink – French. Indeed, Frenchness itself forms a frequent line of appeal. A generic ad for sugar in 1998 quoted a specialist in lifestyles as saying: 'The years of eating "light" are over. It's no longer fashionable to eat products which are sugar- or fat-free (or with reduced fat or sugar content); we've come back to the well balanced foods produced from our home soil'. While the argument may be self-serving and erroneous, there can be no doubt of the emotional force of the idea of local produce. Anything grown in our home soil, like sugar beet for example, must surely be balanced and wholesome. A television ad for an SEB pressure cooker, broadcast at Christmas 1998, took up a similar theme. Through lush country settings, a middle-aged man pushes a big old-fashioned wheelbarrow laden with home-grown vegetables. He stops by his friendly neighbours, busy with their own produce, and exchanges his carrots for their leeks and cabbages. Cut to the kitchen where his wife is showing him the vegetables simmering in the SEB casserole, but there are no carrots: he's given them all away. These images of an idyllic self-sustaining agrarian society, of generous barter with friendly neighbours, of hunter-gathering male and house-keeping female may in fact seem light-years away from the life of the average French consumer: urban, isolated, buying vegetables with cash from the local super- or hypermarket. That is, of course, their attraction. But in one sense, they are not so far removed from reality. The great exodus from the countryside to the cities did not take place in France until the 1950s. The benefit of this SEB pressure cooker is that it takes you back to the country. Many French foods come with their local origin attached to their name: Camembert de Normandie, Brie de Meaux, choux de Bretagne, galette de Pleyben. The same is even more true of wine, of which the place of origin, marked on the label, is an essential factor defining taste and quality. Through food and wine, even the most urban of French are linked to mythical roots in the soil of France: they are transported back to their own origins and they appropriate other regions by consuming them. Munster cheese and 'les vins d'Alsace' are the daily proof by touch, smell and taste of the assimilation of that once disputed province.

In a world flooded with images, advertisements have to stand out but be understood quickly; for that reason they use stereotypes, seeking orginality by giving them a new twist. Some food and drink ads set positive connotations of Frenchness against negative connotations of foreignness. Here are two examples which demonize the Japanese: in one television ad of the mid-1990s, Japanese tourists, male and female, file soberly, two-by-two, into a French restaurant. After drinking Badoit water with their meal, they spill out of the restaurant singly or in laughing, chattering groups. Thus what the French see as the grimness of Japanese collective discipline has been transformed by French water into virtues perceived to be French: individualism and sociability. In another TV ad from some years before, two formally-dressed Japanese men take snapshots of a plump chicken strutting in the French countryside. The voice-over, from a good-looking young farmer in his shirt-sleeves, comments: 'A healthy, calm, well-fed life, in the open air, makes some people pretty envious. Free range chicken from the Orléans countryside: an inimitable taste.' A discomfited Japanese echoes: 'Inimitable'. This little fable of industrial espionage actually represents in stereotyped form the French fear of Japanese technological and economic supremacy. Yet, cooped up in their cities, the Japanese will never produce anything to compare with a French country-bred chicken. Once again, the appeal is to patriotism; buying a French product enables the purchaser to identify with values which are held to be embodied in the French countryside: balance, peace, the natural life. The patriotic appeal is reinforced here by two extra connotations of the product: the 'poulet fermier de l'Orléanais', defying the foreign threat, evokes visually the Gallic cockerel and verbally Joan of Arc, the Maid of Orléans.

But French food and drink are not sold simply on the strength of patriotic associations. Taste also matters – or rather, taste heightened and magnified by advertising into a sensual experience. Two of the most frequently recurring words in food ads are 'la gourmandise' (that is, enjoyment of food, more or less discriminating) and 'le plaisir': Sveltesse – 'la gourmandise vous va si bien' 'enjoying food suits you'; Tutti Free – '4 fois moins de calories et tout le plaisir du sucre': '4 times fewer calories and all the pleasure of sugar'. A 1997 ad for sugar explicitly singled out this attitude to food as a characteristic of Latin, Catholic countries, distinguishing them from their Protestant Anglo-Saxon neighbours:

The tradition of pleasure

There is a real difference between Anglo-Saxon and Latin ideas of food, probably related to the peculiarities of the Protestant and Catholic faiths. The Anglo-Saxons, more Puritan, regard eating as no more than fulfilling a vital function (it's almost unseemly to make too much of it), while the Epicurean Latins appreciate fine fare. For them, it's so true that enjoying food can be no sin.

Marie Claire, 1998, 163

Here pleasure and patriotism run in tandem: to enjoy food is to be truly French – so eat more sugar!

In other French ads, sensual appeal takes more erotic form, addressing both heterosexual and homosexual publics. Ads in the gay press became visually and textually explicit in the early 1980s when a Socialist president and government, elected with gay backing, ushered in a less repressive climate. In the 1990s, images of well-built, semi-undressed young men have appeared more and more frequently in mainstream and in the new 'lad' magazines, for example advertising aftershave lotions. The male body is now sometimes portrayed as an object of desire, reinforcing the desirability of the product. Women's bodies have long played this role in advertising. Since the 1960s, the bath salts manufacturer Obao has been using nude female models to demonstrate the use of its products. Contrast this with the storm of complaints which finally constrained Neutralia Gel to withdraw a UK commercial shown in 1994 and 1995 because for a moment a woman's nipple was visible. The video cassette of commercials issued by the French agency RSCG in 1989 to celebrate its twentieth anniversary showed examples of sex and female nudity being used to sell everything from cars through holiday tours and wallpaper to mail order firms (Henry 1989, 48–9). A comparative survey of French and German TV ads found that a sensual relationship between a couple featured in 7 per cent of the German ads compared to 16 per cent of the French (Walliser and Moreau 1998, 15).

As this might suggest, French public opinion is much less concerned about the use and possible abuse of representations of women in advertising than is British or US opinion. As long ago as 1975, a BVP recommendation nevertheless set out various ways in which the dignity of women should be protected in advertisements. Women should not be represented in ways which denigrated them or which provoked scorn, ridicule or lack of respect. They should not systematically be used to advertise products and services either unrelated to women or designed for the use of both men and women. In addition: 'Advertising must not suggest the idea of a natural, or even acquiesced in, inferiority or subordination of women to men, or reduce the role of women to looking after the home or performing household tasks, thus disregarding women's aptitudes and aspirations' (BVP, 1979). In March 1983, the Minister for Women's Rights, Yvette Roudy, attempted to introduce legislation which would have reinforced this recommendation. Her proposed bill would, amongst other things, have made it illegal to publish advertisements giving 'a stereotyped, demeaning or degrading image of women' and would have given voluntary organizations the right to take to court anyone they considered had infringed the law. Despite the backing of her Socialist Cabinet colleagues and of Simone de Beauvoir in *Le Monde*, Mme Roudy's bill was ultimately withdrawn, defeated by an alliance of the libertarian left, the advertising lobby and the free market right. *Libération* called it 'a G-string law', while the Managing Director of Havas branded it 'a curb on freedom' (Smyth 1983; Roudy 1985, 162–68).

This was the high-water mark of attempts to legislate in this area; there is not much evidence that French attitudes have changed since then. Certainly, in the 1980s, conventional images showing female subordination to males began to be supplemented by images of role reversal and of independent, assertive women (Cornejols 1992). In the 1990s, some ads for Kookaï fashions showed bright young women adopting conventionally male attitudes towards the opposite sex: love them and leave them. And women began to appear in ads as drivers and buyers of cars, as well as in the old role of associated object of desire for the prospective male purchaser: ads for the Renault Mégane used both these images. On the whole, however, although sexism is now sometimes sugar-coated with humour, French advertising largely continues to purvey stereotypical gender roles, particularly on television (Gunther 1992). Out of 430 separate ads broadcast during peak-hour viewing on TF1 in the week before Christmas 1998, women appeared in 210; in only eight of these did women play a professional role outside the home, and five out of the eight were models. Men appeared in 215 ads, of which 36 showed them in professional roles. By contrast, only 13 men appeared in domestic roles compared to 80 women (Park 1999).

Conclusion

Despite globalization and Europeanization, advertising in France remains distinctive in several respects. The state intervenes more and more firmly to control advertising than in most European countries. Even the recommendations of the BVP come close to having the force of law. Ads for some products are French in style and content, and reflect values which are part of a stereotyped, positive French self-image. While there is considerable freedom in the use of sex and, some would say, sexism in French adverts, this goes hand in hand, at least in the mass media, with a broadly conservative representation of gender roles.

Conclusions, however, must be drawn with caution since advertising changes quickly. It reflects and exploits new social trends – all the more so since advertising agencies are supported by increasingly sophisticated research on lifestyles and aspirations. For instance, despite the BVP guide-

INDÉFINISSABLE
ET TOTALEMENT IRRÉSISTIBLE.

ALLURE
LE NOUVEAU PARFUM DE CHANEL

Figure 14.1   In this 1997 ad for an archetypal French product, the model, Mak
Gilchrist, is English and her photopher, Herb Ritts, is American; the bottle of
perfume was photographed by Daniel Jouanneau, a Frenchman.

lines on the use of children in ads, a flurry of ads in 1998 and 1999 showed
youngsters defying their parents – and the French public laughed and made
no objection (Amalou 1999). The impact of new technology also hastens
change. In 1998 less than 0.5 per cent of total advertising expenditure was
devoted to the Internet: but that was an almost 300 per cent increase on
1997. By September 1999, 44 per cent of small and medium-sized enterprises had a website and 19 per cent more planned to have one before the
millennium (*Challenges,* Nov. 1999, 96). Of larger firms to take to the
Internet, the leaders were travel companies (like Dégriftours and Club
Med), computing suppliers, and the bookseller FNAC (Rivaud and Stiel
1999). In June 1999 Axa was the first French insurance company to launch
a major campaign by paying the main search engines to have its name
appear as a banner insert whenever Internet browsers entered key words
associated with financial services. Since the number of Internet users in
France grew from just over 400 000 in January 1998 to over 1 400 000 by
April 1999, advertising on the net cannot but continue its exponential
growth. It allows one-to-one marketing and detailed profiling of customers.
But it is not cheap, and so far seems most effective when combined with
advertising in other media (Mitrofanoff 1999).
   Whatever the changes to come, advertising will continue to offer a means
of understanding some aspects of French society. The examples discussed in

the second part of this chapter have been from two industries in the main, but one can easily undertake small-scale surveys of others. For instance, the study of foreigners or different races in advertising is interesting because it is the other side of the coin of values and virtues which are held to be French. A number of textbooks and previous studies offer methods of analysing advertisements; I mention some of these in the bibliography. It is not difficult to get a selection of ads which lend themselves to comparative study: record some television ads off satellite at comparable times from comparable channels or buy comparable magazines or journals. Although your sample may be too small to be statistically reliable, you will learn some French and something more about French society and its values.

References

AMALOU, F. 1999: La publicité télévisée s'empare des 'sales gosses'. *Le Monde*, 19 October, 24.

BOURDON, J. and GRUNBLATT, C. 1986: Publicité et télévision: une longue histoire. *Médiapouvoirs* 3, 60–70.

Bureau de Vérification de la Publicité 1997: Langues et publicité. Paris: *BVP Echos* 153.

Bureau de Vérification de la Publicité 1996: Les avis définitifs relatifs aux messages télévisés avant diffusion. Paris: *BVP Echos* 149.

Bureau de Vérification de la Publicité 1979, updated 1992 and 1998: *Recueil de recommandations du BVP.* Paris: BVP.

Bureau de Vérification de la Publicité 1992: *Règles relatives à la publicité et au parrainage.* Paris: BVP.

Challenges 1999: Sondage: les PME françaises sont plus branchées qu'on ne le croyait, 94–96.

Conseil Supérieur de l'Audiovisuel 1995: *Réglementation et régulation auiovisuelle en France.* Paris: CSA.

CORNEJOLS, C. 1992: Gender roles in French advertisements in the 1980s. *French Review* 66, 201–15.

CLUZEL, J. Communication audiovisuelle, 1996–97: Sénat, *Rapport général sur le projet de loi de finances pour 1997* 3, annexe 8.

European Marketing Pocketbook 1999: London: NTC Publications.

FRANCESCHINI, L. (ed) 1996: *Les questions clés de l'audiovisuel.* Paris: Dixit.

GREFFE, P. and F. 1995: *La publicité et la loi.* 8th ed., Paris: Lifec.

GUNTHER, R. 1992: Equal but different: gender images in contemporary French advertising. in CHAPMAN, R. and HEWITT, N. (eds) *Popular culture and mass communications in twentieth-century France.* Lewiston, NY: Edwin Mellen Press, 69–82.

HENRY, S. 1989: Body count. *Campaign,* 14 July.

JOSPIN, L. 1997: La déclaration de politique générale. *Le Monde,* 21 June.

Marie Claire July 1997.

Marie Claire July 1998.

MARTIN, M. 1992: *Trois siècles de publicité en France.* Paris: Odile Jacob.

MICHEL, H. 1995: *Les grandes dates de la télévision française.* Paris: PUF.

MITROFANOFF, K. 1999: Avis de coups de pub sur Internet. *Challenges,* September, 88–90.

PARK, S. 1999: Roles and representations of women in contemporary French advertising. University of Stirling (unpublished BA dissertation).
RIVAUD, F. and STIEL, N. 1999: Les galeries Internet. *Challenges*, April, 107–12.
ROUDY, Y. 1985: *A cause d'elles*. Paris: Albin Michel.
SCHROEDER, M. 1991: France-Allemagne: la publicité. L'existence de deux logiques de communication. *Recherche et application en marketing* 35, 1, 66–71.
SÉGUÉLA, J. 1999: Pas de pub, pas de vote. *Le Monde*, 18 June.
SMYTH, R. 1983: 'Virile hand' behind attack on sexist ads. *The Observer*, 20 March.
STEELE, V. 1998: *Paris fashion. A cultural history*, 2nd ed. Oxford/New York: Berg.
WALLISER, B. and MOREAU, F. 1998: Comparaison du style français et allemand de la publicité télévisée. *Cahier du Cesag*, Université Robert Schuman, 98 11 1/11.

Further reading

B. Brochand and J. Lendrevie, *Le publicitor*, Dalloz, 4th ed., 1993, is the standard textbook on the advertising industry in France; a basic introductory text is A. Dayan, *La Publicité*, PUF, 8th ed., 1998. The weekly advertising magazines *CB News* and *Stratégies* give up-to-date information on trends in France. Consumer behaviour and lifestyles have been studied over many years by B. Cathelet, for example in *Publicité et société*, Payot, 1992. A more critical view of the role of advertising in society has been taken by A. Mattelart, for example in *La Publicité*, La Découverte, 1994. Different appoaches to the analysis of adverts forms part of G. Dyer's usefully readable *Advertising as communication*, London: Routledge, 1982. R. Barthes touched on advertising in *Mythologies*, Seuil (Points), first ed. 1957, and in 'Rhetoric of the image', reprinted in *Image, music, text*, London: Fontana, 1977. Judith Williamson used some of Barthes's insights in her seminal work on analysing the structures and ideology of adverts in *Decoding advertisements*, London: Marion Boyars, 1978. The classic text on representations of women in print adverts remains E. Goffman, *Gender advertisements*, London: Macmillan, 1979. A. Lelieur and others, *Négripub*, Paris: Somology, 1994, is a beautifully produced and documented history of the representation of blacks in French advertisements. Useful sources of information in Paris are the Bibliothèque Forney, 1 rue du Figuier, for its fine collections of posters and books, and the Musée de la publicité, 167 rue de Rivoli (website at http://www.ucad.fr/pub/). To keep up to date with changes which may have occurred since this chapter was written, you should consult, for example, the website of the Ministry of Culture (http://www.culture.gouv.fr/culture/actualités).

|15|

A night at the theatre

BY CHRISTOPHE CAMPOS

It is 100 years since moving pictures challenged the role of theatre in providing group entertainment through simulations – an extremely successful challenge, since by the 1930s scores of small playhouses in Paris and the large provincial cities had closed or been converted into cinemas. It is 50 years since television in its turn challenged both cinema and theatre, so that by the 1960s it was commonly said that both these forms were in a state of crisis and would not survive without state support. Today, video, multi-channel television and the prospect of various kinds of enlarged electronic access to information and entertainment are again modifying the scene. Why, then, is theatre still worth mentioning in a survey of present-day France?

Theatre is far from being a majority pursuit, but interest in it is very widespread. Broad social surveys (Busson 1986) show that 60 per cent of French adults would *like* to attend a performance, even though only 18 per cent actually do so in any one year. A wider spectrum of age-groups and social categories frequent theatres than do any of the other performing arts, even though the upper socio-economic groups and people aged 30 and above are most strongly represented. This is not due to early 'hands-on' experience. School theatre productions are few and far between, and the majority of schools do not offer teaching in theatre arts, though they are a possible option at the *baccalauréat*. Nor is there an established tradition of amateur dramatic or operatic societies, such as one finds in other European countries, including Britain. Theatre, however, is considered to be an important part of the French cultural heritage. Schoolchildren are often taken in groups to see professional productions of plays studied in class, and syllabuses for those aged 12 and above always include plays from the classical French repertoire. This is associated with an underlying respect for the power of verbal rhetoric and with a preference for institutionalized cultural activities, both of which are fundamental to French attitudes.

The French tendency to establish dependence on central subsidy and control is very apparent in the field of theatre, which is seen as a national institution, and, as such, deserving of protection and promotion as well as regulation. The *Ministère de la culture et de la communication* includes a department devoted to theatre, the *Direction du théâtre*. There is a sizeable national budget to subsidize theatre, of which part is spent centrally and part in the regions, in association with regional and municipal funding. Here, as in other fields, the habit of looking to the state for care and support is offset by the equally strong tradition of rejecting over-stringent guidance in the name of individual freedom. In fact, *direction du théâtre* is an optimistic and quite misleading phrase, since 'theatre' in France is made up of at least three sets of overlapping cultural practices.

Metropolitan entertainment

Theatre is a ceremony involving two groups – a group of actors and a larger group of spectators, and from both points of view it is an intensely social ceremony. Spectators are aware of each other's presence and reactions to the play (in a way that is not possible in a darkened cinema), they may observe each other before, during and after the performance, they discuss their response to it in intervals or at the end. So theatre has thrived in Europe in circumstances where a relatively small class of theatregoers has made the playhouse or the opera a regular meeting place as part of its social round. This was especially so in Paris in the middle of the nineteenth century, when the effects of trade development and the growth in the production of luxury goods made the French capital overtly wealthy, with a rich and recently-established upper middle class seeking, through conspicuous consumption, a means of expressing its economic dominance.

Between 1860 and 1910, during what came later to be known as *la belle époque* (i.e. the society that was to be swept away by the First World War), theatre and opera thrived in this atmosphere. Playhouses and opera houses were not only places one visited to see the latest play, but also places one wanted to be seen at. The favoured 'Italianate' shape of the auditoria (with balconies facing each other and providing observation points for the stalls) emphasized this social feature. Novels of the time often mention that so and so was seen with so and so at the theatre, often disregarding what they were watching. The play was little more than an entertaining backdrop to a social event, and the authors and composers associated with this period (Offenbach, Labiche, Feydeau) were often highly productive in a formula-driven way, writing plays and musical entertainments reflecting in a lightly satirical and joyous mode the marginal inefficiencies of bourgeois codes of conduct. With the development of rail transport, the Parisian entertainment scene acted like a magnet. Just as Parisians from the lower middle classes came to participate in the entertainments of the better-off, so provincials travelled to Paris to view the glittering life of the capital, and foreign visitors in turn went there to experience the swaggering public style of the French metropolis.

As we saw, the success of moving pictures caused the more popular basis of theatre to collapse. But the 'metropolitan' function survived this cultural change: in the darkness of the cinema, it is not so easy to show off one's fashionable clothes or companions or one's ability to purchase expensive seats. In a survey of French theatre immediately after World War II, it was noted that Paris still retained 52 playhouses (most of them continuing to produce a repertoire very similar to that of the 'belle époque') while the rest of France put together could only muster 50 (most of them opening only occasionally for productions on tour from Paris). Even today, there are still 15 playhouses of this kind, mostly grouped in two areas: around the 'grands boulevards', a string of avenues linking the Opéra with the Place de la République, and around Montparnasse (Corvin 1989). The style of drama typically produced there is known, somewhat derogatively, as *comédie de boulevard*. Plays resembling those of Feydeau and Labiche (typically, they portray families with domestic servants) provide a comforting vision of life amongst the wealthy classes, including some light-hearted satire on their social mores: plots turn on divergences from sexual codes, conflicts between generations, inheritances and minor misunderstandings with provincials and foreigners. Playwrights who wrote in this vein in the 1930s (for instance Sacha Guitry) are also regularly revived. Provincial and foreign visitors now have the added thrill of seeing film and television actors in the flesh on stage, there being a considerable amount of overlap between these branches of the performing arts in France. The current native authors operating in this narrow sphere include Marc Camoletti, whose play *Boeing Boeing* has been produced almost constantly since 1960: never have the thrills and spills of three air-hostesses on an overnight stop in Paris failed to entertain.

Onto this purely Parisian phenomenon, and still in the same 15 or so playhouses, privately owned, designed in the Italianate style described above and appealing to an audience of some 200 000, has been grafted an international repertoire of translations of plays from other, similar western metropolitan contexts, mainly London's West End and New York's Broadway. Parisians who have been on business trips to London and New York can see French versions of plays by Alan Ayckbourn, Harold Pinter or Edward Albee, and visiting businesspeople with cultural aspirations a little higher than the shows at the Crazy Horse or the Moulin Rouge can see plays they know or have heard of, in French translation.

The above description of theatre and audiences also applies pre-eminently to the spectators at the opera, considered by many, in the nineteenth century and now, to be a superior version of theatre. The main Paris opera (now called Opéra-Garnier, after its architect, since the opening of a second establishment, the Opéra-Bastille in 1989) has functioned throughout the past 100 years, with audiences of up to 1900, though its seasons have varied considerably in length. In the 1960s, it absorbed the refugee operettas and their audiences from the now-closed Opéra-Comique. The fact that Paris now supports *two* opera-houses, each with its international links and picturesque directorial history and repertoire, says a great deal about the cultural interests of its inhabitants. Modern opera is, however, more an international than a national cultural phenomenon. The repertoire is European (with more German and Italian than French works), and the directors and star performers move in international circuits. There are also several provincial opera-houses (in Strasbourg, Lyon, etc.).

Incidentally, a British or American observer in France would be surprised at the near-absence of the more popular 'musicals', which form a considerable proportion of the repertoire in English-speaking theatrical traditions. There is one large playhouse devoted to operettas and musicals (the Théâtre du Châtelet), but the French tradition of plays with musical interludes, whose last productive period was the *belle époque*, is now extinct, and there are practically no French translations of the Broadway and West End repertoire, though audio recordings in English are popular.

We have dealt so far with theatre as popular entertainment. But the more culturally sophisticated Parisian theatre-goers also like to frequent two establishments where they find productions which enable them to renew their acquaintance with French heritage theatre. The main one is the Comédie Française, an institution which dates back to 1680, when, on Molière's death, his troupe was given protective patents by the king. Since then, it has had three important functions – to prolong and pursue acting traditions by training and co-option; to continue to produce Molière's plays; and to put on a repertoire of plays considered at various times to have been important to French culture. This company has existed more or less continuously since 1680, with only minor hiccups during the revolutionary period. It is directed by an *administrateur*, usually, but not invariably, someone from the theatre profession, whose appointment is in the personal gift of the President of the Republic. The latter thus continues to exercise, here as in a number of other spheres, a royal prerogative in cultural affairs first instituted by Louis XIV. Politics has come into this patronage, and new appointments to the Comédie Française always provoke widespread comment.

The Comédie Française is also the only theatre to be granted a subsidy considered as 'comfortable', i.e. enough to ensure that it can maintain a permanent company of over 50 actors and put on a varied programme without too much worry about audience numbers. In return, it is also the most active theatre in France: it offers performances almost every day of the year (an average of nine a week, all available to students prepared to queue for cheap seats) at its main theatre, the Salle Richelieu, installed in a wing of the Palais Royal (where the Conseil d'Etat is located); it has also, in recent years, kept a second playhouse going, at the Théâtre du Vieux Colombier on the Left Bank. It rarely travels more widely in France, though it makes very occasional appearances abroad.

The current repertoire of the Comédie Française is a good gauge of the contemporary interest in the official French theatrical tradition. Molière is of course a statutory activity of the company, so the presence of his plays is no surprise, though one may note a current stress on those dealing more controversially with the position of women in society and in the family (*L'Ecole des femmes, Les Femmes savantes, Le Misanthrope, Le Tartuffe*). Productions of other seventeenth-century plays are few and far between, with Corneille and Racine not making more than one appearance a year. The same now applies to the historical plays and comedies written by the French Romantics in the early nineteenth century. On the other hand the complex eighteenth-century comedies of Marivaux, with their stress on role-playing and illusion, which is also a major preoccupation of modern writing for the theatre, have been regularly revisited in the last ten years. The comic stock of the *belle époque* is also drawn on. So are the works of Claudel and Giraudoux, belonging respectively to the first and second quarter of the twentieth century, and who, though quite different in style, are perceived as establishment figures, because of their concern for the survival of French spiritualist ideologies as well as the high status they enjoyed in the French civil service. The Comédie Française has in recent years added to its repertoire the works of three major dramatists of the twentieth century, Beckett, Genet and Ionesco, and it was instrumental in helping to promote Jean-Claude Grumberg. Foreign plays are also present: Shakespeare, who has fascinated French audiences since Romantic times, early modern German playwrights and, occasionally, tributes to Goldoni, Pirandello, Ibsen, Strindberg and Chekhov.

European theatre is, however, mainly to be found at the Théâtre de l'Odéon, situated in the Latin quarter but close, like the Comédie Française, to the symbolic seats of power, in a former wing of the Luxembourg palace, now home of the French Senate. It has been known since 1990 as *Odéon – Théâtre de l'Europe,* and its management has twice been entrusted to directors from other European countries. Its brief has been to present to Parisians, either in French or in the original language with earphone translation or sur-titling, the best of the modern European classics produced by such eminent nationally-sponsored theatre companies as the Piccolo Teatro (Milan), the National Theatre (London), the Abbey Theatre (Dublin) and the Comédie de Genève. This European interest is reflected in Paris, though less so in the provinces.

Theatre as public service

A quite different conception of theatre appeared in the years following World War II, under two very strong impulses. The first was provided by the actor-director-manager Jean Vilar who, on being entrusted in 1951 with the very large auditorium under the Palais de Chaillot (over the river from the Eiffel Tower), revived the name Théâtre National Populaire, which dated back to experiments in popularizing theatre in the early years of the century.

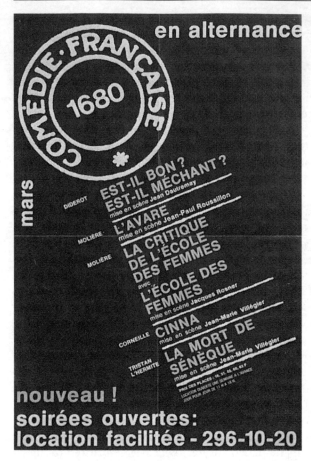

Figure 15.1
Comédie Française poster emphasizing three centuries' allegiance to a classical repertoire and the primacy of word and name in the clever angling of the text in relation to the logo.

According to him (Vilar 1975) the state has a duty to provide all its citizens (not only the wealthy and leisured ones) with a theatrical forum displaying their cultural heritage and emphasizing its political potential. The TNP auditorium could seat up to 1600 spectators, and Jean Vilar arranged for audiences to be bussed in from the suburbs and from provincial towns through contacts in educational organizations and works councils. The plays he produced were mainly from the French classical repertoire, and they were chosen to provide indirect comment on the main political questions of the time.

The second impulse, without which the Vilar experiment might have remained a Greater-Paris phenomenon, came from the revival of provincial identities instigated by the Vichy government between 1940 and 1944 in an effort to revitalize France from its provincial roots, the capital having being perceived by Vichy as having been corrupted by 'cosmopolitan' (i.e., in the fascist dictionary, Jewish) influences. Local theatre companies had been encouraged in centres such as Lyon, Grenoble, Toulouse and Saint-Etienne. After the war, these centres survived and fulfilled a new role in counterbalancing the cultural dominance of Paris.

These two forces were harnessed and spurred on in the early years of the Fifth Republic (1959–1965) by France's first Minister of Culture, André Malraux, under a general policy which came to be known as *décentralisation théâtrale*. A network of provincial theatres was revived or created under the aegis of the state and of regional authorities, and it naturally took on the ideals of Jean Vilar: decentralization was also made to stand for state-sponsored culture, with all the tensions between artistic freedom and state control that this implies. Typically, a playhouse belonging to this network would consider itself responsible for extending the social profile of its audience as much as possible. It employs staff to create and maintain contacts with potential groups of spectators (e.g. schools, professional associations, *comités d'entreprise*) and offer them special tickets. It publishes a newsletter (ranging from a broadsheet to a sophisticated magazine) intended to break down the mythical barrier between backstage and front of house through news of the productions in rehearsal, interviews with directors and actors, plans for the future, and comments on relations between playhouse and sponsors. These sponsors are usually the state, the region and the town council, and their support normally ensures that productions only have to cover their own expenses, without too many overheads. In return, the director of the playhouse is expected to provide entertainment for the local citizens: commonly three home productions and two guest productions a year. So each playhouse in the network expects to take at least one of its productions on tour to other similar establishments during the year.

The 'public service' playhouses have had their ups and downs under the Fifth Republic, having been on the whole favoured by left-wing governments, who tend to support the idea that culture needs to be subsidized from the centre and disfavoured by others. But they are much in evidence in France at present and form the bulk of theatres outside central Paris: this includes the *suburbs* of Paris, so that a visitor may be surprised to find theatres largely frequented by Parisians and easily accessible by métro or RER, such as Créteil, Nanterre, Aubervilliers or Gennevilliers, claiming to be part of 'decentralization'. Their size varies from large multi-purpose *maisons de la culture* (e.g. Nanterre, Bourges, Grenoble) with a permanent staff of 20–30, organizing exhibitions and concerts as well as drama, to medium-sized or small *centres dramatiques* (with national or regional status, depending on type of funding) with a smaller staff, which may not include actors, these being hired (often from Paris) for specific plays rather than forming a 'company'. The network does not cover France evenly and still bears some traces of the division between German- or Italian-occupied and Vichy-governed France: it is most dense in the North-East, the Rhône-Alpes and the Languedoc-Roussillon areas and most sparse in Aquitaine, Brittany and the Channel coast. The playhouses that stand out among the 24 *centres dramatiques nationaux* and the 19 *centres dramatiques régionaux* and often achieve something of a resident company of actors and house style are those associated with the Grenier de Toulouse, the Comédie de Caen, the Théâtre populaire de Lorraine (Metz), the Comédie de Saint-Etienne, the Théâtre de la Criée (Marseille), the Théâtre de la Salamandre (Lille – Tourcoing) and the Théâtre du Cothurne (Lyon). One company has a special status: the Théâtre national populaire, based at Villeurbanne, just north of Lyon, whose brief is to act, under the internationally known actor-director Roger Planchon, as a national touring company.

The civic role of these establishments can also extend to providing the local elites with a smaller version of the Parisian glitter. Very occasionally, operatic productions are invited; and modern dance companies, which are thriving in contemporary France, are frequently part of the offering, as are classic or foreign film seasons. However, theatre still remains a broadly-based prestige activity, and managers of centres usually have a theatrical background, being themselves actor-directors. Since the 1970s, it has become clear that the earlier aims of attracting large numbers of spectators from the less favoured classes (manual workers, the unemployed, immigrant communities) would be difficult to achieve, even though inspired local management in towns like Villeurbanne, Nanterre and Metz, did progress in this direction. The audiences have mainly been extended into intellectually responsive groups such as schools and further education colleges or professional groups in touch with municipal life and local politics.

The repertoire of these theatres relies fairly heavily on the sort of plays appealing to school groups and those recognizing the titles, or at least the playwrights' names, from their school days. Molière (who enjoys status both from the repertoire of the Comédie Française and as the seventeenth-century playwright whose language and traditional plots are familiar from comprehension exercises in school) is therefore over-represented, and 'easy' plays of his such as *Dom Juan* and *Le Bourgeois gentilhomme* are done over and again. The more 'difficult' dramas of Corneille, Racine, Hugo and Claudel, still in the Parisian repertoire, tend to be neglected. Shakespeare is the one foreign dramatist to appear regularly in translation. Twenty years ago Brecht was his immediate follower in the stakes, because many directors in the *décentralisation* movement were socialists who saw in Brecht's dramatic principles a way of making the theatrical experience more relevant to modern political life. Today, Brecht and a few French playwrights inspired by him (Michel Deutsch, Jean-Pierre Faye, Pierre Laville) appear only occasionally in the programme of one of the survivors of that generation.

The relationship between *décentralisation* theatres and local writing has been slight, though it may be improving with a very recent tendency to appoint playwrights in residence. One benefit of the system as seen through one of its overt aims (to regenerate French culture from its provincial roots) could have been to help local writers establish a reputation outside Paris. By and large, this was not achieved in the first 30 years, mainly because the playhouse managers, whose contracts were renewed every four years or so, usually by the Ministry, concentrated on productions that might attract the attention of the national press, and even perhaps of ministry scouts, if invited to tour in the suburbs of Paris. They thus achieved a rather spurious effect (not unknown in other sectors of French political and cultural life) – that of spreading to the provinces, under the banner of 'decentralization', the attitudes and interests of the metropolis. Nevertheless, a number of talented contemporary playwrights with non-Parisian roots have, over the last 20 years, been successfully promoted in this fashion through the *décentralisation* movement, e.g. Bernard-Marie Koltès (Nanterre), Annie Zadek (Lyon), Serge Valletti (Marseille), Gildas Bourdet (Tourcoing), Joseph Danan (Rouen) and, one might add, Roger Planchon (Villeurbanne), though this was more a case of the playwright/actor/director promoting himself. Koltès (1948–1989) is the one of this generation whose works are most often staged abroad.

By and large, then, the repertoire of the *décentralisation* network remains closely related to that of the Parisian establishment playhouses (though without the *boulevard* element). This is not surprising once one realizes that those responsible for theatre in the provinces are in the main Paris-based actors, hired for a play or a season, and directors and managers whose ambition is often to finish their career in or near the capital. The rags-to-riches career of the actor/director Marcel Maréchal is typical in this respect. Born in Lyon and having very little education or training in drama, he founded a small company, the Théâtre du Cothurne, which was successful at Lyon's small Théâtre du huitième. Having been noticed on tour in Paris (and doubtless because of his local reputation), he was appointed in 1981 as the manager of what became the harbour-side Théâtre de la Criée in Marseille (a *décentralisation* playhouse set up with strong support from a proactive and proud town council in the former market where fish used to be sold by auction – *à la criée*). After two renewals of his contract, he was selected as manager of the Théâtre du Rond-Point in the Champs-Elysées in Paris – a playhouse which used to be run by the prestigious Madeleine Renaud-Jean-Louis Barrault company for Parisian elite audiences. Four years later, in 1999, he was considered insufficiently sophisticated by spectators previously nurtured on highly refined dramatic recitations such as those of Marguerite Duras, and had to resign.

The one area in which the *décentralisation* movement has really renewed French theatrical practices is that of production. The system has built or converted several dozen sizeable playhouses to a fairly standardized shape – an elongated cube with variable-shape but straight rows of spectator accommodation (gone are the curved balcony lines of the Italianate playhouses), with infinitely adjustable lighting and acoustic devices built into a dual-level ceiling grid. Productions can tour between these playhouses with minimal disruption to their staging arrangements, which can therefore be more ambitious. Since the director is one of the few permanent staff of the establishment, the system has also favoured director power against actor power. Paris spectators will go to see Gérard Depardieu as Tartuffe in a revival of Molière's play or a new comedy with Jacques Villeret; but *décentralisation* will promote 'Planchon's *Tartuffe*' or 'Savary's *Cyrano de Bergerac*' almost to the extent of disregarding the name of the original author (Molière and Rostand). Directors with generous funds for productions (though they all plead poverty) and a great deal of rehearsal time (two to three months) will go in for sophisticated and inventive designs and styles. The best-known modern directors, such as Antoine Vitez (1930–1990) and Patrice Chéreau (b. 1944), have made excellent use of these facilities, and public-service theatre in the French provinces and the suburbs of Paris can sometimes be technically more accomplished and exciting than in the capital.

Over the past 10 years, the *Direction du théâtre* has reacted against the tendency of *décentralisation* to rest on its classical laurels by designating a new national theatre, the Théâtre de la Colline (Ménilmontant, Paris), as a centre for dramatic experimentation, and by increasing its subsidies to successful individual directors or companies of various kinds. One of these is the *Théâtre ouvert* organization, which began by holding public play-readings by professional actors to give new playwrights the chance to be heard at the Avignon theatre festival and now also holds such events in Paris, where it sponsors half a dozen proper performances of such works and publishes playtexts for circulation amongst potential producers. Other well-established companies working in part for contemporary playwrights are the Théâtre de la Tempête (directed by Philippe Adrien), La Manufacture, Les Athévains (ateliers théâtraux du vingtième arrondissement) for Paris and the Théâtre populaire de Lorraine and the Chêne noir (Avignon) for the provinces.

This contemporary writing is uncertain in its general direction, having emerged from the radical critique of theatre conducted by the absurdist playwrights of the 1950s and 1960s (Ionesco, Beckett) and the reaction against the widespread politicization of theatre which took place in the 1960s and 1970s under the influence of Brecht. The stress is on the solitary confessional (following Beckett) or on the appropriation of historical, geographical or imaginative landscapes by the individual mind or groups of minds, subject to processes of fragmentation and collage rather than harmonization.

Theatre as an alternative society

The third ideological strand which goes into the making of the French theatre scene is closely connected to the 1968 revolution – sometimes referred to as the abortive student revolution, because it did not manage to bring about a change in the political regime. But it did bring to the surface a number of undercurrents which have had a profound effect on contemporary society.

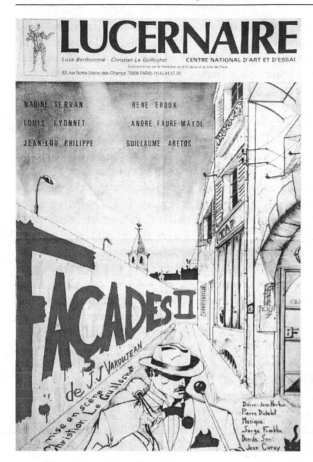

Figure 15.2 This poster for the Lucernaire, a small experimental theatre near Montparnasse, refers to other cultural artefacts (graffiti, elaborate glass awnings, and the 1930s spiv).

Theatre is a profoundly conservative form of art, because it relies on pre-agreement between audience and performers on the type of representation to be expected: whether this be the relationship between 'real' reality and stage reality or the choice of permitted subjects (a variable number of them being considered at any one time as 'ob-scene', i.e. not to be staged), or the degree of political/practical reference to the issues of the day. As such, it is not surprising that it did not respond immediately to the events of 1968, as, indeed, it had not in previous critical events such as the Revolution of 1789–1793 or the Commune of 1871. However, one of the undercurrents emphasized in the years following 1968 was concerned with alternative social models. Some of the more uncompromising *soixante-huitards* went off to set up rural communes where they tried to reshape family relationships and economic conventions and to live off goats. Others found similar comfort in the life of a theatre company which naturally marginalizes itself from conventional society as it changes work into play, night into day, imagination into reality. In this they had been inspired by a number of tours in the early 1960s by American companies such as the Living Theatre or the Bread and Puppet, who demonstrated a blend of political radicalism, dramatic representation and communal living. Indeed, this movement was spurred on, rather than created, by 1968.

The most famous and successful example is the Théâtre du Soleil, a company started in 1965 by Ariane Mnouchkine, an extremely talented director and radical social thinker whose career took on a new turn in 1970 with an unsigned play, *1789*, billed as a *création collective*, i.e. the result of many months of communal study of the subject, conception of scenes through improvisation and dedication to making by hand all aspects of the production (from the communal meals to the trestle stages). *1789*, which was to become a foundation myth for modern 'alternative' theatre in France and elsewhere, had a stated political aim: to re-enact the events of that first French revolution, so familiar to readers of school textbooks, with the added experience gained from the events of 1968. It also had an overt, though less explicit ambition: to demonstrate what actors can do if freed from the dictates of authors, established playhouses, theatrical suppliers and the hierarchy of parts and allowed to rediscover the communal life of the traditional closely-knit travelling company dating back to a time before metropolitan entertainment had been taken over by capitalist modes. Furthermore, the sets and general lay-out of the interface with the audience before and during the performance were intended to break down the traditional client/professional divide: recognizable members of the cast served in the bar, the actors dressing and making-up did so in an area on view to the public, spectators were encouraged in various ways to move around during the performance rather than staking a proprietary (capitalist?) claim to a seat.

In the 1970s, several dozen 'théâtres communes' based on this or similar models flourished in various parts of France. In the end improvisation, it was realized, could not always replace the coordinating role of a director or the discursive underpinning of a playtext. Many communes foundered through internal dissension or over-idealism. But several have had a brilliant history, and still survive, usually through state funding, which recognized their potential creative role side by side with the *décentralisation* establishment. The Théâtre du Soleil, with the Théâtre du Chaudron, the Théâtre de l'Epée de bois and the Théâtre de l'Aquarium, all based in a series of converted ammunition storage warehouses in the Bois de Vincennes, combine to form a kind of experimental theatre ghetto, within easy reach of the city yet keeping its distance from the city. The Soleil itself has an international as well as a French following; more than 100 people a month apply to join its new-style company. In Avignon, André Benedetto's family-based group has been producing its own plays for many years. The group formed around the powerful radical and poetic personality of Armand Gatti (*la tribu*), and though it existed before 1968, has thrived from this ideal. Occasionally, a successful group of this kind has ended up by accepting institutionalization: Jérôme Savary's Grand Magic Circus, which began as a touring company specializing in sending up established culture, now applies its director's considerable talents to providing popular productions of classics at the Théâtre de Chaillot, the distant descendant of Jean Vilar's Théâtre National Populaire. And perhaps this is the place to mention the maverick genius Peter Brook, who made Paris his base for his international company, working out of the Bouffes du nord from 1974 until the 1990s.

Though this sort of alternative theatre is now much less prevalent than in the 1970s, it has had an extensive effect on the balance of professional/amateur practices in the theatre, and on the constitution of social groups living in the margins of theatre. Acting has always been attractive to a much larger number of young people than the professional theatre could employ, and in France, where there is no actors' union with closed-shop agreements, there have for many years been 20 unemployed self-professed actors for one in work. There are regional acting schools (*conservatoires*) and private schools run by well-known actors, but one can only really have a good chance of fairly regular work if one has graduated from the Conservatoire national, where there are 80 applicants for one place. In the past 20 years, the attractiveness of theatre as alternative way of life has increased because of the success of some of the communal ventures. With a large number of small groups attempting to create viable projects, usually in their spare time, the frontiers of professional theatre have been blurred still further. *Faire du théâtre* no longer means hoping to play Phèdre at the Comédie Française one day, but rather getting up a play with some friends, looking for public sponsorship, attending workshops run by other companies, obtaining a small part in a summer festival production, while possibly also pursuing part-time work in a more mundane occupation. In keeping with its general support of the theatre, the French state has a rather generous system of unemployment benefits for occasional actors or self-employed technicians, known as *les intermittents du spectacle*.

The resulting ferment allows some 50 000 people to be involved in theatre in some way and occasional opportunities for individuals or groups to move out of the twilight into the limelight. This state of affairs was given a boost as a result of the 1981 elections, when the new Mitterrand government, following the well-established left-wing tradition, almost doubled the amount of public money spent on theatre and, especially, introduced allocation rules which spread it over a much larger number of individual projects and small companies. If you open the weekly *Officiel des spectacles* for the Paris area between October and May, you will find some 180 theatrical events every evening. More than half of these are the work of small semi-professional groups or one-person shows, quite a few in *cafés-théâtres* which work like night-clubs: for an expensive drink, there is an opportunity to be entertained and tip the performers. Here, dramatic art merges with other types of performance – comedy routines, dramatized readings from literary classics (which bear famous names acting as bait, even if the author never intended to write for the theatre), circus arts – which are difficult to relate even to experimental theatre. Paris is an exceptional case because of the concentration of these marginal forms, but they are also present in several other large towns (Lyon, Grenoble, Lille, Montpellier) and they abound at the main annual professional theatre jamboree, the Avignon festival, where, for the last three weeks in July, this small southern town is overrun by official and semi-official events in which companies show off their wares in the hope of being noticed and invited to tour.

Conclusion

In the 1980s, Bernard Pivot famously banned theatre from his well-known television review of books and the arts, *Apostrophes* (and its contemporary successor, *Bouillon de culture*), on the grounds that nothing significant was afoot in this field. It is true that since the absurdist school of playwrights (1950s and 1960s), not many creative writers have brought modern ideas into startling focus on stage or in texts for the theatre. On the other hand, France spends £200 million a year on helping to keep the cost of theatre seats down to half their real value, plus £80 million a year on building or restoring playhouses, while 4 million spectators visit theatres every year in Paris alone and 1000 actors work there every evening. The live presence of spectators and actors within the same space continues to be attractive in a world threatened by its virtual incarnations.

References and further reading

BRADBY, David, 1991: *Modern French drama 1940–1990*. Cambridge: Cambridge UP, 2nd edition. A good account, in English, of the formative period of modern French theatre.
BRADBY, David and SPARKS, Annie, 1997: *Mise en scène: French theatre now*. London: Methuen. An extended programme of the 1997 French theatre season in London, containing a great deal of up-to-date information on people and places.
BUSSON, Alain, 1986: *Le Théâtre en France. Notes et études documentaires*, La Documentation française, 4805. Provides a full survey and excellent notes and references.
CORVIN, Michel, 1989: *Le Théâtre de boulevard*. Paris: PUF. Provides a good historical and contemporary survey of this Parisian phenomenon. Que sais-je?
DEGAINE, André, 1993: *Histoire du théâtre dessinée*. Paris: Nizet. A personally crafted and hand-illustrated account of theatre seen from a modern French perspective.
DORT, Bernard, 1979: *Théâtre en jeu*. Paris: Seuil. A collection of articles summarizing the modern debates on the role of theatre, by one who was professor of Theatre Studies, and also, for a time, responsible for the *Direction du théâtre*.

VILAR, Jean 1975: *Le Théâtre, service public*. Paris: Gallimard. A collection of various seminal writings on theatre from the 1950s.

VINAVER, Michel, 1987: *Le Compte rendu d'Avignon. Des mille maux dont souffre l'édition théâtrale et des trente-sept remèdes pour l'en soulager*. Paris: Actes-Sud. A significant report on publishing playtexts by a contemporary playwright quite well known outside France.

|16|

Cinema in a nation of filmgoers

BY SUE HARRIS

France has a more buoyant and internationally successful domestic film industry than any other West European nation. And the French are fiercely and notoriously protective of their cinema. This combination of pride and defence was very much in evidence at the GATT talks in 1993, when French politicians gained recognition for the status of French cinema products as *l'exception culturelle*, a cultural exception not subject to the imperatives of the free-trade market. The talks attempted to dismantle what were perceived as France's unfair policies of providing subsidies to the domestic industry, and of limiting international competition by imposing strict quotas on the numbers of imported (foreign) films distributed in France in any one year. This attack was resisted by the French at every turn, and ultimately came to nothing: the French film industry today remains as protected and as generously subsidized as ever.

But what explains the motivation of the French to mount such a vigorous defence of their film industry rather than any other cultural medium? The reasons have to do with history, tradition and economics. The French were, of course, the pioneers of the late nineteenth-century film technologies, and have since led the way in innovative cinematic practice. French practitioners and critics have also been in the front line of developing new theories within the discipline of film studies: since the 1950s, discussions and analysis in the pages of journals like *Cahiers du cinéma* (founded 1951) and *Positif* (founded 1952) have set the parameters for debate in world cinema. Furthermore, France has led the way in state funding for the arts: since the Liberation, a generous system of state aid resulted in one of the most heavily subsidized and professionally accessible cinema industries in the world: new young filmmakers in France have benefited for nearly half a century from the *avance sur recettes* which provides loans for new projects to be set against future profits. Most importantly, however, the cinema is what makes modern French culture distinctive in European terms, setting it apart from its neighbours and competitors in the European Union, and providing a major platform for the promotion of the nation's identity on the world stage. '[A] hundred years after the Lumières' breakthrough in 1895, the film industry remains the barometer by which the French measure the cultural state of their nation' (Austin 1996, 1).

For many foreigners, the knowledge that we have (or think we have) about the French – their habits, lifestyles, key preoccupations and concerns – has been mediated through French films. This mediation has taken a particular shape on foreign markets, where French cinema is commonly perceived in terms of a number of consistent traits: at the top of the list is that it is a cerebral and self-consciously artistic form of expression. Difficulty for the foreign viewer lies in large measure with the language which has to be dubbed or subtitled. The peculiarly intimist cinematic style of many French *auteur* movies has also frequently been read as a sign of an intellectual approach to filmmaking, demanding more spectator input than the dynamic, physically active modes typical of a great deal of American cinema: foreign audiences have become skilled at identifying as 'typically French' the verbosity and emotional intimacy that has characterized much exported French film of the last few decades. French movies, especially in the UK and the US, have become synonymous with 'foreign films' – films which are more daring, more stylish and more intellectually conceived than mainstream Hollywood products.

French films in the UK– even Luc Besson's English-language blockbuster *Léon* (1994) or Jean-Marie Poiré's phenomenally successful comedy *Les Visiteurs* (1993) – are rarely screened outside regional art-house cinemas or, if televised, are relegated to the late-night 'intellectual' scheduling spots on BBC2 and Channel 4. Popular French stars and industry personnel are also little known outside their own country. Faced with the task of naming the Gallic equivalents of contemporary luminaries such as Harrison Ford, Martin Scorsese, Susan Sarandon and Julia Roberts, very few figures come immediately to mind. In the past, figures such as Maurice Chevalier, Jean Renoir, Brigitte Bardot, Jeanne Moreau and Louis Malle all achieved significant success beyond the borders of the Hexagon. But mostly this occurred when they worked in the English language, or Hollywood productions. Thus, in spite of their high-calibre status on home territory, the few (mostly male) actors and directors who have recently made the leap across the Atlantic – Gérard Depardieu, Isabelle Adjani and Luc Besson are significant examples – have been little more than occasional visitors in a foreign country and culture. Apart from a minority of international art film enthusiasts, the longer careers of these French ambassadors tend to be known and appreciated only by French and francophone audiences.

While these received opinions about French cinema may owe more to popular wisdom than to reality (see below), these perceptions have some basis in its evolution over the twentieth century. French cinema's position as the representative of the European industry on the world stage appears to be bound up with the idea that opposition to the might of the Hollywood dream factory must be the very antithesis of what the latter has deemed cinema to be. While American cinema (predominantly populist, easily assimilated, costly and commercially driven) tends to be regarded principally as a leisure pursuit, French cinema, by a process of opposition, is looked to for something challenging, 'arty' and self-consciously 'cultural' – something that is 'other' than the Western norm. To understand how this situation has been arrived at, a brief survey of the French cinema industry may be helpful. This will allow us to assess the state of the industry today in France, and to draw some conclusions about where cinema fits into present-day French culture.

A brief historical overview

It is generally accepted that the first public projection of a film, the Lumière brothers' *L'arrivée d'un train dans la gare de La Ciotat*, took place in Paris on 28 December 1895, and French cinema quickly became the commercial and cultural benchmark of global cinema. Production and distribution companies such as Méliès's Star-Film company, Gaumont and Pathé were created, and many now familiar popular genres (detective film, fantasy, documentary, historical reconstruction and the serial film) were first established in France in the years before World War I. From the first decade of the twentieth century, French cinema became associated with a literary tradition adapting stage plays for screen, and relying on professionals trained in a theatrical mode. France went on to produce many experimental and avant-garde artists (not just in filmmaking) including the surrealists of the 1920s and, in the inter-war years, some directors embraced a highly stylized, almost literary form of filmmaking, now known as poetic realism. This was quite at odds with Hollywood filmmaking of the period which tended towards frothy musicals and large-scale visual spectacles. This is sometimes seen as French cinema's *âge d'or*, but the failure in the under-capitalized industry to anticipate the impact of new sound technology and to develop it sufficiently quickly meant that France soon found itself losing out in global terms to American films. French cinema's strength was the value it placed on a craftsmanlike (rather than purely commercial) approach to filmmaking, but this meant that 'classic' French films began to take on an aura of esoteric intellectualism, privileging mood and atmosphere over plot and action.

What is less well appreciated beyond France, however, is that French cinema of the interwar years did not consist entirely of the classic masterpieces which appealed to sophisticated international audiences. Indeed, besides films by 'serious' directors like Jean Renoir and Marcel Carné, the 1930s saw a tremendous vogue for popular comic films with their roots in performative media such as theatre and music hall. The *comique troupier* film, or bawdy 'military comedy', was a particular favourite on home ground, with *Ignace* (1937) starring Fernandel outselling Renoir's *La Grande Illusion* at the French box office, to emerge as the most popular French film of 1937 (Vincendeau 1996, 58).

The German Occupation dealt a further blow to the industry. Domestic production decreased dramatically in 1940, as the occupying forces took control of the economic infrastucture, and the industry remained relatively small scale throughout the four years of the Occupation: in this time, only 220 feature films were made in France (Williams 1992, 253). Directors Max Ophuls, Jean Renoir and René Clair quickly left France for the safety of the United States, while other prominent figures fled to the unoccupied zone, leaving production facilities behind them in the North. Jewish personnel from technicians to producers were excluded from filmmaking by anti-semitic Vichy legislation, and many, such as Joseph Kosma and Alexandre Trauner, went into hiding – and professional inactivity – in the South. Nevertheless, both Kosma and Trauner contributed clandestinely to Carné's epic *Les Enfants du paradis* (1945), one of the most lavish French films ever to be made. British and American films were banned from France, and replaced with German and Italian films screened in dubbed versions. Paradoxically, what developed in France in this period was a dynamic – if strictly regulated – home production base controlled by German finance through production companies like Continental. This gave new life to the French industry, and resulted, according to many historians, in the rebirth of a cinema of some pictorial beauty, but characterized by stasis, escapism and distance from contemporary social reality. Whatever the stylistic result, the Occupation years served as a period of consolidation for an industry cut off from international competition.

The Liberation, however, saw the lifting of restrictions prohibiting American films, and post-war French audiences welcomed these with great enthusiasm: in early 1945, 60 per cent of the films screened in French cinemas were of foreign origin. The 1946 Blum-Byrnes agreement which allowed American films to flood the French market, and drastically reduced the potential screen time of French films from 100 per cent to 30 per cent, alarmed industry personnel and cultural commentators. It was feared that France's competitiveness could never be reestablished under such conditions. The newly formed Centre national de la cinématographie (CNC) therefore took it upon itself to grant significant financial support to 'quality projects', which included adaptations of French literary classics, and elaborate costume dramas. These films, with their high production values and major French stars, stood up well against Hollywood films, and were instrumental in reestablishing the international credibilty and commercial effectiveness of French cinema in the 1950s.

In the post-war period, enabling funding structures, new technology (lightweight cameras, rapid film stock), and rapid change in social habits all contributed to an evolution in French cinema. Various *lois d'aide* (financial aid measures) were introduced after the war, the most significant of which was the *avance sur recettes*, introduced in 1960. This subsidy was a key factor in the revitalizing of film style and production which took place in the 1960s. The experimentalist innovations of New Wave directors (of whom the most well known are Jean-Luc Godard, François Truffaut, Eric Rohmer, Jacques Rivette and Claude Chabrol) were directly concerned with the relationship between aesthetics and representation, and theirs was often an explicitly political or ethnographic form of cinema. The five directors named above quickly found themselves singled out as an 'intellectual school' of filmmakers, largely because of the critical stance that they shared vis-à-vis post-war French films: in their writing and their practice, this 'family' of young directors rejected the classic narrative realism and bourgeois performance tradition of what they called the *'cinéma de papa'* (that is 'quality' films of the 1950s outlined above), and overturned the established conventions of film construction.

Although they worked closely from time to time, and were associated as writers with *Cahiers du cinéma*, the five were not a unified movement, and produced very different kinds of films. In creative terms, part of the fun of their cinema lay in the way in which they took pre-existing popular forms such as the American film noir, and turned them into something new (the *polar*, or crime thriller), something that overtly interrogated the processes of cinematic construction. Their debates about *auteur* theory – that the director is an original creative force in the process of film construction, as much the author of his or her material as any painter or literary artist – resulted in a fresh reappraisal of the work of well-known but critically underestimated Hollywood directors such as Alfred Hitchcock, John Ford and Howard Hawks, as well as native talents such as Jacques Tati. Other directors such as the stylish maverick Louis Malle were also associated with this generation. Much of the cinema produced in France at this time is now categorized as being within the *auteur* tradition of filmmaking, that is to say it is held to embody self-consciously 'intellectual' traits such as self-reflexivity, discursiveness and cultural awareness. As it was exported, French New Wave cinema appealed to the more cosmopolitan and well educated sectors of international audiences, and inevitably gained the label of 'alternative' or 'art house' cinema. This is the categorization which still prevails today.

Filmmaking in France took a markedly different direction in the 1970s. Essentially, the relaxation of censorship laws after the death of Charles de Gaulle allowed for a boom in the production of sexually explicit adult-rated films, which have contributed to French cinema's enduring reputation for sexual explicitness and *risqué* content. Depictions of on-screen sexuality had always been more explicit in European films than in American films, a legacy of the Hayes Code on cinematic production (in operation since the 1920s) which censored potentially erotic and violent images in the name of 'taste and decency'. However, the liberalizing changes in French legislation after 1974, initiated by Valéry Giscard d'Estaing, resulted in an unprecedented upsurge in pornographic and sexually explicit films: between 1975 and 1979, around 50 per cent of all French production was within this vein. These films, such as the *Emmanuelle* series by Just Jaekin, in which visible sexual activity overshadows plot, dialogue and characterization, were dubbed and exported world-wide. The recuperation of sexual explicitness by *auteur* directors for the art house environment gave further credence to the view that French cinema is obsessed – some say pathologically – with sex. The content of films by directors such as Jean-Jacques Beineix (*37°2 le matin/Betty Blue*, 1986) and Bertrand Blier, whose *Trop belle pour toi* (1989) was an international art house hit, scandalized the British and American press, and French cinema at the end of the twentieth century continues to shock foreigners in this way: one of the most controversial films of recent years has been Catherine Breillat's *Romance* (1999), a film which figures the Italian porn star Rocco Siffredi, and explores, in graphic and apparently unsimulated detail, the sexual fantasies and erotic capacity of a woman protagonist.

And yet the post-1968 decade also saw a flowering of the work of historically marginalized groups in cultural expression such as women filmmakers, of which Breillat is herself an example. The emergence of Diane Kurys and Coline Serreau alongside Agnès Varda, already productive before the New Wave, gave voice and image to issues relating to the women's movement and established new priorities in areas of representation: the domestic environment, female desire and social and economic pressures. Women filmmakers in France have since gone from strength to strength: Claire Denis, Catherine Corsini and Tonie Marshall are just some of the most prominent female directors whose work has been showcased at international film festivals. However, industry accolades for these artists have been few and far between: to date, no woman director has ever received the César for Best Director, and only Coline Serreau has received a Best Film César for her 1986 smash hit *Trois hommes et un couffin*, later remade in the United States as *Three Men and a Baby* (Nimoy, 1987).

The success of women in the industry was paralleled by the emergence of other previously marginalized voices in filmmaking, most notably *beur* filmmakers, who came to prominence in the 1980s and 1990s. Medhi Charef (*Le Thé au harem d'Archimède*, 1985) and Malik Chibane (*Hexagone*, 1993; *Douce France*, 1995) are typical of the genre in that they focus on working-class immigrant (or second-generation immigrant) families, set their action in an often menacing (for outsiders) urban *banlieue* (or inner city), and engage with problems of integration and cultural deprivation. The huge success of a film like Mathieu Kassovitz's *La Haine* (1995), not a *beur* film but nevertheless a direct descendant of this genre, is a testament to how far modern cinema has embraced the need to represent a multi-cultural and ethnically plural France and its attendant problems. The intensity of the film's treatment of social exclusion, and the huge critical and public response to the film as social artefact (awarded César for Best Film in 1996; commented upon by Jacques Chirac) is a revealing indication of how far so-called 'alternative' cinema has been embraced by mainstream audiences and directors.

The 1980s saw a number of high-profile initiatives, taken mainly under the auspices of Mitterrand's dynamic Minister of Culture, Jack Lang. These sought to address French filmmaking's reputation for being esoteric, and to repopularize domestic cinema both for home audiences and for export. The blame for falling attendance figures, and fear for the health of the industry in France, were laid at the door of television; between 1960 and 1980 access to television had expanded nationwide, with the proportion of households owning televisions rising from 10 per cent to 90 per cent (Hayward 1993, 57). Estimates at the end of the 1990s put ownership at over 97 per cent. The threat to cinema production had spurred the government to promote a still popular, but culturally valuable (that is potentially educative) form of cinema, for which large subsidies were available. Deregulated television companies (especially Canal Plus) and private investors were encouraged to support the cinema industry financially, and have some input into the films they would distribute or screen.

These initiatives resulted in a vogue for a historico-literary form of cinema which adapted classic works of French literature (*La Gloire de mon père* [Robert, 1989], *Cyrano de Bergerac* [Rappeneau, 1990], *Madame Bovary* [Chabrol, 1991], *Germinal* [Berri, 1993]), celebrated the life of heroic figures (*Danton* [Wajda, 1981], *Camille Claudel* [Nuytten, 1988], *Lucie Aubrac* [Berri, 1997]), and recounted moments (glorious and inglorious) in France's past: *Une Affaire de femmes* (Chabrol, 1988), *Indochine* (Wargnier, 1992), *La Reine Margot* (Chéreau, 1994). The common denominator in films like the above, which proliferated throughout the 1980s and 1990s, was the very high production values that they embodied. Visually spectacular, frequently depicting rural/provincial/touristic France, these films placed a great store on 'authenticity', and on a nostalgic appeal to the French cultural consciousness. Many of these films were a huge popular success in France; but as successful exports on continental European television, and on the UK and US art-house circuits, they also confirmed for many foreign spectators France's predisposition to high quality 'cultural' products. The progressive involvement of established *auteurs* such as Claude Chabrol, Patrice Chéreau and most recently Diane Kurys in some of these projects (*Un enfant du siècle*, 1999) only added yet more intellectual kudos to the genre(s).

Finally, the 1980s saw the emergence of a new generation of filmmakers who quickly came to be known as the New New Wave. Like the New Wave directors before them, Jean-Jacques Beineix, Luc Besson and Léos Carax were not a coherent 'school' of filmmakers, and yet the key influences on them were sufficiently similar to suggest that they were indeed working within a common aesthetic culture: the video culture of pop and rock music, product advertising, and a concern to embrace in film images the qualities of 'designer chic' apparent elsewhere in French youth culture led to the labelling of their style as '*style Forum des Halles*', a reference to the ultra-modern, luxury shopping complex opened in Paris in 1979. Beineix's *Diva* (1980) is the emblematic film of both the style and the period: a labyrinthine *polar* involving plots, sub-plots and sub-sub-plots, the film both encapsulates the essence of, and provides a blueprint for, much filmmaking that followed. The film is typical in its narrative focus on 'sub-cultures' – here marginalized youth and underground criminals – and in the depiction of these within a familiar yet artificially stylized urban environment, rich in consumer goods and highly technological.

Critics were somewhat confused by the use of a semi-fantastic mode to depict contemporary types and cultures: the more generous categorized the style as 'neo-baroque', heavy on ornamentation, visual extravagance and spatial and temporal complexity. The less enthusiastic deemed it to be a '*cinéma du look*', a superficial exercise in style, mere pastiche underpinned by little narrative substance. Like *Diva*, however, *Subway* (Besson, 1985), *37°2 le matin/Betty Blue* (Beineix, 1986) and *Les Amants du Pont Neuf* (Carax, 1991) among others went on to gain cult status, most especially among young French audiences, but also on the 'art house' circuit outside France. Ultimately, however, these films have done little to challenge the foreigner's view that French cinema is first and foremost an intellectual exercise: despite the popular cultural references, the emphasis in these films is on visual and narrative complexity, and this takes precedence over more conventional narrative constants such as plot, story and characterization. These films have therefore had little effect on changing the dominant stereotypes about the 'intellectuality' of much French cinema.

The industry today

The diversity of the French market is part of its strength and its perceived weakness. French cinemagoers are fortunate to be faced with a large number of choices: between watching films in French or other languages, between domestic genres and styles and those more common to the American industry, between home-grown actors and those who shine on the global stage. The richness of their potential viewing is both a source of great pride – a regular diet of international films as compared to the singularity of choice that tends to dominate in English-speaking countries – and of anxiety, the fear that French production and distribution suffer because of the influx of foreign products onto a relatively small viewing market. This fear about the 'Cocacolonization' of French culture, that French youth (who will determine future trends) will inevitably be seduced by the international glamour of American cinema, has been articulated in many forums. The most high profile of these was no doubt the GATT talks during the formulation of the Maastricht Treaty in the early 1990s. But this anxiety has a much longer history: the post-Liberation government, fearing the saturation of the industry with a backlog of American films unreleased in France during the Occupation, progressively opposed the Blum-Byrnes agreement and opted to introduce systems of quotas and financial aid packages which have remained in place in various guises since. This protectionist policy has been regarded with considerable suspicion by those outside France, which is hardly surprising given that this approach appears to undermine the ethos of modern culture in the global market: that value will be decided by audiences rather than by some anonymous and elitist dirigiste body.

The answer to whether or not the threat of American cultural imperialism is as real as cultural policy makers and commentators fear is both yes and no. Yes, it is true that the French market is dominated by US cinema; if we look at what French audiences go to see, we find that France was no more immune than other European countries to the 'Titanic effect', which saw James Cameron's film alone take 12 per cent of the 1998 box office. *Titanic* was seen by a staggering 21 million spectators in France, leaving the year's top French hit, *Le Dîner de cons* (Veber, 1998), far behind at just short of 9 million. In fact, it took the combined result of the year's top French productions to better *Titanic*'s success, with *Le Dîner de cons, Les Couloirs du temps* (Poiré, the sequel to *Les Visiteurs*) and *Taxi* (Pirès, 1998) drawing a total audience of 23 million.

Other American (and more significantly American-*style*) action movies have had enormous success in France in the 1990s. Besson's *Le Cinquième Elément*, the top film of 1997, is a case apart in French production. Made by a celebrated French director, with French money and using a French production and design team, but filmed in English and starring Bruce Willis (of *Die Hard* fame), the film's appeal for the general public clearly lay more in its generic style than in any overtly Gallic flavour. Like the second most successful film of that year, *Men in Black*, and the previous year's huge success *Independence Day* (1996), *Le Cinquième Elément* was shown to a majority of French audiences in a dubbed version – dubbed into French that is. What is of note in this example, however, is the fact that while French audiences may flock to the same popular films as anyone else in the Hollywood catchment area, they prefer to watch these films in the French language, with the cachet of traditional 'v.o.' screenings (*version originale*, that is to say subtitled rather than dubbed films) reserved for more obviously art-house, lower budget international products.

This leads us to qualify our response to the question whether or not French culture has been fundamentally threatened by Americanization. In spite of the buoyancy of American blockbusters of the type outlined above, the French market has not been overwhelmed by US cinema to such an extent that the domestic industry has become invisible in France. Films in French are valued and appreciated by most French viewers. Indeed, there is much evidence in today's figures to allow us to conclude that French cinema is healthier than ever, with production at such levels that industry commentators in the pages of *Le Film Français* have begun to speak of a new *âge d'or*.

The French industry is supported and kept in the public eye in many ways. There is a calendar of annual festivals of which Cannes is the most well-known internationally. Founded in 1938, established since 1946, Cannes is the event that puts French cinema culture on the world stage, premièring, showcasing and rewarding home talent as well as international stars as diverse as Akira Kurosawa, Quentin Tarantino and Roberto Benigni. The world's media descend every May on Cannes, transforming it from a chic Mediterranean resort to a global cinema hall. Other major annual festivals include the *Festival du cinéma américain de Deauville*, the *Festival du film policier de Cognac* and the *Festival International de Films de Femmes de Créteil*.

All of the major festivals have a system of awards: at Cannes the coveted *Palme d'or* promises both international visibility and commercial recompense. The *César* (the term is officially used only in the singular), or French Oscars, are the most highly prized industry awards. Created in 1975, and voted for by the Académie des Arts et Techniques du Cinéma, a body of nearly 3000 industry professionals, *Césars* reward French actors, directors and technicians. The awards ceremony is broadcast every year on national television and is presided over by an eminent figure from the industry: the first president was Jean Gabin, the last of the twentieth century Isabelle Huppert. *La Nuit des Césars* is traditionally one of the most watched television broadcasts of the year and certainly encourages audiences back into the cinema: in 1997, both *Ridicule* (Patrice Leconte) which obtained four *Césars* (including Best Film and Best Director) and *Microcosmos* (Nuridsany and Pérennou, 1997; five *Césars*) saw their audiences increase overnight by 45 per cent and 60 per cent respectively.

Audiences have also been encouraged back into the cinemas by a variety of high-profile political initiatives. *La fête du cinéma* was established in 1995 by Jack Lang to mark the centenary of French filmmaking. The event, which encouraged French audiences to attend the cinema for a token sum of only one franc, was such a huge success that it was retained in the national calendar and has gone from strength to strength: in 1998 *la fête du cinéma* lasted three days, drawing audiences of over three million.

Statistically, comedy has long been the mainstay of the domestic industry, and this genre gives us some clue as to how French cinema resists the bland internationalism of the global market. The French have made this genre their own, and they show both great loyalty (consistently high attendance figures and ratings on television) and great affection for it (many comic films have gained cult status in France). *Les Visiteurs* (1993), *Les Anges Gardiens* (1995), *Gazon Maudit* (1995), *Le Dîner de cons* (1998) and *Astérix et Obélix* (1999) are some of the recent films that have set records for first-day takings. Similarly, Palaud's *Un indien dans la ville* drew the biggest audience of the year for a film broadcast on terrestrial television in 1997.

The reasons why these films should be so little acknowledged or even known beyond France are quite straightforward: film comedy, in France as elsewhere, often relies on a family of well-loved character actors whose comic persona is consistent and progressively intensified from film to film (Raimu, Fernandel, Louis de Funès, Christian Clavier, Thierry Lhermitte, Josiane Balasko). The films rely on language and very specific – culturally and geographically localized – references: topicality, familiarity and immediate recognition of verbal and visual cues are behind the success of satirical comedy. Just as the success of the Carry On series of films in the UK is linked to traditions of seaside humour and pantomime, so in France much comic action and characterization draws on the farcical tradition as represented by the work of Labiche and Feydeau. The strength of the café-théâtre comedians in cinema is to be seen in the anarcho-comic style and quickfire verbal jousting of cult films like *Le Père Noël est une ordure* (Poiré, 1982), *Papy fait de la résistance* (Poiré, 1983), *Les Visiteurs* (Poiré, 1993) and *Le Dîner de cons* (Veber, 1998). Cinematic comedy's most successful export was, for a whole generation, Jacques Tati, whose style of humour, rooted in slapstick and physical dexterity, can be traced to established traditions of French theatre performance going back to mime. The scarcity of dialogue in this director's work may also account for its international success, but the films cited above, with the exception of *Les Visiteurs* (which was the biggest grossing French film abroad of the 1980s and 1990s) but including the phenomenally successful *Le Corniaud* (Oury, 1965) and *La Grande Vadrouille* (Oury, 1966), have never 'made it' in the Anglo-Saxon markets. In 1998, entirely European films (that is those made with no financial input from the US) attracted barely 1.6 per cent of the American audience.

Where French cinema has 'made it' abroad is, perhaps unsurprisingly, in Francophone countries and in neighbouring European countries where English is not the national language. The Swiss import the greatest number of French films per capita, while Germany, Belgium and Portugal are the biggest markets for French films on television. Co-productions, especially with Italy, have been well supported by state finance and have been commercially successful in both countries. Unsurprisingly perhaps, Europe as a whole constitutes France's biggest market with European consumption in 1996 accounting for 62.5 per cent of the year's exports of French films.

Conclusion

So what does all this tell us about the French? There is no doubt that the French nation is a nation of cinemagoers, and never more so than in the present: attendance records rose constantly in the 1990s, with the magical figure of 150 million tickets per year reached at the end of the decade. The legacy of the ciné-club tradition has proved to be an enthusiastic and receptive modern audience which sustains both big commercial interests and more small-scale 'cultural' projects, especially in Paris, where hundreds of films are showing in any given week (see *Officiel des Spectacles*). While *cinemas d'art et essai* (regional film theatres) are not proliferating in France, their presence is not threatened by commercial expansion such as the rapid growth in multiplexes: 45 such cinema complexes had been established in metropolitan France by the end of 1998, with up to 60 by the year 2000.

In terms of viewing habits and preferred leisure pursuits, one might safely conclude that the French public itself does not feel as threatened by American cultural imperialism ('Cocacolonization') as French cultural policy would suggest. While it is true that the improved audience figures cited above have chiefly benefited the American film industry and not France (where in 1998 only five domestic films drew an audience of more than one million), the French continue to watch films predominantly in the French language. Furthermore, the preference for popular genres of filmmaking displayed by French audiences favours home-grown products such as the comic film.

Further reading

ABEL, Richard 1998: *The ciné goes to town*. Berkeley: University of California Press.
AUSTIN, Guy 1996: *Contemporary French cinema*. Manchester: Manchester University Press.
CRISP, Colin 1997: *The classic French cinema 1930–1960*. Bloomington: Indiana University Press.
FORBES, Jill 1992: *The cinema in France: after the New Wave*. London: Macmillan.
HAYWARD, Susan 1993: *French national cinema*. London and New York: Routledge.
HUGHES, Alex and READER, Keith 1998: *Encyclopedia of contemporary French culture*. London: Routledge.
JEANCOLAS, Jean-Pierre 1979: *Le Cinéma des Français: La Vème république (1958–1978)*. Paris: Editions Stock.
PREDAL, René 1991: *Le Cinéma français depuis 1945*. Paris: Nathan.
WILLIAMS, Alan 1992: *Republic of images: A history of French filmmaking*. Cambridge, MA and London: Harvard University Press.
VINCENDEAU, Ginette 1996: *Companion to French cinema*. London: BFI/Cassell.

Readers are also directed to a number of academic journals which regularly feature articles on French cinema. The most useful are *French Cultural Studies* and *Modern and Contemporary France*. The specialist cinema journals *Cahiers du cinéma* and *Positif* are essential reading for those interested in contemporary French cinema. For non-French readers, the monthly publication *Sight and Sound* carries regular articles on French cinema written by leading British critics and academics. More detailed studies of individual films are provided by books in the *BFI Film Classic* series, and Manchester University Press's *French Film Directors* series is an invaluable and up-to-date resource which gives new appraisals of the work of key French directors. See also the new *Journal of French Film Studies* from 2001.

|17|

Festivals and fêtes populaires

BY SUE HARRIS

Festivals are an important and distinctive feature of French cultural life. The national festival, celebrated every year on 14 July, the anniversary of the taking of the Bastille prison by the Parisian crowd in 1789, is a date which is as immediately recognizable to those outside France as it is to those within her borders. The celebration of republicanism which takes place on this day is as much a feature of the Western cultural calendar as American Independence Day or St. Patrick's Day. This holiday is just one of a great many that occur annually in France: a quick glance at any diary reveals that France has one of the highest numbers of public holidays (*jours fériés*) per year in Europe (eleven in total). In addition to common European public holidays such as Christmas, New Year and Easter, the French officially mark the following dates with official holidays: 1 May (*la fête des travailleurs*: May Day or international Labour Day), 8 May (*la fête de la victoire*: dedicated since 1981 to marking the end of World War II), 14 July (*la fête nationale*: formally adopted in 1880 to commemorate the establishment of republicanism in France), 15 August (*la fête de l'assomption*: the Feast of the Assumption), 1 November (*la Toussaint*: All Saints' Day), 11 November (*l'Armistice*: date of the 1918 Armistice, commemorated by a public holiday since 1922). Some overseas departments and territories like French Guyana (DOM) and French Polynesia (TOM) celebrate additional public holidays which mark historical and cultural events in the local calendar: for example, French Guyanans celebrate the Abolition of Slavery on 10 June every year, and French Polynesians mark occasions such as Missionary Day (5 March) and Internal Autonomy Day (8th September).

French holidays, as the above makes clear, encompass both civic and religious events. They provide official spaces in the annual calendar to reflect on events and beliefs that have made France what it is today: a secular state with a strong Catholic tradition and an awareness of the relevance of national history to contemporary life. These holidays are enshrined in the French consciousness and are respected and enjoyed by employers and employees alike. One only has to look at the tradition of taking public holidays on the exact date on which they fall, be it mid-week or at the weekend, for evidence that this is so. In Britain, public holidays tend to be moved around to take account of a predominantly commercial calendar, hence the tradition of Bank Holiday Mondays. But in France, the situation is rather different: although a holiday is effectively 'lost' if it occurs on a non-working day such as Sunday, more often than not the French use mid-week holidays to *faire le pont* (literally 'to make a bridge'). In practice, what this means is that if a public holiday falls on a Tuesday, Wednesday or Thursday, then the days between the holiday and the weekend are often taken as a holiday too by the great majority of French workers.

The many designated public holidays which take place in France every year are supplemented by a great number of non- or semi-official *fêtes* and festivals. The number and type of festivals taking place in France has grown rapidly over the last few years. In 1993, it was estimated that up to 500 festivals were taking place on French soil every summer (Saint Pulgent 1993); by 1997, this figure had reached 800 (Drillon 1997) and by the year 2000 approximately 1000. These festivals fall into three distinct categories. First, there are designated artistic and cultural festivals, 'official' festivals at which awards are often given and where the emphasis is on both celebration of the best examples of and assessment of the current state of a given art form such as theatre, cinema, *bande dessinée* or comedy. Second, there are local municipal and regional festivals which have their roots in local history, products and attractions and which invite visitors to appreciate the work, environment and heritage of a given community. The third category is that of what we might term 'invented' festivals, that is those which have recently come into being as a direct result of government policy, involve large numbers of the population and have, for the most part, become an established part of the cultural fabric of the nation in a very short space of time.

That this third category should exist at all is down to the dynamic intervention in French cultural affairs of post-1981 governments. Jack Lang, the Minister of Culture from 1981 to 1986, and again from 1988 to 1993, proved to be a trailblazer in matters of cultural innovation, arguing for the arts, obtaining greater subsidies than ever before and facilitating the positive development of the audio-visual and performance industries. The promotion of both local and national culture has been a large part of the mission of this ministry, and the creation of new country-wide festivals is one of the most tangible examples of this policy in French cultural life. The reason for this is very simple: as has been made clear in the recent French contributions to international debates about the status of cultural products, for the state, sponsorship of the arts is perceived as a matter of more than just money: it is a way of keeping debates about language, citizenship and 'Frenchness' itself at the front of the national agenda. Cultural products and manifestations of community activity are perceived in France as being fundamental to the formation and projection of a sense of national identity, and therefore worthy of the active support of the state. Festivals are, in many ways, the modern secular mode of the former religious ceremonies, uniting communities and diverse social groups in acts of commemoration, celebration and (more or less spontaneous) festivity.

The organization, promotion, and subsidizing of French festivals is the responsibility of the Ministère de la culture et de la communication. This ministry has many branches which have remits to deal with a diverse range of French cultural media: architecture, museums, books, cinema, *arts plastiques* and language are all within the domain of this branch of government. Since 1998, festivals have come under the specific jurisdiction of the Direction de la musique, de la danse, du théatre et du spectacle (formerly two separate ministries dealing with music and dance on the one hand, and with theatre and performance on the other). The mission of this body is 'de favoriser l'expérimentation et le développement des formes artistiques nouvelles', that is to support, carry out research into, and where necessary legislate in favour of artistic activity and creativity. Thus, traditionally marginalized activities such as festivals and *fêtes foraines* and traditionally marginalized participants such as amateur artists have gradually found themselves with a privileged official status in France; in practical terms this has meant access to generous funding structures and public visibility. The *direction* also maintains links with the Ministère de l'éducation nationale, promoting music, dance, drama and performance at the level of national education, and safeguarding the quality of professional and advanced academic training within these disciplines. Subsidiary organizations such as Lieux publics and HorsLesMurs have emerged from these governmental structures: the role of Lieux publics (Centre National de Création des Arts de la Rue), created in 1983, is to facilitate the practical aspects of performance in urban spaces, and this has resulted in, among many other things, the creation of a dedicated annual festival of street theatre, the *Festival Eclat* at Aurillac (see below). HorsLesMurs is an associated body, founded in 1993, which provides a specialist information and resources centre for professionals working within the field and produces materials such as guides and journals for public use. As we can see from this, the French authorities accord considerable importance to what many countries might regard as cultural curiosities or insignificant (in national terms) 'alternative' or traditional practices.

Arts festivals

The festivals that most foreigners know something about are those which we might term 'designated festivals', that is discipline-specific arts events which tend to obtain a high level of international press coverage. One of the most immediate examples is the *Festival international de Cannes*, one of the cinema world's most important and prestigious annual events. The first festival, scheduled to take place on 1 September 1939, is notable for being one of the first casualties of World War II, being abandoned almost in mid-flow in the wake of Hitler's ultimatum to Poland on 29 August 1939. The outbreak of war meant that only one film, William Dieterle's *The Hunchback of Notre Dame*, starring Charles Laughton, was projected, before the festival was postponed indefinitely. It was successfully staged for the first time in September 1946, although problems of funding meant that it remained a somewhat sporadic event throughout the remainder of the 1940s, finally establishing itself as a landmark annual event in the cultural calendar from 1951 onwards. Since 1951, the festival has taken place every year except 1968 when protests by critics and directors who sympathized with the May events forced its closure. Its major award is the *Palme d'or* (sometimes known in the past as the *Grand Prix du Festival*) which is awarded to the film judged overall best in the competition: French talents such as Henri-Georges Clouzot, Jacques Demy and Maurice Pialat have been recognized in this category, but the festival is perhaps even more renowned for its tradition of rewarding innovative non-French directors, among whom one finds Luis Buñuel, Federico Fellini, Quentin Tarantino and Mike Leigh.

The *Festival d'Avignon* was also a post-war creation, first taking place in 1947 under the direction of Jean Vilar. Vilar's decision to initiate a major theatre event outside Paris was part of the political trend towards decentralization which prevailed in the 1940s and 1950s (see chapter 15), and was a key factor in the decision to appoint Vilar as the director of the Théâtre National Populaire in Paris in 1951. Vilar's appointment in Paris strengthened the status of the festival, by facilitating professional links in terms of both repertoire and personnel. The main venue for the Festival today remains the *Cour d'Honneur* of the *Palais des Papes*, a spectacular open air courtyard which, in its day, was evidence of the rapidly changing agenda in French theatre about the nature of 'performance space'. Vilar's decision to stage classic dramatic works in a vast outdoor arena was unusual then, but was indicative of a trend towards the revitalization of modern performance which took hold in the 1960s and 1970s and which endures in venues such as Avignon today. The festival now lasts for three weeks in the summer and attracts vast numbers of participants to both the official festival and, since 1970, the 'fringe' or 'Off' festival. Here, as in other international theatre festivals like Edinburgh and New York, the fringe is an outlet for young, often experimental amateur groups to perform innovative work which they may have difficulty staging in more conventional dramatic environments. Today, the importance of the festival can be seen in the extent to which it has expanded to encompass much of the space available in Avignon, a town whose name has become synonymous with French theatre: the official festival boasts around 30 regular venues, while the fringe occupies up to 100 venues, and puts on up to 500 productions every summer.

Many music festivals are known beyond France, and regularly attract participants from all over the world. The *Printemps de Bourges* (Bourges spring festival) is a major celebration of French song which takes place at Easter, and which has attracted an estimated audience of over 2 million since its inception in the 1970s. This festival has regularly attracted French stars of the calibre of Charles Trenet, Maxime Le Forestier, Renaud and Alain Souchon, and remains a dynamic high point of the French musical year. Aix-en-Provence is host to a well-attended annual festival of classical music, and La Rochelle hosts an increasingly popular music festival, *Les Francofolies*, at the height of the summer season in July. Many towns such as Albi, Amiens, Laval and Nevers host yearly jazz festivals, which often have a significant international dimension. Furthermore, the numerous *Festivals d'humour*, such as those held around the country in towns such as Aubagne, St Gervais and Toulouse, attract *fanfare* bands who combine traditional music and song with makeshift instruments and comic performance. All of this is evidence of the importance of live music in French cultural life.

Less well known outside France, but incredibly popular within its borders, are dramatic festivals such as the *Festival des Arts de la Rue 'Eclat'* which takes place every August in Aurillac (inaugurated in 1985) and the *Festival du Théâtre de la Rue* which is staged annually in Chalon-sur-Saône. These festivals take dramatic performance into the public spaces of urban environments and embrace the conception of theatre as *fête populaire*: a participative community event. In both cases, the town itself is the stage on which performance is enacted. Innovative and experimental young theatre companies have been the lifeblood of these festivals: groups such as *Royale de Luxe* and *Illotopie* have pioneered the use of 'grandes installations' or purpose built large-scale urban 'stages' which form the backdrop for their performances, a mode of performance that has since been taken on the road (literally) to a range of French community festivals. These companies use the levels and dimensions provided by the streets and buildings of a town to create spectacular visual tableaux which extend around the crowds of ambulant spectators. By extension, the spectators become an integral part of the performance, themselves a key component of the *spectacle vivant*, or 'living spectacle'.

Local and regional festivals

Many French festivals take place at a very local level, and are a high point of the municipal or regional timetable for the year. Carnivals, *fêtes foraines* and *fêtes patronales* – festivals which celebrate the patron saint of a town, and frequently, as in Brittany, revolve around a Catholic mass – tend to have their roots in local history and culture and are attended principally by local residents and tourists. These festivals are marked in the community calendar by visits from *manèges* (fairgound rides) or may be the occasion for a *braderie* (street or flea market) or a *brocante* (bric-à-brac or antiques sale). Some such festivals are constucted seasonally around harvests of local products or related culinary traditions such as snails or mussels (*la braderie de Lille*). The appeal to tourism means that all such festivals provide good opportunities for local commerce and for the municipality, which may organize *son et lumière* spectacles to promote visits to local attractions such as cathedrals and *châteaux*.

The local and regional has taken on a national and even international profile in some cases, most notably in Brittany. The last few decades have seen the increasing popularity of Breton festivals which promote and celebrate the language and culture of the region as well as the culture of other Celtic communities. The *Festival interceltique de Lorient* is perhaps the best known of the festivals, attracting audiences of up to 400 000 from a geographically diverse Celtic community which includes Scotland, Ireland, Canada, Cornwall, and Galicia. Similar festivals include the *Celtofolies de Lanouée*, the *Nuits celtes de Muzillac*, the *Week-End de Saint-Nolff* and Quimper's *Festival de Cornouaille* which have all come into being fairly recently. The phenomenal success of the *Vieilles Charrues* festival at Carhaix gives an idea of how rapidly this phenomenon has taken hold in France: the festival has gone from attracting audiences of only 500 in 1992 to over 100 000 in the summer of 1997. Like the smaller-scale local festivals outlined above, larger-scale town-festivals of this kind are often extensions of pre-existing municipal festivals, and are therefore traditionally accompanied by a series of animations such as *bals populaires* (public dances), *défilés* (parades), *fanfares* (comic or traditional musicians) and fireworks. Increasingly, these might feature invited professional artists like *Royal de Luxe* or *Illotopie* or have open-air screenings of popular films: an example was the projection of the science-fiction blockbuster *Men in Black* outside the *Maison de la Culture d'Amiens* on 11 August 1999, the day of the last total eclipse of the sun of the twentieth century. For this event, as for many of those connected with local festivals, admission was free; 'le principe de gratuité' is something which is greatly cherished in French policies relating to community culture.

National festivals

The most internationally significant of France's national festivals is 14 July, the *fête nationale*. This event is marked throughout France by a public holiday, which begins with a local dance such as the traditional *bal des sapeurs pompiers* (Firemen's Ball) on the night of 13 July. In the provinces, as in Paris, this event is accompanied by fireworks and by a general '*esprit de fête*'. It is a more sombre affair on 14 July, with focus centred on Paris and on the military parades which take place in the presence of the French President and high-ranking foreign guests. This commemorative parade is repeated on a smaller scale up and down the country by local dignitaries and officials. The bicentennial celebrations in 1989 were the most extravagant to date, with the official parade in Paris created by Jean-Paul Goude (see chapter 12).

Of the numerous other examples of national festivals which bring the French population together in moments of shared focus, many are much more recent than the above. The *fête de la musique* which takes place at the summer solstice (21 June) is one of the most successful of recent years and is a good example of how 'invented festivals' have taken hold in French cultural practices. The *fête de la musique* first occured in France in the summer of 1982, just a year after the election of the first left-wing regime in France since the 1930s. The initiative to inaugurate the festival was taken by Jack Lang, then newly appointed Minister of Culture, in collaboration with Maurice Fleuret, the government's then *Directeur de la Musique et de la Danse*. A survey of cultural habits conducted in 1982 had revealed that as many as 5 million French people played a musical instrument, and that participation in choirs, amateur musical associations and contemporary groups was at an extremely high level. The decision was therefore taken to inaugurate a new musical festival that would be an outlet for individual and group talent within the context of the local community. France's thousands of amateur musicians were invited to dedicate half an hour of the traditional pagan festival of the summer solstice (used previously in France as 'bonfire night', the *feux de Saint Jean*) to musical performance in streets the length and breadth of the country. The success of the venture was immediate and widespread, extending well beyond the designated half hour (from 8.30 to 9 p.m.), such that only three years later, in the European Year of Music in 1985, the festival had taken on a significant international dimension. At the end of the 1990s, over 80 countries mark the *fête de la musique*, and many towns and countries have signed up to the Music Festival charter, an accord which has given the festival a permanent cooperative international status.

The punning slogan of the festival is 'faites de la musique' ('make music'), an invitation and an instruction which puts the emphasis firmly on participation and community activity. As in many other instances of festival life, this festival is one which takes place in the streets and exists for and because of the people who participate in it. *La fête du cinéma* (see chapter 16) is another of Lang's initiatives which follows the same organizational pattern: a moment of shared activity which occurs in discrete local environments but which unites the country at state level. *La Mission 2000 en France*, a series of events to celebrate the millennium, is the most recent example of the proactive cultural legacy provided by Lang which has quickly become part of the cultural specificity of the French nation.

There is, of course, a great deal of overlap between the categories outlined above; they are not meant to be exclusive or restrictive in their classification of French events and cultural tendencies, but rather seek to give a broad outline of a diverse range of related practices which function rather differently in France than they do in other nation states. The notion of the festival is one that we see translated into many other aspects of French life, including politics and sport. One-off festival-type events have become popular ways of drawing attention to political and social causes: the *fête de l'Humanité* is a regular event in Paris which promotes the PCF in a way which takes politics out of government buildings and party offices. The organization SOS Racisme, which assembled around a festival event in Paris in 1984, brought the slogan 'touche pas à mon pote' ('hands off my mate') into the public domain and made the debate about racism accessible to young people. In 1995, the community of La Seyne sur Mer held a festival to protest at the victory of a National Front mayor in the neighbouring town of Toulon: performers and personalities as diverse as NTM, Patrick Bruel and Bernard-Henri Lévy were brought together in an event which coincided with the national festival and counted grandparents, young people and infants among its participants. In another fortutitous example of timetabling, France's Football World Cup victory in 1998 coincided with the national festival and with an atmosphere celebrating the inclusiveness of contemporary republican culture: the 'black-blanc-beur' motto underpinned both celebrations and media commentary and added significantly to the festive euphoria which overtook the population. On a more regular note, the annual Tour de France cycle race has something of the status of a mobile festival, an event which moves around the country, drawing enormous crowds out into the streets and focusing attention on local communities. The race, which towns compete to have pass through their streets, is more than simply a sporting event in France: it is a further example of a peculiarly French event which brings a large part of the population together in a combined holiday, party and community performance.

Conclusions

Festivals are a distinctive feature of French community life. In their concern to involve a 'non-traditional' public, and to bring the events into the urban, inhabited environment, festivals respond to something that has long concerned cultural policy makers: festivals are a concrete manifestation of alternative uses and functions of '*l'espace public*', a reappropriation of public space by the people themselves (see chapter 11), and succeed in engaging those whom 'official culture' (theatre, opera, art, museums) tends to exclude for reasons of education. What Jean Vilar termed the *non-public*, or those who have no access to conventional cultural outlets, is here involved in a participative role as the people who make culture happen and who make it happen on their own terms. As such, festivals are a cultural phenomenon which may be regarded as achieving, where other cultural forms have failed, a sort of 'classlessness'. The success of a festival like the *fête de la musique* lies in the way in which it unites generations, social groups and different tastes in a shared experience: whether one favours classical music or *bal musette* (traditional accordion music), *chanson à textes* or rap, such a festival has something for everyone. As such, it arguably achieves the democratization of culture which has been a recurrent concern of French cultural policy since the beginnings of the Third Republic.

As stated above, this trend is a quite distinctive feature of French cultural life and one which sets it apart from its neighbours. The increasing number of festivals from year to year, the increased participation by huge numbers of ordinary French people in the events, is evidence of a frequently unexpected quality of conviviality, festivity and spontaneity in the French *mentalité*. Indeed, perhaps nowhere else is the founding value of *fraternité* so well expressed in French culture. It is to be hoped that such a view of French culture will give the outsider a new perspective on a culture that is more habitually associated with 'intellectual' traditions, such as the literary and the philosophical.

Further reading

There is very little information in English about French festivals. The most useful source currently is Alex Hughes and Keith Reader, *Encyclopedia of contemporary French culture* (London: Routledge, 1998). One can find articles in the French press (usually in the summer) and special supplements in daily newspapers such as *Libération*. Articles consulted in the preparation of this chapter include: Maryvonne de Saint-Pulgent, Ode aux festivals, *Le Point*, 3 March 1993 and Jacques Drillon, Neuf festivals inattendus, *Le Nouvel Observateur*, 26 June 1997. By far the most useful sources of information about festival culture are French websites, which have the advantage of being updated regularly. Those that I have found of particular interest include the French Ministry of Culture and Communication site: http://www.culture.gouv.fr. Others include http://www.horslesmurs.com and http://www.lieuxpublics.com. A very useful search engine is provided by Yahoo at the following address: http://www.fr.fir.yahoo.com/artsetculture/Artsduspectacle.

|18|

From press barons to digital TV: changing media in France

BY JEAN-CLAUDE SERGEANT

It is difficult to identify the specificity of the French media by going back over history. In fact, what strikes the observer is the similarity between the development of the press on both sides of the Channel, particularly during the second half of the nineteenth century. In both France and Britain, at about the same time, the combination of the growth of an increasingly literate public with the relaxation of state controls over newpapers resulted in soaring circulation figures. The growing affluence of society, together with the spreading of a new entrepreneurial spirit, boosted investment in the newspaper sector whose development depended on the use of state-of-the-art equipment.

In France the refreshing liberalism of the 1881 law on the press, still in force today, was seen as an encouragement to journalists with commercial flair to set up business and launch popular newspapers on a large scale. A typical example of this new breed of publishers was Jean Dupuy who in 1879, although not a journalist by training, started *Le Petit Parisien*, which he fully owned ten years later. By the turn of the century, circulation passed the one million mark, two years before Alfred Harmsworth's *Daily Mail*, which bore some resemblance to *Le Petit Parisien*. Like Harmsworth, who visited him before launching the *Daily Mail* in 1896, Dupuy had high political aspirations which, unlike his English counterpart, he fulfilled beyond expectations. He held several Cabinet posts after 1909 and was even invited by the then President of the Republic Georges Clemenceau to form a new government, an honour which he wisely declined.

As in Britain, therefore, but perhaps even more so, newspaper power in France went hand in hand with political ambitions, a characteristic which was to endure until recently. Robert Hersant, the owner of the newspaper empire which bore his name and who died in 1995, was a prominent, if not always assiduous, member of the National Assembly. The current head of the regional publishing group La Depêche du Midi was a member of a recent Socialist government. Conversely, politicians occasionally launched newspapers to serve their political creeds and interests. Thus Gaston Defferre, who during the 1980s was Minister of the Interior (equivalent to the British Home Secretary), had earlier founded *Le Provençal*, a daily based in Marseille, and went on controlling it until his death in 1986.

On the whole, however, direct links between politics and the press are less obvious today, with the exception of *L'Humanité*, the official mouthpiece of the Communist Party, even if every national daily and a few regional dailies reflect a degree of partisanship which may vary with a change of ownership. A recent example of this is the shift towards the centre of the political spectrum of the editorial policy of *France-Soir*, a paper which had impeccable conservative credentials before its sale in April 1999 by the publishing group Socpresse, owner of *Le Figaro*.

Current situation of the national press

The fate of *France-Soir*, sold for one symbolic franc to Georges Ghosn, a relative newcomer in the field of newspapers, is a good illustration of the slow erosion of the national press. Founded after the Liberation of Paris in 1944, like other well-known titles such as *Le Monde* and *Le Parisien*, *France-Soir* soon became the archetypal French popular daily under the stewardship of Pierre Lazareff who left his mark on popular journalism even among broadcasting journalists. By the mid-1950s, *France-Soir* had become the best-selling daily with a circulation of 1.4 million. Ten years later, the 'daily of the rue Réaumur', as it was called, still dominated the scene with a significantly diminished circulation slightly in excess of one million. *The News Chronicle*, on the other hand, a British liberal daily with a similar circulation, had to fold at about the same time. The contrasting fate of these two newspapers reflected the vastly different scales of circulation across the Channel. Increasing competition from television and the 1968 upheaval dealt a serious blow to popular dailies, with younger potential readers turning to new titles – *Libération* in particular – which had managed to reflect the tastes and values of a new generation. Faced with what looked like an unstoppable decline of the title, the publishing group Hachette, which had owned *France-Soir* since 1946, sold it to Robert Hersant in 1976. In spite of various alterations to its lay-out and a change to the tabloid format, *France-Soir* never managed to recover enough readers. Writing in 1983, Pierre Albert, a leading historian of the French press, was already speculating about the daily's future (Albert 1983, 91). And with a circulation of less than 200 000 copies today, it is difficult to see how this ailing newspaper will be able to stem the tide.

Not all of the 11 national dailies have had to face such critical problems, but only a handful of 'general information' dailies can be reasonably optimistic about their future, as Table 18.1 suggests.

Table 18.1   Circulation figures of the national dailies (in thousands)

	1998	1988
Le Parisien/Aujourd'hui[a]	471	384
Le Figaro	346	432
Le Monde	341	387
Libération	160	195
France-Soir	149	255
La Croix	83	104
L'Humanité	51	109
Les Echos	111	96
La Tribune	81	n.a.
L'Equipe[b]	359	230
Paris Turf	97	105

Source: OJD (figures do not include sales abroad)
[a] *Aujourd'hui* is the national edition of *Le Parisien* which is sold only in the Paris region
[b] Figures for mid-week editions of the sports daily

In the past ten years, only *Le Parisien* has managed to increase its circulation by producing two different editions every day. Under the title *Aujourd'hui*, one is aimed at the national market; the other, which includes pull-out sections reflecting local interests, is as much a Paris or, more precisely, an Ile-de-France regional daily as a national daily. *Le Parisien* has also toned down its former popular style and tried to acquire a more mid-market personality with an increased number of political stories and a commitment to express the views and comments of readers by means of a daily survey of five different people on the major stories of the day. This new formula seems to have found an encouraging response in the public and suggests that dailies can adapt to the changing expectations of the readers.

If the only success story in the category of general information dailies is *Le Parisien*, however hybrid its identity, the four titles which do not belong to that category have also shown that they can respond to the growing demand for financial and economic news and for sports coverage. *Les Echos*, owned by the British media group Pearson, is slowly consolidating its reputation as the preferred daily of the business class, while *L'Equipe*, part of the Amaury publishing group which also owns *Le Parisien*, has become the indispensable companion of the growing constituency of sports devotees. In 1998, the Monday edition which carries the results of weekend sports events had an average circulation of 478 000: 120 000 more than on any other day except Saturday.

If we leave aside the four specialized titles, there remain only the seven titles in the upper section of the table, a very small number indeed in a country where democracy has always been equated with wide-ranging expression of opinion. Moreover, these seven titles sell mostly in the Paris area, even though they are widely distributed across the country. About ten years ago, *Le Monde*, *Le Figaro* and *Libération* tried to attract more regional readers by starting local editions based in Lyon, the second largest city in France. This experiment did not bring about the expected results and ended after a couple of years. Only the small Catholic daily *La Croix* seems less centered on the Paris area. Founded in 1880, *La Croix*, which in September 1999 transformed itself from an evening to a morning daily, sells 90 per cent of its copies to subscribers, an advantage which cuts the number of unsold copies and ensures stable revenues.

Such a steep decline of the French national press could not have been foreseen 60 years ago, on the eve of World War II, when 32 dailies were published in Paris. Twenty titles were started between August and December 1944, and by 1945 28 dailies could be found on Parisian news-stands. The turbulent years which followed 1968 stirred ideological debates and spawned some shortlived journalists' outlets (*Rouge, Le Quotidien du Peuple, L' Humanité Rouge*). These did not compensate for the loss of more traditional titles which had acquired a high reputation but could not attract enough readers to keep them going (*Paris Presse, Paris Jour* and *Combat*, which disappeared in 1970, 1972 and 1974 respectively). In 1939, national dailies accounted for two-thirds of the overall circulation of all French dailies of general interest. The proportion is now less than a quarter.

The crisis in newspaper reading, particularly as regards the national papers, does not affect France alone but its magnitude on this side of the Channel certainly has something to do with the high cover price of the dailies. Quality papers (*Le Figaro, Libération*) sell at 7fr, even 7fr50 in the case of *Le Monde,* while the more popular titles (*France-Soir, Le Parisien*) sell at 5fr, as does *L'Equipe* (4fr90). While at the beginning of the century it was accepted that as a basic commodity the daily newspaper should not cost more than an inland postage stamp, the gap between the two has kept widening over the years. An average mid-market daily (*La Croix* for example) now costs twice as much as the stamp for letter post at normal speed anywhere in France or in the EU.

High cover prices reflect a somewhat imbalanced cost structure in which distribution and wages bills are the dominant factors. Nearly 37 per cent of the overall costs are accounted for by the national system of distribution run by a co-operative company called NMPP (*Nouvelles Messageries de la Presse Parisienne*) in which Hachette has a 49 per cent stake. Wages and salaries represent a third of the average costs, since the Paris print union, to which nearly all the 2500 print workers belong, has managed to maintain enough pressure on management to retain hefty salaries and bonuses, although the union has moderated its demands since 1990. Furthermore, a deal was signed in 1993 with the print union which provided for the gradual shedding of 1000 of the older print workers.

On the other hand, the national press is faced with diminishing advertising revenues, tapped by TV channels both public and commercial. Between 1975 and 1998, the advertising resources of the daily newspapers were slashed by more than half. National and regional dailies account for only

14.5 per cent of the total advertising spend in media, while the share of TV over the same period has gone up from 14 per cent to 34 per cent in 1998. Admittedly, all newspapers do not derive an equal proportion of their revenues from advertising. It represents 21 per cent of the total resources of *Libération* against 50 per cent for *Le Figaro* – largely classified ads – and even 54 per cent in the case of *Les Echos*.

One way of restoring a level playing field would be to impose a levy on TV advertising takings to feed a fund which would then share the proceeds of this new tax between daily titles. Such, at least, was the proposal made recently by Jean-Marie Colombani, chairman and editor of *Le Monde* (see Assemblé nationale report 1997, 78). This additional source of funding, approved by the government, would increase the already significant amount of public financial support available to the press. In 1998, the overall total of direct and indirect subsidies to the press as a whole amounted to 7.8 billion francs (about 12 per cent of the total turnover of the press industry) out of which the most important item (95 million) concerned the sums paid by the Government to compensate for the reduced rate applied to the transportation of printed publications by the *SNCF* (French railways). Less substantial but no less important symbolically is the aid given to national dailies of general information with low advertising receipts. In 1997 only *La Croix* and *L'Humanité* were eligible for that kind of subsidy which in previous years had also benefited the extreme right daily *Présent*. Even more crucial to the press is the reduced postal rate worth about 5 billion that *La Poste* applies, in exchange for a government contribution of a much lesser amount. Other forms of aid include the reduced rate of VAT (2.1 per cent against the standard lower rate of 5.5 per cent) and the 45 million franc funding granted to developing home delivery of newspapers which is still being experimented with by national dailies,[1] whereas this is common practice in northern and eastern parts of France.

Part of state funding is also intended to help publishers to invest in multimedia operations and to develop on-line versions of their papers. At the beginning of 1999, nearly all dailies with the exception of *L'Equipe* and *France-Soir* could be consulted on a website. A minority of them however provide a full on-line version of the paper. Those who do, *Les Echos* and *Le Monde* in particular, tend to charge a fee for the consultation of back numbers and specialized files; otherwise access is free (see chapter 2). If display advertising in electronic versions is currently rather small, this is surely a source of revenue which is bound to grow as well as e-commerce available on newspaper websites. Electronic newspapers are proving extremely successful. *Libération*'s site had an average of 27000 daily visits at the beginning of 1999; at about the same time a total of 16 million pages were read every month on *Les Echos*' site. On-line papers are not yet the alternative to paper editions but they have become the indispensable complements of every publication and more crucially so in the case of national dailies.

The regional press

This group of newspapers includes different categories of publications. Alongside the well-known traditional dailies, about 300 weekly or bi-weekly papers with limited circulation are very often the preferred choice of reading of the 55 million French people who live outside the Paris area. Regional dailies reach on average 45 per cent of the population (IPSOS 1999), of whom a third live in rural areas. Unlike the national dailies whose readers are predominantly men (60 per cent), the readership of the regional dailies is almost evenly shared between men (51 per cent) and women (49 per cent). As might be expected, fewer readers belong to the younger age group (26.4 per cent of readers in the 15–34 age bracket) than is the case for national dailies (37.3 per cent). Another characteristic of the regional press is the loyalty of its readers. In Alsace but also in Brittany, two-thirds of the local population read a regional daily. In one-third of all French regions, one person in every two will read a local paper for an average of 32 minutes per day.

This loyalty certainly reflects the satisfaction of the readers who find in their local papers the sort of practical news they need to feel at home in their areas. Cheap compared to national papers (from 4fr60 to 5fr), local dailies are an essential mirror of micro-realities which shape the daily routine of millions of readers. Multiple local editions of metropolitan dailies are therefore necessary to capture the interest of groups of readers with strong parochial identifications. A typical example of this diversified approach to local needs is provided by *Ouest-France*, the best-selling French daily with a circulation of 757 000 copies, which prints about 40 local editions serving seven million people scattered over seven *départements*. *La Dépêche du Midi,* founded in 1870 and based in Toulouse, is equally active and sells its 18 local editions in ten *départements*. This daily is run by the eponymous publishing group which also owns two other dailies, two weeklies and two advertising agencies and has a stake in local radio and television.

On the whole, the seven million copies of regional titles sold every day are published by a dozen groups offering more than one title as well as numerous editions of the most widely distributed papers, ultimate control resting, in a number of cases, with a larger national media group such as Hersant,[2] which has a majority stake in or full control of ten of the 62 dailies published in mainland France. Less vulnerable than the national press because of its easier accessibility through home delivery and also because of the large degree of monopoly it enjoys over nearly one half of the country, the regional press has become the dominant segment of the daily press. Among the ten largest selling French dailies, seven are regional dailies, as Table 18.2 shows.

Table 18.2   The seven largest French regional dailies

	Circulation in thousands	Town where printed
Ouest-France	757	Rennes
Sud-Ouest	337	Bordeaux
La Voix du Nord	323	Lille
Le Progrès	262	Lyon
Le Dauphiné libéré	259	Grenoble
Nouvelle République du Centre Ouest	251	Tours

Source: OJD, 1998

Despite its apparent prosperity, the regional press has also been affected by the decline in the number of readers. The combined circulation of all regional dailies has fallen back to what it was by the end of the 1960s. The growth in local television opt-outs siphons off the display advertising revenues which until recently local papers had only to share with commercial radio. The projected opening up of TV advertising to retailers – which the government is currently considering – would contribute further to the erosion of the regional press's financial base, 27 per cent of which is actually provided by the large retailing groups. This risk might be deflected by the launching of a series of local TV channels which regional publishing groups could supply with local news programmes. Such is at least the proposal that 16 leading regional press owners have submitted to the broadcasting regulating Authority (CSA), which has yet to decide on its response.

Weeklies and magazines

One of the reasons for the decline of the traditional dailies is probably to be found in the availability of a large and diversified magazine press which caters for every taste or interest, however exotic or specialized. The presence of about 500 free weeklies with a combined circulation of 40 million adds to the pressure weighing on full-price dailies. As in Britain, French publishing groups have responded to the threat by moving into the free papers market where companies controlled by *Ouest France*, *Sud-Ouest* and *La Nouvelle République du Centre-Ouest* have become dominant players. Additionally, regional dailies have tried to enlarge their readership with Sunday editions complete with colour supplements, a development which national publishers have not emulated, with the exception of *Le Figaro* (*Le Figaro Magazine* and *Le Figaro Madame* are sold with the Saturday edition of the daily).

Despite the efforts of the daily newspaper publishers, both national and regional, to revamp their products – all national dailies, with the exception of *Libération*, have recently altered their make-up, the latest face-lift being that of *Le Figaro* at the end of November 1999 – the future of the daily press is at best unstable. It seems that one of the reasons for this lack of public support lies in competition from magazines that can capture the latest changes in lifestyle trends. By the end of the 1990s, about 250 new titles were launched every year on the magazine market, only a few of them managing to find a lasting niche in that market which attracts half of all the advertising revenues of the press sector.

With a daily combined readership of over 35 million people, the French magazine market has attracted foreign publishers – EMAP, Bertelsmann – who have bought existing titles and launched new products with substantially cheaper cover prices than established rival titles. Prisma Presse, for example, a subsidiary of Bertelsmann, set up at the beginning of the 1980s, is now the second largest magazine publisher in France after Hachette Filippachi (*Elle, Paris-Match*). Through its cost-conscious policy, Prisma has contributed to revitalizing the ailing women's magazine market. *Femme Actuelle* has now become the leading title among women's weeklies with a circulation of over 1.6 million (1996) while *Prima*, a concept duplicated in Germany and Britain, sells over a million copies each week. The Prisma Presse empire also includes best-selling titles such as *Géo*, *Gala* and *Capital*, a popular business magazine, which have explored new concepts in the field of magazine journalism.

The third largest publisher of magazines, EMAP, entered the French market in 1994 by buying a number of magazines and specialized weeklies, among which is the well-known *L'Auto Journal* from Hersant. With a portfolio of 40 titles, EMAP is trying to diversify its range of products, which received a new addition in June 1999 with the launching of the French edition of *FHM*, the notorious British men's magazine with a somewhat brash reputation. As in Britain, the attention of magazine publishers has turned to that traditionally neglected segment. If not quite overcrowded today, the men's magazines market includes a substantial number of competing titles – *Max, M Magazine, Men's Health* and the newly launched *Kromosom* – some of them already threatened with extinction.

If the French magazine market, like all other markets of the kind in industrialized countries, is dominated by TV listings magazines – the French leading title in that segment is *Télé 7 Jours* with a weekly circulation of 2.6 million – it includes some specific components which are more developed in France than elsewhere in Europe. The news magazines in particular are remarkable for their diversity and resilience. The oldest of them were launched in the 1950s as weekly newspapers with definite political views, often close to those of left-wing parties. The shift to a new format, imitating the US *Time Magazine*, took place in 1964. This was accompanied by a less militant editorial policy and the broadening of the news coverage. Devoting as much attention to culture and society as to politics, *L'Express* and *Le Nouvel Observateur* became the successful forums of the elite. By the early 1970s, *L'Express* had a circulation of around 700 000 even though a rival title – *Le Point* – had been started in 1972 by a group of journalists who had defected from the *Express*, considering it to be too left-wing. In 1985, Jean-François Kahn, a former history teacher with iconoclastic views about the press in general and magazines in particular, launched *L'Evénement du Jeudi*, soon nicknamed l'EDJ, which offered a less conventional coverage of the week's events and, above all, a more light-hearted treatment of the news. After the failure of l'EDJ, which had to be sold to Hachette, the same tireless innovator started another weekly in 1997 which he called *Marianne*, after the name of the traditional personification of the French Republic. Costing ten francs, half the price of the traditional news magazine, *Marianne* was meant to stir the reader with provocative news stories and a dazzling cocktail of diagrams, cartoons and photographs.

Even if the combined circulation of all major news magazines hardly reaches 1.5 million – the most popular of them, *L'Express*, had a circulation of half a million in 1998 – their influence is not to be neglected. Not only do they provide in-depth coverage of a wide variety of topics but they also increasingly launch politically embarrassing investigations – a speciality of the *Canard Enchaîné*, the satirical weekly started in 1916 which sells 459 000 copies every week and whose revelations have often shaken the political establishment to its foundations.

More recent magazines have also been able to find a substantial readership in non-political fields. *Télérama* is one of them. The best-selling title of the Catholic press group La Vie, *Télérama* started as a rather bland TV and radio listings weekly in 1950. Nearly 50 years on, *Télérama* can claim to be the leading cultural magazine of the educated classes. TV listings as well as the radio programmes of the week are still there but they now occupy less than half of the 200 pages that a current issue will normally offer. Regular sections devoted to the latest productions in the various art forms and an exhaustive review of the latest cultural events combine to make *Télérama* the quality guide to cultural life in France. The weekly also reflects some of the major controversies of the time – the war in Kosovo and the World Trade Conference in Seattle are among the more recent topics – always envisaged from the moral angle characteristic of this progressive Catholic publication. With a cover price of ten francs, *Télérama* is finding its way into an increasing number of homes: its circulation of 653 000 in 1998 was twice that of 20 years ago.

Other examples suggest that culture sells well in France. *Les Inrockuptibles*[3] originated in 1986 as a rock music magazine published every other month by a small group of young independent students who wanted to explore aspects of the rock and popular music world ignored by major record companies. Their success was such that by 1992 *Les Inrockuptibles* became a regular monthly which changed itself into a weekly in 1995. When celebrating their tenth anniversary, the editorial team pledged never to renounce 'the spirit of the idle, confrontational student eager to make new discoveries' (editorial, 78, 6–12 November 1996) which fed the early issues of the magazine. Selling about 60 000 copies a week, *Les Inrockuptibles* has widened the range of its interests to include books, painting and even classical music. The style of the weekly however remains equally abrasive and studiedly relaxed, though not always reader-friendly for afficionados over 30 years of age.

The same cultural bonanza is tapped by FNAC, the leading book and music shop with branches in major French cities. Describing itself as a 'cultural agitator', FNAC launched a customer magazine called *Epok* with a large editorial component made up of the usual books, films, music and exhibitions sections. The first issue of the magazine, published in November 1999, included special features dealing with the new literary season and DVD technology as well as a six-page report on the situation in Algeria. According to François-Henri Pinault, the chairman of FNAC who wrote the editorial for the first issue, *Epok* is meant to echo all the cultural, social but also technological forces shaping our mindset as we begin the new millennium. Perhaps it should be mentioned that Pinault, who runs the retailing group 'Printemps-Redoute', also owns *Le Point*, the news magazine bought from Havas – a Vivendi subsidiary – in 1997. Culture has become a lucrative commercial sector.

Broadcasting

The French broadcasting scene was long dominated by the role of the state which had imposed a monopoly over the programming and transmission of French radio and television services. The monopoly was in fact the direct continuation of the control the state had exerted over wireless communications enforced in 1903. Various public corporations with limited degrees of autonomy were established to provide broadcasting services to the country: Radio-Télévision française (RTF) from 1949 to 1964, the Office de Radio-Télévision française (ORTF) until 1974.

It was President Giscard d'Estaing who decided in 1974 to break up the broadcasting corporation into seven independent units, three of them corresponding to the three TV channels of the time, transformed into private companies with the state as sole shareholder. But the government retained responsibility for appointing members of the boards of directors and in particular their chairpersons and for defining their policies and constraints. These seven companies, with the exception of the production company SFP, were mainly financed out of the proceeds from the licence fee to which were added advertising revenues, capped to a 25 per cent limit of total resources.

It was not until July 1982 that the government surrendered its monopoly over the provision of broadcasting programmes, a way of legalizing the dozens of pirate radio stations which had sprouted on the FM waveband. However, the Socialist government of the day kept its monopoly over the transmission of signals which was the preserve of Télédiffusion de France (TDF). A more symbolic provision of the 1982 law was the setting up of a regulating body which was supposed to sever the umbilical cord which had hitherto linked governments to state broadcasting companies. In practice, the responsibility of appointing the officials running those companies was transferred to the new regulator, along with responsibility for monitoring the performance of the channels and their compliance with their remits, still defined by the government. Later, the regulating body, whose composition and title varied over the years,[4] acquired wider powers in terms of awarding franchises to commercial radio and TV companies and granting authorizations to foreign channels broadcasting over the national territory.

Radio

The legislation of the 1980s led to the creation of literally thousands of private local radio stations on the FM band. Regrouping and takeovers have somewhat rationalized their number though today 'they can no longer be considered very free or local' (Pedley 1998). A few of them have gone on to become household names, mostly for the music they play: examples are NRJ for mainstream up-to-date music, Nostalgie for golden oldies and Skyrock for the further out. All are subject to the ruling, effective from 1996, that 40 per cent of songs must be in French (cf. chapter 19). Other private stations are run by religious minorities or local groups. But a large share of the audience for private radio still tunes in to the big three, RTL (Radio-Télévision Luxembourg), RMC (Radio Monte Carlo) and Europe I, collectively known as the *radios périphériques*, which transmit from just over the French borders and were once the only antidote to state-controlled broadcasting. As well as music, these stations run quiz-shows and topical interviews and features. The state broadcasting network, Radio France, based in the Maison de la Radio and financed very largely out of the licence fee (*la redevance*), still retains about 20 per cent of the total audience. Its mainstream channel is the general-interest France-Inter, and it also runs a continuous news programme, France-Info, as well as the long-established France Musique (classical and jazz) and France Culture. Radio plays an often unacknowledged role in most people's private *paysage audiovisuel*, playing in the background when they eat breakfast, do the chores, mind the children or drive the car.

Television

The new broadcasting law of September 1986, introduced by a new right-wing government, removed the last shred of state monopoly over transmission systems, except for public broadcasting services, still dependent on TDF facilities, and, more importantly, provided for the privatization of TF1, the most popular of the three public TV channels. This decision was to further destabilize the television sector, to which three commercial channels had already been added between 1982 and 1986 without any prior consultation of parliament.

After the completion of the sale of TF1 in 1987, French viewers could choose between six different terrestrial channels, two of them public (Antenne 2 and FR 3), the other four funded through advertising (TF1, La 5 and TV6) or subscription (Canal Plus).[5] At the time TF1 remained the most popular channel with a market share of 40 per cent, A2 trailing behind with 33 per cent. La 5, awarded to a consortium made up of Hersant, Berlusconi and Seydoux (Chargeurs réunis), was the third most popular channel with an audience share of 15 per cent, twice that of FR 3, the other public channel. Three years after its launching, Canal Plus, the new pay-TV channel, had slightly over 3.5 per cent of the market while TV6, the music channel run by the Luxembourg based company CLT, had hardly any impact on the audience (1 per cent).

More than 20 years later, the context has changed substantially as a result of the withdrawal of some operators and the ensuing alterations in the kind of programmes available. In particular the collapse of La 5 in 1992 after the decision by Hachette, its ultimate owner, to pull the plug on the debt-ridden channel, freed a frequency awarded to La Cinquième-Arte. The air time of the channel is now split between La Cinquième, a public learning channel set up in 1994, and Arte, a Franco-German channel established on the basis of a treaty signed in 1990. TV6, renamed M6, has now restructured its programme schedule and offers more series – mostly American – and docudramas than music programmes. The wind of change has not spared the public channels either. In 1989, the government decided to bring the two channels together into a holding called France Télévision, run by a single chairperson. Thus A2 and FR3 gave way to France 2 and France 3 respectively.

Yet the pecking order of the different terrestrial channels on the basis of their audience shares has not been dramatically altered, except in the case of M6 and the fifth network (La Cinquième-Arte), as Table 18.3 shows.

Table 18.3   Audience shares for the week 7 to 13 December 1998

	Viewing time (minutes)	Audience share (%)
TF1	73	36.8
FR2	42	21.1
FR3	32	15.8
Canal Plus	10	5.0
M6[a]	26	13.1
Fifth network[b]		
(La Cinquième/Arte)	7	3.5
Other TV[c]	10	4.7
Total TV	200	100

Source: Médiamétrie
[a] M6 is available in 93 per cent of households with TV
[b] The fifth network which includes La Cinquième and Arte is available in 90 per cent of households with TV
[c] Other TV = non-terrestrial TV

Obviously the emergence of cable and satellite TV combined with the launching of the cultural channel on the fifth network vacated by La 5 was bound to have an impact on the viewing share of TF1 and of the two major public channels which suffered most. The apparently sluggish growth of Canal Plus, the pay-TV channel, conceals in fact an unexpected success story which has led Canal Plus to become the leading group of pay-TV in Europe, where 11 million people are subscribers to the channel (7.5 million in France alone). M6 (Métropole Télévision) – a subsidiary of CLT and the utility company Lyonnaise des Eaux – has also managed to strengthen its brand image in the crowded sector of terrestrial general public television. Its original programme schedule, which deliberately tries to avoid the conventional structure of the three major channels, includes such hits as the weekly *Capital* (a business programme with an average audience of 3.2 million) and *Zone interdite* (an investigative current affairs programme which gets a regular audience of nearly three million). But audience figures really peaked with the weekly episode of the *X Files* series (four million). Originally aiming to reach the 15–35 age group, M6 has recently widened its audience target to the under-50s as well as to the 4–14 age group, with whom it has become the second most popular channel after TF1.

M6 is also the channel where week after week younger viewers will follow the riveting adventures of *Ally McBeal* (the episode of 20 October 1999 was watched by six million people). The same, together with their slightly older fellow viewers, would not miss *Melrose Place,* shown every day on TF1 from 5.35p.m. to 6.25p.m. *Seinfeld* (Canal Plus) and *Friends* (currently repeated on the cable channel Canal Jimmy) are also among the most popular TV programmes watched by people in the 14–24 age groups. All these programmes are American and so is *Les Feux de l'Amour,* shown every day on TF1 and proving immensely popular with older women. But the programmes that still attract the larger audiences are game shows (*Le Bigdil,* TF1) and the news programmes, in particular the FR3 *Journal Télévisé* in the access prime time period, 7–8.30p.m. Later in the evening, feature films, football or series – this time mostly French, such as the long-standing *Navarro* police series – will pull audiences in excess of 15 million. Teenage viewers would probably have deserted the living room by that time after watching *Nulle Part Ailleurs,* the daily iconoclastic cultural chat show on Canal Plus, including the savagely satirical *Guignols* sequence in which latex puppets of famous personalities, mostly politicians, are held up to public ridicule.

However, French television cannot be equated with the whole television supply available. Cable television was introduced in France in 1985 and did not begin to take off until the mid-1990s. By the end of 1998, over seven million homes had been cabled and two and a half million of them had subscribed to one of the 'packages' offered by one of the three cable operators, France Télécom, Lyonnaise Câble and NC Numéricâble (in which Canal Plus has a 63 per cent stake). The penetration of cable was thwarted by the availability of satellite TV, among other factors. The Astra satellites offered a range of about 60 channels, most of them in foreign languages, which, in the case of the large Arabic-speaking community, explained the greater attraction of satellite TV as opposed to cable.

The launching of digital satellite TV in 1996 revived the demand for non-terrestrial TV, so much so that at the turn of the century 25 per cent of all TV homes have access to digital television which, in the homes where it is available, accounts for 28 per cent of the total audience (1998 figure). In 1998 the number of subscribers to any one of the three satellite TV opera-tors (Canalsatellite, TPS and AB Sat) had gone up by half to 1.7 million. Rather unexpectedly France finds itself the leading European country in the field of satellite digital television and far from inhibiting the growth of cable television, this development has led to an increase in the number of chan-nels, nearly all of them thematic, that can be accessed through satellite or cable. Today, French viewers can choose from 70 non-terrestrial channels, the most popular of them being, as might be expected, sports channels (Eurosport), premium film channels (Ciné Cinémas) or documentary chan-nels (Planète, Voyage). Cultural channels (Paris Première) and news chan-nels (LCI) also attract large audiences.

The sudden success of digital satellite television is likely to have an impact on the overall structure of French broadcasting; the public stations will find it increasingly difficult to compete with cash-rich TF1 and the new stations. The concept of public service broadcasting is likely to be further eroded, but, on the other hand, television will gain in diversity which may very well lead to that fragmentation of the sense of national identity that successive governments have long tried to avert. Watch this space.

Notes

1   In 1998, 19 536 subscribers to *Libération* in the Paris area had the daily delivered at home. Yves de Chaisemartin, chairman of *Le Figaro* and President of the *Syndicat professionnel de la presse parisienne* (the equivalent of the British National Publishers' Association) felt that national dailies could only survive if delivered at home, failing which 'they will simply be wiped out of the scene at least in paper form'. *Rapport d'information de la Mission d'information com-mune sur la presse écrite*, op.cit. 265.

2   The Hersant group also owns *Le Figaro* and associated weekly titles – *Le Figaro Magazine, Le Figaro Madame* – through its subsidiary SOCPRESSE.

3   The title is a spoonerism based on the French title of the American vintage TV series *Les Incorruptibles* (*The Untouchables*). As a matter of fact, the magazine borrowed its title from a rock music programme broadcast in the early 1980s by a small independent radio station in a Paris suburb.

4   The successive incarnations of the regulating body were the following: *Haute Autorité de la communication audiovisuelle* (1982–1986), *Commission nationale de la communication et des libertés* (1986–1989), *Conseil supérieur de l'Audiovisuel* (1989 to the present day).

5   The attribution of a national terrestrial frequency to a private encrypted channel

was not the most natural decision expected of a socialist government. The hatching of the Canal Plus project is chronicled in Chamard and Kieffer 1992.

References and further reading

ALBERT, Pierre 1983: *La Presse française*. Paris: La Documentation Française.
Assemblée nationale 1997: *Rapport d'information de la Mission d'information commune sur la presse écrite* (Auditions), rapport 3512, April.
BOON, M., RYST, A. and VINAY, C. 1990: *Lexique de l'audiovisuel*. Paris: Dalloz.
CAYROL, R. 1991: *Les Médias: presse écrite, radio, telévision*. Paris: PUF.
Guide de la radio 1995: Paris: Télérama.
CHAMARD, M.E. and KIEFFER, P. 1992: *La télé: Dix ans d'histoires secrètes*. Paris: Flammarion.
HUGHES, Alex and READER, Keith (eds) 1998: *Encyclopedia of contemporary French culture*. London and New York: Routledge. (Contains over 50 entries on individual papers, stations and people as well as longer articles by Raymond KUHN, Alan PEDLEY and Pam MOORES on TV, radio and the press respectively.)
IPSOS 1999: Media Survey for the *Syndicat de la presse quotidienne régionale* (the French equivalent of the Newspaper Society), September.
KUHN, Raymond 1995: *The media in France*. London and New York: Routledge.
PEDLEY, A. 1998: see HUGHES and READER 1998.

The weekly *Télérama* is the best current periodical for up-to-date information, programmes, etc.

Most newspapers, TV stations and radio stations have their own websites. See chapter 2 for a discussion of general search engines, such as Yahoo! France, which has a link to virtually everything under the title Actualités et médias. Examples: www.nrj.fr and www.radio-france.fr

|19|

From Messiaen to MC Solaar: music in France in the second half of the twentieth century

BY MARY BREATNACH AND ERIC STERENFELD

'France,' André Malraux famously stated in 1965, 'is not a musical nation.' Is that a serious proposition? This chapter will explore contemporary French musical culture, both classical and popular, and question that judgment.

'Art' or 'classical' music in France since 1945

Malraux, who was de Gaulle's Minister of Cultural Affairs when he made the above remark, was not the first person in France to express this negative view. In 1753, the philosopher Jean-Jacques Rousseau claimed to have shown that 'there is neither measure nor melody in French music', concluding that 'the French have no music and cannot have any'. Yet France has produced many composers of stature, and some of real genius, and in 1831, the Polish-born composer Frederic Chopin claimed to have found 'the best musicians in the world' in Paris. In terms of world-class figures, the second half of the twentieth century is no less rich than earlier periods of French history. For example, cellist Paul Tortelier (1914–1996) and flautist Jean-Pierre Rampal (b. 1922) are household names and among some of today's best-known soloists are pianists Pascal Rogé (b. 1951) and Jean-Yves Thibaudet (b. 1961), and violinists Jacques Kanterow (b. 1945), Pierre Amoyal (b. 1949) and Raphael Oleg (b. 1959). In particular, two of the most influential figures in post-war European music, Olivier Messiaen (1908–1992) and his pupil Pierre Boulez (b. 1925), have been Frenchmen. In different ways, the careers of these two men illuminate many of the problems and contradictions that have dogged French musical life for more than 200 years.

In 1945, musical life in France was very much as it had been before the war. The musical establishment was notoriously conservative and (despite the innovators of the early twentieth century) prejudice against modern trends was vigorous. Neither in the regional conservatories nor in the Conservatoire National Supérieur de Paris – the main centre of musical education in the country – had methods of instruction changed significantly since the 1880s. In composition, for instance, Nadia Boulanger (1887–1979), a champion of neoclassicism and the most influential teacher at the time, advocated techniques which looked back to the nineteenth century, seeking to preserve rather than innovate. Passionately interested in exploring new territory, the young Messiaen, who studied at the Conservatoire from 1919–1930, was a product of this system, but found no place in it as a teacher. Despite a brilliant student career, he was seen by the establishment as an outsider and at an official level everything was done to minimize his influence. Eventually, in 1941, he was appointed to teach traditional harmony at the Conservatoire National Supérieur, but this decision was influenced by the fact that he had been a prisoner of war. One of his greatest masterpieces, the *Quatuor pour la fin du temps* (*Quartet for the End of Time*), had been composed while he was in captivity and, under astonishing conditions, had received its first performance in the camp, Stalag VIII A at Goerlitz, on 15 January 1941. On his release, the musical authorities were no longer able totally to exclude this remarkable man from their ranks.

Messiaen became a highly influential teacher, both at the Conservatoire and privately at the home of Guy Bernard Delapierre, an Egyptologist and composer of film music whom he had met in the camps. His fame spread and his seminar soon became a focus for gifted and independent-minded young musicians, among them the French composers Serge Nigg, Michel Fano and, most famously, Boulez, as well as the Greek composer Iannis Xenakis and Karl-Heinz Stockhausen, who later became leader of the German avant-garde. The pianist and renowned executant of Messiaen's piano works, Yvonne Loriod, whom he later married, was also a member of this class. Messiaen provided an environment in which not only the music of acknowledged twentieth-century masters but also that of the Second Viennese School was studied seriously for the first time in France. The works of Debussy, Bartok and Stravinsky were analyzed alongside those of Schoenberg and his pupils, Berg and Webern. It was no accident that seminal works such as Schoenberg's *Pierrot lunaire* or Berg's *Lyric Suite* for string quartet, respectively 1912 and 1925, were virtually unknown in France until after World War II. As one might expect, the antagonism between France and Germany discussed in chapter 3 had had profound and far-reaching artistic repercussions as well as political consequences. From the time of the Franco-Prussian war of 1870–1871, and especially after the two world wars, cultural interchange between the two countries diminished. It took a crusading spirit such as Messiaen to penetrate the barriers that had been built up.

Messiaen's position in musical history is a paradoxical one. In his creative work and also on a personal level, he combined the attributes of a great innovator with those of a profoundly simple human being whose natural instincts were deeply rooted in tradition. Both sides of his character are reflected in the two main sources of his inspiration: birdsong and a life-long, unwavering Roman Catholic faith. Though the first might suggest a superficial prettiness and the second a daunting austerity or even stuffiness, no such characteristics are to be found in his extraordinarily sensuous and original music.

But though Messiaen's pupils admired his work as a composer, it was not through his music that he influenced them most. His real legacy as a teacher was his breadth of vision, his openness to all the musics of the world and his enthusiasm for the music of his own century. In the case of Boulez, his most gifted pupil, this enthusiasm led to a break – short-lived on a personal level, but radical on an artistic level – with Messiaen. Captivated by the work of the Second Viennese School, Boulez embraced wholeheartedly the system of composition used by these composers, a system known as serialism. Unlike the traditional tonal system which, using major and minor keys, treats one or two notes as focal points in a piece, serialism treats all 12 tones equally. First used by Schoenberg in 1912, it is exemplified in Boulez's famous piece, *Le Marteau sans maître* (*The Hammer Without a Master*), which was premiered at the Darmstadt Festival in 1954. Based on poems by René Char, and scored for alto voice and instrumental ensemble, *Marteau* established the young composer's reputation as the leader of the European musical avant garde. Serialism was for him a means to an end: to write music that reflected the times in which he lived. With the same end in view, he began, in the early 1950s, actively to explore the possibility of using machines to create new sound worlds, something he later developed in striking ways (see below). In the meantime, Boulez's zeal manifested itself in other areas of musical life. He began his life-long mission of building up an audience for twentieth-century music.

In 1953, he persuaded the actor Jean-Louis Barrault to put on four concerts of contemporary chamber music at the Petit Marigny Theatre in Paris in order, as he said later, 'to provide a means of communication between the composers of our time and the public that is interested in its time'. First called the Concerts Marigny and later the Domaine Musical, the series was an immediate artistic success. In this tiny theatre, Boulez made his debut as a conductor. Today he enjoys an international reputation as one of the great conductors of twentieth-century music, working with the world's finest orchestras, including the BBC Symphony, the New York Philharmonic, the Cleveland Orchestra, the Chicago Symphony and the Berlin Philharmonic.

In order to understand some of the problems Boulez faced at this period, we need to look at the position of art music in the cultural politics of post-war France. Traditionally, music was seen by the French as less important than the other arts. For generations, it had been underfunded by successive governments. Indeed it has been suggested that musical culture in France never really recovered from the impact of the 1789 Revolution and that church music in particular continued to suffer well into the twentieth century from the troubled relations between Church and state. With the dispossession in 1789 of the institutions which supported it – the Church and the court – music itself arguably lost much of its patronage. If one then considers the reluctance of successive post-war governments to invest in any effective form of musical education for the nation's children, one begins to discern a correlation between official neglect and the absence of a vibrant musical life in the community. Rather than being an innate characteristic, as Malraux suggested in the quotation cited at the outset, the lack of 'musicality' among the French might be the result of a kind of cultural deprivation.

What France lacked for so many years was not exceptional individual musicians, but a generalized or institutional musical culture within the population as a whole. One reason for that was undoubtedly the failure to teach music effectively in schools. Neither at primary nor at secondary level was the subject given a significant place in the curriculum. This is by no means a peculiarly French problem: in Britain too the complaint is often heard that music is given low priority compared with other parts of the curriculum. But in post-war Britain some form of music – usually singing – was an integral part of every child's experience at primary school as well as at the nursery and infant stages, and church choirs and choir-schools continued to maintain a strong choral tradition. In post-war France, music had virtually ceased to figure in the school timetable. Officially, one hour of music a week was a compulsory part of the programme. However, teachers often ignored the injunction and no attempt was made to enforce it. There were opportunities to learn outside school, in the Conservatoires régionaux, the counterparts of local music schools in Britain. Then as now, these institutions provided musical instruction for children and young people aged between six and 25. They were, however, few in number and were run on ossified lines. For example, before being allowed to study an instrument, students were – and still are – obliged to spend at least a year learning *solfège*, the elementary principles of musical notation. Rather than fostering enjoyment of musical activity, this rigorously theoretical approach often discouraged it and undoubtedly contributed to the absence in France of an equivalent to the lively tradition of amateur music-making prevailing in Britain – though the system has of course produced many excellent musicians.

In 1962, however, Malraux set up a committee chaired by the composer Marcel Landowski (b. 1915), to study the organization of music in France. This led to the publication in 1966 of a 10-year plan for musical development in the French regions. Known as the *Plan Landowski*, the plan conformed to Malraux's requirement that music, like other aspects of French cultural life, should be democratized and decentralized. The reforms were ironically stymied during Malraux's time by lack of adequate financial support; implementation began in earnest only in 1969, under the presidency of

Georges Pompidou. The Ministry then increased considerably the proportion of the national budget dedicated to music, allowing the plan to bear fruit. By 1978, state expenditure on musical education had risen twelvefold. 1970 saw the institution of a music option in the *baccalauréat*. Numbers of students taking the exam are, however, still low (only 300 of the 175 061 candidates who sat the *baccalauréat* in 1995 took music) and given the slow rate of change in primary schools, it seems unlikely that they will increase for some time to come. The number of regional conservatories was increased to 31 and, in 1979, a second Conservatoire National Supérieur was opened in Lyon. The number of orchestras was also increased: there are now 32 permanently employed orchestras in France, of which nine are in Paris. Among the latter are the Orchestre national de France, L'Orchestre philharmonique de L'ORTF and the Orchestre de Paris. Provincial orchestras include the Orchestre national du Capitole de Toulouse, the Orchestre national de Lyon and the Orchestre philharmonique de Strasbourg. The readiness to support so many orchestras and the willingness in recent years to appoint world-class foreign conductors such as Daniel Barenboim or Myung-Whun Chung to high-profile positions testifies to the greater importance attached to music.

Ironically, however, Malraux's reforms had alienated Boulez. In an open letter entitled 'Pourquoi je dis non à Malraux' (*Nouvel Observateur*, 25 May, 1966) he explained his objections to the *Plan Landowski* and accused Malraux of perpetuating jaded, backward-looking methods on a grander scale. Disillusioned and incensed, he left France for Germany where he believed music was controlled by specialists with a thorough understanding of the problems relating to the organization of music. This clash was symptomatic of a deep rift between those who, like Boulez, saw the funding and promotion of *contemporary* music as the main issue, and those like Landowski who did not. However, given Boulez's standing as a leading figure in the world of contemporary music, his decision to live and work in exile could not be ignored.

Accordingly, in 1970, in an unprecedented gesture, President Pompidou summoned him to the Elysée Palace and persuaded him to return to Paris. The incentive was the opportunity to fulfil a long-standing ambition: the setting up of a sophisticated research institute equipped with the most up-to-date technology and dedicated to the advancement of musical techniques and sound production. Handsomely funded by the state, the Institut de recherches et de coordination acoustique/musique (IRCAM) opened in 1977 under Boulez's directorship. As a conductor, Boulez's aim was to educate public taste for the music of the twentieth century. At IRCAM, he aimed to provide the composers of that music with the means to develop their working methods and an environment where the new technology, now rapidly permeating all areas of life, could be harnessed to serve the needs of contemporary music. In 1976, he created the Ensemble Intercontemporain, a resident group of first-class musicians, to perform the music. The artistic success of the Institute is sometimes questioned, but its presence in Paris has certainly ensured the city's reputation as one of the most important centres in Europe for musical research.

In spite of its close association with the popular Pompidou Centre at Beaubourg, IRCAM is viewed by the general public as an elitist organization having little to do with the ordinary, everyday life of Paris. In 1995, a more obviously people-oriented centre opened its doors. The much-talked-of Cité de la Musique at La Villette in the north-east of Paris is, in the words of the architect Christian de Portzamparc, 'a small town dedicated to music'. Portzamparc has sought to create an environment in which the public, and especially the young, are encouraged to experience all types of music and to engage in all kinds of music-related activities. The Cité comprises the Conservatoire national supérieur and a museum containing musical instruments and manuscripts from many periods and cultures, as well as information accessible on computer, CD-ROM and the Internet. Perhaps the most adventurous aspect of the whole project is the adaptable concert hall which the architect designed in close collaboration with Boulez. Unlike conventional concert halls, conceived with the orchestra of the nineteenth century in mind, the hall at La Villette is designed to cater for the very different and widely varying needs of the contemporary repertoire. It is, in Boulez's words, 'a concert hall both for the present and for the foreseeable future'.

But there is another side to musical life in France. Despite the thriving experimental scene described above, no visitor can remain unaware for long of the French predilection for composers of the baroque period. Public performances of early music, especially if a counter-tenor is involved, are guaranteed an audience. Weekend performances in local churches of works for various small ensembles by composers such as Gabrieli, Corelli, Vivaldi, Telemann, Bach and others are a familiar feature of Parisian musical life. Often free of charge, these concerts are extremely popular. Of the two radio stations specializing in classical music, France Musique devotes more time to baroque music than to any other, while Radio Classique's output is almost 100 per cent baroque. The difference between the two stations is arguably less than that between their British counterparts, BBC Radio 3 and Classic FM.

Public taste may still be attracted to the old and familiar, but it is clear that in the field of so-called classical music, France's preeminence on the world stage is primarily as a centre for contemporary music. This is in part due to enlightened political decisions taken in recent years. Without the vision of highly influential artists such as Messiaen and Boulez, however, such a situation would never have come about.

Rock, popular and world music in France

In 1980 the French popular music scene looked rather jaded. Musical culture was seemingly wedded to practices that had stayed unchanged since the

1960s if not before. Why was this? The fairly dramatic changes that would take place over the next two decades can be explained by a number of social, cultural and political factors. The transformations of French society in the 1980s and 1990s resulted in a very different landscape, and popular music benefited in several ways. To put this in context, we need to go back briefly to the years just after World War II.

After 1945, France, and especially Paris, was gradually being overtaken in artistic matters by other countries, in particular America. It is true that in these post-war years, some of the pre-war French performers re-surfaced and had a kind of Indian summer, from Maurice Chevalier to Edith Piaf and Charles Trenet. Their tradition, the famous French *chanson*, had its origins in the music-hall. With poetic or witty lyrics over haunting but quite simple and repetitive melodies, they produced a distinctive 'French' sound still popular at home and valued by Francophiles abroad (Piaf's 'Je ne regrette rien' for instance). Newer voices emerging in Paris cabarets and clubs, such as Jacques Brel, Georges Brassens, Bobby Lapointe, Léo Ferré and Serge Gainsbourg, were thought of as poet-composer-singers. With their unorthodox and sometimes anarchist songs, they had success in the 1950s and early 1960s in France, and to some extent abroad. For a while, 'existentialist' Left Bank cabaret was in vogue, with singers like Juliette Greco singing lyrics by Jacques Prévert. A similar clientele would be found in the post-war jazz clubs, listening to a mostly modern and cool form of jazz, particularly prized by French intellectuals.

But by the early 1960s, rock'n'roll and its derivatives had hit France and teenagers took to them with enthusiasm. Rock, rooted in R&B, seemed to be the first kind of music directed straight at 15–20 year-olds. These were the 'yéyé years' and they lasted through the decade, bringing fame to a generation of singers born in the 1940s: Johnny Hallyday, Eddy Mitchell, Sylvie Vartan, Françoise Hardy, Jacques Dutronc, Claude François, etc. They became youth icons in magazines like *Salut les copains* and sang lyrics about teenage preoccupations to a vaguely rock'n'roll backing or did cover versions.

Thanks to the booming record industry and the first EP (45 rpm) discs, France was by now importing more and more music from across the Channel and the Atlantic. French audiences discovered and appreciated the Beatles, Rolling Stones and co. This transitional phase lasted until 1968, the date that really marked the break with the old wartime and post-war order, for the younger generation. The youth audience now turned decisively to British and American music, since the singers and groups of the 'protest years' – Bob Dylan, Joan Baez, Jimi Hendrix, Frank Zappa – voiced their feelings much more clearly than the *yéyés*. This was a complete and massive break with the past, and it started a move away from the indigenous French rock singers (who had emerged only ten years earlier, but were now ten years older). To French audiences, US and British music represented energy and protest, while the local product, still suited to the French variety show, began to look old-fashioned and *ringard* (corny). This important turning-point in cultural practice would have a powerful influence on all the participants on the popular music scene in the coming years. Later generations had been brought up to be much more aware of music from abroad. Even if they didn't always understand the words, they identified with the sentiments, creating a sort of cultural consciousness completely divorced from any French roots. At the same time, there were the first signs of expansion and democratization in the music industry (broadcasting, record companies), but it still remained very limited since at this stage, the media and cultural institutions lagged behind public taste.

So by the late 1970s, the French musical scene was rather fractured. Part of it was still embedded in the all-French tradition, with the artists who made their names in the 1960s still around. Not having managed to adapt to the new generation, their musical style remained within the French format, and since they had not broken into foreign markets either, French popular music was an example of *l'exception culturelle*. On the other hand, young people who had cut their teeth on Anglo-American music were looking for their own means of expression, to which we now turn.

Looking back, it should be acknowledged that 1981 made a big difference. The new socialist-led government brought in measures which would revivify French cultural life. The state took an active role in developing French popular music, especially during the Lang years (see chapter 4). Noting that French music was not very competitive, the Ministry of Culture introduced a programme of financial support, both at national level, and at regional level with the DRACs, a strategy intended to encourage French music. In 1981, the FM radio revolution took place, when the government allowed the creation of new private radio stations, which quickly came to represent particular strands of music (Radio Montmartre for old-fashioned song, NRJ for an international mix, etc.). A government policy of quotas (mooted in 1993, effective in 1996) meant that at least 40 per cent of the material broadcast had to be of French origin, to encourage the home industry. TV changed too, with new channels such as M6, ex-TV6 (started in 1987) with a policy of concentrating on youth entertainment. The music press produced more magazines, fanzines and specialized publications. In 1993, an export bureau for French popular music was set up in cooperation with various industrial companies (SACEM, ADAMI, SNEP etc.) to obtain a greater share of markets abroad.

All these changes together or separately modified not only the structures of musical production but also the way the French public related to popular music. Whereas the French radio audience in the 1970s switched on mainly to hear the news, 20 years later they were tuning in to hear music. A Louis Harris poll in 1996 reported that this change affected over 70 per cent of the population. Much the same happened with TV, since the most popular shows in terms of ratings are now recorded live concerts or variety shows, for which there is an increased demand. Attendance at concerts is going up, especially among young people. In 1992, it was estimated that 15 per cent of 15-years-olds and upwards had been to a rock or jazz concert in the 12 previous months, compared to 6 per cent in 1973. And of course people have music at home: 73 per cent of French homes now have a hi-fi/CD player compared to only 8 per cent as recently as 1973. More people are learning to play instruments too.

The last 20 years: some of the key players

The punk movement started in 1977 in Britain with groups like the Sex Pistols, Sham 69, the Clash and so on, bringing a new dimension to rock, with nihilist overtones ('no future') and libertarian tendencies. It seemed like a complete break with previous rock idols, who were now being criticized for cosying up to showbiz and making large amounts of money – rebels no more.

In France, after a long period of conservative rule, the 1981 socialist election victory raised expectations of a new era of freedom of expression. Younger musicians gravitated either towards punk (Metal Urbain, Oberkampf) or towards New Wave (Taxi Girl, Indochine, Kas Product). These groups were all in fact still influenced by the British model, even if this time the lyrics were in French (the French language had until then been thought a major obstacle, since it is not easily adapted to rock music – a handicap for would-be song-writers/musicians). Attitudes to the music industry altered too: while some groups went on dreaming of the famous contract with a record company, others decisively rejected this road, and went for do-it-yourself methods.

A libertarian and non-conformist movement emerged, becoming known as 'alternative rock' and seeking to create a new kind of music which would take on board the contradictions inherent in French culture and shake off for good the inferiority complex towards Anglo-American music. Steering clear of the big record companies and traditional circuits of the music industry, this movement set about getting known via home-made labels and cooperatives: names include Bondage Records, VISA, Disques du Soleil et de l'Acier, Disques du Crépuscule. New bands were formed: Lucrate Milk (arty punk), Les Endimanchés (industrial java), Ludwig von 88 (rock), Ausweis (reggae dub rock), Berrurier noir (clown rock), Achwgha nei wodei (experimental Dada), Washington Dead Cats (rock), VRP, Babylon Fighter and others.

These bands were energetic at organizing themselves and setting up associations to produce their records or sponsor concerts in new venues, such as squats. (Squats – the English term is used – were fairly new in France in the early 1990s and several of them became centres for creative arts.) The state helped the newcomers extend their audience by subsidizing new concert spaces. The Garçons Bouchers helped create new bands with different styles

– Los Carayos (country musette), Pigalle (bringing the accordion into the line-up) – and also issued records under their own label, Boucherie Productions. The success of the new generation prompted the big record companies to take an interest: some bands accepted invitations to sign up with them, others didn't. But one way and another, a different French musical identity was beginning to appear, with a better match between the French public and the performers. More high-profile bands began to make a name for themselves even outside France: Les Négresses Vertes, Mano Negra, Les Rita Mitsouko, drawing attention to the change. These groups, the first on the alternative rock scene to sign big record contracts, drew partly on their own cultural heritage, the twentieth-century *chanson française* with foregrounded lyrics (as sung by Piaf, Brel, Brassens, or even Fréhel, a singer of the 1920s whose songs evoked the Paris music-halls of the day). This trend has been carried on to the present by groups like Les Têtes raides, La Tordue, Les Ogres de Barback, Las Patatas Espantadas. Other bands set out to mix the different ethnic origins of the present-day population in their music (Cartel del Barrio, Raffik, Les Dupuiz) which combined Latin American, Arab and rock influences.

By the 1990s, French popular music was looking very different: there is now a real market for it, not only with the standard labels but from many independents, and the media regularly promote French music. The state and larger cities have developed structures such as festivals where the new sounds are transmitted (le Printemps de Bourges, Eurorockéennes in Belfort, Francofolies in La Rochelle, Trans-musicales in Rennes).

But as well as all this, some completely new music has now appeared on the French scene, most strikingly world music. The spectacular growth of traditional music from the South combined with contemporary sounds and rhythms has made France one of the most important centres for world music in post-colonial times. By the 1980s Paris was already the world capital of African music and saw the arrival of famous African musicians like Salif Keita, Papa Wemba, Mory Kanté, Angélique Kidjo, Youssou N'Dour, Ray Lema, Xalam, Touré Kounda and others. All these performers gave a platform in France and elsewhere to new sounds and rhythms previously known only to a few.

Simultaneously, the French population of Maghrebi origin, especially the young generation, discovered a kind of music which started in Oran in the 1920s (it was created by Moroccan women who sang amongst themselves, being denied any other outlet for expression) and has been given a modern twist with new technology. This is *rai*, of which the longest-established performer is Rainette, a woman from Oran. It became possible to hear young Maghrebi performers like Cheb Khaled (Cheb means 'young' as opposed to Cheik), Cheb Mami, Cheba Fadéla, Faudel and Lounes Matoub, who worked out his own special style singing traditional Berber melodies, and was assassinated in 1998 by religious fanatics. The group Carte de Séjour (residence permit) came to prominence and its lead singer Rachid Taha went on to have a solo career, successfully combining techno music with traditional North African and western rock. These performers, Cheb Khaled in particular, were able to get their music played throughout the Arab world, using networks which brought them star status in these countries and communicating their style to others.

In 1985, the Conseil francophone de la chanson was set up and in 1990 the Association Zone franche, which helped improve the standing of French-African music and secure it a permanent place. By this time, France was coming to the realization that it had a multi-racial population and was willing to accept contributions, particularly in the musical sphere. Young people were not afraid of going out to listen to new kinds of music previously seen as esoteric because they were restricted to a minority audience. The industry realized that a new market was opening up and provided platforms for such music which public taste was coming round to: at big public concerts, French audiences discovered Cesaria Evora, the Gipsy Kings, Les Voix Bulgares (featuring traditional Bulgarian songs, sung by women), who brought out an album with Ray Léma, the Pakistani Qawals (Nusrat Fateh Ali Khan) and music from Eastern Europe: Taraf de Haidouk (Romania), the Kozcany Orchestra (a band from Macedonia); and the Pires, Taraf de Bretagne ('Taraf' means band). Latin-American music (salsa, son, merengue etc.) has also started to catch on.

While many of these new sounds are concentrated in Paris, France has several strong regional cultures. Traditional or folk music from rural areas had always had a local audience, but in the mid-1990s commercial recording success led a wider public to take an interest in their music. The former guitarist from Alan Stivell's famous Breton band Dan ar Braz took part in the Eurovision Song Contest because his record 'L'Héritage des Celtes' was a hit. French audiences also discovered the unsuspected riches of Corsican polyphony (I Muvrini), Basque song and hurdy-gurdy music. Some bands sing in regional languages but with modern songs: Massilia Sound System from Marseille sing in Provençal over a ragamuffin beat, the Fabulous Troubadours of Toulouse sing in Occitan, and Kortatu, Negu Goriak sing rock music to Basque words.

Last, it should be pointed out that rap has become so popular in France that it is now one of the largest markets for it world-wide: from Johnny Go, Destroy Man and Sidney, or Dee Nasty in the 1980s, to Assassin, Doc Gynéco, Passi, Stomy Bugsy, IAM, NTM, and MC Solaar in the 1990s, there has been a flood of French rap which has actually been a supplementary and witty method of spreading the French language abroad. Meanwhile, among new trends, or more precisely from the techno-house camp, the global success of bands like Daft Punk and Air shows that French music has gained in confidence and now has less of a complex about Anglo-American music and performers.

At the same time, singers drawing on the old French music-hall tradition have not disappeared. By the mid-1990s, Johnny Hallyday had become a kind of national institution, after almost 40 years in showbiz, and several *chanson* performers have come up since the 1980s (Francis Cabrel, Florent Pagny, Vanessa Paradis, Bernard Lavilliers, Renaud, Jacques Higelin, Liane Foly).

All in all then, French popular music has gone through a period of massive change in the last 20 years of the twentieth century, showing much more richness and diversity than before. This has happened basically because French society has changed, with post-1980 generations having a very different approach, whether as performers or audience. For example, more women now perform in line-ups these days. Both the record market and institutional structures have encouraged the rise of new performers. However, despite some notable though not very numerous successes outside France, the new scene is showing some signs of losing momentum, once more related to the specificity of the French language. Possibly too the French system is becoming too complacent. It is as if each element has now found its place in the new deal and is simply obeying the market without any real urge to take innovation any further. So what does the future look like? With new technology and in particular the Internet, the way that music is developed and delivered will soon be completely different. Those who have the technology to hand will be able to control creative production from start to finish, bypassing the big record companies. So French popular music may be heading for an unpredictable future in which national cultural characteristics are diluted via cyberspace, and the putative audience will be able to decide for themselves what they want to hear.

References and further reading

Classical/art music: the following items are all introductory; further bibliographies will be found in these sources.

CABANE, Pierre 1981: *Le Pouvoir Culturel sous la Ve Republique*. Paris: Olivier Orban, 175–85.
CHARLTON, D.K. (ed.) 1976: *France: a companion to French studies*. London: Methuen. See: 'French music from 1500–1950' by Hugh MacDonald.
FREMY, Dominique and FREMY, Michèle 1996: *Quid 1996*. Paris: Editions Robert Laffont.
GLOCK, William (ed.) 1986 *Pierre Boulez: a symposium*. London: Eulenberg Books.
GRIFFITHS, Paul 1978: *Modern music: a concise history from Debussy to Boulez*. London: Thames & Hudson.
HILL, Peter 1995: *The Messiaen companion*. London: Faber & Faber.
HUGHES, Alex and READER, Keith 1998: *Encyclopedia of contemporary French culture*. London: Routledge. See articles on 'Music' under classified contents list.
JAMEUX, Dominique 1984: *Boulez*. Paris: Fayard.
MARI, Pierrette 1968: *Olivier Messiaen*. Paris: Seghers.
Ministère de la Culture 1966: La musique contemporaine en France, in *Panorama de la France*. Paris: Documentation Française, 767–71.

PEYSER, Joan 1976: *Boulez: composer, conductor, enigma.* New York and London: Schirmer/Macmillan.
SALZMANN, Eric 1967: *Twentieth-century music: an introduction.* New York and London: Prentice Hall.
Websites: IRCAM on www.ircam.fr

For more information about popular music – performers and *chanson*, jazz, rock, etc. – see the relevant articles (listed in the classified contents list under 'music', many of them by Gérard Poulet) in Hughes and Reader 1998. On the impact of African, Maghrebi and world music, see Chris Warne, 'The impact of world music in France' and Steve Cannon, 'Paname City Rapping', both in Alec Hargreaves and Mark McKinney (eds), *Post-colonial cultures in France* (London: Routledge, 1997).

Accessible works in French include L. Rioux, *50 ans de chanson française* (Paris: Editions de l'Archipel, 1994) and F. Hennion, *Les professionnels du disque* (Paris: Editions Métailié, 1981). See also several reports for the Ministère de la culture: *Les pratiques culturelles des Français* (Documentation Française, 1998); *Les Français et la musique* (Développement culturel 87) and *Les jeunes et les sorties culturelles* (1995). Cf. Assemblée nationale, Commission des Affaires culturelles *La chanson française: rapport d'information*, 1006 (La Documentation Française, 1994). See articles in the magazine *Les Inrockuptibles*, among others.

There are a number of websites which can be consulted, e.g. for performers, www.irma.asso.fr. Most major record companies have their own websites. e.g. www.sonymusic.fr or, for the alternative Boucherie Productions, www.neatbeat.com.

20

Reading books in France: la culture du livre

BY BERNARD C. SWIFT

The airport bookshop

Aéroport de Paris, Roissy-Charles de Gaulle: Terminal 2, Hall F. Wednesday 12 May 1999, 1800 hours. In this vast, new, ultra-modern area of the airport, a few minutes walk from the TGV railway station, the bookshop is a branch of the French 'Relais H' chain, belonging to the Hachette network. Relais H has about 2000 branches throughout the world and is still growing, but the local manager is free to decide which books to stock, and whether to put on special displays. He has set up only one display of books by an individual author today: it is at the back of the shop, past 'Essais', 'Tourisme', 'Suspense' and 'Romans' – and it is devoted to an American writer, Mary Higgins Clark. Her novel, *La Nuit du renard*, 'translated from the American', won the Grand Prix de littérature policière back in 1980 and her novels have been on the best-seller list ever since. Other favourites of the French, according to the manager, are Agatha Christie, Tom Clancy and Stephen King – alongside a whole range of books first published in France itself.

Hachette is also a publishing house, well-known for producing school manuals, children's books and classic French texts, often in pocket editions, which make up the traditional body of French literature and are still thought to define the cultural heritage of well-educated French people: Montaigne, Molière, Racine, Corneille, Pascal, the nineteenth-century novelists and so on. But times have changed. Relais H now has an Internet website, which offers a 'virtual' walk around a typical store. According to some observers, electronic communication threatens to signal the 'death of the book'; here, it is used to spread information about books. 'What books do French people read today?' The manager is pragmatic: he has a pretty good idea which books will sell. When deciding what to stock, he consults the book-trade lists of best-sellers, and takes information from radio, television

Figure 20.1   Advertising for a Mary Higgins Clark *polar*, Shakespeare at the Avignon festival, a reportage on Kosovo and *Télérama* in the Paris metro.

and the press. His choices may be wrong, he thinks, with a touch of commercial caution, but his selection is not random, and time will tell.

Some books are ephemeral; others seem almost to transcend time. Successful books run into many reprints. Prize-winning novels, recipients of such prizes as the Prix Goncourt, the Fémina, Renaudot or Médicis (the French pioneered book prizes) will not necessarily last. Practical books are more likely to be reprinted than other kinds of non-fiction. But in France, the non-fiction 'essai' and the journalistic book on current affairs find a readier market than in Britain or America. The shelf-life of such books may be short, but there is a demand for them from educated readers.

Among non-fiction titles on display in May 1999 there was a wide range of subjects. Geneviève de Gaulle Anthonioz's *La Traversée de la nuit* (Seuil 1999) is an account of her experiences in Ravensbrück concentration camp in the 1940s. World War II continues to exert a particular fascination in France following re-assessment of the French experience. Among the many political titles, several were concerned with Europe: Régis Debray, *Le Code et le Glaive. Après l'Europe, la Nation?* (Albin Michel 1999) contains a republican's reflections on whether Europe will be the undoing of the French Republic, while Alain Duhamel's *Une ambition française* (Plon 1999) suggests the opposite. In *Fort Chirac* (Grasset 1999), journalists Claude Angeli and Stéphanie Mesnier report on political struggle in the

Elysée Palace – politician-watching is a popular publishing phenomenon in France. Religion is personalized, in Jean-Bernard Raimond's account of Pope John-Paul II, *Un Pape au cœur de l'Histoire* (Le cherche midi 1999). The past and the present were represented in various guises: Michel Winock, *Le Siècle des intellectuels* (Seuil, Collection Point, 1997, new edition 1999), on the influence – or lack of influence – of thinkers on public life; *Cent ans de souvenirs et d'événements, 1900–2000*, a popular retrospective seeking to make money out of the new *fin de siècle*, in the form of a *Readers' Digest* compilation; Françoise Giroud, *Les Françaises: de la Gauloise à la pilule* (Fayard 1999), appealing both to a sense of history and to the interest in books about women – one of publishing's growth areas in recent years. Best-selling titles included *L'Art du bonheur* (Robert Laffont) by the Dalai Lama, *La Plus Belle Histoire des plantes: les racines de notre vie* (Seuil) by Jean-Marie Pelt and others, *Les Enfants du soleil: histoire de nos organes* (Odile Jacob) by André Brahic, and *Le Harcèlement moral* (Syros) by Marie-France Hirigoyen – titles which may be thought to represent the preoccupations of many people at the end of the twentieth century.

Expensive, beautifully illustrated books on sale included travel books – on Paris, the Châteaux of the Loire, Indonesia and Thailand. In the cooking and gastronomic section, French cuisine and French cheeses were given great prominence. Books for children included Tintin and the Schtroumpfs (Smurfs), leaders in the *bandes dessinées*, another success story of the late twentieth century. Since these have speech bubbles, they are regarded as 'reading books', and used to encourage young children to learn to read. The word 'reading' – *la lecture* – is regularly taken to mean reading works of fiction: in France, the phrase *les joies de la lecture* tends to imply 'enjoying reading novels'. No twentieth-century poetry was in evidence. Poetry was represented by Baudelaire; there were a few nineteenth-century French novels by Stendhal, Flaubert, Zola and Balzac; but in this bookshop where travellers might look for holiday reading, most space was taken up by detective, mystery, suspense and science-fiction titles and current best-selling novels. In 1999 these included John Irving's *Une veuve de papier* (Seuil), Robert Merle's *Fortune de France, t. II: La Gloire et les périls* (Bernard de Fallois), J.M.G. Le Clézio's *Hasard* (Gallimard), and Tom Wolfe's *Un homme, un vrai* (Robert Laffont), advertised as Wolfe's masterpiece: in France, Wolfe has the high reputation of being 'le Zola américain' (*Le Nouvel Observateur*, 15–21 April 1999, 58–9). Also prominent were Daniel Pennac, *Aux fruits de la passion* (Gallimard), Michel Houellebecq, *Les Particules élémentaires* (Flammarion), and Tahar Ben Jelloun's *L'Auberge des pauvres* (Seuil). It was quite a wide and representative range for an airport bookshop with relatively restricted space, and it included – typically – contemporary foreign novels translated into French: French people are said to read more translations than their Anglo-American contemporaries.

What do readers want?

Is it possible to determine in general what French people are reading today? There is of course plenty of 'instrumental' reading-matter: advertisements, railway timetables, the times of television programmes, instruction manuals for setting up computers, e-mail in cybercafés, ballot papers, leaflets, recipes (on newspapers and magazines, see chapter 18). Books can be used for practical purposes – for help in repairing the Renault, succeeding as a manager, surfing the Internet, finding social, historical, cultural references (why *was* the Tour Eiffel completed in 1889?), identifying one's ailments and their remedies (is it *mal au foie* or is that ulcer playing up again, and will a *cure* help the *guérison*?). And they provide practical help for bookish things, finding references to other books, checking the meanings of words or their spelling (are there two *e* acutes in *événement*?), looking up the grammar of gender agreements, quite baffling to many French people (should the past participle agree with the subject in *elles se sont rendu compte*, and if not, why not?). The answer, where there is one, will most usually be found in a book. But practicality is not incompatible with pleasure. Bibliophiles can find de luxe editions, but the regular French binding is made of paper, and there is less concern about whether a book – either as a practical object or as an object of desire – is manufactured in hard-back or soft-back, than about the size, from standard formats to '*livres de poche*'. In France as elsewhere, the visual 'culture' of the television or computer screen, which offers practical information and entertainment more conveniently and less expensively than a book, cannot replace the 'book culture'. The 'browser' on the Internet is, in French, a *navigateur*, but for the book browser, *ce badaud, intéressé ou oisif, qui feuillette les pages des livres*, there is no single noun in French which readily catches the meaning.

For French book-lovers, as opposed to book users, browsing in bookshops still brings its own delights or frustrations, especially in second-hand bookshops, at bookstalls in a local flea-market, or – more picturesquely – among the prints and books displayed on the *bouquiniste* stalls alongside the Seine in the centre of Paris. The Latin Quarter of Paris contains a concentration of bookshops, new and second-hand, scholarly and popular, specialized and generalist. Readers combing the second-hand stalls and bookshops may find a bookseller specializing in, say, books on Napoleon, detective novels, French colonial cultures of the Far East, moral theology, Astérix, Lucky Luke, sixteenth- or seventeenth-century classics, the set texts for the *baccalauréat* or the *agrégation*. The English and American bookshop close to Notre Dame, 'Shakespeare and Company', is popular with expatriates. Or one may simply riffle the second-hand books looking for the unexpected – an old first edition worth a fortune? One may find something by Jean-Paul Sartre or Albert Camus, no longer so fashionable in France but still widely read in schools and colleges and cheaper second-hand than new.

One may come across last year's new novels, sold by panel judges or blasé reviewers.

Reading and literacy: facts and figures

To read, of course, one needs to know how to read, and there is some anxiety in France about the patchy reading ability of the population. It has been estimated that between 10 per cent and 20 per cent of the adult population – and 37 per cent of the prison population – is to some degree illiterate. A distinction is made between *analphabétisme*, which refers to people who have never had an opportunity to learn a written code in any language, and *illettrisme*, the term for those who have read so little that they have not developed a taste for reading. Compulsory education removes analphabetism, but illiteracy is a matter of degree, and there is particular concern about levels of illiteracy among school children (see Frier 1999, 15–20). Learning how to read is part of learning how to learn, and nursery-school teachers adopt various methods, such as fairy tales, when preparing infants for reading before they reach primary-school age.

Since the late 1980s, national evaluations of pupils' reading ability have been undertaken annually by the Ministry of Education. In 1998, estimates showed that by the age of 11, about 20 per cent of pupils were unable to read with understanding. Children in France, as in other countries, are frequently thought to spend too much time zapping between television channels or playing computer games instead of reading. However, a sociological study published in 1999 under the title *Et pourtant ils lisent* (Baudelot, Cartier and Detrez 1999) claimed that schools *were* succeeding in imparting a taste for reading to younger pupils, though in the lycées older pupils appeared to turn away from reading once it became associated with examinations. Reading was not dying, but the attitudes of teenagers towards reading were changing *(Le Nouvel Observateur*, 4 March 1999, 4–11). Compared with thirty years earlier, reading was no longer thought of as a high cultural activity, a summit of achievement towards which pupils must strive if they were to succeed academically: instead it was regarded as just one activity amongst others. If *Le Monde* noted that 'La lecture ne meurt pas, elle change' (19 March 1999), success in encouraging reading in the earlier school years had apparently made reading appear an ordinary activity – *la lecture s'était banalisée* (Baudelot, *Le Figaro*, 19 March 1999).

A survey of favourite weekend leisure activities among teenagers showed that they rated reading books much lower than listening to music, watching television, seeing their friends, playing sport or reading magazines. Fifteen-year-olds placed reading books at about the same level as playing video games, though eighteen-year-olds placed it higher. The latter more frequently preferred cooking or doing odd jobs. Perhaps unexpectedly, *bandes dessinées* were not so popular either with 15- or 18-year-olds, who all over-whelmingly preferred magazines. The ten authors most frequently mentioned by 15-year-olds were Agatha Christie, Zola, Maupassant, Pagnol, Molière, Stephen King, Jules Verne, Balzac, Steinbeck and Mahmoody. Among 18-year-olds, the favourite authors were Stephen King, Mary Higgins Clark, Maupassant, Voltaire, Zola, Balzac, Agatha Christie, Camus, Sartre and Molière. However, when pupils were asked to say what they had read most recently outside school, 36 per cent of boys and 17 per cent of girls could not name a single book. In general, girls were clearly more regular readers than boys, a finding reflected in the reading habits of women and men in the population as a whole (see below).

While the French Ministry of Education has an obvious interest in reading habits, the Ministry of Culture and Communication and the Ministry of Industry also have particular responsibilities. In the 1960s, Culture Minister André Malraux made a short-lived attempt to increase reading culture by distributing novels to newly married couples. The Ministry of Culture exists to protect and promote French culture inside and outside France (see chapter 4) and has a substantial budget. Within the Ministry the existence of a section called the 'Direction du livre et de la lecture' illustrates the importance which the French attach to books and reading. The Direction du livre is responsible for the national library, the Bibliothèque nationale de France (since 1998 located in a vast new building on the Left Bank of the Seine, designed with four corner towers in the form of half-open books), the Public Information Library, the Centre national du livre and the French National Archives. It advises and inspects public libraries outside Paris, promotes French books, conducts research into reading habits, and organizes conferences. Under its aegis, the Centre national du livre offers support to publishers and encourages the production of high-quality books. It offers grants, based on the quality of the work, the degree of risk run by the publisher and willingness to distribute the book widely. It provides loans or grants for translations, and through a scheme called 'Les Belles Etrangères' it arranges programmes for foreign writers to visit France. It also supports large-scale projects like the Librairie du Bicentenaire de la Révolution, and encourages a wide range of local activities – such as the creation of public or mobile libraries – designed to promote reading throughout France. One of its functions is to encourage the decentralization of cultural activity.

Les Pratiques culturelles des Français. Enquête 1997, a report carried out by Olivier Donnat for the Ministry of Culture and Communication (1998), confirmed a number of general tendencies in the habits of French readers, already suggested by earlier reports. Reading was found to be losing out to other forms of activity – notably the use of audiovisual equipment – as a means of access to cultural experience. In 1997, 45 per cent of French people, based on samples aged 15 or over, had more than one television set at home, compared with 24 per cent in 1989. There had been a huge increase in the numbers owning hi-fi, CD-ROM and personal stereo equipment, notably among young people. While the proportion of French people who did not possess a single book had fallen from 27 per cent in 1973 to 13 per cent in 1989 and 9 per cent in 1997, apparently 25 per cent had not *read* a book in the preceding year, about the same proportion as in the 1980s. The proportion who had read between one and nine books in the preceding year had risen slightly, from 32 per cent in 1989 to 34 per cent in 1997, but on average French people were found to be reading fewer books per year. Young people especially – school pupils and students – were reading fewer books, and, except in country areas, this was the case whatever their social background. Many older men were however found not to read at all. Overall, women were reading twice as many books as men, and 36 per cent of women, compared with 14 per cent of men, read detective stories. Women bought books twice as often as men, and talked about their reading with friends and colleagues. While women read more novels, men preferred history books, *bandes dessinées* and scientific or technical works. One of the principal findings of the report was that there had been a marked 'féminisation du lectorat'. The use of mobile libraries – the *bibliobus* – had grown, and membership of public libraries had risen from 10 per cent in the early 1980s to 17 per cent in 1989 and 21 per cent in 1997 – with the largest increase among women, 15–19 and 35–44 year-olds, Parisians, and people with qualifications in higher education. Book borrowing is, of course, a common alternative to book buying, though in one town at least, Perpignan, the actual numbers of books borrowed fell in the late 1990s. Many libraries have developed into 'médiathèques' and resource centres as well as places where books may be consulted and borrowed. The greatest increase in bibliothèque/médiathèque visits had been amongst non-member users, but the main activity remained the consultation or borrowing of books: 82 per cent of users consulted or borrowed at least one book during the preceding twelve months, compared with 36 per cent for records, 22 per cent for video-cassettes and 10 per cent for CD-ROMs. Women were rather more likely to visit a library or médiathèque, especially if they had children (Donnat, 1998, 167–214, 241–3; Fabrice Piault, *Livres Hebdo*, 26 June 1998; Robine 1999, 35–7).

The French Ministry for Industry is directly concerned with the economics of book production. It requires the Syndicat national de l'Edition, the publishers' union, to produce annual figures for book sales, based on samples taken throughout France, showing financial turnover and production and sales figures. According to statistics for 1997, there were between 6000 and 7000 publishers in France with at least one title in their list, but only about 800 produced regular catalogues. Sales were subject to price control imposed by the Loi Lang, 10 August 1981, with retailers required in principle to sell at the price fixed by the publisher, a more predictably unpopular with discount stores. By 1997, the book market had fallen behind other sectors of French industry. Turnover was down by an average of more than 7 per cent since 1990, the main fall having occurred during the early 1990s.

Publishers had responded by increasing the number of titles of new books or new editions by 21 per cent. The average print-run in 1997 was calculated to be 8797 copies per title, but the average number of copies sold per title had fallen by 14 per cent, from 8440 to 7254. Total book production for 1997 was 415 347 000 compared with 374 588 000 in 1978. Since 1978, the total number of book titles published per year had increased more sharply, but in fewer copies, from 26 584 in 1978 to 47 214 in 1997. Of these, 24 522 were new or re-editions, and 22 692 were straight reprints. It was concluded that more and more people were reading less and less.

In particular, books considered difficult were less certain to reach their intended public, while low-priced collections for the general public were increasing in popularity. Books were often being bought for practical purposes. More use of libraries, plus the impact of photocopying, was held responsible for the difficulties of publishers. The areas of sharpest decline were encyclopaedias and dictionaries (because of CD-ROMs), art books, down by 21 per cent, and the human and social sciences. Among the latter, mostly bought by academics, professionals and students, the number of *titles* published continued to increase in response to a fall of almost 40 per cent in average sales per title, from 5762 in 1990 to 3509 in 1997.

On the other hand, the number of copies of children's books was rising, with a higher-than-average print-run of 9865 copies: this was due to the higher cost of producing illustrated books, which require a higher turnover to pay their way. Comic books – the *bandes dessinées* – continued to represent a rising market, largely because of the exceptional success of series such as Tintin and Astérix, well-known both in France and abroad. The single best-seller in 1997 was a comic book which sold 490 000 copies. In the same year, over 13 million copies of *bandes dessinées* were sold, representing almost 4 per cent of total book sales (which were reported to have reached nearly 343 million). Novels (26.4 per cent) accounted for the single largest share of the market, followed by children's books (excluding *bandes dessinées*) at 18.6 per cent, school books (17.9 per cent) and practical books (14.8 per cent), including atlases, guides, professional life, do-it-yourself, gardening, gastronomy, sport, etc. Human sciences represented 3.2 per cent, and encyclopaedias and dictionaries 2.4 per cent, scientific and technical books including medicine and management 2 per cent, books on religion and art books 1.9 per cent, current affairs, politics, memoirs and biographies 1.8 per cent, history 1.3 per cent, and law and economics just under 1 per cent. Sales of essays and works of literary criticism amounted to about 1 per cent of the total, but poetry and drama accounted for only 0.3 per cent (*L'Edition de Livres en France*, 1998).

If what French people *read* is broadly in line with the books they *buy*, 'reading' still means predominantly reading novels. Within the sales figures for fiction, the percentages shown in Table 20.1 of the total sales figures for all books were recorded.

Table 20.1 The books French people buy

	Copies sold in 1000s	% of total books sold
'Contemporary'	46 400	13.5
Sentimental	14 177	4.1
Detective, espionage	12 730	3.7
Classic	11 980	3.5
Science fiction, horror	4308	1.3
Erotic	579	0.2

In most of these categories, more reprints than new titles or new editions were published, the exceptions being erotic and sentimental novels, as shown in Table 20.2.

Table 20.2   New publishing v. reprints

	Number of new titles or new editions	Number of reprinted titles
'Contemporary'	2555	2993
Sentimental	650	136
Detective, espionage	515	655
Classic	386	987
Science fiction, horror	253	329
Erotic	147	2

Source: L'Edition de Livres en France, 1997 report

French publishers use the term 'contemporary novels' to indicate those dealing broadly with up-to-date characters and situations but eschewing the rather formula-driven devices of other categories in the table. While 'contemporary' novels were far ahead of the rest in production and sales, the most reliable market in terms of reprints was in classic, detective and espionage novels and in science fiction. The market for *bandes dessinées* was similar to these, based on 554 new titles and 778 reprints. Sales of sentimental novels – romantic fiction like Mills and Boon in Britain – were very buoyant, but more new titles than reprints were evidently judged necessary to supply the market. In human and social sciences, there were more new titles than reprints (in economics there were 913 new titles, 63 reprints, in pure science 496 new titles, 162 reprints, in medicine 423 against 160 and in geography 91 against 21).

The French: exceptional readers?

In the self-image of educated French people, the preoccupation with reading is as central as the price of bread. Literacy, with numeracy, is commonly regarded as the key to the economic and social welfare of the nation and to personal success: it is thought to give individual self-respect and to enable people to control their lives and attitudes. Provided that there is no censorship, reading and the availability of books are seen as marks of the advanced, free society, encouraging independence of mind as well as civic virtues and social solidarity. In radical thought, reading is often seen as an engine of civilized social progress. In France as elsewhere, to be in some measure unable to read is to be stigmatized as being outside cultivated society, that vague, convenient concept. However, the cultural value of reading is also coloured by attitudes towards erudition, by the complexity or difficulty of texts and by the force of social snobbery. In the early 1980s, Theodore Zeldin could write that:

> the Germans, the Dutch, the British all put reading as their favourite leisure pursuit more frequently than the French. The British spend almost 50 per cent more on books, and British lending libraries lend about twelve times more books than French ones do. ... But the French give the impression of being book lovers because they have a literary class for whom books are almost life itself.

Zeldin judged, in addition, that, compared with British readers who were said to have a predilection for reading novels, 'French book readers have a broader interest in the human sciences, history, art, anthropology, literature' (Zeldin 1983, 335–6). Whatever the merits of this earlier judgement, it no longer seems an accurate reflection of the book-buying public.

The crisis in academic publishing is a sign of changed times. Reading habits are undoubtedly one of the measures of the social and intellectual life of a nation: if the exchange of ideas slows down, intellectual publishing houses will feel the effects. In the late 1990s, one of the best known academic publishing and bookselling organizations, the Presses universitaires de France (PUF), ran into financial difficulties. These were attributed to a collapse of interest in the exchange of ideas, which seems to be at odds with French intellectual traditions. In May 1999, the chairman of the PUF, presenting a restructuring plan for the organization, commented that in the France of the late twentieth century there was a crisis in the humanities: intellectual theorists, philosophers and scholars, scientists and public figures were, he said, shying away from the challenges of intellectual battle, and making a virtue of compromise and consensus. The result was indifference, revealed strikingly in the sales figures for translations of social science texts, the basis of the PUF's publishing activity. He reported that texts which sold 7000 or 8000 copies in English, or 3000 to 4000 in German or Italian, were selling only about 700 copies in French. The results were staff lay-offs, a review of marketing policy and a plan for the closure of the main bookshop near the Sorbonne (Michel Pringent, interviewed in *Le Monde*, 12 May 1999, 32). In an age when intellectual *contestation* appeared to have become the norm, the conflict of ideas had itself become banal. Local book

sales at the PUF were also thought to have been reduced by the transfer of
Sorbonne students from the Latin Quarter to buildings in other parts of
Paris and by the availability of photocopying – in French the term 'photo-
copillage' has been invented for the illegal photocopying of copyright material. Still, the PUF's publication activities were not all affected adversely (the
future of certain of its academic journals was reported to be secure), and
where there are high standards combined with commitment, sales can be
guaranteed. Some smaller, specialized publishing houses have been quite
successful: Verdier, Circé, L'Harmattan, L'Esprit du Temps Editions, Galilée,
Cerf Editions or the well-named 'Editions de l'Encyclopédie des Nuisances',
producing works on such topics as genetically modified crops or in vitro fer-
tilization, and 'Les Empêcheurs de penser en rond', specializing in contemporary issues such as ethnopsychiatry (see *Le Nouvel Observateur*, 1804,
3–9 June 1999, 61). In Paris and in some other cities, there are feminist
bookshops, cinema bookshops, religious bookshops, 'green' bookshops
etc., as well as ethnic specialists. The readerships for such works may be limited, but the books are being published. Nevertheless, the art of reading
intellectually demanding books is considered, rightly or wrongly, to be
under threat. Specialists often read only books which relate to their subjects,
and non-specialists may not be interested in those subjects at all. Intellectual
specialization has sometimes led to obscurantist or jargon-ridden expression
which is unappealing to general, educated readerships. In general, an author
may find it fairly easy to have a specialized book accepted for publication,
but it does not sell many copies. Asked in June 1999 what kind of public
was intended for Gallimard's highly respected 'Bibliothèque des sciences
humaines', the director of the Collection, Pierre Nora, replied:

> We have two readerships: academic readers and the general public.
> Both are in the process of disappearing. Primarily because the cultural
> basis which brought these two kinds of reader together has been frac-
> tured. Whole disciplines, such as linguistics and even psychoanalysis,
> now stand by themselves, in isolation. Others have faded away – soci-
> ology, for example, with the exception of Bourdieu. History is holding
> its own, but literary criticism, a traditional discipline in France, has
> sunk almost without trace: apart from Starobinski, Bénichou and
> Fumaroli, there is no hope. You might have thought that the 'death of
> ideology' would have liberated people's minds; it has imprisoned
> them. At the same time, intellectual authority has declined sharply, to
> be replaced by personalities: we didn't expect this.

> *Le Nouvel Observateur*, 3–9 June 1999, 60–61

These personalities who served as a substitute included Bernard Pivot,
anchorman for the television book programme *Apostrophes*. It was as
though an *appearance* of literary culture was replacing the reality of a reading culture. However, books which were discussed on this programme

would sell well, and *Apostrophes* undoubtedly helped to keep books in the public mind and made reading a subject of topical interest.

Despite this crisis in the academic market and some fashionable uncertainty about the 'future of the book', there does not appear in fact to be a *crise de la lecture* in France. But reading habits are evolving, and some bookshops are evolving with them. The great bookstores, such as the FNAC group throughout France or the Joseph Gibert bookshops, prominent on the boulevard Saint-Michel in Paris, continue to trade in considerable and varied book-stocks and are doing very good business, but they do so by also selling CDs and computers, video, audio, telephone or photographic equipment and services. Not only will they sell travel books and maps, they will also act as travel agents, and provide a personal stereo, a mobile phone and books for reading during the trip.

Conclusion

Books still sell, and people still enjoy being told stories. The fundamental rule, recognized by Paul Valéry when writing about the novel, is that the reader must be encouraged to turn the page. So when interesting stories are invented, or when things happen which arouse curiosity, there will usually be people willing to write books about them and others willing to pay for the pleasure of reading them. This is so, especially, when the subjects include personalities linked in some way to historic events. What happened, for example, to the fortune of Henri d'Orléans, Comte de Paris, who died in June 1999 at the age of 90 in the modest suburban bungalow of his mistress? A direct descendant of Louis XIV and pretender to a throne of France, he once possessed a great fortune, including jewellery which had belonged to Marie-Antoinette. Situated in the vague hinterland between the *fait divers* and the movement of history, this kind of event may be expected sooner or later to find its way into a popularizing book, feeding the reader's curiosity. Even the republican French people often seem to delight in stories of the royal family in the United Kingdom.

Is 'French literature' then a thing of the past? Not so long as readers take pleasure in reading older or modern classics, books which last. Balzac, Stendhal, Flaubert, Zola, Proust and many others who have contributed in some measure to the gradual evolution of the curious genre which is the novel are still read, as are Colette, Mauriac, Camus and Malraux. Many of the classic writers were scandalous in their day. A new generation of serious novelists has continued the tradition of provoking controversy: Marie Darrieusecq, Michel Houellebecq and others. The publisher Robert Laffont has enjoyed success with a collection entitled 'Bouquins', including novels as well as other texts which many might consider intellectually demanding. 'Bouquins' illustrates an approach to publishing which seeks to attract readers by producing substantial works – such as Proust's *A la recherche du temps perdu*, the works of Cioran, or a group of novels by Balzac – in one volume, but at a low price. With the supple binding associated with *livres de poche*, yet printed on fine paper, this series competes with the prestigious leather-bound and expensive books of the 'Bibliothèque de la Pléiade' type produced by Gallimard. At the same time, the attraction of more popular works remains very strong and, in terms of sales, predominates: many French people find their entertainment in contemporary books of romantic fiction, horror stories, science fiction or in tales such as those told by Marcel Pagnol, with sales encouraged by film versions of the novels. The suspense novels of the American Mary Higgins Clark – 'MHC' to her French fans – have sold an extraordinary 25 million copies in France – something the author attributes to having had a single translator. It could also be said that she offers the attractions of a transatlantic blend of the Belgian Simenon and the English Agatha Christie which one commentator considers 'très balsamique' (Marc Lambron, *Le Point*, 18 July 1999, 83).

So the French are perhaps not such an 'exception' as they sometimes think, and enjoy formulaic, cathartic or escapist works which they can pick up while they are buying their weekly provisions at the supermarket or waiting for their train or aeroplane.

References and recommended reading

I am indebted to MM. André Béziat, professor of English in the University of Perpignan, and Alain Delmas, journalist at Radio Europe 1, Paris, for their help with establishing documentation for this chapter.

BAUDELOT, Christian, CARTIER, Marie and DETREZ, Christine 1999: *Et pourtant ils lisent*. Paris: Seuil.
BLIND, Camille-Frédérique (ed.) 1999: *L'illettrisme en toutes lettres*. Paris: Ouvrage collectif, France-Culture Flohic Editions, Collection Expressions.
DONNAT, Olivier 1990: *Les pratiques culturelles des Français, 1973–1989*. La Découverte, La Documentation Française.
DONNAT, Olivier 1994: *Les Français face à la culture: de l'exclusion à l'éclectisme*. La Découverte.
DONNAT, Olivier 1998: *Les pratiques culturelles des Français. Enquête 1997*. Ministère de la Culture et de la Communication, La Documentation Française.
L'Edition de Livres en France 1998: report for 1997. Paris Syndicat national de l'Edition.
FRIER, Cathy 1999: Presse et illetrisme: le regard de l'autre. In BLIND 1999, 15–20.
ROBINE, Nicole 1999: L'évolution du rapport à la lecture. In BLIND 1999, 35–37.
ROUET, François 2000: *Le livre: mutations d'une industrie culturelle* (2nd edn). Paris: La Documentation Française.
ZELDIN, Theodore 1983: *The French*. London: Collins.

There are weekly reports on best-sellers in magazines such as *Le Point*, and book-trade reports in *Livres Hebdo*. For a translated selection of new writing with a provocative introduction, see Georgia de CHAMBERET, *XCITés. The Flamingo book of new French writing*. London: Flamingo, 1999. On the Loi Lang, see *Prix du livre. Mode d'emploi 1995*, issued free by the Ministère de la Culture.

|21|

Intellectuals in French culture

BY MARTYN CORNICK

For over a century intellectuals have formed an integral part of French culture. They have intervened in public debate and generated controversy, committed themselves to causes at home and abroad, and have adopted political positions from the extreme left through the centre to the extreme right, with many shades in between. Who are the intellectuals, what do they represent, and where do we find them in France today? These are the principal questions addressed by this chapter.[1]

Definitions and the importance of history

We should first define the term 'intellectuals' (in French, *intellectuels*, or *clercs*). Because of the nature of French political culture, intellectuals and their activities are so bound up with the country's history that an explanation of this context is essential to an understanding of why intellectual culture is like it is today. To reinforce a point made in one of the introductory chapters, intellectuals constitute one of the major sites of memory *(lieux de mémoire)*. In other words, their position within society is such that their role is intimately linked to the specific way republican culture has developed over the last century. It is for this reason that intellectuals in France behave so differently from those in other countries. The definition adopted here is that intellectuals are writers, artists, scientists or educators who use their status to intervene in the public arena in order to pronounce upon given events or *causes célèbres*, for example the Dreyfus Affair, the Occupation, the Algerian War or, more recently, events such as the Gulf War or the conflict in Kosovo. As one historian puts it, 'intellectuals are those who participate in cultural creativity or in the progress of scientific knowledge, as well as those who contribute to the dissemination or the vulgarization of the results of creativity or knowledge' (Sirinelli 1995a, 524). So intellectuals may be creative artists, like writers or novelists, or they may be sociologists or scientists; yet intellectuals are also those who *mediate* knowledge or opinion to the public. Thus their importance lies in their relationship to the manipulation of *political power*, which is why they sometimes stand in a problematic relationship with the media. We shall return to this question further on.

Of course there are other, more complex, definitions of intellectuals (cf. Ory and Sirinelli 1986; Rieffel 1993). Perhaps the most famous intellectual of all in France, Jean-Paul Sartre, devoted a series of lectures to the subject. Here Sartre makes a similar point to that made above, but he expresses it in a slightly different way:

> Originally, the body of intellectuals appeared as diverse individuals having acquired a degree of notoriety through their intellectual endeavours (the exact sciences, applied sciences, medicine, literature, etc.) and who *abused* this notoriety to step outside their own area in order to criticize society and the powers-that-be in the name of global and dogmatic concepts, whether these are vague or precise, of moral intent or Marxist.

> Sartre 1972, 13

Figure 21.1
Roseline Granet's striking bronze 'Hommage à Jean-Paul Sartre' (1987) in the courtyard of the Bibliothèque nationale, Paris.

Thus it is usually understood that a rocket scientist working on a new weapon is *not* an intellectual; if, however, this rocket scientist joins with other scientists or writers to sign a manifesto warning the general public through the media of the dangers of such applications of science, then he or she *is* to be considered as an intellectual (Julliard and Winock 1996, 11).

The contemporary meaning and use of the word originated in the last decade of the nineteenth century. A study by Venita Datta insists upon the emergence around 1890 of avant-garde reviews as 'centers of sociability': without these, groups of writers would not have entered the public stage as they did, self-consciously *as* autonomous intellectuals, to challenge the literary and social status quo (Datta 1999). In one sense though, intellectuals in modern France had antecedents in the eighteenth and nineteenth centuries, as Priscilla Clark (1991) and Paul Bénichou (1999) have shown. Several celebrated writers played a self-conscious and prominent 'public role' in France. During the period of the Enlightenment, *philosophes* (or thinkers) such as Jean-Jacques Rousseau (1712–1778), Voltaire (1694–1778) and Denis Diderot (1713–1784) helped to prepare the philosophical, legal and social ground for the French Revolution. Theirs were the catalyzing forces behind new ways of thinking about human and social relationships: for instance, Rousseau foreshadowed the direction taken by modern thinking on human rights when he wrote (in *Du contrat social*, 1762): 'Man [sic] was born free, and everywhere he is in chains'. What is more, in 1765 Voltaire came to the defence of Jean Calas in a case of religious prejudice and injustice that prefigured the Dreyfus Affair (1894–1906). Writers or historians such as Jules Michelet (1798–1874), George Sand (the pen-name of Aurore Dupin; 1804–1876), Ernest Renan (1823–1892) and Victor Hugo (1802–1885) also achieved prominence as public-political figures during the nineteenth century: without their efforts, their successors could not have evolved in the ways they did.

By the 1890s, the Third Republic (founded in 1870–1) had witnessed a phase of rapid social and industrial modernization. National education policies, increased literacy and the bringing together (via the railways and press distribution) of the regions into a more cohesive whole meant that France was moving rapidly towards mass democracy. Thus were laid the bases of modern French political identity. As Christophe Charle (1990) has shown, against this background changes in the higher education sector and other social reforms created the conditions for the emergence in the 1890s of the 'intellectuals'. But the event which gave rise to the use of the term 'intellectual' in the contemporary sense was the Dreyfus Affair, a *cause célèbre* which continues to have a bearing on French political history. In late 1894 Captain Alfred Dreyfus was falsely accused of spying on behalf of Germany, tried and sentenced to detention on Devil's Island, off the coast of South America. The majority in France believed him guilty, but while Dreyfus languished in his prison exile, a small band of friends, believing him innocent, devoted themselves to his cause. The first intellectual 'acts' proper were when the novelist Emile Zola, convinced too of Dreyfus's innocence, wrote a devastating attack on those in authority, particularly the army high command: this was *J'accuse...!*, published in the daily newspaper *L'Aurore* on 13 January 1898 (Oriol 1997; Pagès 1998). The next day, the same paper published the first of 17 separate lists of names under a text headed 'A Protest' (*Une Protestation*): 'We the undersigned, in protest against the violation of judicial procedures in the trial of 1894...persist in demanding revision' (Julliard and Winock 1996, 371–91). Eventually the authorities had to allow the judicial revision to proceed and, after a sensational retrial in Rennes which was avidly reported by the world's press, in September 1899 Dreyfus was finally pardoned.

The consequences of these first acts of political *engagement* were far-reaching. To begin with, the pro-Dreyfus intellectuals – who argued for Justice, Truth and Reason, all solid republican values – were pitted against the anti-Dreyfusards – including Catholics, nationalists, and sometimes anti-Semites – who argued for the primacy of the national interest over the rights of the individual. To this extent the Affair represented the first major test of French republican identity. Not for the first time in recent history, society was divided over the issue. In the end, the intellectuals helped to stage a 'defence of the Republic' that became a reference point with enduring echoes. For instance, it is instructive for today's student of French culture to look at the coverage of the press surrounding the centenary in January 1998 of the publication of *J'accuse...!* The quality dailies basked in the glorious role played by some of their predecessors in righting wrong, while the magazine *Le Nouvel Observateur* lent its pages to a group of ten writers wishing to highlight a range of *contemporary* cases of injustice. Furthermore, the Prime Minister, Lionel Jospin, became embroiled in controversy when he too readily likened opposition politicians to the anti-Dreyfusards.[2] This is a clear instance of the many links between past and present in France, links which will frequently be found in today's media, especially around anniversaries.

Second, the values for which intellectuals argued – Justice, Truth and Reason – now coincided with those of the Republic, and questions touching on human rights continue to be couched in these terms. As the writer André Glucksmann explained on TV in 1998 to a student audience, when there are unhappy people in the world, 'fortunately there are some sensitive souls who say – we must do something' (Desfons 1999). To this extent intellectuals express the nation's conscience as the guardians of these values. France's international image derives historically (in part at least) from the dissemination of these values across other world cultures. Finally, the Affair set a pattern which was to remain unchanged for many years to come: Sirinelli (1996) provides evidence of how intellectuals of all shades continued to produce manifestos and petitions from World War I onwards, through the ideological upheavals of the inter-war period in the 1920s and 1930s and on into the post-1945 period, with further oppositions over the Cold War,

Algeria and the rest. They continue to do so, one example in 1999 being the manifesto issued against NATO's intervention in Serbia entitled 'Stop the bombing'.[3]

How can we sum up the development of French intellectual history over the last century, a history whose legacy is so crucial today? According to Michel Winock (1997), this history is dominated by three figures each representative of their age: 'the Barrès years', from the Dreyfus Affair to World War I; 'the Gide years' covering the inter-war period to 1944; and 'the Sartre years', from the Liberation until 1980.[4] In his day Maurice Barrès (1862–1923) exercised such an influence over his generation that had he not existed, the intellectuals of the period would have evolved quite differently. Barrès's intensely nationalistic conception of French identity prepared the ground for the opposition between intellectual camps whose terrain was already clearly mapped out at the time of the Dreyfus Affair. Whether on the side of Barrès or against him, French intellectuals were widely mobilized in the 1914–18 war effort against Germany. This was the first *total* war, and writers' talents were deployed in what became a life-or-death struggle between two opposing concepts of civilization, the French (*civilisation*) and the German (*Kultur*) (Hanna 1996).

André Gide (1869–1951) is the dominant figure in the inter-war period. With his own reputation as a writer having already been established by the outbreak of World War I, and once Barrès had died in 1923, Gide's influence was unsurpassed. His 'immoralism', his agonies over religion, colonialism and sexuality, his Communist 'fellow-travelling' phase from 1932 to his dramatic disavowal of the Soviet experiment in 1936 and his influence over the review *La Nouvelle Revue française* (Cornick 1995) are the factors explaining his magnetic appeal for new generations of young writers emerging from the disaster of the Great War. Whether he attracted or repelled, Gide acted as a guiding spirit, both in France and elsewhere in Europe. Great homage was paid to him by Jean-Paul Sartre, who acknowledged, on Gide's death in 1951, that his influence on French thought over the previous 30 years had been as great as that of Marx, Heidegger or Kierkegaard.

With the Liberation in 1944 came the transition to the 'Sartre years'. The division of the world into opposing ideological power blocs led to an intensification and multiplication of French intellectuals' campaigns and battles. The principal figures were Sartre (1905–1980), representing the non-communist and then the revolutionary left, Albert Camus (1913–1960), standing for liberal or left-of-centre humanism, and Raymond Aron (1905–1983), whose position and writings were those of right-of-centre liberalism. One study traces the oppositions between Sartre and Aron, both of whom graduated at the same time from the elite Ecole normale supérieure (ENS)[5] in Paris; their different intellectual trajectories provide an exemplary and striking contrast (Sirinelli 1995b). Around or away from these dominant figures clustered other individuals or (more usually) groups of intellectuals, with their reviews and networks. Finally, with the eventual discrediting during the 1970s of totalitarian socialism and the waning of its appeal for French intellectuals, the figure of Aron has latterly come to 'be recognized as the greatest intellectual dissenter of his age and the man who laid the foundations for a fresh departure in French public debate' (Judt 1998, 182). And when Sartre died in 1980, tens of thousands of people followed his funeral cortege to his final resting place in Montparnasse cemetery; looking back, it seems indeed that the end of an era had been reached. Sartre was the last great public writer – or writer-as-intellectual – whose name and image were immediately recognized by so many people. These public figures having no obvious successors, the very existence of the intellectuals came increasingly to be questioned (Lyotard 1984; Ross 1987 and 1991; Bodin 1997).

Locating intellectuals in France today

Over the last 20 years, in France as elsewhere the impact of the 'new' media – television, videos, satellites and now the Internet – on the production and dissemination of information and culture has radically changed the market conditions in which intellectuals operate. Not long after François Mitterrand had led the left to power in 1981 for the first time in the Fifth Republic (founded 1958), some were troubled by what was perceived as the 'silence of the intellectuals' and looked back nostalgically to the 1930s, the 'golden age' of the Gide years (Cornick 1998). The withering of the 'grand narrative of Marxism' (e.g. Lyotard 1982), the gradual collapse of socialism in eastern Europe and, most significantly, fears over the globalization process (e.g. Chesneaux 1983), all took their toll on the intellectual community, sparking reappraisals of their role. At the end of the twentieth century, however, there is plenty of evidence to suggest that intellectuals continue to play a major public role in France.

Who are the intellectuals in France today, and where do we find them? What are the issues addressed by them? For students of French culture seeking accessible evidence of contemporary intellectual preoccupations, I propose three avenues of exploration. It is instructive to look not just at the work of certain individual personalities, but also to examine the *milieux* or reviews and magazines in which they circulate and operate. Third, intellectuals' reactions to specific events and issues, such as war or political crisis, also repay study. Within the limited space available, I shall point to some prominent and accessible examples of these three key aspects.

Personalities

Until the late 1970s, intellectual culture was based almost entirely on the written word. With the arrival of the mass medium of television, there was a gradual shift away from cultural practices based on the written word, a process analyzed by Régis Debray, a leading contemporary intellectual. Debray is a controversial figure: born in 1940, he excelled in his studies at the ENS and was attracted to the communist cause in the early 1960s, travelling several times to Cuba where he met Fidel Castro. He then engaged in revolutionary activity with Che Guevara in Bolivia, where he was arrested (1967), imprisoned and eventually released in December 1970 after appeals were made on his behalf in Paris. After this experience he turned to literature, and became increasingly involved in socialist politics. Following his critiques of media domination over cultural life in France, with the Mitterrand victory in 1981 he was made adviser to the President and appointed to the government think-tank, the Conseil d'Etat (see Reader 1996). In several works which repay study, he offers a solid defence of the French republican state and tradition against various perceived threats, especially political apathy at home and the forces of globalization abroad (Debray 1989, 1990, 1998, 1999a). In one short and illuminating text 'explaining the Republic to his daughter', Debray uses the traditional terminology of the 'one and indivisible Republic' to extol the virtues of a French system at risk from other (especially American) cultural influences: 'we are moving towards a more selfish society, indifferent to others, in which everyone wants to get rich and attain success individually' (Debray 1998, 7; 11). His intervention in May 1999 over the Kosovo crisis unleashed a storm of controversy, to which we shall return.

In *Le Pouvoir intellectuel en France* (1979), Debray analysed the shifts in the distribution of symbolic power in France. He identified three overlapping 'ages': the university cycle (1880–1930), the publishing cycle (1920–1960) and the media age (from 1968 onwards). The gist of his argument was that since the time of the Dreyfus Affair the pronouncements of the Parisian intelligentsia based around the 'high' intellectual institutions – first the University, the ENS, the Académie française, then reviews, newspapers and publishers – filtered down to the 'lower intellectuals' in the hierarchy and in the provinces; these then communicated with the greater mass of the people through their 'lesser' institutions, including schools and the press. The coming of the mass medium of television, argued Debray, required the reorganization and concentration of cultural power among a few conglomerates able to afford the massive outlay. The act of *communication* became paramount. George Ross (1987) puts it well:

> the 'mediatization' of the product assumed much greater importance than its nature and quality. Moreover, since the media held the keys to cultural success, it became incumbent on the intellectuals to establish a recognizable and favorable media presence to become celebrities. . . . To break through to the general public, intellectuals had to master a new set of networks. If one wanted one's works to be read or discussed beyond a narrow circle, then one had to . . . respond to the incentives

of the media. Most importantly, now one had to become famous in a 'mediacratic' sense in order to establish a publicly recognized brilliant university or literary career.

Ross 1987, 55–6

To ensure the best return on one's intellectual capital, therefore, it became necessary to increase one's media presence. One consequence of this process was that intellectuals became celebrities, TV personalities, 'stars' even, knowing that they would maximize sales of their books by appearing on programmes such as Bernard Pivot's *Apostrophes*.[6] Another consequence was that some intellectuals were now omnipresent in the contemporary media, the most flamboyant example being that of Bernard-Henri Lévy.

Born in 1948, Bernard-Henri Lévy rose to prominence during the 1970s with the publication of *La Barbarie à visage humain* (Barbarism with a Human Face) (1977). This book, an impassioned critique of 'socialist barbarism', sold 100 000 copies, an extraordinary number for such a work. Then in 1981, following the publication of his *L'Idéologie française*, in which a number of French intellectuals (some of them regarded as left-wing) were blamed for the ills of fascism and anti-Semitism, he provoked a further storm of criticism. All this guaranteed his high profile in the media, for since then Lévy has had a constant presence in the press (*Le Quotidien de Paris*, *Le Matin*, *Le Monde*), reviews (including his own *La Règle du jeu*, founded in 1990), and magazines (*Le Nouvel Observateur* and *Le Point*, in which he has written a weekly column since 1993; he also co-founded *Globe* in 1985). Lévy has appeared on countless TV programmes, and has actively promoted the role of intellectuals within society, frequently intervening in issues concerning human rights; thus he was one of the moving spirits behind the founding in 1984 of the anti-racist organization SOS-Racisme (Julliard and Winock 1996, 711). With his youthful good looks and his trademark open-necked white shirts, Lévy's media omnipresence has inspired some mischievous commentaries, one such pointing out his willingness to be interviewed by magazines such as *Elle* and *Jacinthe*, and that he has even been asked to judge beauty contests (Negroni 1985, ch. IV). In a way Lévy's case supports to some extent the thesis about the shift to a dominant visual culture and its emphasis on 'image', a concern having a serious cultural dimension that has been a matter for public discussion (e.g. Debray 1993).

A further change noted over the last 20 years is that major intellectual personalities are now 'experts', especially in the social science areas of economics, international relations or sociology (see Mongin 1998). Intellectuals are no longer necessarily recognized first and foremost as writers who intervene as concerned citizens. This is certainly the case for Pierre Bourdieu (b. 1930), another of the most prominent intellectuals in contemporary France. His interventions in public affairs are undertaken in the interests of justice or human rights because they are based, so he and his supporters argue, upon his expertise and status as France's most celebrated sociologist (Bourdieu 1998a). He has intervened in recent public life not out of commitment to Marxist beliefs (as was the case with Sartre), but rather to uphold the values of the republican tradition (Lane 1999). After a long career in higher education beginning in Algiers in 1958, since 1981 he has held a chair in sociology at the Collège de France in Paris.[7] His work has been translated into several languages, and his reputation extends well beyond the borders of France. Bourdieu's innovative sociological theories have been influential because they are applicable in other disciplines such as aesthetics, history or anthropology. For him and his followers, sociological theory should not simply be deployed to analyse the structures of society and the representations that individuals have of it; such analysis should be brought to bear on these representations in order to change the world. This explains Bourdieu's own willingness to intervene in the public arena, whether on behalf of striking students (as in 1986), striking workers (in December 1995) or against the NATO bombing campaign in Kosovo (Julliard and Winock 1996, 176; cf. note 3 above).[8]

Bourdieu wields considerable power himself in the intellectual field: he edits an established series of books for the publisher Editions de Minuit ('Le sens commun'), and since 1975 he has edited *Actes de la recherche en sciences sociales*, an influential review in which his own work and that of his many disciples is published. In a recent issue he turned his attention to a perceived 'conservative revolution in publishing' in France, with its attendant dangers of concentrating media power and 'symbolic capital' (Bourdieu 1999). Furthermore, he controls a publishing venture called 'Liber-Raisons d'agir', a series that did much to relaunch controversial intellectual debate in the late 1990s (Halimi 1997; Bourdieu 1998a; Duval et al. 1998). Indeed, because Bourdieu exercises so much power in the intellectual field, he has come under increasing attack from various quarters. In the wake of the social unrest in November and December 1995 and the alleged support given to the 'reformist' cause (opposing the strikers) by the reviews *Esprit* and *Le Débat*, a number of Bourdieu's 'disciples' attacked them in one of the 'Raisons d'agir' series (Duval et al. 1998).[9] The editors of *Esprit* countered in their issue for July 1998, accusing Bourdieu and his followers of distortion and intellectual dishonesty; if Sartre invented the 'total intellectual', then Bourdieu, wrote *Esprit,* using the sociologist's own terms, is the *'intellectuel dominant'.*[10] This was the very theme of a further attack later that year in which Bourdieu and his sociology were accused of 'terrorism', relentless self-promotion and of representing the real *'pensée unique'* in France (rather than neo-liberalism) (Verdès-Leroux 1998). And predictably this whipped up another media storm, with one weekly showing Bourdieu on the cover over the headline 'the most powerful intellectual in France' (*L'Evénement du jeudi*, 27 August–2 September 1998).

By now it may have become apparent that the majority of high-profile intellectuals in France are male. There are exceptions of course, the most celebrated being Simone de Beauvoir (1908–1986). This is attributable to historical factors that have borne down with considerable oppressive force. Traditionally most women in France were restricted to the private domain. For centuries women's public expression was forbidden, whether in religious or political arenas. Women were not permitted to speak in church, and for much of the last two centuries it was considered vulgar in polite society for women to talk about politics; moreover, French women only gained the vote in 1944. 'The Word is the prerogative of those who wield power. The Word is power. The Word makes Man [sic]' (Perrot 1998). Given the importance for intellectual rank of the written word and high public profile, it is unsurprising then that in one recent history of twentieth-century France, 'only eight women are included in connection with art, literature, and philosophy, compared with 180 men'. In the domain of 'cultural creation', independent studies showed the existence of 'a ratio of 75 per cent male authors to 25 per cent female', and that 'this ratio ha[d] remained stable' for 40 years, 'despite the rise of the women's liberation movement' (Marini 1994, 309). A similar exercise may be conducted using the index of *Le Siècle des intellectuels* (The Century of the Intellectuals) (Winock 1997) to show to what extent female intellectuals are still in the minority. Having said this, however, things have changed considerably over the last 20 years, and in the cultural domain Marini is optimistic that this 'change has paved the way for a new cultural practice, for a truly *mixed* culture', as opposed to one in which women are trapped in 'a double-bind: they are both students (or teachers, writers, intellectuals) *and* women' (Marini 1994, 300; 317). Today there are a number of high-profile women active in the fields of history (e.g. Mona Ozouf or Michelle Perrot), criticism and psychoanalysis (e.g. Hélène Cixous or Julia Kristeva) and 'women's writing'.[11]

Reviews and magazines

One of the most accessible places to find out about intellectuals' preoccupations is in their reviews, since these remain among the most salient features of the intellectual landscape. France still enjoys a strong written culture, so the existence of a broad spectrum of reviews and newspapers may be said to be symptomatic of a healthy democracy. Indeed, despite all the fears about its culture being submerged or suffocated by (an American-dominated) visual culture, France has a dynamic range of intellectual reviews, among which the most accessible are *Esprit*, *Le Débat*, *Les Temps modernes* and *Commentaire*.

Esprit

Founded in 1932 by the liberal Catholic Emmanuel Mounier, *Esprit* is one of the most dynamic intellectual forums in France, printing between 10 000 and 20 000 copies per issue. It is considered politically to be on the 'progressive' left, having as long ago as the late 1950s militated in favour of a 'new left' distanced from 'traditional' Socialism or Communism. Under Paul Thibaud (editor 1976–88), *Esprit* denounced socialist totalitarianism. In a process begun in 1989 under its current editor, Olivier Mongin, it continues to examine in multiple perspective the different aspects of a modern democratic society, in particular the theme of social justice. Its monthly issues are usually organized around a theme, and in recent years the most important have treated the situation in Algeria, Europe, globalization and the nature and future of work in France. Since 1993, *Esprit* has published over 20 articles specifically on the situation in Kosovo. Its April 1999 issue on 'France and Reformism' is an impressive example of how it can marshal expertise, and Mongin's survey of contemporary intellectual trends will be of interest to those reading this chapter (see Rieffel 1993, 330–58; Mongin 1999).

Le Débat

Published by Gallimard, this review was founded in 1980 by Pierre Nora, the editor responsible for the landmark series *Les Lieux de mémoire*; *Le Débat* prints between 8000 and 15 000 copies per issue depending on the themes covered. It was created to promote the 'human sciences' as successfully as the *Nouvelle Revue française* did for literature. As though symbolically, *Le Débat* appeared on 15 April 1980, the day Sartre died, its *raison d'être* being to stimulate debate. Its opening text laid stress upon 'openness' to what was 'new' in all areas of intellectual concern, the outside world and the young generation. *Le Débat* achieved success partly by drawing on the talents of both well-established and new academics at the Ecole des hautes études en sciences sociales (EHESS),[12] in particular the historians François Furet, Mona Ozouf, Pierre Rosanvallon and Jacques Julliard. It also helped to establish a new generation, including Gilles Lipovetsky, Alain Finkielkraut and Alain Minc, all of whom are now well-known intellectuals. Politically, *Le Débat* is in the centre: it is identifiably 'reformist', meaning that its main concern, as for *Esprit*, is to encourage discussion by multiple voices on a wide range of issues regarding the state of French democratic society. During the early 1980s, it opened its pages to those concerned with the renewal of socialism; in the late 1990s it has links with the Fondation Saint-Simon (founded in 1982 and named after an enlightened early nineteenth-century economist). This 'think-tank' encourages consensual thinking on social or work organization, and as such incurred the wrath of those supporting the strikers in December 1995 (Duval et al. 1998). Its usual format is to group together two or three or more articles on a range of topics: in the September 1999 issue, for example, there was a major piece on the humanitarian aspect of the Kosovo conflict as well as a section of five articles on the 'uncertainties' of the Fifth Republic. There are many articles too on contemporary trends in intellectual life (e.g. Grémion 1999; see also Rieffel 1993, 390–402).

Also worth consulting for contemporary debates are *Les Temps modernes* (founded in 1945 by Jean-Paul Sartre and Simone de Beauvoir), still anchored on the left politically, and *Commentaire*, a review of the liberal right. The latter, launched in 1978 by Jean-Claude Casanova and Alain Besançon, owes much to the thought of Raymond Aron, whose intellectual legacy remains strongly felt in France. Many of the intellectuals mentioned, as well as many others, write for a range of magazines (mostly weekly), from *Le Monde diplomatique*, *Politis*, *Marianne* (Jean-François Kahn) and the mainstream *Le Nouvel Observateur* (Jacques Julliard and Alain Touraine) on the left or in the centre, to *Le Point* and *L'Express* on the centre-right. With minor exceptions, the former apparently unbridgeable gulf between the left and right has disappeared from the written media.

Events and issues

In recent years, intellectuals have reacted more frequently to events at home and abroad than they did at the beginning of the 1990s, and there are no signs that this trend is in decline; they certainly appear to have fully 'reawakened'.[13] Indeed, if one consults the contents pages of their reviews, intellectuals appear stimulated by the historical moment of being on the threshold of a new century. This phenomenon, characteristic of the 'fin de siècle', entails looking back over the past century to see how concerns such as the construction of republican identity, or anxieties over the future of France, have evolved, and how they will determine the future. To take one example: the figure of Charles Péguy (1873–1914) has re-emerged as an intellectual reference point in a way that brings these concerns together. Around 1900 Péguy was renowned as a rather eccentric figure who published his and others' work in his review *Cahiers de la quinzaine*. What marks him out is his curious intellectual trajectory: he campaigned for the Dreyfus cause, became a socialist and then returned to an ardent Catholicism around 1910. From 1905 he predicted that France would go to war with Germany, underpinning his analysis with an intensely patriotic nationalism. He was killed in September 1914 just after the beginning of World War I. Because some of his work was quoted selectively during the Occupation in support of the Vichy regime, he was accused later (e.g. Lévy 1981) of having contributed to a French strain of 'fascism'. So in view of Péguy's radical critiques of money, press power and external threats to France, Alain Finkielkraut and others have revisited his work to find inspiration for their own critiques of 'the modern world' (see Finkielkraut 1991; *Esprit*, December 1997; Plenel 1999). General de Gaulle is another figure with a mythical dimension to have undergone revision by sympathetic intellectuals, on the grounds that the founder of the Fifth Republic represents a *site of reconciliation*, for instance in the face of disillusion with socialism (Debray 1990; Glucksmann 1995). Thus the question of republican identity is a burning one in France, especially in the context of the European Union. With European integration implying the gradual relinquishing of national sovereignty to Brussels, worries continue to be expressed about the stability of republican identity. Such fears underlie the creation of the Fondation Marc-Bloch, a new 'think-tank' (founded March 1998) formed by a grouping of so-called 'national-republicans'; it has sponsored two works outlining their fears clearly (Cohn-Bendit and Guaino 1999; Debray 1999a).

Finally, contemporary intellectuals remain highly sensitive to the issue of war. In the 1980s, when tensions between the USA and the former Soviet Union were still high, an 'Appeal to the World's Intellectuals' was issued by a large group against the deployment of American Pershing missiles in Europe. They published this in March 1984 on their own authority as 'witnesses of their own time, as guardians of the memory of past centuries, and because they worked for the people of the future' (Desfons 1999). The outbreak of the Gulf War in the Middle East in 1991 saw France allied with the US and Britain against Saddam Hussein. Although opinion polls showed that some two-thirds of the public supported the intervention on behalf of the Kuwaitis, pacifist passions were reawakened among the intellectuals. There were reports of vocal opposition to French involvement in the war. At a press conference on 24 January 1991, the writer Gilles Perrault made an impassioned plea against involvement, and even called for French troops to desert. Such seditious remarks drew condemnation from many quarters, but Perrault's action struck a chord, for a few days later an appeal entitled 'Avec Gilles Perrault' was signed by 100 intellectual figures and placed in the press. At another level of debate, in a sometimes bitter exchange of views on France's role in the crisis and on the wisdom of intervening in the war, Debray crossed swords with Jean Daniel and Jacques Julliard in *Le Nouvel Observateur*. Intellectual reaction to the unfolding crisis covered a variety of issues, including human rights, anti-American feeling, North–South relations, the nature of Islam and geopolitical and economic matters.[14]

Given the European context, it is not surprising that the proximity of the war in the former Yugoslavia and the spring 1999 conflict in Kosovo should mobilize intellectuals. In the latter case the issues for and against were coloured by the humanitarian question, some believing that France and the Allies were right to intervene on behalf of the Kosovars because Slobodan Milosevic's Serb forces were again carrying out a policy of 'ethnic cleansing'. Yet doubts were expressed about the NATO bombing of Belgrade, especially when the Chinese embassy was hit. One petition signed by 25 intellectuals (including Bourdieu) called for an immediate halt to the bombing, the organization of a conference bringing together representatives of all the Balkan states, the defence of the principle of self-determination, and finally a debate in parliament on the future of French involvement in NATO. However, the greatest furore was unleashed after the publication in

Le Monde on 13 May 1999 of Régis Debray's 'Lettre d'un voyageur au président de la République' (now reprinted with other texts in Debray 1999b, 195–8). Here Debray deconstructed a statement made by President Chirac justifying NATO intervention in order to argue that the 'evidence' of his own journey to the Balkans earlier in May cast doubts on the validity of the President's case. Controversially, Debray believed that the bombing had negligible effets on the civilian population; that Milosevic was not a dictator since he had been elected twice; that the Kosovars were not the victims of 'genocide'; that Serb forces were not damaged or demoralised; and that an alliance defence minister had lied when he announced that almost a million Kosovars had been displaced. For the next month, the press was awash with articles taking issue with this 'Letter'; the very next day Debray was accused of being the 'defender of the Serb cause', and of 'international cretinism' (B.-H. Lévy, 'Adieu, Régis Debray'; A. Joxe, 'Contre le "Crétinisme international"', *Le Monde*, 14 May 1999). Debray alleged that *Le Monde* had faxed his article *before* publication to Lévy and Joxe in order to manufacture a controversy (Debray 1999b, 203), and these are precisely the grounds on which Debray subsequently defended himself. In the June issue of *Le Monde diplomatique*, in his preferred guise as 'mediologist', or critic-theoretician of the media, he attacked what he called the 'War Machine', arguing that the globalized media stifled real debate because in the case of the Kosovo conflict it was complicit with the military chiefs of the western alliance (reprinted in Debray 1999b, 203–8).[15]

No doubt the issues arising from this controversy, in particular the power of the media, globalization and the future world role and identity of France will be debated for a long time to come. These are the issues which make the headlines, the issues which mobilize the intellectuals. Although for a while it appeared that the public role of French intellectuals had diminished, the evidence from their own work, their networks and reviews suggests that in the political and cultural context of contemporary France, they will for a long time continue to stimulate debate and sow the seeds of memory.

Notes

1 My thanks go to David Drake of Middlesex University for generously making available a number of primary sources for this chapter. Translations are my own.
2 The bibliography on the Dreyfus Affair and its legacy is enormous. For the best recent summary in English, see E. Cahm, *The Dreyfus Affair in French society and politics* (Harlow: Longman, 1996). For the centenary, see *Le Point* (10 January 1998), *Libération* and *Le Figaro* (12 January 1998), *Le Monde* (13 January 1998), and for the protests see *Le Nouvel Observateur* (8 January 1998).
3 'Arrêt des bombardements, autodétermination', manifesto signed by Pierre Bourdieu and others (May 1999).
4 During the autumn of 1999, the television channel France 3 showed five films based on Winock's book. The fifth part was called 'The Media Years, 1980–1998' (Desfons 1999).

5 The Ecole normale supérieure, whose origins go back to 1794, is an elite educational establishment producing teachers and researchers; see Julliard and Winock 1996, 435–7.

6 For more on *Apostrophes*, see Rieffel 1993, 604–14, and INA, 'Littérature et télévision', *Dossiers de l'audiovisuel*, 29 (janvier–février 1990).

7 The Collège de France, whose origins go back to the sixteenth century, is France's most prestigious higher education establishment staffed by the nation's top professors. Its lectures are open to the public; see Julliard and Winock 1996, 281–3.

8 See also the dossier in the magazine *Politis* (18 March 1999) on Bourdieu as a modern-day Zola figure.

9 The strikes of November–December 1995 sparked intense debate about the evolving socio-economic bases of contemporary France. For a spectrum of opinion see the daily press for December 1995, especially *Le Monde*, *Libération* and *Le Figaro*. For a more retrospective appraisal see C. Leneveu and M. Vakaloulis, *Faire mouvement. Novembre-décembre 1995* (Paris: PUF, 1998).

10 As one example among many of contemporary intellectual controversy this debate may be studied by consulting, in order, Duval et al. 1998; P. Bourdieu, 'Pour une gauche de gauche', *Le Monde* (8 April 1998); Bourdieu 1998a; M. Lazar, 'Pierre Bourdieu à la recherche du peuple perdu', *Esprit* 243 (June 1998), 158–61, and O. Mongin and J. Roman, 'Le populisme version Bourdieu ou la tentation du mépris', *Esprit* 244 (July 1998), 158–75.

11 For further references on women's writing, see Marini 1994 and Hughes 1998, and see chapters 7 and 22 in this volume.

12 The EHESS traces its origins to 1948. It became an autonomous higher education establishment in 1975 and is renowned particularly for its historical and sociological research; see Julliard and Winock 1996, 418–20.

13 'Le grand réveil des intellectuels', *L'Evénement* (25–31 March 1999), 55–68.

14 For coverage of some of these issues, see *Le Monde* (27–28 January, 9 February 1991); *Le Nouvel Observateur* (14–20 February and 7–13 March 1991); there is a debate between B.-H. Lévy and Régis Debray in *Globe* (March 1991), 74–83. The defence minister Jean-Pierre Chevènement resigned over French involvement; see *Le Monde* (30 January 1991). Further references will be found in Julliard and Winock 1996, 549–50.

15 Many other intellectuals joined in the debate; see the series of articles in *Le Monde* spanning the whole month after 13 May 1999; *Libération* (14–25 May 1999); Plenel 1999.

A note on sources

As mentioned above, much useful information on intellectual debate may be gleaned from French newspapers reviews and magazines. Recent issues of the following were consulted: *Le Débat*, *Esprit*, *Les Temps modernes*, *Le Monde diplomatique*, *Le Nouvel Observateur*, *Politis*, *L'Evénement*, *Marianne*, and *Le Point*. The daily newspapers *Le Monde*, *Libération* and *Le Figaro* cover intellectual affairs, as do several TV programmes, for instance the weekly *Bouillon de culture* presented by Bernard Pivot (France 2). Much of the press and major TV channels have interactive websites which are well worth consulting, since the best have searchable archives such as those of *Le Monde* and *Libération*. During the autumn of 1999 the TV channel France 3 broadcast a five-part series based on Michel Winock's *Le siècle des intellectuels* (1997). Finally, each issue of the journal *Modern & Contemporary France* contains a Quarterly Periodicals Index including references to intellectual life.

References

BÉNICHOU, P. 1999: *The consecration of the writer, 1750–1830*. Lincoln and London: University of Nebraska Press [French original 1973].

BODIN, L. 1997: *Les Intellectuels existent-ils?* Paris: Bayard Editions.

BOURDIEU, P. 1998a: *Contre-feux*. Paris: Liber-Raisons d'agir.

BOURDIEU, P. 1998b: *On television and journalism*. London: Verso.

BOURDIEU, P. 1999: Une révolution conservatrice dans l'édition. *Actes de la recherche en sciences sociales* 126/127, 3–28.

CHARLE, C. 1990: *Naissance des intellectuels*. Paris: Editions de Minuit.

CHESNEAUX, J. 1983: *De la modernité*. Paris: La Découverte.

CLARK, P.P. 1991: *Literary France. The making of a culture*. Stanford: University of California Press.

COHN-BENDIT, D. and GUAINO, H. 1999: *La France est-elle soluble dans l'Europe?* Paris: Albin Michel.

CORNICK, M. 1995: *Intellectuals in history. The Nouvelle Revue française under Jean Paulhan, 1925–1940*. Amsterdam and Atlanta: Rodopi.

CORNICK, M. 1998: Left intellectuals in Mitterrand's France. In M. MACLEAN (ed.) *The Mitterrand years. Legacy and evaluation*. Basingstoke: Macmillan, 300–13.

DATTA, V. 1999: *Birth of a national icon: the literary avant-garde and the birth of the intellectuals in France*. New York: SUNY Press.

DEBRAY, R. 1979: *Le Pouvoir intellectuel en France*. Paris: Ramsay; translated by David Macey as *Teachers, writers, celebrities, the intellectuals of modern France*. London: Verso, 1981.

DEBRAY, R. 1989: *Que vive la République*. Paris: Odile Jacob.

DEBRAY, R. 1990: *À Demain de Gaulle*. Paris: Gallimard.

DEBRAY, R. 1993: Dictature de l'image? *Le Débat* 74, March–April.

DEBRAY, R. 1998: *La République expliquée à ma fille*. Paris: Seuil.

DEBRAY, R. 1999a: *Le Code et le glaive. Après l'Europe, la nation?* Paris: Albin Michel.

DEBRAY, R. 1999b: *Croyances en guerre. L'effet Kosovo. Les Cahiers de médiologie* 8, Paris: Gallimard.

DESFONS, P. 1999: Les années média, 1980–1998, episode 5 of *Le siècle des intellectuels*, d'après l'ouvrage de M. Winock, FR3, broadcast 27 October 1999.

DUVAL, J. et al. 1998: *Le «décembre» des intellectuels français*. Paris: Liber-Raisons d'agir.

FINKIELKRAUT, A. 1991: *Le Mécontemporain. Péguy, lecteur du monde moderne*. Paris: Gallimard.

GLUCKSMANN, A. 1995: *De Gaulle, où es-tu?* Paris: J.-C. Lattès.

GRÉMION, P. 1999: Ecrivains et intellectuels à Paris. Une esquisse. *Le Débat* 103, January–February, 74–99.

HALIMI, S. 1997: *Les Nouveaux Chiens de garde*. Paris: Liber-Raisons d'agir.

HANNA, M. 1996: *The mobilization of intellect: French scholars and writers during the Great War*. Cambridge, MA: Harvard University Press.

HUGHES, A. 1998: Women's writing. In HUGHES, A. and READER, K. (eds), *Encyclopedia of contemporary French culture*. London: Routledge, 564–7.

JUDT, T. 1998: *The burden of responsibility. Blum, Camus, Aron and the French twentieth century*. Chicago: The University of Chicago Press.

JULLIARD, J. and WINOCK, M. 1996: *Dictionnaire des intellectuels français*. Paris: Seuil.

LANE, J. 1999: 'Un étrange retournement'? Pierre Bourdieu and the French republican tradition. *Modern & Contemporary France*, vol. 7, no. 4, 457–70.

LÉVY, B.-H. 1977: *La Barbarie à visage humain*. Paris: Grasset.

LÉVY, B.-H. 1981: *L'Idéologie française*. Paris: Grasset.

LYOTARD, J.-F. 1982: *La Condition post-moderne*. Paris: Minuit.

LYOTARD, J.-F. 1984: Tombeau de l'intellectuel. In *Le Tombeau de l'intellectuel et autres papiers*. Paris: Galilée.

MARINI, M. 1994: The creators of culture in France. In THÉBAUD, F. (ed.) *A history of women in the west. V. Toward a cultural identity in the twentieth century*. Cambridge, MA and London: Belknap Press.

MONGIN, O. 1998: *Face au scepticisme. Les mutations du paysage intellectuel (1976–1998)*. Paris: Hachette-Pluriel.

MONGIN, O. 1999: 1999, avant et après… Les incertitudes de la vie intellectuelle. *Esprit* 252 and 253, 202–11 and 206–16.

NEGRONI, F. de 1985: *Le Savoir-vivre intellectuel*. Paris: Olivier Orban.

ORIOL, P. (ed.) 1997: *J'accuse! Emile Zola et l'affaire Dreyfus*. Paris: EJL-Librio.

ORY, P. and SIRINELLI, J.-F. 1986: *Les Intellectuels en France, de l'Affaire Dreyfus à nos jours*. Paris: Armand Colin.

PAGÈS, A. 1998: *13 janvier 1898. J'accuse…!* Paris: Perrin.

PERROT, M. 1998: La parole publique des femmes. In *Les Femmes, ou les silences de l'histoire*. Paris: Flammarion.

PLENEL, E. 1999: *L'Epreuve*. Paris: Stock.

READER, K. 1996: *Régis Debray*. London: Pluto.

RIEFFEL, R. 1993: *La Tribu des clercs. Les intellectuels sous la Vᵉ République*. Paris: Calmann-Lévy/CNRS.

ROSS, G. 1987: The decline of the left intellectual in modern France. In GAGNON, A. (ed.) *Intellectuals in liberal democracies*. New York: Praeger, 44–65.

ROSS, G. 1991: Where have all the Sartres gone? In HOLLIFIELD, J. F. and ROSS, G. (eds), *In search of the new France*. London: Routledge, 221–49.

SARTRE, J.-P. 1972: *Plaidoyer pour les intellectuels*. Paris: Gallimard-Folio.

SIRINELLI, J.-F. 1995a: Intellectuels. In *Dictionnaire de la vie politique française au XXᵉ siècle*. Paris: PUF.

SIRINELLI, J.-F. 1995b: *Deux intellectuels dans le siècle, Sartre and Aron*. Paris: Fayard.

SIRINELLI, J.-F. 1996: *Intellectuels et passions françaises. Manifestes et pétitions au XXᵉ siècle*. Paris: Gallimard-Folio.

VERDÈS-LEROUX, J. 1998: *Le Savant et la politique. Essai sur le terrorisme sociologique de Pierre Bourdieu*. Paris: Seuil.

WINOCK, M. 1997: *Le Siècle des intellectuels*. Paris: Seuil.

|22|

The French contribution to contemporary cultural analysis

BY JEREMY F. LANE

'The traditional antithesis of nature and culture gives way to an opposition between culture and cultures.' (*The Fateful Question of Culture*, Geoffrey Hartman, 1997).

You may have been surprised to find that this book is about French cultures, in the plural. It was traditionally assumed that to study French language and literature, in school or at university, was to learn about something called 'French culture', in the singular. That singular 'French culture' was, in turn, held to have achieved its highest realization in the works of France's novelists, philosophers, poets, and playwrights, whose mastery of their own language enabled them to express 'le génie français', something quintessential about the French national psyche and identity. In this rather traditional conception, the term 'culture' was understood in what might be termed its classical or *belle lettriste* sense as referring to the greatest creations of the human spirit, to the sum of humanity's highest artistic achievements. To study 'French culture' was both to become 'cultured', to acquire 'culture' in the sense of enlightenment and refinement, and to learn something fundamental about the French national identity.

If the subject-matter of this volume reflects a concern with sport rather than Sartre, the media rather than Montaigne, and rap rather than Racine, that is because our understanding of what we mean by the term 'French culture', in the singular, has been subjected to a more critical examination. It is now seen less as the expression of a single quintessentially French 'national' identity, than as the expression of one historically dominant identity, that primarily of the educated, (mostly) male middle classes, which was given special status over and above many diverse and sometimes conflicting French identities. Indeed 'French culture' seems a dangerously restrictive concept when faced with the variety of 'French cultures', as does 'French identity' in the face of the many different 'French identities'. In short, the traditional definition of 'culture' has increasingly been displaced by what is often known as the 'anthropological' definition of that term. This implies none of the *belle-lettriste* value judgements ('greatest', 'highest'), but refers instead to the entire set of beliefs, customs, and values shared by any social group, whether that group is defined in terms of nationality, ethnicity, class, sexuality, or gender.

So when we study French culture today, we are increasingly unlikely to focus exclusively on the greatest works of French art and literature, but seek instead to acknowledge the diversity of cultures and identities that find expression within France: the cultures of France's immigrant communities, youth and mass cultures of all kinds, regional identities, sporting cultures and so on. In explaining this shift in our perception of what 'French cul-ture/s' might be, we could refer to a whole series of developments in post-war French society, to say nothing of the changes to secondary and higher education in Britain and other countries where French is studied. But there is no doubt that the work of a series of influential post-war French thinkers has played a key role in forcing us to extend our horizons to embrace the much wider variety of interests and activities that make up the set of diverse French cultures.

In what follows, I can only provide the briefest of introductions to the immense variety of thinking about culture and society produced by post-1945 French thinkers. To focus on the ways such thinkers have encouraged us to broaden our horizons is to take only one of many possible approaches to their work. We cannot impose some spurious identity onto the immense range and variety of thinking about culture produced in France in the post-war period. The influence of these ideas over disciplines as diverse as sociol-ogy, cultural studies, literary criticism, anthropology, film studies and feminist theory has been immense, not simply in France but throughout the world. Indeed, many French thinkers exerted their greatest influence outside France itself, acquiring the status of intellectual gurus for academics in uni-versities throughout the English-speaking world in the 1980s and 1990s. In this context, one could cite the sociologist and anthropologist Pierre Bourdieu (b. 1930), the cultural and literary critic Roland Barthes (1915–80), the psychoanalyst Jacques Lacan (1901–81), the anthropologist Claude Lévi-Strauss (b. 1908), the philosophers Jacques Derrida (b. 1930), Jean-François Lyotard (1924–96), Gilles Deleuze (1925–95) and Luce Irigaray (b. 1932), as well as thinkers such as Hélène Cixous (b. 1937), Michel Foucault (1926–84), Julia Kristeva (b. 1941) and Jean Baudrillard (b. 1929), whose varied writings are less easy to classify in terms of a single academic discipline. (For suggestions of further introductory reading to all these, see end of chapter.)

Quite how this diverse range of French thinkers came to exert such influ-ence over English-speaking academics remains a contentious subject, with some commentators maintaining that their influence has been largely nega-tive. Indeed, they are sometimes lumped together under the single banner of 'Theory' or even 'French Theory', the better to condemn their output for its supposedly wilful obscurity and political irresponsibility. It is important to stress from the outset, then, that there is no such thing as a homogeneous 'French Theory'. If the thinkers generally included under this disparaging banner have all encouraged us to re-think our assumptions about the study of culture, this has not prevented them from pursuing very different lines of enquiry and sometimes arriving at diametrically opposed conclusions. We may need to pay as much attention to the differences between French thinkers as to the similarities.

From high culture to mass culture

In 1957, a new sociological review, *Arguments*, was launched in France. Its editorial board included the literary critic Roland Barthes, and dissident communists, such as Edgar Morin, Henri Lefebvre, and Pierre Fougeyrollas, who had left the French Communist Party in disgust at the 1956 Soviet invasion of Hungary. Although these figures had all been trained in the prestigious disciplines of philosophy and literature, their output from the mid-1950s onwards was marked by an interest in the apparently mundane details of what Lefebvre had dubbed 'everyday life', that is to say everything from adverts for soap powders, to women's magazines, the popular fascination for cinematic icons such as Brigitte Bardot, consumer goods, and the burgeoning tourist industry. The writings of the *Arguments* group represented some of the first attempts to understand the sociological, political and ideological implications of these new mass cultural phenomena. This group was thus highly influential in re-defining the study of French culture, in turning away from an exclusive focus on works of great art and literature and making 'everyday life', in Lefebvre's phrase, a valid topic for serious intellectual study.

These preoccupations need to be understood in the context of contemporary developments in French society. By the mid-1950s, French society was beginning to feel the benefits of the period of post-war reconstruction, modernization, and economic growth known as 'les trente glorieuses', when it seemed that traditional ways of life and culture were being swept away in a deluge of new consumer goods aggressively promoted by advertising campaigns. As the French economy modernized and expanded, large numbers of farmers and their families left the countryside to seek work in France's towns and cities, apparently abandoning an older folk culture in favour of what were then widely seen as more Americanized models of mass culture, swapping their Pernod for Coca-Cola, their regional dress for Levi's jeans, their folk songs for Elvis and Johnny Hallyday. The long-playing record, the transistor radio, the television and the paperback book seemed to many to suggest that high culture, once the preserve of the rich and privileged, was being placed within the reach of all. If folk culture was being replaced by mass culture, then so too was high culture. It was this advent of an era of mass culture and mass consumerism that formed the core of influential works such as Lefebvre's 1947 *Critique de la vie quotidienne* and his later *Introduction à la modernité* (1962), or Morin's *L'Esprit du temps* (1962) and his later study of the effects of mass culture on a rural community in Brittany, *Commune en France: la métamorphose de Plodémet* (1967). However, if there is one work from this period which has, somewhat paradoxically, acquired the status of a classic, it is surely Roland Barthes's 1957 *Mythologies*.

In the first part of *Mythologies*, Barthes collected a selection of the columns he had written for the magazines *France Observateur* and *Lettres Nouvelles* offering a series of wry commentaries on contemporary French society and culture. Barthes wrote about the latest Hollywood films, the rapidly growing market for glossy women's magazines, advertisements for washing powder, the latest model of Citroën to be wowing the French public, the ways in which France's colonies were represented in magazines and exhibitions. Although apparently unconnected, even trivial, the subjects covered by Barthes in fact offer an insight into the issues which were preoccupying many French people in the second half of the 1950s. The second, theoretical section of *Mythologies* was more serious in style and attempted to formalize certain methodological rules for the study of mass culture, drawing particularly on Marx's theories of ideology and the work of the Swiss linguist, Ferdinand de Saussure, whose basic proposition was that languages are systems or structures composed of linguistic signs that are both arbitrary and differential. He defined signs as having two elements, the 'signifier', the set of sounds or letters which make the word 'bush' for instance; and the 'signified', the idea of a kind of vegetation (bigger than a plant, smaller than a tree).

In *Mythologies*, Barthes sought to apply Saussure's insights about the functioning of language to the study of mass cultural forms, arguing that advertising hoardings, magazine covers, soap powder boxes were all *signs* which needed to be deciphered in order to be understood. He took the example of a front cover of the magazine *Paris Match* which carried a photograph of a Black African in a French Army uniform saluting the French flag. At the first, more straightforward level of meaning, what Barthes termed 'the level of language', the collection of colours and shapes that made up the photograph functioned as the signifier, the vehicle which communicated the photograph's meaning or signified, namely 'this is a photograph of a Black French soldier saluting the flag'. Barthes then went on to argue that this first level of meaning, the visual sign, which signified 'a young Negro in French uniform is saluting', itself served as a signifier, a vehicle, conveying another less obvious signified, a second level of meaning, namely the level of 'metalanguage' or 'myth'.

Barthes was writing at a time when France's African colonies were demanding their right to independence. To publish this photograph in the 1950s was to make a very definite political point; it was to reinforce the myth that the indigenous peoples of France's extensive colonies were happy with their lot, that, far from being oppressed, they were the zealous and contented servants of the French Empire. Drawing on Marx's theory of ideology, Barthes argued that such myths functioned by making situations which were in fact the product of a particular history, and hence open to being challenged or transformed, appear to be entirely 'natural', unchanging and beyond question. The front cover of *Paris Match*, for example, made no reference to the history of French colonialism, to France's violent annexation and domination of its colonial possessions and peoples. On the contrary, it presented the fact of French imperialism as a natural and unquestionable phenomenon and colonized peoples' loyalty to France as equally a matter of course.

Barthes's deciphering of the myths communicated by the front cover of *Paris Match* was intended to serve as a model for a more general semiology or science of signs. The role of the semiologist was to decipher the myths communicated by a whole range of mass cultural forms, showing how such myths worked to 'naturalize' phenomena that were in fact the products of a history which might have been different and was open to question. It is easy to see why *Mythologies* was to have such an influence over cultural analysis in France and elsewhere. Armed with Barthes's methodological tools, one could analyse the myths of femininity communicated in women's magazines and advertising of all kinds, the myths of national identity communicated by the Queen's annual speech to the British nation or the military parade down the Champs Elysées every 14 July, and so on. For example, an ad for a washing powder featuring interviews with housewives discussing the difficulties of removing stains from the collars of their husbands' white shirts makes us the viewers take for granted a series of questionable assumptions about the role of women in society. Barthes's insights enable us to challenge such assumptions, revealing them to be myths based on the concealment of the historical processes which have determined the sexual division of labour, the construction of notions of femininity and of the 'proper' role of women in society.

Other peoples, other cultures

If Barthes's *Mythologies* made the most apparently mundane and commercialized forms of cultural expression seem worthy of serious study, his debt to Saussure's linguistics needs also to be placed in the context of the dominance of structuralism over the French intellectual field of the 1950s and 60s. Arguably the most influential figure in popularizing structuralist readings of culture was the anthropologist Claude Lévi-Strauss. In his writings from the late 1940s onwards, Lévi-Strauss applied the structuralist paradigm to the analysis of kinship, gift exchange, myth, and ritual in 'primitive' or 'exotic' societies. He interpreted each of these socio-cultural forms as functioning in a manner analogous to Saussure's descriptions of the system or structure of language; they were kinds of language, permitting a sort of communication between the members of the society in question, communication through the exchange of gifts, or of women from fathers to husbands, and so on.

In *La Pensée sauvage* (1962), for example, Lévi-Strauss turned to the ways in which people in 'primitive' or 'exotic' societies divided up and classified their world: how they grouped plant and animal species or the different clan and tribal groupings which made up their societies. At the core of *La Pensée sauvage* was Lévi-Strauss's insistence that although these supposedly 'primitive' systems of classification were markedly different from those in the West, they were nonetheless complex and sophisticated. Although other peoples and other cultures understood the world in ways which were very different from our own, this understanding of the world revealed just as great a capacity for abstract thought. Lévi-Strauss thus rejected outright the notion, central to many earlier anthropological studies, that there was an essential or fundamental difference between the intellectual capabilities of 'primitive' peoples and their 'modern' Western counterparts.

In rejecting as ethnocentric any essential difference between 'primitive' and 'modern' mentalities, Lévi-Strauss also challenged conventional notions of historical change and progress, arguing that human history could not be understood as a unilinear evolutionary progression from the 'primitive' to the 'modern', with Western societies and cultures as the highest stage of historical development. Drawing on archaeological evidence, Lévi-Strauss showed that human cultural and technological developments had emerged at different times and speeds in different geographical regions. Archaeological evidence showed that around the twentieth millennium BC the nomads who migrated across the Bering Straits into America were far more technologically advanced than their Western contemporaries. Yet, when Columbus 'discovered' America for the West in 1492, it was Western culture which was described as making the greatest advances, and indigenous American peoples were seen to have stagnated, even regressed by comparison. We should acknowledge, Lévi-Strauss argued, that history proceeded 'by leaps and bounds', sometimes rushing forward in one area, only to mark time in another. If the post-Renaissance West had been the site of some of the most significant technological and social advances, that reflected not the region's intrinsic superiority, merely a fortuitous combination of circumstances.

One of the implications of Lévi-Strauss's work was to challenge any claim that Western or French culture might make regarding its own *intrinsic* superiority, and to recognize the immense diversity and richness of other cultures – another way of broadening our horizons. This call had not only a strong moral dimension, it also had a definite political force since it was issued at a time when the colonized peoples of France's empire, often considered by the French to be 'primitive' and hence inferior, were themselves demanding recognition for their own cultures and ways of life in the face of an unjust imperialism.

In the final chapter of *La Pensée sauvage*, Lévi-Strauss had engaged in a detailed critique of the heavily Marxist-influenced theory of history elaborated by the philosopher Jean-Paul Sartre in his *Critique de la raison dialectique* (1960). For Lévi-Strauss, Sartre's understanding of history, despite his left-wing credentials, reproduced many of the ethnocentric assumptions about 'primitive' societies which could be found in classical anthropology. The Lévi-Strauss–Sartre dispute provides a nice example of the way in which the French intellectual field favours both the cross-fertilization and the conflictual exchange of ideas between different disciplines and personalities. If the Lévi-Strauss–Sartre exchange has often been read as a symptom of a broader intellectual shift in post-war France, in which the earlier dominance of existentialism was giving way to the rise of structuralism, then the series of readings of Lévi-Strauss's work offered by the philosopher Jacques Derrida in the late 1960s has been interpreted as marking one further shift, the shift from structuralism to post-structuralism.

In his *De la grammatologie* (1967) and the essay 'La Structure, le signe et le jeu dans le discours des sciences humaines', published in the collection *L'Ecriture et la différence* (1967), Jacques Derrida had offered detailed and sympathetic readings of Lévi-Strauss's anthropological studies. However, whilst acknowledging the latter's contribution, Derrida argued that ultimately Lévi-Strauss's analyses rested on the very ethnocentric oppositions between 'primitive' and 'modern', the non-West and the West he had sought to challenge.

Derrida paid particular attention to Lévi-Strauss's designation of the 'exotic' societies he had studied as 'societies without writing', arguing that the concept of a 'society without writing' was both theoretically and empirically without foundation. Derrida was not seeking to deny the existence of pre-literate societies nor the role that the spread of literacy or the invention of technologies of printing might play in accelerating social and cultural change. Rather, he objected to Lévi-Strauss's use of the absence of writing as an index of 'primitive' societies' essential unity, simplicity, and innocence. In Lévi-Strauss's account, writing was a technology imposed onto 'primitive' societies from somewhere outside, a technology which, if it shattered their state of primal innocence, nonetheless held the key to all future social change and historical progress.

For Derrida this account of the advent of writing and history to 'primitive' societies rested on a questionable opposition between speech and writing. In this view, speech was taken to correspond to the immediate relationship between intention, expression and meaning, an ideal core of sense, which writing contaminated by deferring the self-present expression of meaning in a technological medium of representation. Yet as Derrida showed, even in speech, meaning was never self-present, it was always already deferred, caught up in a structure of differential relations. Speech was always already contaminated by writing – if we understand 'writing' in an extended sense, meaning any structure of difference or deferral which mediated the apparent self-presence of the spoken word. If speech was always already inhabited by its 'other', namely writing, then this held true of the series of other oppositions structuring Lévi-Strauss's anthropology; the West was always already inhabited by the non-West, apparent self-presence by representation, the same by the other, and so on.

Derrida's attempt to 'deconstruct' the oppositions structuring Lévi-Strauss's work had a very definite ethical force. He thought that by romanticizing 'primitive' societies as the sites of some primal unity and innocence, Lévi-Strauss had put forward a view of history as essentially a narrative of fall and redemption. Thus Western technologies, such as writing, might seem to shatter the edenic innocence of 'primitive' societies, occasioning a 'fall' into a modern universe of exploitation and alienation. Yet, paradoxically, those same technologies would also, *within a linear narrative* (such as Lévi-Strauss did not contest), possess a redeeming force, since in certain versions of Marxism, they could be seen to form part of the historical process ultimately leading to a future communist utopia. Within such an account of history, 'primitive' cultures might be romanticized or idealized, yet ultimately their specificity, their characteristic difference turned out to be merely an obstacle to be overcome in the onward march of historical progress. Implicit in Derrida's thought, then, is a call for such differences to be *respected* rather than overcome and subsumed in a narrative of Western progress and reason. This is unlikely to be achieved if they are idealized and romanticized, in a way which keeps the binary opposition between the West and the Rest, modern and primitive, same and other firmly in place. Derrida sought to 'deconstruct' those oppositions, by acknowledging that just as speech is always already inhabited by its other, namely writing, so any form of identity is always already inhabited by its other, whether at the level of the individual (personal identity), of the local or national collectivity (French identity, British identity), or of the wider geo-political region (Western as against non-Western identity). Any attempt to maintain a coherent sense of national identity, in Derrida's view, would always involve repressing, denying, or excluding the other, namely other ethnicities, immigrant groups, marginalized sexualities, women.

For Derrida, then, to imagine an organic link between the French language, French culture, and French national identity would be to effect a gesture of exclusion. To suppose that French culture emerges organically from the French national soil, like a plant from a flower-bed, and that it expresses something fundamental about the French national identity through the transparent medium of the French language is, for example, to exclude those French citizens not born on French soil, to classify them as 'foreign', a possible threat to the identity of the French nation. Any notion of an organic link between French national identity, culture and language will thus always deny or repress the constitutive difference within French identity, the non-

Frenchness concealed within notions of Frenchness, the contribution of other peoples, languages and cultures to what we may still be tempted to term 'French culture'. It is the very inconsistencies implicit in our received notions of national cultures, languages and identities that Derrida asks us to reflect upon when he opens his more recent book, *Le Monolinguisme de l'autre* (1996), by asking us to imagine what it might mean to cultivate and to be cultivated by the French language, or to be born a subject, as he puts it, of French culture.

Derrida's meditations on questions of language, culture and national identity in this work were sparked, in part at least, by his personal experiences as a Jew brought up in French colonial Algeria during World War II, a time when the Vichy authorities removed the Algerian Jews' right to French citizenship with a stroke of the pen, hence highlighting the extent to which national identity is a contingent phenomenon, founded on a gesture of exclusion. The significance of Derrida's thoughts is not limited to his own personal experience, however. On the contrary, his message to his readers seems to be 'Nous sommes tous des Juifs-Français d'Algérie'.

Feminisms

As Derrida had shown in his deconstructive readings of the work of Lévi-Strauss, binary oppositions between the primitive and the modern, the non-West and the West, the other and the same operate by simultaneously idealizing and disparaging the first term in each of those pairs. In the case of Lévi-Strauss, for example, 'primitive' societies were idealized as the sites of some primal innocence, yet they were simultaneously disparaged inasmuch as they were considered essentially static, inherently incapable of any change or progress.

This insight about the tyranny of binary oppositions can be seen as one of the key concepts in the post-1968 generation of feminist thinkers. In 'Sorties', her contribution to the 1975 text *La Jeune née*, Hélène Cixous drew on Derrida's work to argue that the opposition between woman and man functioned according to an equivalent logic. 'Sorties' opens with a series of binary oppositions – activity/passivity; culture/nature; day/night; father/mother; head/heart; intelligence/feeling – each of which, Cixous suggests, are grounded in a fundamental opposition between man and woman. Woman may be idealized as an object of beauty, more in touch with nature, with the lunar cycle, with the emotional rather than the coldly rational aspects of life. Yet ultimately that idealization remains profoundly disparaging; man is seen as the source of all reason, productive activity and progress.

For Cixous, philosophical systems, theories of culture and of society were all characterized by these kinds of hierarchized oppositions which served to marginalize woman, placing her always on the side of passivity. In *De la grammatologie* and elsewhere, Derrida had coined the term 'logocentrism' to refer to the precedence traditionally given to the spoken word over writing, to the assumption that the spoken word, the logos, formed an ideal core of self-present truth and meaning. Cixous used the term 'phallocentrism' or 'phallogocentrism' to refer to those forms of thought which posited the male principle, symbolized by the phallus, as the positive term in the series of binary oppositions between male and female, activity and passivity, and so on. Combating phallocentrism, for Cixous, centred around a particular textual practice known as 'l'écriture féminine', an experimental form of writing which takes as given the subversive power of feminine sexuality and desire and thus challenges the supposed rationality of the male phallic order.

Cixous is often cited alongside two of her contemporaries, the philosopher Luce Irigaray and the psychoanalyst and literary theorist Julia Kristeva, as typifying French feminism's focus on sexual difference as a force which disrupts a symbolic and social order organized around the power of the phallus. For Kristeva it was in the 'semiotic', the dark, repressed side of the patriarchal order which corresponds to the pre-oedipal relationship to the mother's body before the advent of the phallocentric (or father's) symbolic order, that feminists might find a resource for challenging patriarchy. In her 1974 study, *La Révolution du langage poétique*, Kristeva identified certain forms of avant-garde poetic language as expressing the subversive force of the semiotic by re-enacting the pre-oedipal relationship to the mother. In her readings of Freudian psychoanalysis and the Western philosophical tradition in *Speculum de l'autre femme* (1974) and *Ce sexe qui n'en est pas un* (1977), Luce Irigaray contrasts women's irreducible multiplicity and fluidity, expressed in 'l'écriture féminine', with the hierarchized oppositions which structure the traditionally phallic economy of reason.

The interest of Cixous, Kristeva, and Irigaray in theoretical questions concerning philosophy, psychoanalysis and literature, combined with their emphasis on questions of sexual difference, is often taken by commentators as epitomizing the difference between French feminist theory and the more empirical, historical approach favoured in Britain and the United States. This misleading distinction, already referred to in chapter 7, risks overlooking the work of feminists such as Christine Delphy and others associated with the journal *Questions féministes* (re-named *Nouvelles questions féministes* in 1977), who are highly critical of the positions taken by the theorists of sexual difference. For Delphy, the emphasis on sexual difference and 'l'écriture féminine' is based on an essentialized notion of woman and the feminine which overlooks the material and historical processes whereby those two notions are constructed. She calls for a materialist feminism, arguing that patriarchy ultimately has its foundations in economic exploitation, in what she terms 'the domestic mode of production'. Her work has thus been more sociological than philosophical, literary, or psychoanalytic and has focused on issues such as housework or unpaid domestic labour, women's role in consumption and production, marriage and divorce.

Although clearly indebted to the Marxist tradition, Delphy rejects the Marxist assumption of the primacy of class as a determinant of exploitation, arguing that this has served to marginalize the importance of the women's struggle.

In their rejection of the French feminism of sexual difference and their emphasis on the social construction of gender, Delphy and those associated with *Nouvelles questions féministes* can trace a line of allegiance back to Simone de Beauvoir. Beauvoir's 1949 *Le Deuxième sexe*, a two-volume study of the social and historical processes which have forced women to adopt a subordinate role to men, has become a classic both in France and world-wide. Although the book ends with an assertion that a socialist revolution was the necessary precursor to women's liberation, this was a position Beauvoir would reject in the early 1970s, acknowledging, like Delphy after her, that conventional socialist or Marxist politics paid insufficient attention to the specificity of women's oppression.

One of the most interesting aspects of Simone de Beauvoir's classic text, in the context of our survey of French culture, is that as one of the first generation of women to benefit from the classic French system of higher education, she turned that tradition against itself in a pioneering and critical fashion. Just as Barthes's and his colleagues' writings on mass culture need to be set against the background of the social and cultural changes affecting post-war France, and Lévi-Strauss's and Derrida's attentiveness to other cultures and other peoples can be set in the context of decolonization and mass post-war immigration to France, so the provocative and varied range of thinking about gender and sexual difference which has emerged in post-war France needs to be set against the background of the changing role of women in French society of that period, the gaining of the vote, the mass entry of women into the workplace and higher education. Although these thinkers have offered very different, sometimes diametrically opposed, theories of culture and society and although this chapter has only offered the briefest of introductions to the immense variety of post-war French thought, it is possible to see how such thinkers have all, in their different ways, forced us to rethink our assumptions about the relationship between culture, language and national identity and pay greater attention to the diversity of cultures, ethnicities, genders and sexualities that any singular notion of national culture and identity would risk effacing.

Suggestions for further reading

1. Barthes and the *Arguments* group
For a useful introduction to the *Arguments* group, see the special number of *French Cultural Studies*, vol. 3, no. 24 (1997). A more detailed analysis of the work of Henri Lefebvre can be found in Rob Shields, *Lefebvre, love and struggle: spatial dialectics* (London: Routledge, 1999), particularly chapters

7–9. See also Henri Lefebvre, *Critique de la vie quotidienne, I: Introduction* (Paris: L'Arche, 1958, 2nd edition), and *Introduction à la modernité* (Paris: Editions de minuit, 1962). For an introduction to the work of Edgar Morin, see Myron Kofman, *Edgar Morin: from big brother to fraternity* (London: Pluto, 1996). See also Edgar Morin, *L'Esprit du temps* (Paris: Grasset/Livre de Poche/Biblio-Essais, 1962) and *Commune en France: la métamorphose de Plodemet* (Paris: Fayard, 1967). For a concise introduction to Barthes's *Mythologies* see Andrew Leak, *Barthes: Mythologies* (London: Grant & Cutler, 1994). The text itself is available in the accessible Points/Seuil format: *Roland Barthes, Mythologies, suivi de Le Mythe aujourd'hui* (Paris: Seuil/Collection 'Points', 1957).

2. Lévi-Strauss and Derrida

For a concise, if sometimes overly hostile introduction to Lévi-Strauss's work, see Edmund Leach, *Lévi-Strauss* (London: Collins, 1970). Amongst the most accessible of Lévi-Strauss's works is *Race et histoire* (Paris: Denoel/Folio-Essais, 1987 [orig. 1952]); see also *La Pensée sauvage* (Paris: Plon, 1962), and, for an explanation of the application of structural linguistics to anthropological study, 'L'analyse structurale en linguistique et en anthropologie', in *Anthropologie structurale* (Paris: Plon, 1958), 37–62. Derrida's seminal deconstructive readings of Lévi-Strauss can be found in 'La Structure, le signe et le jeu dans le discours des sciences humaines', in *L'Ecriture et la différence* (Paris: Seuil/Collection 'Points', 1967), 409–28, and *De la grammatologie* (Paris: Minuit, 1967). For a concise introduction to Derrida's work, see Christopher Johnson, *Derrida* (London: Routledge/The Great Philosophers Series, 1999) and Christopher Norris, *Derrida* (London: Fontana Modern Masters, 1987). See also Jacques Derrida, *Le Monolinguisme de l'autre* (Paris: Galillée, 1996). Robert Young's *White mythologies: writing history and the west* (London: Routledge, 1990) provides a detailed analysis of the critique of ethnocentrism in post-war French thought from Sartre through Lévi-Strauss and on to Derrida and other 'post-structuralist' thinkers.

3. Feminisms

One of the best introductions to French post-war feminisms remains Toril Moi's *Sexual/textual politics* (London: Routledge, 1988). Rosi Braidotti's *Patterns of dissonance: a study of women in contemporary philosophy* (Cambridge: Polity, 1991) is a more detailed and sophisticated attempt to situate recent French thinking about sexual difference. For an introduction to the work of Julia Kristeva, see Toril Moi (ed.), *The Kristeva reader* (Oxford: Blackwell, 1986). On Hélène Cixous, see Morag Shiach, *Hélène Cixous: a politics of writing* (London: Routledge, 1991), and on Luce Irigaray, see Maragaret Whitford (ed.), *The Irigaray Reader* (Oxford: Blackwell, 1991) and Maragaret Whitford, *Luce Irigaray: philosophy in the feminine* (London: Routledge, 1991). Examples of all three thinkers' writings can be found in the anthology *New French Feminisms* (London: Harvester Wheatsheaf, 1981), edited by Elaine Marks and Isabelle de Courtivon, which provides a useful introduction to the range of French feminist thought, although it is generally seen as paying too much attention to theorists of difference to the detriment of materialists such as Christine Delphy. Amongst the primary texts, see Julia Kristeva, *La Révolution du langage poétique* (Paris: Seuil, 1974), Luce Irigaray, *Speculum de l'autre femme* (Paris: Minuit, 1974) and *Ce sexe qui n'en est pas un* (Paris: Minuit, 1974), and Hélène Cixous, 'Sorties', in *La Jeune née* (Paris: UGE, 10/18, 1975). Delphy's critique of the proponents of 'l'écriture féminine' can be found in two articles, both of which originally appeared in French in 1975 and 1982, but have since been anthologized in the useful English-language collection, Christine Delphy, *Close to home: a materialist analysis of women's oppression*, trans. D. Leonard (London: Hutchinson, 1984). See also Delphy's essay, 'The invention of French feminism: an essential move', in *Another look, another woman: retranslations of French feminism*, special number of *Yale French Studies*, no. 87 (1995), 190–221. More recent examples of Delphy's approach can be found in her *L'Ennemi principal, I: l'économie politique du patriarcat* (Paris: Syllepse, 1997). Beauvoir's *Le Deuxième sexe* is available in two volumes in the Folio-Essais series. For an introduction to her life and work, see Toril Moi, *Simone de Beauvoir: the making of an intellectual woman* (Oxford: Blackwell, 1994).

4. Other French theorists mentioned
Below are some useful introductions to the work of the other French theorists mentioned at the opening of this chapter.

(a) On Jean Baudrillard, see Douglas Kellner, *Jean Baudrillard: from Marxism to postmodernism and beyond* (Stanford: Stanford University Press, 1989); Mark Poster (ed.), *Jean Baudrillard: selected writings* (Cambridge: Polity Press, 1989).

(b) On Pierre Bourdieu, see Richard Jenkins, *Pierre Bourdieu* (London: Routledge, 1992); Jeremy F. Lane, *Pierre Bourdieu: a critical introduction* (London: Pluto Press, 2000).

(c) On Jacques Lacan, see Malcolm Bowie, *Lacan* (London: Fontana Modern Masters, 1991).

(d) On Jean-François Lyotard, see Geoffrey Bennington, *Lyotard: writing the event* (Manchester: Manchester University Press, 1988); Bill Readings, *Introducing Lyotard: art and politics* (London: Routledge, 1991).

Conclusion

Cultural stereotypes die hard. Georgia de Chamberet, the editor of an anthology of recent French writing, translated into English and aiming to put readers in touch with the 'real France' of today, warns them to put out of mind a certain number of 'glorified clichés' which have had a long life:

> cafés and Left-Bank existentialism, sultry sexy sirens and pouting starlets, Godard and Truffaut, Coco Chanel and chic little poodles, châteaux and fine wines, Provence and pastis, brie and baguettes, Magnum Photographers ... Duras and *le nouveau roman*, 1968 and all that
>
> De Chamberet 1999, ix

As an alternative 'real France', her anthology includes an interview with the football player Marcel Desailly, as well as pieces by the avant-garde DJ Christov Rühn aka DJ Tov, and a dozen or so young journalists or fiction-writers, of both sexes and varied ethnic and national origins. They reflect the 'cultural mosaic' of France today, with a special emphasis on the suburbs and inner cities, on youth culture and films like *La Haine*.

De Chamberet's collection lives up to its name (*Xcités*) and certainly works as an admirable counterpoise to a certain professional and rather dated Francophilia. But perhaps there is a slight risk here of assuming that France is slipping straight into a new set of cultural stereotypes. As has been pointed out elsewhere in these pages, the 'multiculturalism' of present-day France cannot either be dismissed or taken for granted. And in many subtle ways, history still clings to France like a garment, clothing its streets with names and statues, its language with expressions like 'A nous deux maintenant!' (Balzac), or 'une certaine idée de la France' (de Gaulle), and certainly affecting the way cultural policy operates.

In a book this length it is not possible to cover all the aspects of French life which could quite properly be called cultural – whether Provence and pastis, or indeed theme parks and the Belgian mussels-and-chips restaurants which are all over Paris. But we have already shown that it is possible to find all kinds of 'Frenchness' sitting side by side, producing many contradictions between old and new. Yes, you can still sit in a café on Paris's Left Bank and see, if not glamorous post-war existentialists, at least plenty of cheerful and intense students. But they will not now be as predominantly white, middle-class and male as they still were in 1968, and their concerns will be very different. The 'sultry sirens and starlets' may not be quite the same as in the old days but a beautiful young 'top model' has been voted for as the model for the new bust of Marianne, to the despair of feminists and historians alike (cf. St John 1999 and chapter 12). At the street-tables of Marseille, elderly southerners will still be sipping pastis, but France is now, perhaps surprisingly, the third producer after the US and Japan of computer and video games (*Guardian*, 21 October 1999).

In this book, all the contributors, some of whom are French, have tried to give an honest picture of France as it seems to them today, warts and all, undergoing all kinds of change very fast, yet retaining a certain something – *un je ne sais quoi*, as they would have said in the old days – that makes it a delight to study and to compare, for better or for worse, with one's own country.

References

DE CHAMBERET, Georgia (ed.) 1999: *Xcités: the Flamingo book of new French writing*. London: Flamingo.

ST JOHN, Margaret 1999: Why French women are different. *New Statesman*, 18 October.

Appendix

A thematic index to chapters in the French paperback edition of Pierre Nora (ed.) *Les Lieux de mémoire* (Paris: Gallimard, consolidated edition in three volumes, 1997).

This guide is intended as a reference aid for students, postgraduates and teachers. Nora's edited collection, written by some of the leading historians and cultural experts in France, is a treasure-house of fascinating scholarship. Although one can criticize the selection for its lacunae and sometimes the emphasis as being idiosyncratic, anyone studying French culture would find it a good starting point for research. Its organization was however dictated by the expansion of the original plan and is, although thematic, slightly eccentric and not always obvious at first sight. It was published in a total of seven volumes between 1984 and 1992. The three-volume paperback edition (whose continuous pagination is followed here) exactly reproduces the order of the original, so this guide should also help readers of the 7-volume edition. The whole collection has not been translated into English, but a selection of key chapters translated by Arthur Goldhammer is published as *Realms of Memory* (Columbia University Press, 1998). In this guide, which regroups topics in what is hoped is a useful set of categories, authors' names are not given and some items may appear twice.

National symbols

The monarchy

Republican and revolutionary symbols and commemoration

Right and left

The state

Administrative divisions

Civil society

War and military history

Foreign and colonial

The Catholic Church

Religious minorities

Geography and landscape

Food and drink

Regions and sites (outside Paris)

Parisian monuments and sites

Museums, monuments and antiquaries

School and pedagogy

The French language

Le 'Grand dictionnaire' de Pierre Larousse	I, 227–39
Les Trésors de la langue	II, 2189–206
L'Histoire de la langue française de Ferdinand Brunot	III, 3385–422
La conversation	III, 3671–76
Le génie de la langue française	III, 4623–86

Writers, remembered or as memorialists

Les centenaires de Voltaire et de Rousseau	I, 351–82
Les funérailles de Victor Hugo	I, 425–64
Les mémoires d'état	I, 1383–432
Les morts illustres	II, 1831–54
La visite au grand écrivain	II, 2131–56
Le Félibrige	III, 3515–54
La 'Recherche du temps perdu' de Marcel Proust	III, 3835–72
Descartes	III, 4475–520

Historiography

Lavisse, instituteur national	I, 239–76
Les 'Grands Chroniques de France'	I, 739–58
Les 'Recherches de la France d'Etienne Pasquier	I, 759–86
Les 'Lettres sur l'histoire de la France' d'Augustin Thierry	I, 787–850
'L'Histoire de France' de Lavisse	I, 851–902
L'heure des Annales	I, 903–56
La génération	II, 2975–3015

Resources and archives

La Bibliothèque des Amis de l'Instruction du IIIe arrondissement	I, 303–26
La Statistique générale de la France	I, 1353–82

Index

Lightning Source UK Ltd.
Milton Keynes UK
UKOW05f1022130913

217126UK00001B/38/P